MW01717273

inside Al Qaeda

global network of terror

Inside Al Qaeda

global network of terror

OTHER LOTUS TITLES

HARINDER BAWEJA (ed.)	*Most Wanted: Profiles of Terror*
M.J. AKBAR	*The Shade of Swords*
M.J. AKBAR	*Nehru: The Making of India*
ANIL K. JAGGIA SAURABH SHUKLA	*IC 814: Hijacked! The Inside Story*
ERIC S. MARGOLIS	*War at the Top of the World*
JAWID LAIQ	*The Maverick Republic*
MUSHIRUL HASAN	*India Partitioned.* 2 vols
MUSHIRUL HASAN	*John Company to the Republic*
MUSHIRUL HASAN	*Knowledge Power and Politics*
RACHEL DWYER	*Yash Chopra: Fifty Years of Indian Cinema*
SUJATA S. SABNIS	*A Twist in Destiny*
V.N. RAI	*Curfew in the City*

FORTHCOMING TITLES

M.J. AKBAR	*India: The Siege Within*
MAJ. GEN. I. CARDOZO (Retd.)	*The Paramvir Chakra Winners*
MAJ. GEN. K.S. BAJWA (Retd.)	*Dimensions of Soldiering*

inside Al Qaeda
global network of terror

Rohan Gunaratna

LOTUS COLLECTION
ROLI BOOKS

Lotus Collection

© Rohan Gunaratna 2002

All rights reserved. No part of this publication may be reproduced or transmitted, in any form or by any means, without the prior permission of the publisher.

Published in 2002 by
C. Hurst & Co. (Publishers) Ltd., UK
First published in India in 2002 by
Roli Books Pvt Ltd
M-75, G.K. II Market
New Delhi 110 048
Phones: 6442271, 6462782, 6460886
Fax: 6467185
E-mail: roli@vsnl.com; Website: rolibooks.com
Also at
Varanasi, Agra, Jaipur and the Netherlands

ISBN: 81-7436-243-6
Rs. 295

Typeset in Bembo by Roli Books Pvt Ltd and
printed at Paul Press, Okhla, New Delhi-110 020

To my wife Anne
and our sons
Kevin and Ryan

PUBLISHER'S NOTE

A wide range of organisations — banks, governmental and non-governmental bodies, financial enterprises, religious and educational institutions, commercial entities, transport companies and charitable bodies — are referred to in this book as having had contact or dealings with Al Qaeda and other terrorist groups. Unless such references specifically state otherwise, they should be treated as nothing other than a suggestion that the organisations concerned were the unwitting tools of those who attempted, successfully or otherwise, to infiltrate, use or manipulate them for terrorist purposes.

ACKNOWLEDGEMENTS

I am indebted to my mentors, colleagues, friends and family for making this book possible.

For sharing their knowledge, experience and time, I am grateful to my teachers — Dr Bruce Hoffman, Vice President, RAND; Professor Paul Wilkinson, Chairman, Centre for the Study of Terrorism and Political Violence, St Andrews University, Scotland; and Dr Gerard Chaliand, former advisor, Ministry of Foreign Affairs, France. For encouraging me to look beyond the Asia-Pacific I wish to express my gratitude to the late Professor Cyril Ponnamperuma, then Presidential Science Advisor to Sri Lanka; Professor Stephen P. Cohen, Professorial Fellow, Brookings Institute, Washington, DC; Professor Martha Crenshaw, Professor of Government, Wesleyan University; and Ambassador Jayantha Dhanapala, Under-Secretary-General for Disarmament Affairs at the UN.

The opportunities and resources to conduct terrorism research provided the space, time and funds to work on this book. On the Asia-Pacific, M.J. Gohel, President, Asia-Pacific Foundation, UK; on Central Asia, Charles Schmitz, President, Global Business Associates, USA; on information operations, Dr Miles Hills of the Cabinet Office, UK; on the mass casualty attacks, Dr John Parachini, former Director, Monterey Centre for Non-Proliferation Studies, USA; on escalation and de-escalation, Dr Alex P. Schmid, Officer-in-Charge, United Nations Terrorism Prevention Branch, Austria; on the maritime threat, Dr David Claridge, Managing Director, Janusian Security Risk Management, UK; on Al Qaeda, Chris Aaron, editor of *Jane's Intelligence Review*, UK; and on the threat of terrorism, Ian Synge, editor, *Jane's Counter-Terrorism Manual*. At the terrorism database at CSTPV, St Andrews, I wish to thank Captain Eric Bray, Kweilen Kimmelman, Benjamin Weber, Catherine Zara Raymond and Christina Hellmich for their dedication and commitment. Many others, working in the shadows, cannot be named. For sharing their insights and know-how, each one of them is in my debt.

I also wish to thank Dr John King and Dr Peter Riddell for their comments on the manuscript.

For their friendship I wish to express my appreciation to Ambassador Barry Desker, Dr Andrew Tan, Dr Kumar Ramakrishna, Zerney Wijesuriya, Ambassador Nanda Godage, Jean-Paul Rouiller, Captain Lasantha Waidyaratne, Brigadier Rizvy Zaky, Major N.G. Chandrasena, Amith Attygalle, Shanaka Jayasekera, Shyam Tekwani, Dushy Ranetunge, Madurendranath Jha, my publisher Christopher Hurst and my editor Michael Dwyer. Before and during editing, Michael read every piece of writing on Al Qaeda. This is Michael's book as much as it is mine. I also thank the dynamic team at Columbia University Press — Peter Dimock, Madeleine Gruen, Anne Routon, Melissanne Scheld, Helena Schwarz and Clare Wellnitz.

Finally, I thank my family who have stood by me in both good and sad times. For their steadfast support and affection, I express my gratitude to my parents and to Kirthi, Selomi, Malkanthi, Kumar, Samantha and Tamara. For their understanding and love I thank my wife Anne and our sons Kevin and Ryan. To them I dedicate this book.

St Andrews, Scotland R.G.
May 2002

CONTENTS

ABBREVIATIONS

AAD	Interior and Security Ministry (Sudan)
ABIM	Islamic Youth Movement of Malaysia
ADF	Allied Democratic Forces
AKK	Ministry of Foreign Affairs (Sudan)
APU	Movement of Islamic Unity
ARC	Advice and Reformation Committee
ASG	Abu Sayyaf Group
BCCI	Bank of Credit and Commerce International
BIC	Benevolence International Corporation
BIF	Benevolence International Foundation
BN	Barisan Nasional
BNPP	Barisan Nasional Pembebasan Patani
BRN	Barisan Revolusi Nasional
CBRN	Chemical, biological, radiological and nuclear weapons of mass destruction
DEHCQ	Darul Ehsan Orphanage and Hifsul Qur'an Centre
DIAS	Daw'l Imam Al-Shafee
DHF	Darul Hijra Foundation
FH	Front Hizbullah
FIS	Islamic Salvation Front (Algerian)
FMIC	Front Malaysian Islamic Council
GIA	Armed Islamic Group of Algeria
GIGN	Groupe d'Intervention Gendarmerie Nationale (French anti-terrorist force)
GRF	Global Relief Foundation
GSPC	Groupe Salafiste pour la Prédication et le Combat
HCI	Human Concern International
Hezb	Hezb-ul-Mujahidin
HNI	Hizb-i-Nehzat-i-Islami (branch of the IRP)
HT	Hezb-ut-Tehrir
HuA	Harkat-ul-Ansar
HUJI	Harkat-ul-Jihad al-Islami
HuM	Harkat-ul Mujahidin
IA	Indian Airlines
ICS	Islami Chhatra Shibir
IDCP	Islamic Dawah Council of the Philippines
IDGI	Islamic Dawah and Guidance International
IED	Improvised Explosive Device
IFM	Islamic Front of Malaysia

IIC	International Islamic Conference
IIEP	International Islamic Efforts of the Philippines
IIRO	International Islamic Relief Organisation
IMT	Islamic Movement of Tajikistan
IMU	Islamic Movement of Uzbekistan
IOC	Islamic Observation Centre
IPC	Islamic Presentation Committee
IRIC	International Relief and Information Centre
IRP	Islamic Renaissance Party (China)
ISCAG	Islamic Studies Call and Guidance
ISD	Internal Security Department of Singapore
ISI	Inter-Services-Intelligence (Pakistan Security Service)
ITFI	IT Forensic Investigation
IWCF	Islamic World Committee Foundation
IWWWM	Islamic World Wisdom Worldwide Mission
JEEMA	Justice Forum (Uganda)
JI	Jamiyatul Ialam
JeM	Jayash-e-Muhammad (Army of Muhammad)
KIMM	Kongress Indian Muslim Malaysia
KMM	Malaysian Mujahidin Group
LBI	Islamic Benevolence Committee
LeT	Lashkar-e-Toiba
LTTE	Liberation Tigers of Tamil Eelam
MAK	Afghan Service Bureau Front
MASYUMI	Council of Indonesian Muslim Associations
MILF	Moro Islamic Liberation Front
MIRA	Movement for Islamic Reform in Arabia
MIYM	Muslim Islamic Youth Movement
MNF	Multi-National Forces (US-led)
MNLF	Moro National Liberation Front
MWL	Muslim World League
NCB	National Commercial Bank of Saudi Arabia
NIF	National Islamic Front (Sudan)
NU	Nahdlatul Ulema
OFAC	The Office of Foreign Assets Control
OPM/SANG	Saudi Arabian National Guard
OSALA	Oromo-Somali-Afar Liberation Alliance
PAI	Pakistan Awami Itehad
PAL	Philippines Airlines
PAS	Parti Islam Se Malaysia
PDF	Militia People's Defence Force
PFLP	Popular Front for the Liberation of Palestine

PIA	Pakistan International Airlines
PLO	Palestine Liberation Organisation
PPP	Development Unity Party
PULO	Patani United Liberation Organisation
RAW	Research and Analysis Wing (India's Foreign Intelligence Agency)
SBG	Saudi Binladen Group
SPLA	Sudan People's Liberation Army
SSP	Sipah-e-Sahaba Pakistan (Army of the Prophet's Companions)
TMSA	Thai Muslim Students' Association
TNSM	Tehreek-e-Nafaz-e-Shariat-e-Mohammadi
TWRA	Third World Relief Agency
UMFF	Ugandan Mujahidin Freedom Fighters
UTO	United Tajik Opposition
USIS	United States Information Service Centre
YMAT	Young Muslim Association of Thailand

INTRODUCTION

"We – with God's help – call on every Muslim who believes in God and wishes to be rewarded to comply with God's order to kill the Americans and plunder their money wherever and whenever they find it. We also call on the Muslim *ulema* [community], leaders, youths, and soldiers to launch the raid on Satan's US troops and the devil's supporters allying with them and to displace those who are behind them so that they may learn a lesson." (Declaration of War by Osama bin Laden, together with leaders of the World Islamic Front for the Jihad Against the Jews and the Crusaders [Al-Jabhah al-Islamiyyah al-'Alamiyyah Li-Qital al-Yahud Wal-Salibiyyin], Afghanistan, February 23, 1998)

Al Qaeda is the first multinational terrorist group of the twenty-first century and it confronts the world with a new kind of threat. The perspectives of the historian and the political scientist are both essential in understanding and addressing Al Qaeda, but they can lead to an underestimation of the phenomenon facing us. Since the contemporary wave of terrorism began in the Middle East in 1968, no groups resembling Al Qaeda have previously emerged. Al Qaeda has moved terrorism beyond the status of a technique of protest and resistance and turned it into a global instrument with which to compete with and challenge Western influence in the Muslim world. Al Qaeda is a worldwide movement capable of mobilising a new and hitherto unimagined global conflict. This book describes in detail the threat posed by Al Qaeda and offers a perspective with which to formulate a counter-strategy in the coming years of conflict.

My book attempts to paint a broad picture of an organization whose global reach and long-term threat have been underestimated until quite recently. Over the last five years I have spent several hundred hours interviewing over 200 terrorists, including Al Qaeda members, in more than fifteen countries in Asia (including Central Asia), Africa, the Middle East and Western Europe. My initial interest in studying the group we now know as Al Qaeda began with a series of visits to Pakistan and Azad Kashmir in 1993–5, when I interviewed almost all the leaders of the Kashmiri *muhajidin* whose ranks had been swelled by the Afghan Arabs after the Soviet withdrawal in 1989.

More recently I have been able to reach and speak candidly with members of Al Qaeda's penultimate leadership and its rank and file. Through my work as a consultant on terrorism to governments, I have been in contact with the authorities in over a dozen states in charge of interviewing prisoners and detainees being held because of their suspected association with or direct membership of Al Qaeda's network. Both my pre-9/11 and subsequent interviews have allowed me to piece together the comprehensive picture of Al Qaeda I present here. Cumulatively they have also allowed me to assemble the portrait drawn below of Osama bin Laden and to emphasize his single-minded determination not just to take over MAK (Maktab al Khidmat lil Mujahidin al-Arab, or Afghan Service Bureau)/Al Qaeda but to turn it — contrary to the vision of Abdullah Azzam, its founder and intellectual leader — into a global terrorist front. I have also spoken with many government specialists on Islamist terrorist groups, including Al Qaeda.

My knowledge of the links between Al Qaeda and its associate groups in the Middle East, Asia and Europe is based partly on interviews with Al Qaeda members and by reading hundreds of telephone, email and other communications. These include communication transcripts between Al Qaeda leaders and associate leaders such as those between Osama bin Laden and Hasan Hattab, head of the GSPC (Groupe Salafiste pour la Prédication et le Combat), and between Osama's then operations chief, Abu Zubaydah, and Hashim Salamat, head of the MILF (Moro Islamic Liberation Front). The urgency of the times and the degree of the threat posed by Al Qaeda have led me to set forth my conclusions in the strongest possible terms on the basis of what I have been able to learn and the patterns I have discerned from my years spent examining terrorist and official documents and interviewing members of terrorist organisations.

The conventional wisdom among intelligence specialists was that the emerging pattern of terrorism was one based on autonomous cells acting independently of each other, largely because we were unaware of how Al Qaeda and other groups had cleverly reverted to one-to-one contact, primarily via couriers, as a means of keeping in touch that circumvented governments' technical means of intelligence-gathering. This explains why the fact that Al Qaeda's German, British, Spanish, Dutch and Belgian cells were acting in concert was overlooked, something discovered only during *post facto* investigations into the background of Mohammad Atta and the other 9/11 conspirators.

By perpetrating the world's greatest terrorist outrage on September 11, 2001, Al Qaeda demonstrated the magnitude of the escalating threat and the sophistication of its methods. It is a pioneering operational vanguard of a global Islamist threat posing the likelihood of long term, more or less continuous conflict with the West. To manage and counter that threat, a comprehensive understanding of Al Qaeda is required, and it is the purpose of this book to provide it.

Where did Al Qaeda spring from? And why did we begin to hear about it so recently, even though Osama bin Laden has been known of for far longer? The trap to be avoided here when evaluating Al Qaeda as an organisation is the assumption that what drives terrorist groups is publicity in pursuit of their broader goal. If that were so, neatly typed communiqués claiming responsibility for Al Qaeda attacks would have been sent to the press. Until 9/11 Osama bin Laden never used the term "Al Qaeda", nor did his close cohorts. Al Qaeda is above all else a secret, almost virtual, organisation, one that denies its own existence in order to remain in the shadows. This explains why it always uses other names and identities (such as the World Islamic Front for the Jihad Against the Jews and the Crusaders) when referring to its actions, beliefs or statements, thereby keeping us guessing about its true motives, its true intentions. Al Qaeda maintains its practice of absolute secrecy even when dealing with Islamist parties and armed groups that share its aspirations. To them too it is an enigma, a shadowy body that many of them aspire to "join" but which accepts only a tiny proportion of those eligible for enrolment, given the very strict selection criteria it imposes.

Two momentous events in 1979 — the Islamic revolution in Iran and the Soviet invasion of Afghanistan — marked the rise of a new wave of Islamist movements which toppled the Shah of Iran and eventually drove the Soviet Union from Afghanistan. And it was the enduring impact of the Iranian Revolution and the defeat of communism which precipitated the creation of over one hundred contemporary Islamist movements in the Middle East, Asia, Africa, the Caucasus, the Balkans, and also in Western Europe.

Its founders had painstakingly built Al Qaeda al-Sulbah (The Solid Base) for the sole purpose of creating societies founded on the strictest Islamist principles. The Palestinian-Jordanian ideologue Abdullah Azzam conceptualised Al Qaeda in 1987. Defining its composition, aims, and purpose, he wrote in *Al-Jihad*, the principal journal of the Afghan Arabs:

> Every principle needs a vanguard to carry it forward and, while focusing its way into society, puts up with heavy tasks and enormous sacrifices. There is no ideology, neither earthly nor heavenly, that does not require such a vanguard that gives everything it possesses in order to achieve victory for this ideology. It carries the flag all along the sheer, endless and difficult path until it reaches its destination in the reality of life, since Allah has destined that it should make it and manifest itself. This vanguard constitutes Al-Qa'idah al-Sulbah for the expected society.[1]

Azzam — the ideological father of Al Qaeda — was the mentor of Osama bin Laden. After co-founding the Maktab al Khidmat lil Mujahidin al-Arab (MAK, or Afghan Service Bureau) in Peshawar,

Pakistan, in 1984, Azzam and Osama then ran it together for several years. Via MAK they disseminated propaganda, raised funds and recruited new members through a network of offices (including thirty in US cities) in thirty-five countries. MAK housed, trained and financed the anti-Soviet Afghan *jihad*. As this, ultimately successful, campaign was drawing an end, Azzam was keen to redirect the *mujahidin* rank and file into another, ideologically worthwhile, project. If not, he feared "those carrying arms could turn into bandits that might threaten people's security and would not let them live in peace."[2] Azzam, the then spiritual leader of the international Islamists, laid down eight guidelines for training Al Qaeda, the "pious group and the pioneering vanguard", in early 1988. Al Qaeda's founding document, published in *Al-Jihad*, states:[3]

> It must jump into the fire of the toughest tests and into the waves of fierce trials.
> The training leadership shares with them the testing march, the sweat and the blood. The leadership must be like the motherly warmth of a hen whose chicks grow under its wings, throughout the long period of hatching and training.
> This vanguard has to abstain from cheap worldly pleasures and must bear its distinct stamp of abstinence and frugality.
> In like manner it must be endowed with firm belief and trust in the ideology, instilled with a lot of hope for its victory.
> There must be a strong determination and insistence to continue the march no matter how long it takes.
> Travel provision is among the most important items on this march. The provision consists of meditation, patience and prayer.
> Loyalty and devotion
> They must be aware of the existence of anti-Islam machinations all over the world.

Today, these are the very qualities that are clearly evident among Al Qaeda members — in Afghanistan or elsewhere. Whether in hospital, in a prison in Afghanistan, or a courthouse in Virginia or in New York, its fighters seem to us to have conquered the fear of death. As well as serving as a pioneering vanguard, the Islamist cadres of Al Qaeda, spawned and sustained by Azzam's ideology, are an inspirational model for other Islamists. To put into practice Azzam's pan-Islamic ideology, Osama and Al Qaeda's leadership built an organisation with a worldwide network.

At the end of the anti-Soviet Afghan *jihad*, the perennially fragile political situation in the Middle East and Afghanistan facilitated the internationalisation of Al Qaeda. Having defeated the "evil empire", and driven by Islamist zeal, most Arab and Asian *mujahidin* (warriors of God) who returned home from the internationally supported *jihad* (holy war) in

Afghanistan wanted to precipitate radical social and political change. They joined opposition political parties, religious bodies and other groups in their own countries, campaigning against dictatorial Muslim rulers and their corrupt regimes. Their very presence served as a catalyst for religious debate, social instability and political unrest. While non-violent campaigns turned violent, violent campaigns escalated. While many governments imprisoned these erstwhile *jihadi* heroes, others were denied entry, expelled, or made stateless. As the political conditions in Afghanistan deteriorated and international pressure forced Pakistan to expel the remaining *mujahidin*, MAK provided them with a safe haven.

Even before the departure of Soviet troops in 1989, MAK's socio-economic, political and military infrastructure had steadfastly begun evolving into Al Qaeda. The resources at MAK's disposal were diverted by Al Qaeda away from Afghanistan into regional conflicts where Islamist guerrillas were involved, principally in Kashmir and Chechnya, but also in Mindanao, Tajikistan, Uzbekistan, Somalia, Malaysia, Indonesia, Georgia, Nagorno-Karabakh, Azerbaijan, Yemen, Algeria and Egypt. In most of these countries the governing regimes were openly hostile to Islamist movements, often repressing them ferociously. Al Qaeda, using the humanitarian cover of MAK and some Islamic charities, infiltrated many of these conflicts, sending cadres to train further recruits and take part in the actual fighting.

Al Qaeda was uncompromisingly distinct from most other Islamist groups in history, its avowed position being: "Islamic governments have never been and will never be, established through peaceful solutions and cooperative councils. They are established as they [always] have been by pen and gun by word and bullet by tongue and teeth."[4] As progress in these domestic campaigns — from Saudi Arabia to Egypt and Algeria — was slow, a second front was initiated by Al Qaeda to target the United States and its allies. Without directly challenging Western military power, economic strength and cultural influence, the Islamists perceive that they cannot bring about change in their home countries, because a group of Western countries, led by the USA, steadfastly supports Israel and the unrepresentative Arab regimes of the Middle East.

To intervene successfully in conflicts where Muslims were affected, Al Qaeda established ideological, political, financial and military control over several Islamist terrorist groups. Although Afghanistan was Al Qaeda's principal military training base, it also trained recruits in Sudan, Yemen, Chechnya, Tajikistan, Somalia, and the Philippines. For instance, when Al Qaeda trainees had difficulties entering landlocked Afghanistan through Pakistan after the East Africa embassy bombings in August 1998, Osama phoned Hashim Salamat, the leader of the MILF, in mid-February 1999, asking him to set up new training camps in the

Philippines. Later, these MILF camps — "Hodeibia" and "Palestine" in the Abubakar complex — were staffed by Al Qaeda trainers providing instruction for foreign recruits.[5] With the dismantling of their infrastructure in Afghanistan due to the American military campaign launched on October 7, 2001, Al Qaeda's critical training needs will depend increasingly on other overseas camps.

To function at a global level, Al Qaeda created a worldwide strategic framework of Islamist military and political organisations. From the early 1990s onwards, Osama invited representatives of Islamist terrorist groups and Islamic political movements to join Al Qaeda's *shura majlis*, or consultative council. Al Qaeda also established relationships with thirty Islamist terrorist groups, inspiring and assisting them, both directly and indirectly, to attack targets at home and abroad. As Al Qaeda's policy was not to claim these operations as their own, and because these attacks occurred mostly in Asia and the Middle East, scant attention was paid to them in the international media. For instance, Al Qaeda bombed a Philippines Airlines flight over Japan, killing one Japanese and injuring other passengers in 1994, while in 1996 it murdered two German nationals in Libya. Although "*Oplan Bojinka*" — an operation to destroy eleven US airliners over the Pacific, to crash an explosive-laden aircraft on to the Pentagon and the CIA headquarters and assassinate President Clinton and Pope John Paul II in Manila — was exposed, Al Qaeda was not vigorously monitored, nor were its leaders hunted down. Moreover, when Al Qaeda recruited, trained and financed Ramzi Ahmed Yousef to bomb one of the World Trade Centre towers in New York on February 23, 1993, the international intelligence community failed to assess accurately and respond decisively to this highly dangerous international terrorist organisation.

Most vulnerable to Al Qaeda infiltration and targeting are the Western liberal democracies wherein it has fully exploited the tolerance and freedom of association enshrined in their constitutions and laws. In addition to their ideological penetration of Muslim communities by recruiting *imams* and other mosque officials, Al Qaeda has set great store by establishing, infiltrating and trying to gain control of many Islamic NGOs, be they government-registered charities engaged in socio-economic, educational, or welfare projects. According to the CIA, one-fifth of all Islamic NGOs worldwide have been unwittingly infiltrated by Al Qaeda and other terrorist support groups. By forming such front organisations — some registered as non-profit and others as charitable — Al Qaeda and its associates have sought to radicalise and mobilise the Islamic diaspora. The carefully crafted Islamist propaganda disseminated by some Islamic associations and societies has exploited the political impotence felt by some Muslim migrants and left them vulnerable to Al Qaeda indoctrination. Throughout Western Europe and North America there are many first- and second-generation Muslim migrants from the Middle East who share Al Qaeda's vision and mission. Some are willing either to join Al Qaeda's campaign against the West or secretly support the group, politically, financially, and logistically. By working among ordinary European, North American and Australian Muslims, Al Qaeda has gained strategic depth at the very heart of Western communities.

To prepare the pioneering Islamist vanguard, Al Qaeda emphasises the physical as well as psychological aspects of warfare training. The average Al Qaeda fighter is better trained and better prepared for his mission than any other Islamist guerrilla or terrorist. For example, of the twenty 9/11 hijackers it is remarkable that not one of them flinched, not one had second thoughts; all went willingly to their deaths, even the very young. Because he firmly believes that Allah guides him and rewards the principle of sacrifice, he is driven by a relentless, fearless energy.

The *fatwa* (Islamic decree) issued by Al Qaeda and its associates illuminates the motivation of Al Qaeda's martyrs to kill and their supreme indifference to death. It should be borne in mind, however, that the force of a *fatwa* depends entirely upon who pronounces it, and none of the recognised Islamic authorities (Sunni or Shia) regards Osama bin Laden as a person capable legitimately of issuing one:

> ...a martyr's privileges are guaranteed by Allah; forgiveness with the first gush of his blood, he will be shown his seat in paradise, he will be decorated with the jewels of Imaan [belief], married off to the beautiful ones, protected from the test in the grave, assured security in the day of judgement, crowned with the crown of dignity, a ruby of which is better than Duniah [the whole world] and its entire content, wedded to seventy two of the pure Houries [beautiful ones of paradise], and his intercession on behalf of seventy of his relatives will be accepted.[6]

By designing specialised courses and constructing secret camps to train its volunteers for martyrdom operations, Al Qaeda institutionalised the techniques of suicide terrorism. More than in any other Islamist group, the culture of martyrdom is firmly embedded in its collective psyche. The indoctrinated bomber aims to inflict maximum damage on the enemy target by fearlessly striking it, in the process also destroying himself. As the first terrorist group to conduct suicide attacks on land (US embassies in East Africa, 1998), sea (USS *Cole*, Yemen, 2000) and in the air (September 11, 2001), Al Qaeda has expanded and refined this deadly repertoire.

Another hallmark of an Al Qaeda attack is its huge investment in the planning and preparatory stages. To ensure success, Al Qaeda has an elaborate, highly skilled organisation for mounting surveillance and reconnaissance of targets. After gathering critical data on the intended target, its cadres study it patiently and meticulously before rehearsing and executing an operation. Al Qaeda spent one and a half years training its operatives before targeting the US on September 11. As such, its preference is for qualitative rather than quantitative targeting. By selectively attacking high prestige, symbolic targets, Al Qaeda aims to denigrate its opponent, expose his vulnerability and prompt further retaliation. After it bombed the US embassies in Kenya and Tanzania, the CIA knew that it was planning further attacks, but the American government lacked the political will and public support to intervene in Afghanistan in the wholehearted fashion required. Referring to Osama bin Laden, the CIA assessed the threat he posed as follows: "We believe he is planning future operations and are particularly concerned that his use of the word 'qualitative' is a signal for increasing the degree of damage future attacks may inflict."[7] As was demonstrated on September 11, 2001, the combination of suicidal terrorists and shrewdly chosen, psychologically damaging, high-profile targeting led to massive death and destruction. Terrorism is here to stay, and Al Qaeda will not be brushed aside easily.

According to Western intelligence sources, which vary quite alarmingly in their estimates, between 10,000 and 110,000 recruits graduated from Al Qaeda training camps in Afghanistan between 1989 and October 2001.[8] Considering that there were several other terrorist groups operating training camps in Afghanistan in the 1990s, and that Al Qaeda recruited only 3,000, or 3% of those it trained in terrorism and guerrilla warfare, this suggests it has more than enough manpower to draw on, now and in the future. Rather chillingly, it also demonstrates the very high degree of selectivity Al Qaeda depends on to screen out all but the most committed, most trustworthy and most capable operatives. Islamists from all over the world regard it as the very highest honour to be accepted as a full Al Qaeda member; in fact they almost fight to get in, such is the high regard in which it is held. Even if 1,000 Al Qaeda members were killed or captured during the "Third Afghan War", there are, even by very conservative estimates, still several tens of thousand trained Islamist terrorists or would-be terrorists at large.

Whether it is being fought in Afghanistan or elsewhere, destroying Al Qaeda will be nothing but a protracted campaign. The longer foreign troops remain in Afghanistan, the greater the risk of segments of the local population supporting Al Qaeda and the Taliban; yet withdrawing the peacekeeping contingent and élite US and British troops could have the chilling outcome of possibly once again plunging the country into chaos. Although when he and his associates planned the September 11 attacks Osama bin Laden never anticipated that the US would induct ground troops into Afghanistan, Al Qaeda's leadership has always wanted to draw the US into a protracted battle, especially one where its soldiers would find themselves based in a hostile environment, open to hit and run attacks. Osama has continually stressed the need to preserve the strength of his forces and the virtues of patience, whether in long-term planning for terrorist attacks or in waiting for an opportunity for the tide to turn against the presence of foreign troops. Al Qaeda's strategy for ousting US troops from Saudi Arabia is likely to provide a guide to their next move in Afghanistan:

> ...due to the imbalance of power between our armed forces and the enemy forces, a suitable means of fighting must be adopted, i.e. using fast-moving light forces that work under complete secrecy. In other words, to initiate a guerrilla warfare, where the sons of the nation, and not the military forces, take part in it. And as you know, it is wise in the present circumstances for the armed military forces not to be engaged in conventional fighting with the forces of the Crusader enemy (the exceptions are the bold and forceful operations carried out by the members of the armed forces individually) unless a big advantage is likely to be achieved; and the great losses induced on the enemy side that would shake and destroy its foundations and infrastructure, and help to expel him defeated out of the country. The mujahideen, your brothers and sons, request that you support them with the necessary information, materials and arms. Security men are especially asked to cover up for the mujahideen and to assist them as much as possible against the occupying enemy; and to spread rumours, fear and discouragement among the members of the enemy forces.[9]

Al Qaeda has appealed to members of the Northern Alliance to assist them on the basis that "Muslim should support Muslim".[10] Thankfully, this support is unlikely to emerge in the short term because most Afghans, except those aligned previously to them, fear the Taliban's return to power. In the wake of the US-led campaign, the Taliban failed immediately to mobilise support for a guerrilla war, but in the months since the fall of their regime, the Taliban and Al Qaeda elements that eluded the Northern Alliance and US forces have merged into one military unit dedicated to waging a protracted guerrilla war against their enemies, the American forces in particular. This merger has acted as a force multiplier for Al Qaeda/Taliban fighters, and it is highly likely that they are planning a campaign that will last many years. This guerrilla campaign will be augmented by going after American and allied targets overseas (hence Osama's claim that "the battle lines should be widened from 100 metres to 300 metres").

Al Qaeda's relationship with other Islamist groups has long been one of its trump cards. When it struck on September 11, many Islamists rejoiced, some discreetly, others in public. Many groups — including Parti Islam Se Malaysia (PAS), Palestinian Hamas, Palestinian Islamic Jihad, and Lebanese Hezbollah — condemned the attacks, first because they disliked what they saw as public posturing, and second, to avoid potential retaliation from the US and its allies. No Islamist group either disagreed with, or condemned Osama or Al Qaeda's aims and objectives. For many, only the timing was wrong. "Osama acted too early. The Muslim world was not yet ready to openly and fully support his action," claimed one Islamist.[11]

Since the US intervention in Afghanistan in October 2001, Al Qaeda has lost its main base for planning and preparing terrorist operations. Hence the Al Qaeda leadership is relying on its wider network to plan and execute new operations with the support of its associate groups. After relocation, the current, or new, leadership will reorganise the group's lines of command and communication. Al Qaeda is structured in such a way that it can operate without a centralised command. Its regional bureaux function as the nodal points of its horizontal network outside Afghanistan and liaise with associate groups and Al Qaeda cells. For instance, the regional node in Bosnia, Albania and thereafter in Turkey coordinated operations in the Balkans, its counterpart in Georgia handles the Caucasus, African operations are run from Yemen and Somalia, and Malaysia and Indonesia look after Asia. The severe disruption to Al Qaeda's command and communication structures in 2001/2 has only emphasised the usefulness of such a decentralised structure.

To adjust to the new reality, Al Qaeda is rapidly learning from its mistakes. With the sustained targeting and hunting down of its cells, their cadres are bringing forward many operations. Other Al Qaeda cells have tactically retreated, either "sleeping" for the time being or seeking the protection of their allies operating in disrupted zones in Asia, Africa and in the Middle East, where they will regroup, rearm and conduct further operations.

At a tactical level, Al Qaeda's resilience has been tested before, however. It survived the international investigation in the aftermath of the attacks on the US embassies in East Africa and the bombing of USS *Cole* and still managed to execute the multiple suicide attacks on 9/11. Functional and regional compartmentalisation of the organisation — both in its infrastructure and networks — ensures that the highest standards of operational security are maintained.

It also has a proven capacity to regenerate new cells: its networks are intertwined in the socio-economic, political and religious fabric of Muslims living in at least eighty countries. The West's reliance on traditional tools of law enforcement has brought only partial success in detecting and destroying Al Qaeda, while the effectiveness of diplomatic measures has been limited by the group's mobility. For instance, when Western pressure forced it out of Sudan to Afghanistan in May 1996, it maintained ties with Middle Eastern and African groups such as the GIA

(Armed Islamic Group of Algeria) and Ittihad al-Islami of Somalia, but forged fresh alliances with Muslim guerrillas and terrorists as well as Muslim communities in South, Southeast and Central Asia. As a result, Al Qaeda includes Uzbeks, Kazakhs, Kirgyz, Turkmens and Tajiks in Soviet Central Asia; Uighurs in Xingjiang in China; Pakistanis, Kashmiris, Indians and Bangladeshis in the subcontinent; Rohingayas in Myanmar; and Malaysians, Singaporeans, Indonesians, and Filipinos in East Asia. It is now a truly transnational organisation, operating throughout the Asia-Pacific, from Asiatic Russia to Australasia.

Since the modern era of terrorism began in 1968, when the Popular Front for the Liberation of Palestine (PFLP) began its campaign of plane hijackings, the counter-terrorism community has never encountered a group like Al Qaeda. Is it an aberration, or the norm? What is clear is that it is the first multinational terrorist organisation, capable of functioning from Latin America to Japan and all the continents in between. Unlike the terrorists of the 1970s and 1980s, Al Qaeda is not guided by territorial jurisdiction — its theatre of support, as well as its operations, is global. Instead of resisting globalisation, its forces are being harnessed by contemporary Islamist groups, constantly looking for new bases and new targets worldwide.

At the time of writing, seven months into the American, Allied and coalition partner campaign against Al Qaeda, several of its key leaders have been apprehended, including Abu Zubaydah. Most of Al Qaeda's leadership, in this author's view, remains in the lawless tribal areas straddling the Afghan and Pakistan borders, where even the Pakistan Army and its intelligence organisation, the ISI (Inter-Services-Intelligence), find it hard to operate freely.

Although its ideology is puritanical, Al Qaeda is an essentially modern organisation, one that exploits up to date technology for its own ends, relying on satellite phones, laptop computers, encrypted communications websites for hiding messages and the like. Its modes of attack range from low-tech assassinations, bombings and ambushes to experiments with explosive-laden gliders and helicopters and crop-spraying aircraft adapted to disperse highly potent agents. It will have no compunction about employing chemical, biological, radiological, and nuclear weapons against population centres. Although the intelligence community reported in the late 1990s that Al Qaeda had acquired uranium in Khartoum and hired Egyptian and Pakistani physicists to research the development of unconventional weapons,[12] it seems the group may have been duped. Intelligence sources now believe that criminals sold Al Qaeda irradiated canisters purporting to contain uranium stolen from Russian army bases, whereas in fact the contents would have had no military value whatsoever had it been passed on to rogue nuclear scientists.

Al Qaeda's sophisticated use of communications exemplifies its truly global reach and the sheer range of its activities and ambitions. In late 1998 Osama realised that his Compact-M satellite phone was being monitored by Western security and intelligence agencies, so Al Qaeda developed a system to deceive those monitoring his calls.[13] Western security and intelligence agencies were soon able to monitor the new system, which was based on transferring international calls within safe houses in Pakistan to make them seem like domestic calls. Al Qaeda's most important operative, Abu Zubyadah, regularly phoned Al Qaeda-supported groups such as the MILF and GSPC. while analysis of bin Laden's billing records from 1996-8 revealed that nearly a fifth of his calls (238 out of 1,100) were made to hardwired and mobile phones in Britain.[14] The second largest volume of calls (221) .was to Yemen,[15] Al Qaeda's regional node for the Middle East since May 1996. Al Qaeda used the phone number it called in Yemen as a switchboard — that is to divert and receive calls and messages from the region and beyond. In many ways, Britain and Yemen were the two hubs of Al Qaeda's overseas political and military operations in the late 1990s. Not surprisingly, Iran received nearly 10%[16] of the outgoing calls, confirming the Hezbollah-Iran relationship with Al Qaeda. Other countries frequently called were Azerbaijan, Pakistan, Saudi Arabia, Sudan and Egypt

Ideologically Al Qaeda differs markedly from the groups of the past. It has taken the first steps to breaking the Shia-Sunni divide that has traditionally kept apart two terrorist groupings. By forging a tactical relationship with Hezbollah, Al Qaeda mastered the art of bombing buildings. Al Qaeda has persistently argued that Islamist groups should shed their doctrinal differences and unite to take on the real enemy, the West, and strike the US — "the head of the snake". Its broad-based ideology, integrated horizontally and vertically, appeals to, and resonates among, the affluent and the less affluent, the educated and the less educated. Al Qaeda cuts across historical and sectarian barriers, drawing its membership from all strata of society. However it remains an overwhelmingly Sunni group, doctrinally and otherwise.

Another of Al Qaeda's strengths is its wealth. In addition to benefiting from the largesse of Osama bin Laden, its business and financial committee generates significant revenues from its companies, charities and worldwide investments. The penetration of one fifth of Islamic NGOs by Al Qaeda and other Islamist groups is another source of funding, along with voluntary contributions collected clandestinely in some mosques. Al Qaeda also generates funds from its business operations in the money and share markets and through crime, though there is little evidence of Al Qaeda having been involved in the production or sale of drugs, despite repeated US claims to the contrary. The Taliban raised a lot of money through the trade in narcotics, however. Although Al Qaeda has received funding from state sponsors (Sudan, Afghanistan, Iran) its financial robustness clearly lies in its own non-state sources of support. Very few groups have acquired financial assets and independent resources to the extent that Al Qaeda has. Despite a US-led worldwide effort to close down its financial networks, Al Qaeda continues to operate through the *hawala*, or unregulated, banking system, based on the use of promissory notes for the exchange of cash and gold. Al Qaeda also benefited from copying many of the financial models and networks devised by the disgraced Bank of Credit and Commerce International (BCCI), which collapsed in 1991. It was used extensively by terrorists, state sponsors of terrorism and by various security and intelligence organisations.

Al Qaeda's unprecedented mobility, motivation and capacity to generate wealth pose multiple challenges to international security. Is it the prototype of other terrorist organisations which the world is likely to confront in the future? It is clearly very different from "traditional" terrorists and any of the other groups that we are familiar with today. As a multi-dimensional entity, leading the fight against the "unbelievers" and encouraging Muslim migrant communities to side with it, Al Qaeda has raised the profile of the Islamist threat and increased the likelihood of long-term, more or less continuous, conflict with the West.

Islamist groups such as Hezbollah, Palestinian Islamic Jihad and Hamas remain potent threats despite sustained action against them by Israel and its allies for two decades. Nonetheless, history shows that every terrorist group has a lifespan. Statistically, most guerrilla and terrorist campaigns last between thirteen and fourteen years.[17] The global challenge, especially for the West, is how to shorten the life-span of Al Qaeda, the most destructive international terrorist group in history.

The most effective state response would be to target Al Qaeda's leadership, cripple its command and control, and disrupt its current and future support bases. Although the American government has launched several covert operations to kill or capture Al Qaeda's leadership since August 1998, and done so more steadfastly and on a far larger scale since October 2001, the US intelligence community and military has had only limited success. Although destroying the leadership must remain the central objective, the immediate challenge before the international community is to neutralise Al Qaeda's capacity to plan and execute terrorist strikes, such as Richard Reid's failed attempt to blow up flight AA63 from Paris to Miami on December 22, 2001.

As Al Qaeda's reach is global, only a truly multinational approach to degrading its widely dispersed human and physical infrastructure can bring lasting results. Building and maintaining an anti-terrorist coalition, which is a paramount objective in meeting this challenge, is an arduous task. Although Al Qaeda has suffered greatly in Afghanistan, its infrastructure overseas remains virtually untouched in certain parts of the world. Wearing it down will be painstakingly slow, and even with the benefits of close international cooperation, there are grave limitations to attempts to annihilate it. Its sleeper and active cells and its support network of pro-Al Qaeda politico-religious groups in developing countries — such as Indonesia, the most populous Muslim country in the world — will remain in place so long as they are tolerated politically. Similarly, Al Qaeda's infrastructure may now extend to the remote area where the borders of Brazil, Argentina and Paraguay meet, building upon extant Islamist cells. Likewise, except in parts of East Africa, Al Qaeda's infrastructure in Sub-Saharan Africa remains intact. Although its presence in Africa remains small, lawlessness, poverty, civil strife and the continent's enormous size greatly increases its potential for survival.

The mid-term response should focus on targeting pockets of Al Qaeda trainers and members in conflict zones. In addition to the US assisting the Philippines to target the Abu Sayyaf Group (ASG) — an associate group of Al Qaeda — the international community ought to consider a range of diplomatic, political and military responses to end the conflicts in Chechnya, Kashmir, Somalia and Algeria, among others, where Al Qaeda members can blend in easily with domestic terrorist groups.

While Al Qaeda can be tackled militarily, it is only by challenging the Islamists' misinterpretation and misrepresentation of the Koran that the international community can inflict long-term strategic damage on the group. Although the Koran constantly insists that Prophet Muhammad did not come to "cancel out" the revelations delivered by the previous prophets — Abraham, Moses and Jesus — Al Qaeda subscribes to a very different view.[18] For instance, the Koran commands Muslims to speak with great courtesy to "the people of the book — say to them: we believe what you believe — your God and our God is One."[19] But, aiming to galvanise the spirit of its supporters, Al Qaeda corrupts, misrepresents or misinterprets the Koranic text:

> These youths know that their rewards in fighting you, the USA, is double their rewards in fighting someone else not from the people of the book. They have no intention except to enter paradise by killing you. An infidel and enemy of God like you cannot be in the same hell with his righteous executioner.[20]

In the absence of a powerfully articulated counter-ideology, Al Qaeda can come to represent the truth for some Muslims and would-be *mujahid*. Therefore, an integral part of the strategy against Al Qaeda should include non-military measures, such as exposing its heretical nature. As long as the ideology of the group remains appealing, Al Qaeda recruiters will enlist more and more members, thus replenishing its losses. While the coalition response to Al Qaeda has been largely military and financial, Islamist groups have a broader agenda, challenging their enemies on the political, religious, social, cultural and educational planes, as well as the military. If the US, its Allies and coalition forces overlook the non-military factors and conditions that strengthen Al Qaeda and other Islamists in the long term, including the status of the Palestinians, the Kashmiris and the corrupt, autocratic governmen ts of the Middle East, the community of nations is highly unlikely to win a strategic victory.

Inside Al Qaeda is my contribution to understanding the organisation and formulating and executing the international response to it. I examine Al Qaeda's reach, the strategic and tactical threat it poses, its mindset, determination and messianic culture. I look at how Al Qaeda thinks and acts, and discuss the strategies and techniques developed by Al Qaeda to advance its Islamist objectives, as well as how the threats posed by its associate groups can be countered.

My motivation for writing this book began many years ago, when I first investigated the Islamist movements of Central, South and South East Asia and the Middle East. A defining moment, however, occurred on the day in March 2001 when I stood by helplessly on the Uzbek-Afghan border as the Al Qaeda-influenced Taliban regime in Kabul ordered the demolition of the giant statues of the Buddha in Bamiyan, a priceless archaeological treasure that had withstood the ravages of both invasion and the elements. Notwithstanding this more recent catalyst, I had developed a sustained and deep interest in Islamist guerrilla and terrorist groups during my many visits to Central Asia, including Afghanistan, during the last decade. I also interviewed law enforcement, immigration and intelligence officers, thus evaluating both the threat and the government response. Among the documents I consulted were several Al Qaeda manuals, including the ten-volume *Encyclopaedia of the Afghan Jihad*, dedicated to both the master, Azzam, and his protégé, Osama bin Laden.

1

WHO IS OSAMA BIN LADEN?

"The West, and the rest of the world, are accusing Osama bin Laden of being the prime sponsor and organizer of what they call 'international terrorism' today. But as far as we are concerned, he is our brother in Islam. He is someone with knowledge and a mujahid fighting with his wealth and his self for the sake of Allah. He is a sincere brother and he is completely the opposite to what the disbelievers are accusing him of. We know that he is well established with the mujahideen in Afghanistan and other places in the world. What the Americans are saying is not true. However, it is an obligation for all Muslims to help each other in order to promote the religion of Islam. Osama bin Laden is one of the major scholars of the jihad, as well as being a main commander of the mujahideen worldwide. He fought for many years against the Communists in Afghanistan and now is engaged in a war against American imperialism." (Ibn-ul-Khattab, military commander of the *mujahidin* in the Caucasus)[1]

Al Qaeda's Emir-General, Osama bin Muhammad bin Laden, was born in Riyadh, Saudi Arabia, on July 30, 1957.[2] The son of migrants, his father Muhammad bin Awdah bin Laden, also known as Muhammad bin Laden, came from Yemen and his mother Hamida from Damascus, Syria. Osama was the seventeenth son of fifty-two children, his father having had four wives and many concubines, although he also married and divorced several women he met during his travels. He provided for them all, including the children, wives and mistresses living in houses scattered throughout Saudi Arabia. Osama had no brothers from his mother, only sisters, including one who would later marry Muhammad Jamal Khalifa.[3] His mother, Hamida, is still alive, had re-married and was till recently in contact with her son.

Osama's father, Muhammad bin Laden, hailed from the Hadhramat, in Yemen, his family having moved to Saudi Arabia in the 1930s. It is well known how he rose from poverty, starting off as a dockworker in the port of Jeddah, to become Saudi Arabia's foremost construction magnate. He refrained from politics yet saw his Saudi Bin Laden Group — as the company is now known — win huge infrastructural projects in the Arabian Peninsula and elsewhere. His contracts included the renovation of the holy cities of Mecca and Medina, including its mosques, and he rebuilt the al-Aqsa mosque in Jerusalem. Thus the 300-strong bin Laden family became highly respected in the eyes of Saudi royals and commoners alike.

Osama was raised in Medina and the Hijaz under the influence of his Syrian mother. After schooling in Jeddah he married a Syrian, a relative of his mother, and later attended King Abdulaziz University where he studied economics and management with the intention of joining the family business. An average student, he was especially interested in government and international politics, but left during his third year. While at university in Jeddah, Osama was taught Islamic studies by Muhammad Qutb, the brother of Sayyid Qutb, the ideologue of the Muslim Brotherhood, and Abdullah Azzam, both of whom created a deep impression on him.[4] Contrary to press reports, however, he did not study engineering, nor did he complete his degree. Nor for that matter did he visit Sweden in 1971 or learn to fly near Oxford in England.

There was much respect and affection between the Saudi King, Faisal ibn Abdul Aziz, and Muhammad bin Laden. When the latter was killed in a helicopter crash in Saudi Arabia in 1968, the King was visibly upset, and some 10,000 people, including Osama, attended the funeral. Immediately afterwards King Faisal met the bin Laden family and told the children he was placing them under royal decree. Muhammad bin Laden's estate was placed in trust to a committee appointed by the King. Apart from Ali, who was twenty-one at the time, all the others accepted the arrangements. Ali took his share of the inheritance and has since lived in Lebanon and Paris, apparently regretting his decision.

Muhammad bin Laden had always urged his children to refrain from politics and religious debate, declining general political posts offered by the King. After Muhammad bin Laden's death, in keeping with his advice, another of his sons also politely turned down a cabinet post. The only member of the family to take a sustained interest in politics, from about 1973 onwards, was Osama. While working for the family business he focused his energies and resources on the advancement of Islam and Islamism. In particular he supported the Saudi-based Islamists of South Yemen who were fighting to oust the Communists. Although very little is known of his role at this time, Osama was for nearly two decades one of the key players in this struggle, even after his return to Saudi Arabia from Afghanistan in 1989.

Within a month of the Soviet invasion of Afghanistan on December 26, 1979, Osama left Saudi Arabia for Pakistan to assess the situation. There he saw the Afghan leaders Burhanuddin Rabbani and Abdur Rab Rasool Sayyaf, whom he had met on the Hajj.[5] A teacher of theology, Rabbani led the Jamaat-i-Islami, and Sayyaf, a *mullah*, the Itehar-i-Islami. They were among the seven principal commanders that spearheaded the anti-Soviet *jihad* with the military, logistical and financial support of a multinational coalition organised by the CIA and comprising the United States, Britain, Saudi Arabia, Pakistan, China and several other countries. Intelligence and military personnel from most of these countries were active on the ground in Afghanistan and neighbouring Pakistan, funding and training Afghans and Arab volunteers to fight the Soviets.

The other five Afghan leaders were Gulbuddin Hekmatyar, a student activist and leader of the Hizb-i-Islami; Yunus Khalis, a *mullah*, and chief of the Hizb-i-Islami; Nabi Muhammadi, a *mullah*, the driving force of Harakat-i-Inqilab Islami; Syed Ahmed Gailani, a spiritual elder [*pir*] who led the Mahaz-i-Milli; and Sibghatullah Mujaddidi, another *mullah*, who led the Jabha-i-Nitaz-i-Milli. Osama also met Ahmed Shah Masood, the celebrated military commander of Jamaat-i-Islami and an associate of Rabbani.

When Osama arrived in Peshawar there were only a few dozen Arab *mujahidin* in Afghanistan preparing for the anti-Soviet *jihad*. Within a few months, Osama fell under the influence of the Jordanian Palestinian, Sheikh Dr Abdullah Azzam, one of the leading Islamists of his generation. Azzam — a stalwart of the Jordanian Muslim Brotherhood — influenced Osama's thinking for the next ten years. As well as teaching at the International Islamic University in Islamabad, he played a key role in formulating and articulating the *jihad* doctrine that mobilised Afghans and Arab volunteers to fight the Soviets.

Azzam was born in 1941 in the village of Selat al-Harithis, in northern Palestine. Later he joined the Muslim Brotherhood "before he had even come of age",[6] and after studying and teaching obtained a bachelor's degree in *shariah* (Islamic law) from Shariah College, Damascus University. In the wake of the Israeli annexation of the West Bank in 1967, he went to Jordan and joined the resistance to the Israeli occupation, during which he also studied *shariah* at al-Azhar University in Cairo. With the expulsion of the Palestine Liberation Organisation from Jordan in 1968, he left for Egypt where he both taught and studied for a doctorate in Islamic jurisprudence at al-Azhar University in Cairo. Azzam was expelled from King Abdul-Aziz University in 1979 for Islamic activism, after which he left for Pakistan.

Together with Osama, Azzam set up the Afghan Service Bureau (MAK) in 1984. Also known as the Afghan Bureau, the Office Bureau or the Service Bureau, it catered primarily for the foreign *mujahidin*, above all Arabs. As an organisation staffed and managed by the *mujahidin*, it played a decisive role in the anti-Soviet resistance. In addition to recruiting, indoctrinating and training tens of thousands of Arab and Muslim youths from countries ranging from the US to the Philippines, MAK disbursed $200 million of Middle Eastern and Western, mainly American and British, aid destined for the Afghan *jihad*. Osama also channelled substantial resources of his own to the cause, a gesture that resonated with his fighters, raising his credibility and allowing him to raise more funds and recruit even more volunteers.

At the height of the influx of Arab and other foreign Muslim fighters from 1984-6, Osama spent most of his time in Afghanistan, moving in 1986 to Peshawar in Pakistan, where he worked from offices in a two-storey villa in the university district.[7] Osama and Azzam built his first camp, al-Ansar, in Jaji, in Afghanistan's Paktia province, bordering the North-West Frontier province of Pakistan.[8] He was fully immersed in fieldwork, which he described as "*jihad*".[9] Azzam also travelled widely, recruiting *jihadists* from among the Muslim Brotherhood and others, as well as raising funds, especially in the Arab world. He also travelled to Germany and to the US, where he lectured to Muslim communities and was welcomed and feted by Muslims worldwide for his role in the war against the Soviet Union. At one meeting organised by the Muslim American Youth Association (MAYA) in Fort Worth, Texas, in 1982, the audience included Essam al-Ridi, a flight instructor. He was so inspired by Azzam's rhetoric that he later joined Al Qaeda, serving both as a procurement officer and as Osama's personal pilot.

Occasionally Osama returned to Saudi Arabia, especially to consult with Saudi intelligence about the Afghan campaign. His wife remained there too, but his son Abdullah, then aged twelve, visited him in Afghanistan.[10] After the anti-Soviet campaign began in earnest, his family rarely saw Osama. For instance, his half brother Yeslem, the eighth or ninth son, claims to have seen him on only a handful of occasions, mostly family functions, till the mid-1980s. Meanwhile Salem, who was educated in Britain and had married an Englishwoman, took over the family business. It was he who transformed it into a global enterprise with offices around the world; but, like his father, he was killed in a plane crash — in Texas, in 1988. Bakr, another brother, then succeeded Salem as chairman of the Saudi Bin Laden Group. Osama invested most of the wealth he inherited from his father's fortune overseas. Intelligence sources differ over the sums involved: the Swiss, with access to superior banking information, opt for a figure of $250-500 million.[11] The Australian government believes it to be over $250 million,[12] while the British estimate is $280-300 million.[13] In fact Osama inherited between $25-30 million, which through prudent investment was soon generating a very healthy annual return, according to intelligence sources.

To improve Al Qaeda's social and military infrastructure, Azzam and Osama built for the Arab *mujahidin* several training camps and guesthouses, including Beit al-Ansar (House of the Companions), Ma'sadat al-Ansar (House of Lions) and the Sidda camp. With Arab fighters in Pakistan and Afghanistan in the early 1980s now numbering 400, the

Pakistani government asked the Saudi royal family to dispatch someone to lead this international brigade, and Osama, who had cultivated a close relationship with Prince Turki ibn Faisal ibn Abdelaziz, the Saudi chief of security and intelligence, was the natural choice. As aid for the *mujahidin* increased, by the mid-1980s Osama was drawing on his family skills, importing heavy machinery, building roads and cave complexes, and supervising the blasting of massive tunnels into the Zazi mountains of Paktia which were to hide field hospitals and arms depots.[14] These facilities, spanning several kilometres, provided for the training and accommodation of hundreds of fighters.

MAK's Emir (leader), Azzam, and his Deputy Emir, Osama, worked closely with Pakistan, especially its formidable ISI. They also had close contacts with the Saudi government and Saudi philanthropists and with the Muslim Brotherhood. The ISI was both the CIA's conduit for arms transfers and the principal trainers of the Afghan and foreign *mujahidin*. The CIA provided sophisticated weaponry, including ground-to-air "Stinger" missiles and satellite imagery of Soviet troop deployments. The Saudi Chief of Intelligence, Prince Turki, worked closely with Osama to coordinate both the fighting and relief efforts, while two Saudi banks — Dar al-Mal al-Islami founded by Prince Turki's brother Prince Muhammad Faisal in 1981 — and Dalla al-Baraka, founded by King Fahd's brother-in-law in 1982 — supported the anti-Soviet campaigns.[15] The two banks channelled funds to twenty NGOs, the best known of which was the International Islamic Relief Organisation (IIRO). Both IIRO and the Islamic Relief Agency functioned under the umbrella of the World Islamic League led by Mufti Abdul Aziz Bin Baz. In addition to benefiting from the vast resources and expertise of governments channelled through domestic and foreign sources, MAK developed an independent global reach. Several mosques and charities, including the Kifah refugee centre in Brooklyn and its mosque, served as MAK outreach offices in the US.

Osama's philanthropy only made him more popular in Afghanistan. Although he came from a privileged background, his commitment to the *jihad*, his humility and simplicity and his ability to befriend and communicate with fighters on the ground appealed to the *mujahidin*. To quote one of them:

> "He not only gave us his money, but he also gave himself. He came down from his palace to live with the Afghan peasants and the Arab fighters. He cooked with them, ate with them, dug trenches with them. This is Bin Ladin's way."[16]

Among the *mujahidin*, he became known as Shaykh Osamah Bin Muhammad bin Laden, *alias* Osama Muhammad al Wahad, *alias* Abu

Abdallah, *alias* Al Qaqa.

While Osama was living on the Afghan-Pakistan border, his religious convictions deepened. He built close relationships with several religious authorities, including Sheikh Umar Abd al-Rahman, who came to Pakistan in 1985. Although Osama played a support, rather than a combat, role he participated in battles in the later stages of the campaign, especially in the 1986 attack on Jalalabad.

In 1987 the *mujahidin* mounted a daring and spectacular attack against a powerful Soviet offensive involving land and air power. It was one of the most famous battles of the whole war and, due to the high risk encountered, was known as the "Lion's Den Operation". Many notable *mujahidin* participated in it, such as Osama, Abu Zubair al-Madani and Shaykh Tameem Dnani. Shaykh 'Abdullah Azzam was "in the second line of the front".[17] Osama was exposed to Soviet poison gas attacks and also suffered minor injuries, as revealed in an interview with Peter Arnett of CNN. And in 1989, Osama fought at Jaji, one of the campaign's decisive battles, further bolstering his reputation in the eyes of many *mujahidin*. By winning this battle against the Soviets he showed how their huge military machine could be defeated by unconventional methods.

Osama's wealth, influence and fearlessness made him a natural leader of the Arab *mujahidin* — most of whom were Saudis, Yemenis, Algerians or Egyptians — in the late 1980s. Until 1989, MAK kept no records of the number of foreign and Afghan *mujahidin* serving in Aghanistan, hence we have no precise tally, only estimates. These too vary greatly, with estimates of 25,000-50,000, and their Afghan counterparts numbering some 175,000-250,000.[18]

While Osama spent much of his time on the front line, Azzam was popularising the concept of *jihad* on the Pakistan-Afghanistan borders. His writings on the political dimension of Islam also influenced other Islamist movements, while some consider him to be one of the founders of Hamas. Contrary to public perception, it was Azzam who conceptualised Al Qaeda, primarily to stabilise and harness the massive *mujahidin* organisation his ideology had helped to create. Nonetheless, Osama's aim of re-creating the Caliphate, or uniting the whole Muslim world into a single entity, appealed to the Arab *mujahidin*. At a practical level, Osama and his Egyptian-dominated *mujahidin* grouping wished to establish Islamic states where rulers deemed too secular held power, beginning with Egypt.

The broad outlines of what would become Al Qaeda were formulated by Azzam in 1987 and 1988, its founding charter being completed by him during that period. He envisaged it as being a organisation that would channel the energies of the *mujahidin* into fighting on behalf of oppressed Muslims worldwide, an Islamic "rapid reaction force", ready to spring to the defence of their fellow believers at short notice. Towards the end of the anti-Soviet Afghan campaign, Osama's relationship with Azzam deteriorated, and in late 1988 and in 1989 they disagreed over several issues. One of these concerned the al-Masada *mujahidin* training camp on the Afghan-Pakistan border. In early 1989 Osama asked Azzam whether it could be turned over to Al Qaeda in order to become its principal base. Azzam refused, notwithstanding Osama's continued entreaties. Despite these differences, the two men maintained a public show of unity and continued working together. After Azzam's death in 1989, Osama was one of the surviving few among the senior *mujahidin* who organised and supported the anti-Soviet campaign at a strategic level. Privately, Osama took credit for the expulsion of the Soviets from Afghanistan. He firmly believed that it was the actions of the *mujahidin* primarily supported by the Muslim world that led to the collapse of the Soviet Union and the ending of the Cold War. He also believed that the US had achieved its goal of becoming the sole global superpower through what he and his fellow *mujahidin* had achieved in Afghanistan. Osama later justified his actions by stating that MAK and its Islamist allies were being persecuted by "an ungrateful United States" who had also taken credit for the defeat of the Soviets.

Although Osama and Azzam agreed on the principal issues of supporting Muslims who were persecuted for their religious and political beliefs, especially those engaged in ethno-nationalist campaigns such as Chechnya and Kashmir, worldwide and on the creation of Al Qaeda, they disagreed on tactics. The tension between the two came to a head over a proposal by MAK's Egyptian fighters to train the *mujahidin* in terrorist techniques. The Egyptians were keen to build a force to mount a campaign back home, but Azzam insisted that MAK's funds were to be used only in Afghanistan. Having lived in Egypt, he knew the futility, danger and limits of launching a terrorist campaign there and hence issued a *fatwa* stating that using *jihadi* funds to train in terrorist tactics would violate Islamic law. On killing non-combatants, Azzam's writings ly reflect the finer points of the issue, as well as his position:

> Many Muslims know about the *hadith* in which the Prophet ordered his companions not to kill any women or children, etc, but very few know that there are exceptions to this case. In summary, Muslims do not have to stop an attack on *mushrikeen* [polytheists], if non-fighting women and children are present. But, Muslims should avoid the killing of children and non-fighting women, and should not aim at them...Islam does not urge its followers to kill anyone amongst the kufar except the fighters, and those who supply mushrikeen and other enemies of Islam with money or advice, because the Qur'anic verse says: "And fight in the cause of Allah those who fight you".[19]

However Osama was already plotting against Azzam, even though he was his designated successor. He wished to reconfigure MAK and the nascent Al Qaeda in his own image, as an unflinchingly hostile global terrorist force, established with the aim of destroying America and Israel and re-establishing the Caliphate by means of a worldwide *jihad*. As tensions between mentor and protégé grew, Osama split from Azzam and moved to Khost in Afghanistan and then back to the Peshawar suburb of Hayatabad. There he established new guesthouses and training camps with the intention of creating an infrastructure for Al Qaeda separate from MAK. When Osama tried to designate the al-Masada camp as Al Qaeda's headquarters, Azzam disagreed in the strongest possible terms. After Azzam was killed, an extremist faction of MAK joined Osama. but the *mujahidin* who had been close to Azzam constantly quarrelled with Osama. To seize control of MAK's offices overseas and its headquarters in Peshawar, Osama had to rely on his Egyptians allies. After the split, Osama briefly used the term "Islamic Army" to describe the *mujahidin* force aligned to him. Meanwhile, the Egyptians had attempted to gain control of MAK's finances, hitherto overseen by Azzam. At their request but with his encouragement, Osama called for the establishment of a financial committee, and again Azzam resisted.

The power struggle between Osama and Azzam had to culminate in the removal of one of them, it being in the interests of Osama and MAK's Egyptian faction to have Azzam out of the way. The Egyptians had won over Osama to their cause before they assassinated Azzam, on the condition that he backed their strategic shift towards terrorism, a move he wholeheartedly endorsed.

On November 24, 1989, a bomb containing 20 kilos of TNT, activated by remote control, killed Azzam and his two sons, Ibrahim and Muhammad, while he was driving to Friday (Jummah) prayer in Peshawar The attack was carried out by at least six members of the Egyptian "family". Osama has never publicly criticised Azzam and still refers to him in a reverential way, praising his achievements in setting up MAK, conducting *jihad* and laying the groundwork for the establishment of Al Qaeda. All this is of a piece with Osama's exceedingly duplicitous nature. He has never attacked in print, in speeches or in conversation the mentor whose murder he sanctioned, if not condoned, and in his writings Osama only praises him. By acquiescing in Azzam's murder, Osama freed the organisation from being constrained by its founder's guiding principles and rules, allowing him to refashion it in his own image, and channel it in directions he preferred. He is not an original thinker but an opportunist, a businessman at heart, who surrounds himself with a good team, manages it well but borrows heavily from others. His cunning was also demonstrated by the fact that he left Pakistan for Saudi

Arabia in the year that Azzam died. It has been impossible to pin down when exactly he left, and no sources on this have been forthcoming, but one should not in the least be surprised if it transpires he was not in Pakistan when Azzam was murdered, furnishing himself with a sound alibi and allowing him to distance himself from the act as much as possible. With the arrest in early 2002 of several longstanding members of Al Qaeda, the identity of the Egyptians and Osama's precise role in Azzam's assassination are likely to be made public.

Nearly a decade later, a Palestinian Al Qaeda member, Muhammad Saddiq Odeh (*alias* Muhammad Sadiq Howeida), told his Pakistani and later his American interrogators that Osama "personally ordered the killing of Azzam because he suspected his former mentor had ties with the Central Intelligence Agency (CIA)".[20] In my view it is highly unlikely that Azzam had ties of any sort with the CIA which, rather than working directly with the *mujahidin*, preferred to let the ISI act as go-between, if only to maintain "deniability" of the Agency's involvement.[21]

Although Soviet troops withdrew from Afghanistan in February 1989, the Russians installed in power in Kabul Muhammad Najibullah, a pro-Communist leader. Hence MAK continued to fight the Najibullah puppet regime and to channel resources to other international campaigns where Muslims were perceived as victims. To complete Al Qaeda's takeover of MAK, Osama loyalists were appointed to key positions. For instance, the MAK representative in New York, Mustafa Shalabi, who was close to Azzam, was killed on March 1, 1991. Although there is no evidence to indicate that Osama ordered his death, it is clear that Shalabi was not with the Egyptians who backed Osama. Furthermore, his body was found, with multiple stab wounds and shot through the head, in the New York apartment of Mahmud Abouhalima, Umar Abd al-Rahman's driver, who was a member of the Al Qaeda team that bombed the World Trade Centre in 1993.

At the time of his assassination in Peshawar, Azzam was the acknowledged leader of the international *jihadists*. He was succeeded by the spiritual leader of the Egyptian Islamic Group, Umar Abd al-Rahman, the "Blind Sheikh", with whom Osama had developed a strong rapport since his first visit to Pakistan in 1985 and subsequently in 1990 in Afghanistan. While in Pakistan the Blind Sheikh was seen in the company of, and was taken round by, Muhammad Shawki al-Islambouli, the brother of Khaled al-Islambouli, President Sadat's assassin. Thereafter Muhammad al-Islambouli joined Al Qaeda and managed one of its terrorist training camps. Osama admired Umar Abd al-Rahman and acknowledged him as the undisputed leader of the international *jihadists* after Azzam's death. Before Umar Abd al-Rahman's arrest in the US in 1993, he had assumed the role of spiritual leader of Al Qaeda. The Blind

Sheikh travelled widely, preaching, recruiting and raising funds for the international *jihad*, meeting Islamists in South Asia, the Middle East, Europe and North America. After his arrest his two sons, Ahmed and Muhammad, both then in exile in Pakistan, joined Al Qaeda, working closely with Osama in Afghanistan

Before his death Azzam had been a determining influence on Osama's thinking and actions, especially his stressing of the need to build support via radical rhetoric rather than indiscriminate killing. In his absence Osama was to mature as a radical under the guidance of the Egyptian Dr Ayman Muhammad Rabi' al-Zawahiri. Ten years younger than Azzam, he gradually filled the ideological void created by the latter's death. Al Zawahiri was born on June 9, 1951, and came from one of the most influential and respected families in al-Sharqiyyah, Egypt.[22] His grandfather was Sheikh Rabi' al-Zawahiri of the Al-Azhar mosque and his father was a professor of medicine. Al Zawahiri's mother is the daughter of Dr 'Abd-al-Wahad 'Azzam, dean of the School of Arts and President of Cairo University, who became Egypt's Ambassador to Pakistan. As a member of a highly-regarded medical family, al-Zawahiri himself qualified as a physician in 1974 and later married a student from the School of Arts in 1979.

Joining an Islamist organisation at the age of fifteen, al-Zawahiri has since accumulated over thirty years of expertise in clandestine operations, operating under the aliases of Dr Abd-al-Wahhab, Salah 'Ali Kamil, Sami Mahmound El Hifnawi and Amin Othman. Amid persistent attempts by the Egyptian security services to destroy it, he built up one of the two most feared terrorist groups in Egypt, Egyptian Islamic Jihad.

After he was tried for, and acquitted of, the assassination of President Sadat, al-Zawahiri left Egypt in 1985. Osama met him for the first time in 1986, in Peshawar, where al-Zawahiri had come to review funding for the Afghan *jihad* and treat injured *mujahidin*, though both men knew of, and admired, each other beforehand.[23] Largely due to al-Zawahiri's influence, Osama was perceived as favouring the two Egyptian Islamist terror groups — Islamic Jihad and the Islamic Group. In fact he was so impressed by al-Zawahiri that many of his followers thought he was lending more support to the Egyptians than to Al Qaeda members and their families.[24] Gradually Osama used his influence to resolve many of the differences, which he thought of as reconcilable, that separated the two Egyptian groups. These pertained to doctrinal and leadership issues and structures, especially those relating to the *shura,* or consultation, process.[25] As the Egyptian Islamic Group leader Rifa'i Taha 'Ali (*alias* Rifai Ahmed Taha) disagreed on the organisational structure and the appointment of Sheikh Umar Abd al-Rahman as the group's new international leader, al-Zawahiri and Taha agreed to preserve their organisational structures, retain their leaderships and cooperate under Osama's direction.[26]

Many insiders, including al-Zawahiri's former lawyer Muntasir al-Zayyat, have argued that Osama was transformed from a guerrilla into a terrorist by al-Zawahiri. What is undeniable is the influence that al-Zawahiri wields over Osama. In nearly every media and public appearance after Osama moved to Afghanistan al-Zawahiri has been by his side. *Al-Hayat* stated that he often determines and controls Osama's "actions and reactions."[26] Al-Zawahiri also provided the crucial, practical, know how Osama lacked and helped him develop his organisational capability, turning his ideas into reality. And if one examines Al Qaeda's leadership, it reflects how al-Zawahiri positioned his fellow Egyptian loyalists as Osama's key aides. Al Qaeda's first military commander, Ali al-Rashidi (*alias* Abu Ubadiah al-Banshiri), was an al-Zawahiri loyalist. An Arab *mujahidin* commander in Afghanistan, he was named Abu Ubadiah al-Banshiri after fighting the Soviets in the Panjsher valley.[27] Al-Banshiri, al-Zawahiri's closest aide, was formerly a Cairo police officer, dismissed for Islamist activities. According to Europe's leading specialist on Al Qaeda, al-Banshiri "won" Osama's "heart" and "dominated" his "mind", although there is evidence that al-Banshiri was as much manipulated by Osama as the other way round.[28] Al-Banshiri, who was not only Al Qaeda's military commander but also its Emir, drowned in Lake Victoria, Kenya, on May 21, 1996, while preparing the East African embassy attacks. He was a passenger on the Bukova-Mwanza ferry which capsized with 480 passengers on board, having been overloaded with cargo. Osama despatched two teams from Al Qaeda's Tanzanian cell to investigate the circumstances of his death, but it had clearly been a genuine accident. The loss of al-Banshiri had a profound effect on Osama and continues to haunt him today. Al Banshiri had been travelling on a Dutch passport, attending to a host of Al Qaeda matters, both military and business, in Africa, from the Somalia operation to dealing in gold and diamonds. His deputy and successor, Subhi 'Abd-al-'Aziz Abu-Sittah (*alias* Muhammad Atef), was also an al-Zawahiri loyalist. Although US forces announced that he was killed in a precision bombing attack in Afghanistan in November 2001, there has been no independent verification of the claim and it remains disputed by some European intelligence agencies. Al-Zawahiri has been Osama's personal physician since at least 1996 and it is likely that the two men are in close proximity, if not in everyday contact.

Al-Zawahiri and Osama are archetypes of a new generation of terrorists, many of whom come from educated and well-to-do families, as did the 9/11 hijackers — a clear demonstration that Islamist terrorist ideologies appeal equally to all classes and strata of society. Although al-

Zawahiri held no administrative or military position in Al Qaeda during its formative stages, he was present from its inception. In addition to attending all the important Al Qaeda meetings from 1989 onwards, al-Zawahiri influenced the thinking of both Osama and the organisation. He was head of the religious committee, one of the key Al Qaeda bodies that issued *fatawa,* or legal rulings, and of the consultative council — the *Shura Majlis*. Under his influence, Osama assigned a high priority to the organisation's military wing, appointing Al Qaeda's military commander also as Emir, or head, of the organisation. Successive military commanders dominated meetings and decision-making, and in public were always seated next to Osama. After al-Banshiri's death, Atef worked closely with Osama and al-Zawahiri.

Both al-Zawahiri and Osama are followers of the Salafi strand of Islam, which is associated with Wahhabism. Salafis are known as the pious pioneers of Islam, and the Salafi Dawah (Call of the Salafis) is Islam in its totality, addressing all humanity irrespective of culture, race or colour. It is this aspect that enabled Osama to reach beyond the Sunnis, because Salafism empowered Al Qaeda to forge links with Shias and hence establish a working relationship with groups such as Hezbollah. The Salafi strand aims to return the entire nation to the sublime Koran and the Prophet's authentic Sunnah. It also strives to revive Islamic thought within the boundaries of Islamic principles (meaning the presentation of realistic Islamic solutions to contemporary problems) and to establish a true Islamic society governed by Allah's laws. It is pure and free from any additions, deletions or alterations. As such, for an Al Qaeda member the Salafi school is complete, perfect in its methodology of understanding Islam and of acting according to its teachings. As one Al Qaeda member put it: "The Prophet said that the Salaf are the best generation of Muslims. Those who come after them have been guaranteed success, victory, salvation and safety from the fire [i.e. hell]. In our generation, Osama is a Salafi."[29]

When the Soviets withdrew from Afghanistan in February 1989, Osama returned to Saudi Arabia. As the experienced leader of the valiant *mujahidin* he was treated with respect and helped Saudi intelligence to create the first *jihad* group in South Yemen under the leadership of Tariq al-Fadli, which was seeking to oust the Communist regime. Although Osama resumed work for the family construction company, his thoughts lay elsewhere. Meanwhile, on the pretext of supporting a group of Kuwaiti revolutionaries opposed to the ruling Sabah family, Iraq invaded Kuwait on August 2, 1990, and occupied the oil fields. As the Saudi royal family discussed inviting US troops to repel the Iraqis and establish a presence in their country, Osama approached them with an alternative plan, namely to offer his services to forge an anti-Saddam Hussein Arab coalition to defeat the Iraqis by enlisting 5,000 *mujahidin* veterans who were still in Afghanistan. His proposal was rejected, US troops were invited into the Holy Kingdom, and Osama was humiliated. To reinforce Saudi defences against Iraq, the US launched Operation Desert Shield by dispatching paratroopers, an armoured brigade, and jet fighters to Saudi Arabia on August 7. Osama detested the very idea of armed non-Muslims even entering the land of the two holy mosques, and expressed his displeasure to Prince Turki. The Saudi royal family assured Osama that US troops would remain only until the threat receded. However, their failure to honour the pledge to withdraw foreign troops after Kuwait was liberated only reinforced Osama's sense of betrayal.

Osama did not begin his campaign against the Saudi regime until after the Iraqi troops were defeated in Kuwait in February 1991. When he expressed his displeasure publicly at the continuing presence of US troops, which he regarded as "infidels", on Saudi soil, he was sidelined. By making common cause with the forces opposed to the Saudi monarchy, Osama initiated a subtle campaign against them. In a *fatwa* issued by Al Qaeda much later, again without any formal sanction, he explained what happened at that time, referring to the actions of the Saudi government:

Ignoring the divine shari'ah law; depriving people of their legitimate rights; allowing the Americans to occupy the land of the two Holy Places; imprisonment, unjustly, of the sincere scholars…Through its course of actions the regime has torn off its legitimacy.

(1) Suspension of the Islamic shari'ah law and exchanging it with man-made civil law. The regime entered into a bloody confrontation with the truthful ulamah and the righteous youths ...

(2) The inability of the regime to protect the country, and allowing the enemy of the ummah, the American crusader forces, to occupy the land for the longest of years. As the extent of these infringements reached the highest levels and turned into demolishing forces threatening the very existence of the Islamic principles, a group of scholars who can take no more — supported by hundreds of retired officials, merchants, and prominent and educated people — wrote to the King asking for implementation of corrective measures. In 1411AH (May 1991), at the time of the Gulf War, a letter, the famous letter of Shawwaal, with over four hundred signatures was sent to the king demanding the lifting of oppression and the implementation of corrective actions. The king humiliated those people and chose to ignore the content of the letter; and the very bad situation of the country became even worse. People, however, tried again and sent more letters and petitions. One particular report, the glorious Memorandum of Advice, was handed over to the King on Muharram, 1413AH (July 1992), which tackled the problem, pointed out the illness and prescribed the medicine in an

original, righteous and scientific style...As stated by the people of knowledge, it is not a secret that to use man-made law instead of the shari'a and to support the infidels against the Muslims is one of the ten 'voiders' that would strip a person from his Islamic status. [...] In spite of the fact that report was written with soft words and very diplomatic style.. ..those who signed it and their sympathisers were ridiculed, prevented from travel, punished and even jailed...Clearly after belief (*iman*) there is no more important duty than pushing the American out of the holy land. [...]There is no precondition for this duty and the enemy should be fought with one's best abilities. If it is not possible to push back the enemy except by the collective movement of the Muslim people, then there is a duty on the Muslims to ignore the minor differences among themselves [...] Man-made laws are put forward permitting what has been forbidden by Allah such as usury (*riba*) and other matters. Banks dealing in usury are competing for land with the two Holy Places and declaring war against Allah by disobeying His order. [...] All this taking place in the vicinity of the Holy Mosque in the Holy Land. [30]

Clearly Osama had now joined the ranks of the Saudi dissidents, those who claimed that the country's rulers were false Muslims (*jahiliyya*) who had to be overthrown and replaced by a true Islamic state. After being warned that the government was planning to arrest him, Osama left Saudi Arabia for Pakistan in April 1991, where he launched a campaign against the land of his birth. In addition to re-establishing communication with, and lending support to, the dissidents he had cultivated in Saudi Arabia, Osama dispatched Al Qaeda cadres to build cells within the kingdom, where they have a significant presence. The wave of bombings against British and American nationals in 1998-2001, which have been attributed by the Saudi authorities to rivalries among alcohol smugglers, may in fact have been the work of Al Qaeda operatives, working either alone or in conjunction with disaffected Saudi police and intelligence forces, but this remains open to speculation. Osama's speeches and lectures, both as pamphlets and cassettes, began to circulate in private homes and mosques, and other dissident Saudis soon joined him in Pakistan, especially after the regime cracked down on those suspected of having links to Osama.

Meanwhile, the National Islamic Front (NIF), led by Dr Hasan al-Turabi, its spiritual head, which came to power in Sudan in 1989, sent a delegation to Peshawar. Drawing from the Soviet experience, al-Turabi argued that the Americans too could be taken on and defeated by the united force of Islamists. The NIF's three-man delegation brought with them a letter from Sudan's spiritual leader to Osama, expressing the keenness of the new government of Sudan to develop a relationship with Al Qaeda. Acceding to the envoys' requests, Osama agreed to train NIF members in guerrilla warfare to oppose the largely Christian Sudan

People's Liberation Army (SPLA) fighting for independence in the southern part of the country. Before their return, the delegation conveyed the expressed wish of al-Turabi to invite Al Qaeda to establish a presence in Sudan.

Two factors prompted Osama to relocate Al Qaeda's infrastructure to Sudan. First, Saudi Arabia and Pakistan enjoyed close relations, not least because several thousand Pakistan Army troops helped guard the Saudi royal family, and Osama realised the danger of remaining in Peshawar. Furthermore, Osama's influence in Pakistan had waned after he funded a failed no-confidence motion against the Pakistani Prime Minister, Benazir Bhutto, and subsequently attempted to assassinate her on two occasions.[31] Second, Al Qaeda members were getting restless, due to inactivity on the Afghan front now the Russians had gone; they favoured relocating to Sudan in the belief that they could "go to work again". At a meeting attended by Abu Ubaidah al-Iraqi, Ayoub al-Iraqi, Abu Fadl al-Iraqi, Abu Hammam al-Saudi, Abu Unays al-Saudi and Ali Haroun (*alias* Abu Hassan al-Sudani), discussion focused on relocating to Sudan because of its proximity to the Arab world, from where most of those present originated.[32]

While accepting al-Turabi's invitation to move to Sudan, Osama remained cautious. Moving Al Qaeda's men and material, not to mention their families, to another continent would be one of his biggest challenges. He therefore dispatched a delegation to examine the conditions on the ground before he made the final decision. Osama's delegates reflected the composition of Al Qaeda: Abu Hammam al-Saudi, from Saudi Arabia; Mamdouh Salim, *alias* Abu Hajer al-Iraqi, from Iraq; Abu Hassan al-Sudani from Sudan; and Abu Rida al-Suri, from Syria. In Sudan they met the NIF leadership and were presented with publications written by the al-Turabi. On their return, they met with Osama in private and a core group from Al Qaeda's main base, the Farook camp in Khost.

Osama rarely attended large gatherings, preferring one-to-one briefings or meeting with small groups. Apparently satisfied by Al Turabi's Islamist credentials and vision, he welcomed the offer, although some Al Qaeda members questioned whether they should trust a European-educated Islamist (al-Turabi had studied at the Sorbonne). One of the delegates responded that al-Turabi had memorised the Koran and was an expert in Koranic law with forty years' experience of Islamic study and preaching.

An Al Qaeda advance party — including a member from its Sudanese group — went to Sudan and rented farms and homes to accommodate the group's single and married members as well as for training purposes. Only after Osama visited Khartoum and met al-Turabi was the bulk of the infrastructure transferred to Sudan. From late 1989 to late 1991, most of Al Qaeda's best trained and experienced fighters (*c.*1,000-1,500) moved to Sudan, although Osama retained an extensive training and operational infrastructure in Afghanistan and Pakistan. In addition to the MAK office and several guest houses in Peshawar, camp complexes in Afghanistan included Darunta, Jihad Wal, Khaldan, Sadeek, Khalid ibn Walid and al-Farouq.

Osama did not allow his departure to Sudan to weaken Al Qaeda's training program in the subcontinent. Al Qaeda's top instructor, the Egyptian-born Ali Muhammad, formerly of the US Special Forces, trained Al Qaeda recruits in Afghanistan in 1992. For specialised training he moved between Sudan, Bosnia and other theatres of conflict. Only a few hundred of Al Qaeda's newly-trained recruits remained in Afghanistan or Pakistan. After completing their ideological and physical training, most returned to their home countries, while others left to fight in the Balkans, the Caucasus, Africa and elsewhere.

While in Sudan, Osama played a dual role, both as terrorist and businessman. In keeping with Sudan's clandestine support for Islamist movements around the world, he built a parallel organisation to augment Khartoum's efforts. After establishing links with about twenty Islamist groups engaged in guerrilla warfare and terrorism, he supported them with funds, training and weapons.

As emerged in US court proceedings, by investing his inherited wealth, Osama diversified his businesses and established some thirty companies in Sudan, from high-tech labs engaged in genetic research to civil engineering. Osama entrusted Al Qaeda's Egyptian group, especially al-Zawahiri and Abu Ubaidah al-Banshiri, who had supervised the relocation to Sudan, with plans to develop Sudan's infrastructure. Al Qaeda purchased two huge farms, including one north of Khartoum, bought in the name of a Sudanese Al Qaeda member, for $250,000. This was where al-Zawahiri lived. Salt Farm, near Port Sudan, 1,100 km. from Khartoum, was also purchased, for $180,000

The first commercial firm established by Osama in Sudan was Wadi al-Aqiq.[33] The Sudanese President, Brigadier Omar Hassan Ahmad al-Beshir, issued a letter to Wadi al-Aqiq, the main holding company, providing for the protection of Al Qaeda while operating in Sudan. This enabled Al Qaeda to import goods without inspection or payment of tax. Under Wadi al-Aqiq Al Qaeda established Laden International, an export-import company, and Taba Investment, a moneychanger. Another Al Qaeda company, al-Hijra Construction, bought supplies for road and bridge construction as well as explosives for blasting rock. Al Hijra Construction also built roads and bridges, including the 83-mile road between Damazine City and Kormuk City. The "Tahaddi" road —

"Revolutionary Highway" — between Khartoum and Port Sudan made Osama a household name throughout Sudan.

Although he paid attention to detail, Osama mostly macro-managed his business empire. For instance, al-Hijra Construction was at first managed by Dr Sharif al-Din Ali Mukhtar.[34] To improve its efficiency he later replaced him with four of his best men who operated under the pseudonyms Abu Hassan al-Sudani, Abu Hammam al-Saudi, Abu Rida Suri, and Abu Hajer al-Iraqi.[35] Gradually, Al Qaeda expanded its business into agriculture and manufacturing. It also owned Blessed Fruits, a fruit and vegetable company located in the Sajana Tower in Khartoum, and ran a trucking firm called al-Qudurat Transportation. In the outskirts of Damazine City, at the organisation's Damazine farm, Al Qaeda members grew sesame, peanuts and white corn, these and other products being processed and sold by another of its companies, al-Themar al-Mubaraka, both inside Sudan and overseas. The farm had another role: it was used for refresher training in weapons and explosives for Al Qaeda members (the organisation's explosives trainers from Afghanistan, Salem el-Masry and Saif al-Adel, another Egyptian, were based there, and, as one would expect, there were always several Sudanese too, such as Abu Talha al-Sudani).[36] When members of Egyptian Islamic Jihad were being trained in the use of explosives in late 1991, the sound of detonations led local residents to complain to the police. The latter arrested a few Al Qaeda members but Sudanese intelligence, who were working closely with Al Qaeda, intervened and ensured their speedy release. With Osama providing funds for the Sudanese government's campaign in the South, the NIF reciprocated by allocating him land for Al Qaeda training camps.

To protect himself and his organisation, Osama retained business interests and ties with Sudan's political leadership, the intelligence community and the military. In addition to maintaining a close relationship with al-Turabi, he cultivated the President, ministers, and heads of government departments. He also invested some $50 million in a bank which is closely linked with the Sudanese élite. As such, Al Qaeda was treated with respect. The Sudanese intelligence service was the bridge between it and the Sudanese government. In addition to cooperating at a tactical level, Al Qaeda provided special assistance to Sudan's intelligence services. As Sudan had opened its doors to several other Islamist groups other than Al Qaeda, from 1992 onwards the Sudanese intelligence service's delegation office responsible for screening new arrivals relied on Al Qaeda to identify spies. While in Sudan, Al Qaeda capitalised on its Sudanese members: a US court trial revealed that Jamal Ahmed Muhammad al-Fadl, *alias* Abu Bakr Sudani, was the link man with the Sudanese government while Abu Hassan al-Sudani ran Taba

Investments.[37]

Osama recognised talent but spent prudently. For instance, Jamal Ahmed Muhammad al-Fadl worked for two companies — Taba Investments and Laden International Company — and therefore received two salaries.[38] As the cost of living in Sudan was low, the monthly salary for working for both the companies was $200, that for an Al Qaeda member being $300. Those who worked harder were paid more. Notwithstanding the complaints directed to Osama, Abu Hajer al-Iraqi was paid *c.* $1,500, Wadih El Hage (*alias* Abu Abdullah Lubnani) from Lebanon, about $800, and Abu Fadhl al-Makkee a similar sum.[39] Al Qaeda members who made a profit received additional incentives and everyone received gratis supplies of essentials such as sugar, tea, and vegetable oil from Abu Ahmed el-Masry. They and their families were also reimbursed for any medical or hospital expenses. Osama was known not to show anger with his staff. Even when one employee stole several thousand dollars, he only asked him to pay back the money. Dismissing him would have exposed the organisation to greater scrutiny.

Osama's first office in Sudan was in a complex of nine rooms in El Mek Nimr street, Khartoum, but he spent much time in the three-storey Al Qaeda guesthouse in Riyadh City in Khartoum, where he lived simply, with only a few bodyguards at hand. Often Osama prayed with his fellow recruits, shared meals with them and sat in the open discussing Islam, *jihad* and Al Qaeda. On the second floor of the guesthouse he had a spacious room where he worked. He was meticulous in documentation: just as Al Qaeda created a database in Afghanistan of all the *mujahids*, in Sudan it maintained files on each employee, his family details, his aliases, how much money he had made for Al Qaeda if he was engaged in business, and if he was engaged in military operations, what his role in the fighting had been. Osama studied these files carefully before entrusting a particular task to anyone. He promoted and appointed people based on merit, ability and performance. Under his direction Al Qaeda expanded, doubling its personnel and infrastructure within the first five years of its existence. With the recruitment of civilian employees to its businesses, the group's non-combatant strength grew to about 1,000 in Sudan, while the training of recruits from around the world boosted its fighting strength from 1,000 to about 2,000.

American court proceedings have further revealed that Osama moved his office to Riyadh City in 1991, where Al Qaeda purchased a building for Wadi al-Aqiq.[40] Osama shared it with Abu Hassan el-Masry and Dr Mubarak al-Doori, who managed the Themar al- Mubaraka Company. Once again, another Sudanese Al Qaeda member, Al Qubashi El Sudani, worked closely with Osama in the same office until June 1993, when he was succeeded by the Egyptian Al Qaeda member, Sheikh Sayyid el-

Masry, who was in charge of payroll matters. Other Al Qaeda cadres who were closely associated with Osama during his stay in Sudan were Abdel Rahman, a Somali, and the Saudis Omar al-Makkee, Dr Sharif al-Din Ali Mukhtar and Khalid Ali Waleed.[41] Osama was not rigid about having only Al Qaeda members working for him; his non-Al Qaeda employees included Khalid Ali Waleed,[42] an accountant. Similarly, many NIF party members were employed by Al Qaeda. One of these was Motassem Sadeek Abu Sashl,[43] whom Osama appointed to head the Al Qaeda group of companies, which were being hard hit by international sanctions against Sudan and eventually ran at a loss.[44]

While Osama was in Khartoum, the Saudi government monitored his activities and urged him to return home. Not surprisingly, he refused, so the Saudi authorities responded in February 1994 by revoking his citizenship and freezing his assets A month later Osama's brother, Bakr, expressed through the Saudi media his family's "regret, denunciation and condemnation" of Osama's activities. Later Osama claimed that through the media the Saudi regime had attempted to defame his character in Saudi Arabia and internationally.[45] In retaliation, he established in July 1994 the Advice and Reformation Committee (ARC), which issued press releases, pamphlets and letters critical of the Saudi government. In his writings and speeches, Osama's anger towards the Saudi regime became increasingly apparent. When referring to Saudi Arabia, Osama refrained from using the term "Saudi", the name of the ruling family of his native country. He now felt he had little option but to strike targets inside Saudi Arabia.

It is believed that an assassination attempt by Saudi intelligence was mounted against him in February 1994. Furthermore, a member of al-Takfir Wal Hijra (Renunciation and Exile), known only as "al-Khulayfi", attacked worshippers at Umdurman's Ansar al-Sunnah (supporters of Sunnah) mosque in the suburb of Al-Thawrah. He then headed for Osama's house in a car, intending to kill him, but was shot and apprehended by police, who wounded him in the arm and leg. Bin Laden was not at home at the time although his house was damaged by gunfire.[46] According to Isam, the son of Hasan al-Turabi, al-Khulayfi was deranged: "Al-Khulayfi was absolutely doing the right thing because those who instigated him made him believe that Islam had enemies from within, such as Ansar al-Sunnah [proponents of the Prophet's sayings and doings], whose aim was to undermine and destroy the Islamic faith."[47] Isam added that an attempt was also made on the life of Osama's elder son, Abdallah, the attack being carried out in Khartoum's central market area. These two episodes brought home to Osama in dramatic fashion the dangers confronting him and his family. Thereafter he scaled down his social activities in Sudan, ceased horse-riding and going to horse races, which he had done in the company of Isam. A few days later Ali Muhammad, Al Qaeda's top trainer, then living in California, arrived in Khartoum, where he selected and trained Osama's team of Al Qaeda bodyguards who protected him night and day, even after he returned to Afghanistan.

Believing that the Saudis were behind the attempts on his life, Osama stepped up his campaign by providing arms, ammunition and explosives to anti-Saudi regime cells and also by dispatching trusted Al Qaeda operatives to recruit new members and select suitable targets. In keeping with the guidelines laid down by its Emir-General, Osama, Al Qaeda's code forbade its membership from publicly identifying its organisation or claiming credit for its attacks: "By claiming credit, we were told that the group will earn the wrath of the target state. Everyone knows that we were behind it and responsible for that action. Why claim credit and become identified and then hunted down?"[48] As such, Al Qaeda did not admit responsibility for its bombing of the National Guard Building in Riyadh on November 13, 1995 that killed seven people, or of the Khobar Towers military facility in Dhahran that killed nineteen Americans and injured several hundred more. However, he added: "I have great respect for the people who did this action. What they did is a big honour that I missed participating in."[49]

From Sudan, Al Qaeda began to spread its network worldwide, developing an unprecedented communications network linking its regional offices in London, New York, Turkey and other centres. Latterly great stress has been put on the use of encrypted email messages and websites, some of which were being hosted from locations in the tribal areas of Pakistan in March 2002, according to American electronic warfare specialists. While in Sudan, Osama forged links with several groups and many Islamists from around the world joined Al Qaeda. As the Islamist threat loomed large, many Arab veterans of the Afghan campaign were being arrested by their regimes. In response, the options they faced were to return to join Islamist groups in Afghanistan, Tajikistan, Algeria, Chechnya, Bosnia, Kashmir and Sudan. This created a free-floating pool of Arab *mujahidin* extending from New York via Algeria to the Philippines. The resources at Al Qaeda's disposal in the Sudan brought many of them there for refresher training and finance, some returning either to fight in ongoing conflicts or launch Islamist groups at home.

Meanwhile, India was pressuring the US government to designate Pakistan a terrorist sponsor in the wake of the World Trade Centre bombing of 1993, which was carried out by Afghan-trained and Pakistan-based terrorists, and in response the Americans demanded that Islamabad expel or register the *mujahidin* based in Pakistan. As many of them who had failed to register with the authorities were arrested,

Osama paid for the passage of several hundred of their number who wanted to leave Pakistan. Although over 5,000 *mujahidin* — 1,142 Egyptians, 981 Saudis, 946 Algerians, 792 Algerians, 771 Jordanians, 326 Iraqis, 292 Syrians, 234 Sudanese, 199 Libyans, 117 Tunisians and 102 Moroccans — had registered, Pakistan was eager to see the back of them.[50] Although the US at that time was unaware that the British-educated bomber Ramzi Ahmed Yousef was financed by Osama, they knew of the threat posed to it by the Pakistan- and Afghanistan-based *mujahidin*. As Osama concealed his hand in most operations, including the 1993 bombing, the multinational nature of his organisation had largely escaped the attention of the CIA. In fact, when Ahmad Ajaj — who accompanied Yousef from Peshawar to New York in September 1992 — was detained at JFK Airport on immigration charges and later released, he was carrying with him a training manual entitled "Al Qaeda", which was mistranslated as the "basic rule".[51] Referring to the network created by Al Qaeda in the early 1990s, the CIA stated:

Increasingly, Middle Eastern extremists, particularly Sunni fundamentalists, are working together to further the cause of radical Islam, most importantly the installation of Islamic theocracies in their home countries. The suspects tried and convicted in the World Trade Centre bombing and the second group of extremists who plotted to bomb other landmarks in New York City, including the UN building, did not belong to a single, cohesive organisation, but rather were part of a loose grouping of politically committed Muslims living in the New York City area. They were followers of Egyptian Imam Shaykh Umar Abd Al-Rahman and included non-Egyptians. Of the six original WTC suspects, only one is an Egyptian. The group includes three Palestinians, one Pakistani, and one Iraqi. The 15 individuals indicted in the second New York City case include Egyptians, Sudanese, and a Palestinian. The transnational character of these groups is also underscored by their ability to travel and operate in a variety of countries.[52]

It was in Sudan, as his thinking changed and the military increasingly took precedence over the political and economic, that Osama expressed interest in the use of chemical, biological, radiological and nuclear (CBRN) weapons of mass destruction. Al Qaeda's clandestine research into the CBRN option was initiated with the support of elements of the ruling National Islamic Front (NIF) and the Sudanese military. Its laboratory was based in Khartoum, and initially it designed and developed explosive devices. According to the CIA, Osama also purchased one kilogram of uranium from South Africa and hired an Egyptian nuclear scientist. [53] A US intelligence official subsequently reported: "Osama is directly involved himself with the Sudanese government, trying to get it to test poisonous gases in case they could be tried against US troops in Saudi Arabia."[54] He also recruited an American pilot, Essam al-Ridi, and purchased a military trainer aircraft from the US. Born in Cairo in 1958, Essam al-Ridi was educated in Kuwait and Pakistan. He earned a commercial pilot's licence after training at the Ed Boardman Aviation School from 1979 through 1981.[55] Both for the Afghan *mujahidin* in the early 1980s and for Al Qaeda in the late 1980s, he purchased from Britain two sets of scuba-diving equipment and six range-finders, night vision goggles and scopes from the US and video equipment and other high tech, dual use gear from Japan, Kuwait and Saudi Arabia. In addition to taking in person a second set of eleven night vision goggles from the US for Al Qaeda, he shipped twenty-five 50 calibre Barratt sniping rifles from America to Afghanistan[56] and at Osama's request sighted the scopes for the heavy calibre guns.[57] Within a year of arriving in Sudan from Afghanistan on a private plane, Osama set out to buy his own aircraft for both his personal use and to transport arms (he was planning to transport "Stinger" ground to air missiles from Peshawar to Khartoum in order to target US passenger aircraft), other Al Qaeda members, visiting dignitaries and other cargo. Although Osama flew mostly in private planes chartered by Al Qaeda through its front companies, he disliked flying intensely, having lost both his father and eldest brother in aircraft accidents. Osama instructed al-Ridi to purchase an aircraft in the US and fly it to Sudan. To this end $230,000 was wired from the Shamal Bank in Sudan to a bank in Texas in 1993. Al-Ridi purchased a T389 military aircraft — equivalent to a civilian Sabre-40 — in Tucson, Arizona, and after modifying the plane with a new set of avionics and refurbishing it he obtained FAA approval of its safety. Al-Ridi flew the aircraft, which has a maximum range of 1,500 miles, from Dallas-Fort Worth to Khartoum by heading towards almost the North Pole. His route took him from Dallas-Fort Worth to Frobisher Bay and Fervershaw Bay in Canada, then to Iceland, Rome, Cairo and Khartoum International Airport. The journey was marred by technical problems and bad weather (the temperature was -65F in Fervershaw Bay, which resulted in a loss of hydraulic power and a crack in the window) and lasted two weeks.[58] Al-Ridi was tasked to learn about crop-dusting before returning from the US, a technique that can also be used to disperse chemical or biological agents. Six weeks later he flew a five-man Al Qaeda team and Muhammad Atef from Khartoum to Nairobi, from where his passengers went to Somalia in a King Air aircraft, a private plane with a range of *c.*1,000 miles.[59] In November 1993, Ridi returned to Cairo and began to work for an Egyptian airline. In mid-1994, he returned to Khartoum via Nairobi and prepared the aircraft to fly with a US-educated colleague. While on the runway, the aircraft lost the main hydraulic system, the alternate brake system and even the handbrake. Al-Ridi shut down the engines to reduce the aircraft's propulsion and at about 60 knots

Osama's aircraft crashed into a sandbank just off the runway. Al-Ridi returned to Cairo via Addis Ababa in order to hide the fact that he had been in Sudan. He was given a green card in 1987 and received US citizenship in 1994. He was questioned by the FBI only after the East Africa bombings in August 1998.

Beginning with the failed attempt to assassinate the US President Bill Clinton and the Philippine President Fidel Ramos in Manila in late 1994 and early 1995, Al Qaeda also plotted to kill the Egyptian President Hosni Mubarak, a decision reached in the *shura majlis* in mid-1994. An Al Qaeda team attacked Mubarak's presidential motorcade in Ethiopia in June 1995, but he escaped unharmed. Under Osama, Abu Ubadiah al-Banshiri and Abu Yasir, head of the Egyptian Islamic Group in Sudan, coordinated the "Egyptian Operation". Ibrahim Ahmad Muhammad travelled to Ethiopia twice in the planning stage and Al Qaeda provided funds and security to the assassins' commander Mustafa Hamza, formerly an employee of Wadi al-Aqiq, Osama's first company in Sudan.

Although the regimes in the Muslim world that did not, in Osama's eyes, govern by the tenets of Islam, including the Saudi and Egyptian, were destabilised by the bombings and assassination attempts, none of them was threatened, let alone overthrown. Osama therefore convinced al-Zawahiri of the need to change Al Qaeda's strategy by attacking US and Israeli targets. It would prevent the media from exploiting the reactions to civilian deaths in Egypt; it would widen the scope of the Islamists' activities;[60] and it would lessen the human costs to the Egyptian Islamists of their campaign (thousands of their members had been jailed, and caring for their families was proving a huge financial burden). After the attempt to kill Mubarak the pressure on Sudan to expel Osama became intense, with Egypt being joined by other countries, including the US and Britain, in raising the stakes. When Sudan seemed unwilling to yield to international pressure, the US stepped up military assistance to its often hostile neighbours Uganda, Eritrea and Ethiopia with the intention of containing Sudan. Even after Osama departed, his clandestine training facilities remained in use and the pressure on Sudan did not relent.

Ultimately Sudan bowed to world opinion and Al Qaeda was asked to leave, but with Osama's departure to Afghanistan, the capacity of the international intelligence community to monitor it was lost. In response to questions whether Sudan had expelled the Arab *mujahidin* in May 1996, the Sudanese Information Secretary responded:

> The Government of Sudan did not deport Sheikh Osama Bin Laden or the other Arab brothers. They left Sudan of their own volition knowing the pressures which Sudan is facing and so that they can destroy the opportunity for the enemies of Islam and the Sudan. Sudan will remain a country for every Arab and

every Muslim. Sudan does not bow to the pressures of others. If it did, it would not have faced these trials and tribulations. Our enemies offered to improve our image if we would leave our Islamic directions, and they would also drown us with assistance, grants and loans. However, we would not agree to incur the wrath of Allah in order to gain the pleasure of this country or that.[61]

Osama had in any case decided not to test Sudan's hospitality any longer. Together with his entourage, he had limited the choice of returning to either Pakistan or Afghanistan, and he opted for the latter, in May 1996. But after the arrest there of Ramzi Ahmed Yousef, Osama realised that Pakistan could no longer be counted upon as a safe haven. Although he knew that Pakistan would not welcome him, Al Qaeda's infrastructure there was to play a critical role in the organisation's future plans. Osama's main office in Pakistan was in House 10, Street 11, section H1, Phase II, Peshawar. Operating under the cover of MAK, Osama's able and trusted ally Abu Zubaydah managed Al Qaeda operations in Pakistan, keeping him informed of developments. After Osama arrived in Afghanistan accompanied by his three wives and many children, he drew even closer to Abu Zubaydah who, in addition to liaising with Islamic NGOs, was responsible for receiving recruits before departing for Afghanistan and keeping in touch with Islamist terrorist groups and political parties in Asia. Occasionally, Abu Zubaydah would visit Osama to discuss critical matters and supply the goods and services necessary to sustain the relocated Al Qaeda network. Al Qaeda members such as Abdul Muizz, Abu Ayman, Abu Sayyaf, Samir Abdul Motaleb, and Muhammad Yusuf Abas worked with Abu Zubaydah in this capacity.

In the five years after Osama came to Afghanistan a new force called the Taliban (seekers of knowledge/students) had quickly seized control of two-thirds of the country, aided and abetted by Pakistan's ISI. During Prime Minister Benazir Bhutto's second term, the Government of Pakistan decided to create an alternative force to the various Soviet-era *mujahidin* factions that had shaken off the control of their Pakistani mentors. As these factions were battling among themselves for power, Pakistan felt compelled to take control of the near-chaotic situation in Afghanistan, its immediate neighbour. Although not publicly, Pakistani intelligence officials blamed the United States for having "abandoned" both Afghanistan and Pakistan after the American aim of defeating Soviet expansionism had been achieved.[62] Pakistan could not afford to have two unfriendly countries on its borders, hence the force to be created had to be loyal to it alone, rather than to its traditional adversary, India, which sponsored other Afghan factions in the north of the country.

Taliban membership was drawn largely from Afghan youths who had grown up in Pakistan during the Afghan war and some *mujahidin* leaders living in Pakistan. A strong supporter of Osama over the years, the Jamiat Ulema Islam leader, Maulana Fazlu Rehman, controlled a complex of *madrasas* (Islamic schools) in Pakistan which also provided ardent recruits for the Taliban.[63] The latter had local roots on which it drew for support, based on the Deobandi school of sub-continental Sunni Islam and the Tablighi-i-Jamaat organisation, a Muslim reform group with a strong presence in India and Pakistan. At the request of Pakistan's Interior Minister, retired Major General Naseerullah Babar, the ISI got the military wing of the Taliban off the ground in August 1994, providing them with munitions, supplies and advisers.[64]

Once in Afghanistan Osama kept a close eye on the political situation. In May 1996 the Hezb-e-Islami leader, Gulbuddin Hekmatyar, allied himself with Ahmed Shah Masood, the revered guerrilla commander from the Panshir valley, and under the terms of their agreement, Hekmatyar became Prime Minister. This provoked an immediate response from the Taliban — first, the capture of Spina Shaga, in Paktia, an old ammunition dump used as a base by Hekmatyar, and then the major prize, Kabul, which fell to Taliban forces on the night of September 26, 1996. The Taliban was supported, and soon recognised, by three states — Pakistan, Saudi Arabia and the United Arab Emirates (UAE) — while the Northern Alliance was backed by Russia, India, Iran, Tajikistan and Uzbekistan (at this time the US did not support the Northern Alliance, Western policy favouring a broad-based government acceptable to all factions under the auspices of the UN). Despite the extremist interpretation of Islam supported by the Taliban, the US urged it to form a representative government and effect a reconciliation process.

Osama was quick to consolidate his links with the Taliban leadership, and by financing and materially assisting the regime he soon had widespread influence over it. After a while Al Qaeda developed a guerrilla unit especially to assist the Taliban in the fight against the Northern Alliance. Known as the 055 brigade, Al Qaeda's guerrilla component of 1,500-2,000 Arabs was integrated into the Taliban fighting forces, with the result that Al Qaeda and Taliban fighters camped, trained and operated together. Although they functioned strictly as two separate organisations, the structures were integrated for the purpose of fighting the Northern Alliance. In certain camps which housed Al Qaeda and Taliban troops together, there was a common inventory for weapons, but the inventory sheet identified the individual owner of each weapon.

The regime reciprocated Osama's assistance by giving him and Al Qaeda sanctuary, and by providing weapons, equipment and training facilities. Furthermore, Al Qaeda was permitted to use Afghanistan's national aircraft to transport members, recruits and supplies from overseas. As such, their relationship was reciprocal.

After the capture of Kabul, the Taliban formed a six-member interim *shura* under Mullah Muhammad Rabbani and a 17-member cabinet to run the government.[65] After inviting about 1,000 Afghan clerics to a gathering on April 3, 1996, the Taliban leader Mullah Muhammad Omar styled himself Amirul Momineen (Supreme Leader of the Faithful). Mullah Omar, who was born in Uruzgan province in 1962, and educated in Pakistan, had no previous relationship with Osama, having served as deputy commander of Harkat-i-Inqilab-i-Islami (Party of Muhammad Nabi Muhammad), and had lost an eye in combat against the Soviets. On Osama's arrival in Afghanistan, Mullah Omar sent a delegation to meet him, conveying the message that he would be "honoured to protect him, because of his role in the Jihad against the Soviets".[66]

Osama stayed in Jalalabad for nearly a year, relocating much of Al Qaeda's infrastructure to Afghanistan and recruiting more and more followers. At the time he lived in a newly built house at Hadda farm in Jalalabad which also housed the elderly Hezbul-i-Islami leader, Mullah Yunus Khalis. The house had formerly belonged to the *mujahidin* commander Engineer Mahmood and was now guarded continually by 20-30 bodyguards. Ever adept at image manipulation, Osama usually agreed to meet visiting journalists in nearby caves, projecting the image of a pious man who had abandoned the riches of Saudi Arabia to live in Afghanistan. Osama followed the tenets of Islam to the letter, whether in prayer or in his utterances. A calm and serious man, he reflected at length before he spoke on any subject, and spoke little. Openly, he is kind, compassionate and evinces his love for all Muslims whereas in private his is utterly ruthless, single-minded, never doubting that what he wants to happen will become a reality. His use of symbolism tells us more about Al Qaeda's Emir-General that what he preaches or writes. By observing his deeds, body language and belongings, one can gain some clues into his thinking. In several posters which are widely available throughout Pakistan, Osama is depicted as a saint riding a white horse. Although horse riding is his favourite recreation, his approval of this image for dissemination is symbolically significant. For one thing it is meant to remind the viewer of images of the Prophet, who also fought on a white horse. Moreover bin Laden also tries to reinforce notions of his religious authority by dressing appropriately. The use of the Palestinian *keffieh,* or headdress, relates to Jerusalem's Al Aqsa mosque, one of Islam's holiest sites; and when Osama chooses to be filmed or photographed wearing a plain white turban, this too signifies his near-clerical status. He has not however been seen or photographed wearing a black turban, which would identify him as belonging to the Prophet's family. At his waist

Osama also wears a knife typical in design of the Arabian Peninsula, one that is usually the preserve of rulers and others in authority, again reinforcing his historical legitimacy. And whenever he makes an important declaration — such as his calls to *jihad* in 1998 (once) and 2000 (twice) — he sports a ring containing a black stone set in silver. From a strictly Islamic point of view, the stone symbolises the Ka'aba, which in turn is the symbol of Mecca, the most revered holy place of Islam. This reminds us the viewer that Osama's principal goal is to free Mecca and the Arabian Peninsula from both foreign unbelievers (America and its allies) and the house of Al-Saud.

Although the Saudi regime remained his principal foe, Osama's wider campaign against the US and Israel was his other preoccupation. In this connection he issued three *fatawa*; the first, in August 1996, and the second, in February 1997, clearly demonstrated the Taliban's support for Osama's views and activities within three months of his arrival in Afghanistan (the third, issued on February 23, 1998, is discussed later in this work). Gradually, however, the *fatawa* became more vitriolic. For example, Osama personally named and challenged the US Defense Secretary William Cohen in the second *fatwa* of February 1997, extolling the virtues of his suicide fighters :

> These youths love death as you love life. They inherit dignity, pride, courage, generosity, truthfulness, and sacrifice from father to father. They are most steadfast at war.[67]

Soon after issuing the February 1997 *fatwa*, Osama moved at the request of Mullah Omar to Kandahar, where the Taliban protected him. All the while, however, his inner ring of bodyguards were always Al Qaeda members, not Taliban fighters. Throughout his stay in Afghanistan he travelled widely, often staying at the al-Badr camp in Khost —part of the Al Qaeda complex, Zawwhar Kili Al Badr — near the Pakistan border. Osama also spent time in the Zhawar camp in Khost belonging to the former *mujahidin* commander Mullah Jalaluddin Haqqani.

Meanwhile, the Saudi and Pakistani governments continued to aid his hosts, the Taliban. For instance, the Saudi intelligence chief Prince Turki al-Faisal visited Kandahar and gave money to the Taliban in order to buy the loyalty of several opposition *mujahidin* commanders.[68] On another occasion the Saudis donated 400 pickup trucks to the Taliban, which they arranged to be flown to Kandahar.[69] In addition to replenishment of material losses, regular Pakistan army troops, often disguised as Taliban members, fought against the Northern Alliance. In addition to building a hospital, India financially supported the Northern Alliance.[70] As an ISI officer put it, "We had no option because countries unfriendly to

Pakistan were aiding the Northern Alliance."[71] What is clear is that without the strategic advice, logistics and manpower of Pakistan, the Taliban could never have brought nearly 90% of Afghan territory under its control.

In the name of religion the Taliban inflicted great tribulations on a country that had already suffered the deaths of a million people and seen 1.5 million injured and 6 million displaced or made refugees. As the Taliban enforced its writ, the agony of the people of Afghanistan increased. With the exception of a few doctors, women were denied education and employment, and had to wear the veil. Sexual intercourse outside wedlock was punishable by 100 lashes or stoning to death; homosexuality was punishable by toppling a 15 foot brick wall on the guilty person with the aim of killing him; the hands and feet of thieves were amputated; television was banned, as were photography, singing, flying kites or playing or listening to music; prison was mandatory for those who failed to pray five times a day or did not fast for 30 days during Ramadan; Western hairstyles and the shaving or trimming of beards was outlawed, as were gambling, pigeon-racing and dog racing.[72] While these *hadd* punishments were not the Taliban's invention, having also been practised in Saudi Arabia, they were carried out with especial zeal in Afghanistan.

The longer Osama stayed in Afghanistan, the more his sway over Mullah Omar, the leader of the newly-styled "Islamic Emirate", increased, leading to much speculation about their relationship. Contrary to press reports, Osama's daughter did not marry Mullah Omar, nor did his daughter marry Osama. The Taliban's goal was to create the perfect Islamic state; this suited Osama, and was fully compatible with Al Qaeda's vision and mission.

As Western criticism of the Taliban regime grew, so the Islamic Emirate isolated itself from the rest of the world. For the Taliban the global state system was divided into Dar al-Kufr, the lands of infidels (India, Russia and other non-Muslim states); Dar al-Munafiqin (hypocritical and irreligious states, such as Iran and Turkey) and Dar al-Islam (good Muslim states, e.g. Pakistan, Saudi Arabia and UAE, that recognised their regime).[73] By imposing conditions on NGOs in the late 1990s, now the only source of Western foreign aid to the country, the Taliban terminated international economic assistance. With the withdrawal of the NGOs after the killing and kidnapping of some aid workers, the socio-economic conditions in Afghanistan deteriorated sharply. Acute poverty in some parts of the country led to starvation, with people eating leaves and grass and others even forced to sell their children to survive.

Meanwhile throughout 1997 and early 1998 Osama was painstakingly brokering alliances with several Islamist groups which sent deputations to meet him in Afghanistan, telling their leaders of the need to forge a coalition to mobilise the Muslim masses against the Americans. Osama's *fatwa* gave three main reasons why they should target the United States:

The Arabian Peninsula has never — since God made it flat, created its desert, and encircled it with seas — been stormed by any forces like the Crusader armies spreading in it like locusts, eating its riches and wiping out its plantations. All this is happening at a time in which nations are attacking Muslims like people fighting over a plate of food. In the light of the grave situation and the lack of support, we and you are obliged to discuss current events, and we should all agree on how to settle the matter. No one argues today about three facts that are universally known; we will list them, in order to remind everyone.

First, for seven years the United States has been occupying the lands of Islam in the holiest of places, the Arabian peninsula, plundering its riches, dictating to its rulers, humiliating its people, terrorizing its neighbours, and turning its bases in the peninsula into a spearhead through which to fight the neighbouring Muslim peoples. If some people in the past have argued about the fact of the occupation, all the people of the peninsula have now acknowledged it. The best proof of this is the Americans' continuing aggression against Iraqi people using the peninsula as a staging post, even though all its rulers are against their territories being used to that end, but they are helpless.

Second, despite the great devastation inflicted on the Iraqi people by the Crusader-Zionist alliance, and despite the huge number of those killed, which has exceeded one million...despite all this, the Americans are once again trying to repeat the horrific massacres, as though they are not content with the protracted blockade imposed after the ferocious war or the fragmentation and devastation. So here they come to annihilate what is left of this people and to humiliate their Muslim neighbours.

Third, if the Americans' aims behind these wars are religious and economic, the aim is also to serve the Jews' petty state and divert attention from its occupation of Jerusalem and murder of Muslims there. The best proof of this is their eagerness to destroy Iraq, the strongest neighbouring Arab state, and their endeavour to fragment all the states of the region such as Iraq, Saudi Arabia, Egypt, and Sudan into paper statelets and through their disunion and weakness to guarantee Israel's survival and the continuation of the brutal Crusade occupation of the peninsula.

All these crimes and sins committed by the Americans are a clear declaration of war on God, his messenger, and Muslims. And *ulema* [scholars] have throughout Islamic history unanimously agreed that the *jihad* is an individual duty if the enemy destroys the Muslim countries. This was revealed by Imam bin-Qadamah in Al-Mughni, Imam al-KisaI in Al-Bada'i, al-Qurtubi in his interpretation, and the shaykh of al-Islam in his books, where he said 'As for the fighting to repulse [an enemy], it is aimed at defending sanctity and religion, and it is a duty as agreed [by the *Umma*, the world Muslim community] Nothing is more sacred than belief except repulsing an enemy who is attacking religion and life.[74]

Instead of focusing its resources and energies on campaigning against

Muslim rulers who did not adhere strictly to Islamic precepts, Al Qaeda had clearly opened a second front against the United States, or "King of Satan", the temporal power that facilitated the rule of "false [*jahiliyya*] Muslim regimes". What Osama and his followers object to, as exemplified in the quotation above, is not so much the American way of life, not so much Americans themselves, as what they perceive the American government, in the shape of its foreign policy, is doing to Muslim countries, including Saudi Arabia, the occupation of which is intolerable to Osama.

In building its anti-American coalition Al Qaeda received significant support from both state and non-state actors. These included Sudan, Iran, Iraq and Afghanistan while it also had strategic and tactical relationships with two dozen or so Arab and Asian Muslim political, guerrilla and terrorist groups. It was this conglomerate of disparate groups that gave Al Qaeda the global reach it required to harness the untapped resources of the Muslims living in the West, as well as to mount surveillance of, and target its enemies. Due to the harsh and often brutal domestic counter-insurgency measures of both Middle Eastern and Asian regimes, many of their guerrilla and terrorist groups developed a robust external presence specifically to target those regimes abroad. Furthermore, the conjunction of instability in Afghanistan throughout the 1990s and the relative stability of the Middle East in the second half of the 1990s, following the Oslo Peace Accords, shifted the terrorist centre of gravity to Afghanistan.

On February 23, 1998, Osama announced the formation of his alliance: the World Islamic Front for the Jihad Against the Jews and the Crusaders (al-Jabhah al-Islamiyyah al-'Alamiyyah Li-Qital al-Yahud Wal-Salibiyyin). In addition to Osama, the signatories of the agreement were al-Zawahiri, leader of Egyptian Islamic Jihad; Taha, leader of the Islamic Group of Egypt; Shayakh Mir Hamzah, secretary of the Jamiat-ul-Ulema-e-Pakistan; and Fazlul Rahman, leader of the Jihad Movement of Bangladesh. However, for reasons of security, neither the alliance partners nor Osama wished to disclose the wider composition of the alliance. Groups included in the alliance would definitely be targeted by the intelligence community and might suffer infiltration and possible disruption. Unless these terrorist networks were compartmentalised, their usefulness would be compromised. Sections of the European intelligence community believed that the Armed Islamic Group of Algeria (GIA) was a secret signatory, but Al Qaeda-GIA relations were strained at this time and it is unlikely that the GIA signed up.[75]

Stating that the Americans had declared war on Allah, the Prophet, and Muslims, Osama announced that it was the duty of all Muslims to comply with God's order by killing Americans and their allies, both civilian and military, irrespective of location.

The ruling to kill the Americans and their allies, civilians and military, is an individual duty for every Muslim who can do it in any country in which it is possible to do it, in order to liberate the al-Aqsa mosque and the holy mosque [Mecca] from their grip, and in order for their armies to move out of all the lands of Islam, defeated and unable to threaten any Muslim. This is in accordance with the words of Almighty God: "And fight the pagans all together as they fight you all together", and "Fight them until there is no more tumult or oppression, and there prevail justice and faith in God."

This is in addition to the words of Almighty God: " And why should ye not fight in the cause of God and those who, being weak, are ill-treated (and oppressed)? —women and children, whose cry is: 'Our Lord, rescue us from this town, whose people are oppressors; and raise for us from thee one who will help!'"

Almighty God said: "O ye who believe, give your response to God and His Apostle, when He calleth you to that which will give you life. And know that God cometh between a man and his heart, and that it is He to whom ye shall be gathered.

Almighty God also says: O ye who believe, what is the matter with you, that when ye are asked to go forth in the cause of God, ye cling so heavily to the earth? Do ye prefer the life of this world to the hereafter? But little is the comfort of this life, as compared with the hereafter. Unless ye go forth, He will punish you with a grievous penalty, and put others in your place; but Him ye would not harm in the least. For God hath power over all things."

Almighty God also says: "So lose no heart, nor fall into despair. For ye must gain mastery if ye are true in faith." [76]

For Osama the US presence in Saudi Arabia remained the issue of primary concern, as was clearly reflected when Al Qaeda planned, prepared and executed its first major successful operation against the US. The date of the simultaneous bombing of the two US embassies in East Africa, in Nairobi and Dar es Salaam, on August 7, 1998, was the eighth anniversary of the arrival of American troops in Saudi Arabia in 1990. The attack was clearly in revenge for the US presence in the "Land of the Two Holy Places". Although the East Africa bombings killed more Africans than Americans, there was no backlash by Muslims, the widespread antipathy of Muslims towards US policy in the Middle East, especially its support for Israel, dampening criticism of these actions. Although, in keeping with Al Qaeda's policy, Osama did not claim responsibility for the bombing, he praised the act.

In Osama's mind, and in the thinking of his supporters, the Al Qaeda leader had acted according to Islamic principles. In Islamic law an attack on an enemy must be preceded by an Islamic decree, or *fatwa*. The Al Qaeda *fatwa* issued in February 1998, six months before the attacks in Kenya and Tanzania, had clearly called for the death of Americans. Osama had also received the support of forty Afghan clerics who issued a *fatwa* calling for a *jihad* against the Americans on March 12, and another similar *fatwa* by a group of Pakistan-based clerics, signed by Sheikh Ahmed Azzam, in late April 1998.[77] Critics who claimed that Osama had no legal authority to issue a *fatwa* were neutralised when these two bodies issued similar *fatawa*. Although there is no evidence, it is very likely that Osama discreetly prompted these two bodies to issue the ordinances. Al Qaeda's Emir and military commander, Muhammad Atef, faxed the Afghan *fatwa* and urged Khalid al-Fawwaz to place it in the Arabic daily newspaper, *Al-Quds Al-Arabi*. Al Qaeda issued a letter signed by Osama four days after the Afghan *fatwa*, reiterating the call for *jihad* against the US.

On May 26, 1998, a press conference was held at al-Badr where Osama called once again for *jihad* against US troops and announced the formation of the "World Islamic Front for the Jihad Against the Jews and the Crusaders". In addition to Osama, al-Zawahiri and Muhammad Atef, the sons of the Blind Sheikh, Asadallah and Asim, attended the conference. These two distributed a picture of their father praying. The card, calling all Muslims to attack Jews and Christians, stated: "Divide their nation, tear them to shreds, destroy their economy, burn their companies, ruin their welfare, sink their ships and kill them on land, sea and air. [...] May Allah torture them by your hands."[78] Two months before Al Qaeda destroyed the US targets in East Africa, Sheikh Ali al-Hudaifi, the Imam of the Prophet's Mosque in Medina, also supported Osama's call. He too publicly demanded the withdrawal of US troops, in June 1998.[79]

With the specific intention of killing Osama in retaliation for the embassy bombings, the US responded by firing cruise missiles at Al Qaeda residential and training complexes in Afghanistan on August 20, 1998. The Americans also targeted the al-Shifa Pharmaceutical Plant near Khartoum on August 20, 1998. The CIA had succeeded in clandestinely collecting soil samples from its compound, which when tested were found to contain the possible precursor for the deadly nerve agent VX. At the time of writing, however, the conclusiveness of the evidence gathered remains disputed within the wider intelligence community. Both in Afghanistan and in the Muslim world, the US cruise missile response provided Osama with unprecedented international publicity. Overnight the failed assassination attempt propelled him to pre-eminence as the leading *jihadist* among the many Asian and Middle Eastern Islamist organisations. "Osama stood up to the US" was a common Islamist response.[80]

The CIA concluded that until Osama was killed, he would continue to dominate the centre stage of terrorism directed against the West, particularly the US, and hence it launched another clandestine operation to kill or capture him. To this end President Clinton signed an executive order authorising the CIA to kill Osama. The agency was getting very poor intelligence on him, relying, as they did, on technical sources, and not on human assets in the field. However, despite Al Qaeda's intermittent successes against the US, Osama was embittered. There was no sign of the Americans withdrawing their troops from the Arabian peninsula, and all the while since returning to Afghanistan he was suffering from stomach and kidney pain. He came to rely on renal dialysis and had to support himself with a cane. He also suffered from low blood pressure and developed a permanent backache. The ISI, the best-informed intelligence organisation in Afghanistan, was aware of Osama's medical problems and through them Western intelligence agencies came to know of his condition, some of them believing it was only a matter of time before he would die of kidney failure,[81] although he was being given continual treatment by al-Zawahiri. Until US troops entered Afghanistan, they did not know that Osama had bought two renal dialysis machines, one for his personal use and the other for a hospital in Afghanistan. Osama believed that he had been poisoned and suspected that the Saudi regime was continuously plotting to kill him.

Osama's mother visited her son and his family both in Sudan in the 1990s and in Afghanistan in early 2001 and was present at her grandson's marriage. The public perception has been created that ties between the bin Laden family and Osama are non-existent, but intelligence agencies report contact between Osama and his extended family. While in Kandahar in 2000, Osama married his fourth wife, a Yemeni. He already had close relations with the Islamic Army of Aden Abyan, an Islamist group in the south of Yemen. By marrying a Yemeni from the northern tribes, Osama established close relations with the al-Islah Party. Its leader Sheikh Abdullah al-Ahmar is also the leader of the Northern Tribal Alliance. In Yemen, loyalty resides first with the family, then with the clan and then with the tribe.

Throughout Osama's stay in Afghanistan, the US intelligence community received reports of Al Qaeda's attempts to develop an unconventional warfare capability in Sudan. These indicated that the Sudanese had provided assistance with laboratory facilities but little else. Although intelligence on Al Qaeda's attempts to develop CBRN weapons while in Afghanistan was virtually non-existent, Osama's statements on such weapons provided an insight into his intentions. Unlike other terrorist leaders, who concealed their hand, Osama was quite explicit:

> "Acquiring weapons for the defence of Muslims is a religious duty. If I have indeed acquired these weapons, I am carrying out a duty. It would be a sin for Muslims not to try to possess the weapons that would prevent the infidels from inflicting harm on Muslims."[82]

His statement clearly reflected the need not only of Islamist groups like Al Qaeda but also of certain Islamic countries to acquire CBRN weapons. Three days after India detonated two nuclear devices on 11 May 1998, Osama said: "We call upon the Muslim nation and Pakistan — its army in particular —to prepare for the *jihad.* This should include a nuclear force."[83]

As the US was to discover in January 2002, Al Qaeda had been trying to develop a nerve gas capability. Osama's attention was now fully focused on developing Al Qaeda's 055 battalion to fight the Northern Alliance and its overseas terrorist network for action against overseas targets. While designated members managed Al Qaeda's commercial projects and finances overseas, Osama spent time conceptualising, planning, and assessing terrorist operations.

In one daring operation on January 3, 2000, an explosives-laden Al Qaeda suicide boat sank before it reached its target, USS *The Sullivans.* Osama was undeterred by this reverse, saying that his Al Qaeda team had failed to rehearse the operation thoroughly.[84] A second attack in Aden, this time against USS *Cole,* succeeded on October 12, 2000, killing seventeen American sailors. Together with Al Qaeda members and his family, Osama celebrated the successful bombing of a US destroyer. In a video recorded at his eldest son's wedding in January 2001, Osama narrated the following poem:

> A destroyer, even the brave might fear,
> She inspires horror in the harbour and the open sea,
> She goes into the waves flanked by arrogance, haughtiness
> and fake might,
> To her doom she progresses slowly, clothed in a huge illusion,
> Awaiting her is a dinghy, bobbing in the waves.[85]

Unlike its cruise missile response of 1998, the United States chose not to retaliate overtly to the USS *Cole* attack. However, CIA covert operations to capture or assassinate Osama, his lieutenants and other Al Qaeda members continued, albeit unsuccessfully, largely because of excessive reliance on surveillance craft, satellites and technical intelligence.

In addition to unleashing his Al Qaeda forces, Osama also persuaded the Taliban leadership to destroy the ancient statues of the Buddha in Bamiyan in March 2000. This act was in direct retaliation for the sanctions imposed on Afghanistan, a claim borne out by Arabic documents recovered by a Western journalist. Osama's influence was so pervasive that the Taliban ignored the international outrage that greeted their action, although support for Osama among the Taliban leadership was not unanimous, especially after sanctions began to hurt the Afghan people and the Taliban regime. Osama had convinced Mullah Omar that Allah guided his actions, hence the Taliban leader continued to stand by him come what may, even after the East Africa bombings.

As Al Qaeda's team in the US was making its final preparations for the 9/11 attacks, Osama launched the first phase of the operation in Afghanistan itself. He dispatched two Al Qaeda members posing as television journalists to assassinate the Northern Alliance commander, Ahmed Shah Masood, the symbol of resistance to the Taliban, who had defied them since 1994. The two Arab operatives, carrying Belgian passports and a letter of introduction from the Islamic Observation Centre in London, met Masood at his headquarters on September 9. During the interview one of the Al Qaeda members detonated the explosive charge strapped around his waist, fatally injuring Masood, his interpreter, Muhammad Asem and his head of media relations, Asim Souheil.[86] The Northern Alliance representative in India Massoud Khalil, and Fahim Dasty, a journalist close to Massood, were also injured. By assassinating Masood, which was presented as Al Qaeda's "gift" to the Taliban, Osama had undermined the most immediate threat confronting it and Al Qaeda in Afghanistan.

The Al Qaeda attacks against prestige American targets on September 11, 2001, were meant to cripple the economic, military and political power of the United States and critically weaken its capacity for retaliation. Their symbolic importance was, if anything, paramount in the minds of Al Qaeda and explains which targets were chosen and why. While the first two were the World Trade Centre and the Pentagon, the third is believed to have been Congress or the White House, while some analysts remain convinced that it was a nuclear facility, perhaps the Three Mile Island plant. However, Osama's subsequent reference to the 9/11 operation as an attack on America's "outstanding landmarks" suggests that the third target was indeed the White House.

Quite apart from the cost in human lives, the economic repercussions of the Al Qaeda attacks were huge, the magnitude of destruction in New York being comparable to what might have been inflicted by a mini nuclear device. The destruction of the twin towers and adjacent buildings in New York was in insurance terms the costliest single event in history, surpassing the losses inflicted by hurricanes and other natural disasters. The attack also affected the world economy, with trillions of dollars in losses and many millions of people both in the US and elsewhere becoming unemployed or underemployed as demand for goods and services slackened.

After US troops intervened in Afghanistan, Osama made a speech at the Islamic Studies Centre in Jalalabad on November 10, before retreating to the Afghan-Pakistan border. According to those present he said "the Americans had a plan to invade, but if we are united and believe in Allah, we'll teach them a lesson, the same one we taught the Russians".[87] He concluded his address to the 1,000 or so regional tribal leaders in his audience as follows: "God is with us, and we will win this war. Your Arab brothers will lead the way. We have the weapons and the technology. What we need most is your moral support. And may God grant me the opportunity to see you and meet you on the frontlines."[88]

Osama's aim is to mobilise Muslims worldwide and turn them against the West, primarily the United States. The blurring of the political and the religious differences in Islam and the *hadith* explains why he conducts himself and his actions within a religious framework, continually projecting himself in his writings and propaganda videos as a man of God — an image he reinforces by quoting from the Koran and suggesting that his action are guided by Allah. Even in his choice of names for Al Qaeda camps — Beit al-Shuhadaa (house of martyrs), Beit al-Ansar (house of companions) and Beit al-Salaam (house of peace) — he portrays himself, his organisation and his actions in a spiritual light. From the beginnings of his campaign, Osama has projected to the Muslim world the idea that he is a man of peace, justifying his actions as a necessary response to halt the destruction of Islam and the loss of Muslim life and property. He has clearly won a following by tapping into a broader sense of social and political injustice among many Muslim communities who believe that the US is their real enemy. By investing in propaganda, he inculcates the notion of it as "Satan", the root of all evil; and by conducting daring attacks, he has demonstrated that the US is fallible and can be seriously harmed. But, in hindsight, did Osama not grossly underestimate the international reaction to Al Qaeda's multiple attacks against the US?

Worldwide sympathy for the US, outrage against the Taliban and Al Qaeda, the response of Pakistan, the widespread support for the US-led anti-terrorist coalition, the effectiveness of US airpower, the spectacular military success of the Northern Alliance and the introduction of US and Allied ground troops — none of these outcomes is likely to have been anticipated by Osama. After the first phase of sustained bombing, when US troops began to pour into Afghanistan, Osama turned to history, comparing his return from Sudan to Afghanistan to the Prophet Muhammad's *hijra* (flight) in the seventh century from Mecca to Medina, from where he waged a war for eight years until he captured Mecca. Osama compared Medina to Afghanistan, from where he would launch battle after battle. As he had arrived in Afghanistan from Sudan in May 1996, Osama told his followers they would defeat the Americans by

2004, eight years later.

The public reaction to Osama in the Muslim world after September 11 has been divided but increasingly sympathetic to him. Opinion polls taken in early 2002 revealed that most Muslims in the Middle East did not believe the 9/11 attacks were carried out by their fellow believers, choosing instead to attribute them to Mossad or the CIA. As the symbol of resistance to the US, bin Laden has become a hero among many Muslim communities, from Pakistan to Indonesia and from Nigeria to Egypt. Osama memorabilia — cassettes, CDs and DVDs of his speeches, to posters, T-shirts, pens and sweets bearing his imprint and booklets and magazine articles about him — have proliferated. As the authoritarian regimes of the Middle East have prevented their manufacture and distribution, so they have become widely available in South and Southeast Asia. The Osama T-shirts, produced mostly in Pakistan, Thailand and Indonesia, are being sold all over South and Southeast Asia, including countries with small Muslim populations. One produced in Bangkok, showing Osama next to President George W. Bush beside the burning twin towers, carries the slogan "This is Politics, Not War"; while another depicting Osama, and produced in Jakarta, is captioned: "He is not terrorism, he is fighter [*sic*]".[89]

There were demonstrations against US intervention and in support of the Taliban, Al Qaeda and Osama in Europe, and to a lesser extent Africa, but not in the US or in the Middle East. Those in Indonesia were the largest and the longest in duration because the Indonesian government refrained from responding, stating that in a democracy public protests were permitted. Because demonstrators were allowed to carry placards saying "Long live Osama", even in the vicinity of the US embassy, local Islamist parties were emboldened and recruited more members every day. Photographs of PAS (Islamic Party of Malaysia) and FPI (Islamic Defenders' Front) activists holding pro-Osama posters in Malaysia and Indonesia respectively received widespread publicity while tens of thousands of children born to Muslim parents worldwide have been named Osama. A taxi driver in Jakarta who called his new-born son "Osama, my hero" in October 2001 said: "Look at Osama. Look at his face. He is a good man. He is a kind man. He is a man of God. He cares for poor Muslims."[90] Referring to the September 11 attacks, he added: "He did not do this. The Jewish Mossad did it to put America and the West against Muslims."[91] In the immediate aftermath of the attacks Nigerians, who believe that a person's name influences his behaviour, named seven out of ten boys born in the largely Muslim northern city of Kano "Osama".[92] Some of the responsibility for this widespread popular support for Osama is attributable to the US government, which neglected to publicise in Muslim countries Osama's role and expose Al Qaeda's complicity in many other terrorist attacks, although it did manage, very effectively, to mobilise other governments to its side. Many radical Islamic movements exploited this critical time and space to foster the perception that Osama had not been involved in the 9/11 attacks and that the West was using them as a pretext to target Muslims.

In the spectrum of contemporary terrorist leaders Osama bin Laden. has no equal As a leader who has employed violence in pursuit of his political aims and objectives, he stands out in many ways. First, he is the only leader to have built a truly multinational terrorist group that can strike anywhere in the world. For over a decade Osama has inspired, instigated and supported Islamist guerrillas and terrorists, bringing about many deaths and much human suffering. In the World Trade Centre attack alone, the victims were from nearly 100 different nationalities. Second, he has built a popular following throughout the Islamic world, being almost revered in Muslim circles in Asia, Africa and the Middle East and among the first- and second-generation migrants in North America, Europe and Australia. Nor has his popularity waned despite evidence that he masterminded the worst terrorist attack in history. He continues to be regarded as the supreme symbol of resistance to US imperialism. Third, Osama's disposition towards his enemies has not mellowed in the face of the imminent threat to his own life and to his organisation. Even after the US cruise missile attacks in 1998 and intervention in Afghanistan in late 2001, the tone of his statements has remained constant, if not more strident. To his admirers he sets an example of fearlessness; he is unrelenting; neither he nor Al Qaeda will compromise.

With the persistent and constant application of sustained resources, it must be only a question of time till Osama bin Laden is either killed or, to prevent capture, commits suicide. Was the man the movement or has the movement gone beyond the individual? Osama has always been well aware that because of the high-risk nature of his life he will one day be captured or killed. Would that be the end of Al Qaeda? Has he built an organisation that will outlast him? This will be the ultimate test of Osama bin Laden's qualities of leadership.

2

AL QAEDA'S ORGANISATION, IDEOLOGY AND STRATEGY

"Jihad, bullets and martyrdom operations are the only way to destroy the degradation and disbelief which have spread in the Muslim lands." (Commentary from an Al Qaeda recruitment video seized by police in London after 9/11.)

This chapter is largely based on Al Qaeda documents, including training manuals, the full translations of which I have seen. One was recovered by police in Manchester (England) from the home of an alleged Al Qaeda member, and various versions of *The Encyclopaedia of the Afghan Jihad* from Al Qaeda members arrested in Asia, the Middle East and Europe. Two other others were found in Afghanistan after the collapse of the Taliban regime.

Al Qaeda's organisational and operational infrastructure differs markedly from other guerrilla or terrorist groups. As an unprecedented transnational phenomenon Al Qaeda's infrastructure has proved very hard to detect and combat, not least because law enforcement agencies lack the experience to respond effectively to the threat it poses or to counter its influence among Muslim communities. Al Qaeda is also characterised by a broad-based ideology, a novel structure, a robust capacity for regeneration and a very diverse membership that cuts across ethnic, class and national boundaries. It is neither a single group nor a coalition of groups: it comprised a core base or bases in Afghanistan, satellite terrorist cells worldwide, a conglomerate of Islamist political parties, and other largely independent terrorist groups that it draws on for offensive actions and other responsibilities. Leaders of all the above are co-opted as and when necessary to serve as an integral part of Al Qaeda's high command, which is run via a vertical leadership structure that provides strategic direction and tactical support to its horizontal network of compartmentalised cells and associate organisations.

Its mobility and capacity for regeneration were well illustrated after Al Qaeda lost its sanctuary in Pakistan in late August 1998. Almost immediately it relocated to Afghanistan, if anything leaving it in a healthier position than hitherto; and after the American intervention in Afghanistan from October 2001 onwards, its regional nodes provided leadership, recruitment, training and logistics to the global network, allowing the organisation to function largely undisturbed. Al Qaeda's speed of response was put to the test when US troops were despatched to the Philippines in January 2002, ostensibly to seek out the Abu Sayyaf Group (ASG). Al Qaeda's regional node in Mindanao that had, since early 1999, trained several hundred Filipino and foreign Islamists came under severe pressure, but it is likely to mutate and disperse even further into less accessible parts of Malaysia and Indonesia where it can function in smaller cells.

We should not forget that Al Qaeda's antecedents lie in Islamist movements opposed to the harsh regimes of the Middle East, especially those of Egypt, Saudi Arabia and Algeria, hence from the outset it learned to think and act very quickly in order to survive. Despite seeing over 100 suspected Al Qaeda activists arrested in North America and Europe in the six months after the 9/11 attacks, Al Qaeda has regenerated new cells as well as sustaining many of its older ones. Nor has the severe disruption of Al Qaeda's command and control operations in Afghanistan in late 2001 and early 2002 permanently crippled it. Although it has been weakened on a practical level, its ideology remains unaffected and will continue to draw Muslims, especially young ones, to Al Qaeda's ideal of *jihad* against unbelievers. What radical Muslims previously lacked was organisation, which Al Qaeda and several other Islamist groups have built and sustained amid great secrecy.

Al Qaeda got off to a good start: it inherited a fully-fledged training and operational infrastructure that had been funded by the US, European, Saudi Arabian and other governments throughout the 1980s, while for recruitment it drew on the vast *mujahidin* database originally created by Osama for tracking "martyred" or "missing" *mujahidin* in the later stages of the anti-Soviet *jihad*.

For about five years, until 1993, Al Qaeda maintained its own momentum and no government or rival group attempted to disrupt its growth. However, in 1994 the Egyptian, Saudi and other Middle Eastern governments turned on Al Qaeda as they realised the threat it posed, though by then it was well entrenched, having survived the precarious incipient stage of its formation.

Since the murder of Abdullah Azzam in 1989, Osama bin Laden has been the backbone and principal driving force of Al Qaeda. Although his ultimate goal is the re-establishment of the Caliphate, he began supporting campaigns against "false" Muslim rulers (e.g. Saudi Arabia, Egypt, Tajikistan, Uzbekistan, Algeria) and assisting Muslims victimised by non-Muslim regimes (e.g. Philippines, Kashmir, Bosnia and Chechnya). Al Qaeda also forged a coalition linking fellow militant Islamists, from the Abu Sayyaf Group of the Philippines to the Islamic Group of Egypt and the GIA. Those Al Qaeda cadres who were dispatched to help these causes were vanguard fighters and the most accomplished trainers. In Chechnya they constituted the Al Ansar (the followers of the Mahdi were known as the "Ansar") *mujahidin*, the fiercest of the three main *mujahidin* groups responsible for almost all the suicide bombings. In Bosnia the Al Qaeda-trained *mujahidin* regarded their European counterparts as not battle-hardened or zealous enough, and hence developed a *jihad* manual in order to help them become committed Muslims and better fighters. Al Qaeda's successes at this point were minimal, given the Middle Eastern regimes' crushing response, involving executions, mass jailings without trial and skilful surveillance and disruption of Islamist activity.

When the group was first formed it was known as "Al Qaeda" and the "Islamic Army" but Osama discouraged the use of the latter term. His then immediate deputy was an Iraqi, Abu Ayoub al-Iraqi, who was appointed Emir. Having distinguished himself in battle against the Soviets, including in the front line at Jaji, he convened the first recruitment meeting for Al Qaeda.[1] This was held at the Farook camp in Khost, Afghanistan, in late 1989, when a few trusted veterans of the Afghan campaign were invited to join. Hitherto, the Farook camp was where new recruits were ideologically indoctrinated before being trained elsewhere to fight the Russians. Abu Ayoub al-Iraqi arrived for the meeting accompanied by his brother Yasin, whereupon he argued that training should continue even after the expulsion of the Soviets, due to the need to relieve the sufferings of Muslims around the world. Those who wished to join were given a form in triplicate and invited to sign and swear before an internal committee. Among those present, including those using their Al Qaeda pseudonymns, were al-Zawahiri (*alias* Dr Abdel Moez), the leader of the Egyptian Islamic Jihad; Dr Fadhl el-Masry, an Egyptian surgeon; Abu Ubadiah al-Banshiri, formerly an Egyptian police officer; Muhammad Atef, of Egypt; Jamal Ahmed al-Fadl (*alias* Abu Bakr Sudani), a former Sudanese student in the US; Abu Faraj al-Yemeni from Yemen; Abu Musab al-Saudi from Saudi Arabia; Izzildine; Abu Burhan; and a few others, mostly veterans of the Afghan campaign. Although al-Zawahiri and Dr Fadhl el-Masry, both of the *shura,* were present, along with Al Qaeda's Emir, the top military leaders of Al Qaeda administered an oath (*bayat*). This was sworn and signed before the then Al Qaeda Emir, Abu Ayoub al-Iraqi, and al-Banshiri and Muhammad Atef. Within two years al-Banshiri replaced Ayoub al-Iraqi, and after the death of the former in 1996, Muhammad Atef took his place.

Al Qaeda's structure enables it to wield direct and indirect control over a potent, far-flung, force. By issuing periodic pronouncements, speeches and writings, Osama indoctrinates, trains and controls a core inner group as well as inspiring and supporting peripheral cadres. In addition to exploiting Al Qaeda's relations with Islamist groups, parties and regimes, Osama also seeks to influence their thinking and behaviour.

The constituent groups of Al Qaeda operate as a loose coalition, each with its own command, control and communication structures. The coalition has one unique characteristic that enhances its resilience and allows force to be multiplied in pursuit of a particular objective: whenever necessary, these groups interact or merge, cooperating ideologically, financially and technically.

To further advance the Islamist project, in 1998 Al Qaeda was reorganised into four distinct but interlinked entities. The first was a pyramidal structure to facilitate strategic and tactical direction; the second was a global terrorist network; the third was a base force for guerrilla warfare inside Afghanistan; and the fourth was a loose coalition of transnational terrorist and guerrilla groups.

Immediately below the Emir-General in Al Qaeda's structure stands the *shura majlis*, or consultative council, which consists of very experienced members. Among the first to join were Dr Ayman al-Zawahiri, Abu Ayoub al-Iraqi, al-Banshiri, Abu Hafs el-Khabir, Abu Ibrahim al-Iraqi, Dr Fadhl el-Masry, Abu Faraj al-Yemeni, Abu Fadhlal-Makkee (from Mecca), Sheikh Sayyid al-Masry, a Qaricept al-Jizaeri (an Algerian Koranic scholar), Khalifa al-Muscat Omani, Saif al-Liby, Abu Burhan al-Iraqi and Abu Muhammad al-Masry Saad al-Sharif. Periodically *shura* members leave and new members are appointed. To ensure legitimacy and loyalty, Osama appoints prominent personalities and trusted personal followers to key positions. Although Al Qaeda is a political group driven by an interpretive religious ideology, it operates on the basis of a cultural network, recruiting known persons, yet there is no formal procedure for recruitment, appointment or promotion. While it considers merit, ability and performance, Al Qaeda determines its promotions and appointments on the basis of ties of family, friendship and nationality.

Immediately below the *shura majlis* and reporting to it are four operational committees: military; finance and business; *fatwa* and Islamic study; and media and publicity, which ensure the smooth day-to-day running of Al Qaeda, each being headed by an Emir. While the Emir and Deputy Emir have responsibility for each committee, its members also form compartmentalised working groups for special assignments. At times handpicked members of these committees, especially the military, conduct special assignments for Osama or for his designated operational commanders. Some members serve in more than one committee or are rotated between them.

Al Qaeda's military committee is responsible for recruiting, training, procuring, transporting and launching military operations as well as developing tactics and acquiring and manufacturing special weapons. Each camp providing recruits with basic, advanced and specialised training (explosives, communication, computers) is headed by an Emir. The committee is also entrusted with tasking teams to plan and execute attacks, including gathering intelligence via surveillance or reconnaissance of intended targets and rehearsing attacks and mission training. It also allocates trainers, weapons and other resources to assist fellow Muslims in theatres like Chechnya and Kashmir, and oversees clandestine functions. Before they were all but eliminated by the US air campaign from October 2001 onwards, Al Qaeda complexes in Kabul, Khost, Mahavia, Jalalabad, Kunar, Kandahar and depots in Tora Bora and Liza were managed by the military committee.

The military committee appoints agent-handlers who manage an extensive network of cells and agents outside Afghanistan. Before September 11, Al Qaeda local cells, both support and operational, had been detected and neutralised in Italy, Germany, Britain, Canada, the US, South Africa, Tanzania, Kenya, Yemen and Albania. While some states — Singapore, Malaysia, the Philippines, Jordan, Algeria, Libya and Pakistan — have arrested Al Qaeda members, others such as Somalia, Sudan and Indonesia, have failed to act.

Operational cells comprising "commandos" first operated under al-Banshiri. Another experienced and prized instructor, Muhammad Atef, later replaced him and together they refined Al Qaeda's suicide terrorist capability. Al Qaeda also has an internal security service led by Muhammad Mousa that vets recruits, guards leaders, and protects the organisation from "enemy" infiltration.

As a fluid and dynamic, goal-oriented rather than rule-oriented organisation, Al Qaeda is always liable to change its structure, according to circumstances. That structure has evolved considerably since the East Africa bombings, but that of the *shura majlis* and the four committees persists. Although Osama has felt the need to expand his operations, security threats to it curbed many of its overt activities and he and Al Qaeda became increasingly clandestine, choosing to operate through front, cover and sympathetic organisations, the exception being its activities in Afghanistan.

055 Brigade

Al Qaeda's guerrilla organisation — 055 Brigade — was integrated into the Army of the Islamic Emirate of Afghanistan from 1997 to 2001 to fight the Northern Alliance. It was the least publicised component of Al Qaeda. Although financed and trained by it, its fighters were the shock troops of the Taliban and functioned as an integral part of the latter's military apparatus. 055 also formed the strategic reserve of Al Qaeda's terrorist network, providing motivated and experienced fighters for operations as and when required. It consisted of some 2,000 guerrillas, mostly non-Afghans, of whom most served in the front line, with a few hundred deployed overseas, from Mindanao to Chechnya. In numerical order, 055 Brigade's membership originated mostly from three geographic regions:

Arabs, mostly Egyptians, Saudis, Yemenis, Jordanians, Algerians, Moroccans, Sudanese, Tunisians and Libyans;
Central Asians, mostly Tajiks, Ukbeks, Kyrgyzs, and Kazaks;
South and Southeast Asians, mostly Pakistanis, Bangladeshis, Filipinos, Indonesians and Malaysians.

Its ranks also contained Muslims from Western China (Uighurs), Chechnya, Bosnia and other conflict zones. There were also a few Muslims from the diasporas of Western Europe and North America, often designated by a suffix indicating their citizenship; for instance, Ali Abu Saoud, from the US, would be known as Ali Muhammad "al-Ameriki". Al Qaeda cadres, whether fighting as guerrillas or as terrorists, were absolutely forbidden to use their real names, and before being inducted new members always received, or chose, an alias. No one else in Al Qaeda knows that individual's real name or personal details except his country of origin.

055 Brigade was drawn from two overlapping generations of Afghan veterans: the first, who had driven out the Russians, and the second, generally better educated, who had fought elsewhere — e.g. Kashmir, Daghestan, Tajikistan, Nagorno-Karabakh — but been trained in Afghanistan. With the ending of some of these conflicts, many combatants stayed behind, or married local women, or returned to Afghanistan and Pakistan. Among the latter were several hundred fighters originating from those countries who had befriended the foreign *mujahidin* and joined them to continue fighting *jihad* elsewhere. At a time when their own countries had shunned them, Al Qaeda offered them a refuge. They therefore have an intense personal loyalty to Osama, viewing him as both saviour and leader.

055 Brigade was equipped with weapons left behind by the Soviets — no weapons collection or buy-back program, except for "Stinger" surface-to-air missiles, was set up by Western governments after the Russian withdrawal — and others provided by the Sudanese, Pakistani and Taliban governments. Sudan later provided training facilities, and the Taliban passed on to Al Qaeda weapons supplied to them by the ISI. Al Qaeda also had a worldwide network of procurement officers, such as the US citizen Essam al-Ridi, Osama's personal pilot, who obtained

communication equipment from Japan; scuba gear and range finders from Britain; satellite phones from Germany; and night vision goggles and scopes, video equipment, Barrett 50 calibre sniping rifles and a T-389 plane from America. Other Al Qaeda support cells, mostly operating in Western democracies, played a major role in procurement throughout the 1990s. As of 2000–1, there were several reports that Al Qaeda had linked up with both the Russian and Ukrainian mafia to obtain weapons and equipment.

After the US and its allies stepped up support for the Northern Alliance in late 2001, frontline Taliban and Al Qaeda members suffered heavy losses in October and November of that year, especially from American bombing and cruise missiles. Nearly 500 Al Qaeda members fought to the death, were injured in battle or were captured. To preserve his forces in order to fight another day, Osama ordered the remainder of his battered 055 Brigade to retreat to the Afghanistan-Pakistan border with the specific intention of waging a protracted campaign. In December 2001 and early 2002, Al Qaeda's members were re-establishing their lines of communication as well as regrouping and reorganising their scattered forces near Gardez.

The relationship between 055 Brigade and the global terrorist network is reflected in an Al Qaeda internal report recovered in Afghanistan. According to this document, every Al Qaeda member periodically submits to the leadership his preferred course of action, or career move. For example, after serving one tour of duty against the Israelis in Southern Lebanon and another in Afghanistan against the Northern Alliance, Abu Majid al-Ansari, a Palestinian, stated, "I do not wish to serve in the front line anymore. I wish to become [a suicide bomber] and attain martyrdom."[2]

Financial network

The finance and business committee manages the financial resources necessary to sustain Al Qaeda. Al Qaeda is established in most countries with indigenous or migrant Muslim communities; its infiltration is evident wherever Muslims live and work. It can never operate in isolation, as mounting a terrorist operation requires financial and technical-logistical support that has to be in place often years in advance. In the Middle East, especially the Gulf, Al Qaeda has public, though hidden, support and also receives practical help from Islamic philanthropists and foundations, notably from the UAE and Saudi Arabia. In the developing world its infiltration strategies are linked to providing goods and services to local Muslims, whereas in the Western democracies it raises money for needy Muslims overseas, the soliciting and channelling of funds giving it plausible opportunities for building support and recruitment.

Intelligence and security services worldwide, including the CIA and MI6, have never before encountered a global terrorist financial network as sophisticated as Al Qaeda's. Comparisons with other such networks reveal that Al Qaeda has built the most complex, robust and resilient money-generating and money-moving network yet seen. No network resembles Al Qaeda's, although it shares some features with the now defunct Bank of Credit and Commerce International, which channelled funds to the anti-Soviet Afghan *jihad* and was patronised by other terrorist groups in the 1980s. The resilience of Al Qaeda's financial infrastructure is primarily due to the compartmentalised structure it has adhered to since its inception. It assigns a high priority to financial training and management as well as the sustained generation and investment of funds. Al Qaeda's finance and business committee — comprising professional bankers, accountants, and financiers — manages the group's funds across four continents. To move funds clandestinely from source to recipient, Al Qaeda's financial network disguises the true identities of both parties. For this purpose too, Al Qaeda has established several legitimate institutions including state and privately funded charities, banks and companies; in this respect its *modus operandi* is fully compatible with that of other terrorist groups such as the Tamil Tigers and Hamas.

It has been estimated that maintaining its core strength of 3,000 members in Afghanistan and clandestine agents overseas costs Al Qaeda at least $36 million a year, on top of which the group's set-up costs — weapons, technology, infrastructure, camps, offices, houses, vehicles — are thought to have been in the region of $50 million. Al Qaeda's annual budget is under $50 million, an estimate computed by examining the budgets of terrorist groups in relation to their sources of finance, geographic distribution, organisational sophistication, size and other factors.[3] Although Osama inherited 'only' $25-30 million, not the larger figures mentioned in the press, his shrewd investments bring in a not inconsiderable annual income. While some prominent Saudi businessmen support Al Qaeda, there are no links between Saudi Bin Laden Group, Bin Laden Group International or any of the subsidiaries of these companies with Osama or Al Qaeda. Nor is there hard evidence that Al Qaeda profits from the cultivation or sale of narcotics, unlike the Taliban regime, which did so substantially. To buy loyalty, Al Qaeda also funded individuals in various Islamist groups, including the Taliban, to the tune of $100 million according to US intelligence. The group's cash won them influence over the Taliban's political, religious and military leaders, the key ministries especially defence, and operational autonomy inside the country. To ensure the safe passage of goods and persons, Al Qaeda also required funds to pay customs and immigration officials, the police and the military. If ever there was an unambiguous example of "a state within a state" this was it. Traditionally, states that sponsored terrorism controlled terrorist groups. Before October 2001, Al Qaeda became the first terrorist group to control a state — the Islamic Emirate of Afghanistan.

To generate such vast sums, Al Qaeda depends on a range of sources, state sponsorship of terrorism having declined dramatically since the Cold War. Wealthy Arab benefactors in the Middle East, including respected individuals in the UAE, Kuwait, Saudi Arabia and Qatar, are Al Qaeda's financial mainstays. To facilitate such transactions, many businesses and banks in the Gulf are used as "fronts", enabling Al Qaeda to conduct business under cover. US intelligence has tracked some of the money trails, and they make interesting reading. For instance, funds for the attempted assassination of President Mubarak passed through the National Commercial Bank (NCB) of Saudi Arabia, the largest in the kingdom, which transferred several million dollars to Al Qaeda accounts via corresponding banks in New York and London, without the banks being aware of the true nature of these transactions.[4] After enquiries by the Saudi authorities, the NCB chairman, Khalid bin Mahfouz, was placed under house arrest and the bank reconstituted.[5] Al Qaeda also siphons funds from legitimate Islamic charities and NGOs that it infiltrates, while its extensive web of front, cover and sympathetic organisations include businesses ranging from diamond-trading, import-export, manufacturing and transport. Al Qaeda's clandestine penetration of legitimate public and private organisations included one charity that became the unwitting target of such activities and whose board at the time included President Pervais Musharraf of Pakistan.[6] In the mid-1990s, the CIA estimated that fifty Islamic charities "support terrorist groups or employ individuals who are suspected of having terrorist connections." There was no need for Osama to disguise his accounts in Sudan and Afghanistan, and, as mentioned above, US court records reveal that in the former he invested $50 million and, together with wealthy members of the NIF, capitalised a leading bank. In the same trial it was revealed that other Al Qaeda account-holders included Afad Makkee, who had one in his real name, Madani Sidi al-Tayyib; Nidal (*alias* Abu Rida al-Suri); Mamdouh Salim, Abdouh al-Mukhlafi and, in a joint account, Jamal Ahmed Muhammad al-Fadl and Abu Fadhl al-Makkee. Al Qaeda also had accounts in Bank Tadamon Islami, Bank Faisl Islami and also in Bank of Almusia (the Farmer's Bank).[7] Afad Makkee held an account at Barclay's Bank in London while Osama's UK representative, Khalid al-Fawwaz, managed British and foreign accounts on his behalf.[8] Khalifa al-Omani and Ahmed Ali Lootah held a joint account in Dubai,[9] and there were also Al Qaeda accounts in Malaysia and Hong Kong. The commander of Osama's bodyguard, Abdouh al-Mukhlafi, handled his leader's expenses.

In its military training manual, *Declaration of Jihad Against the Country's Tyrants*, Al Qaeda instructs its cadres about the production and use of counterfeit currency and forged documents (the counterfeiting of credit cards was the speciality of Al Qaeda's Algerian "family" in Europe). The group follows five financial security principles: funds should be divided between those invested for financial return and the balance — operational funds — that should be saved and spent only on operations; operational funds should not all be put in one place; only a few of the organisation's members should know the location of its funds; while carrying large amounts of money precautions should be taken; and money should be left with non-members and spent only when needed.[10]

While Al Qaeda support cells generate funds, its clandestine operational cells disburse them. Its banking network operates feeder and operational accounts, transfers from the feeder accounts to the operational accounts usually taking place through several bank accounts in order to disguise their true purpose. The feeder accounts are registered in the names of Al Qaeda-controlled charities and companies; the operational accounts are held either by Al Qaeda members whose identities are publicly not known or by reliable sympathisers. Al Qaeda depends heavily on the *hawala* informal banking system, whereby funds are transferred without financial or governmental scrutiny or accountability. Pakistani bankers estimate that the *hawala* system accounts for $2.5 to $3 billion entering the country each year, compared to only $1 billion via the formal banking system.[11] While Al Taqwa and Al Barakaat, both used extensively by Al Qaeda, have been named by the US Justice Department as having links to terrorism, there are several hundred other unregulated financial institutions in operation. For instance, in Pakistan alone there are over 1,000 *hawaladars*, of which some deals involve as much as $10 million.[12]

Foreign terrorist groups also receive funds from Al Qaeda, although these are probably on the decline and were never as high as has been thought previously.[13] Although the US has targeted Al Qaeda's support and operational network since 1998 (its account in the Dubai Islamic Bank in the UAE was closed under American pressure), Al Qaeda's financial network in the West has proved durable. First, it is highly mobile, and whenever threats arise, the group moves its assets and operatives. Second, many Western countries where Al Qaeda deposited funds, especially in Scandinavia, refused to sign the UN Convention on the Suppression of the Financing of Terrorism, which was opened for signature in 2000. Third, until 9/11 American efforts to suppress Al Qaeda's financial infrastructure were hampered by a lack of international support especially from Canada and Western Europe. Fourth, governments and private donors to Islamic and other charities are unable to control or determine the end users of their contributions. Unless there is a direct threat to the stability of their own governments or societies, or a threat to important bilateral and multilateral relationships, governments are unlikely to develop a framework for monitoring these NGOs. To ensure normative behaviour, transparency and accountability, as well as sanctions to punish those who violate these norms and practices, it would be necessary to develop a framework or code of conduct for NGOs, donors and recipients.

Al Qaeda's global fiscal network is managed by its regional financial officers. For instance, Muhammad Jamal Khalifa managed significant worldwide investments in Mauritius, Singapore, Malaysia and the Philippines. Another was the US-educated Malaysian businessman, Yazid Suffat, who part funded the 9/11 attacks. According to the FBI, Suffat promised Moussaoui, the twentieth would-be hijacker, $2,500 a month and $35,000 to get him started.[14]

A bank in the Gulf was used to fund Al Qaeda operations in Chechnya, and Osama ordered an investigation after it was brought to his attention that Chechen leaders were siphoning off large sums for their personal use. At a global level, Al Qaeda funds were managed by an exiled Saudi businessman in Ethiopia, Sheikh Muhammad Hussein al-Almadi; the Afghanistan- and Peshawar-based Palestinian, Zein-al-Abideen (*alias* Abu Zubaydah); and the Karachi-UAE-based, Saudi-born Mustafa Ahmed al-Hawsawi (*alias* Mustafa Ahmed). The latter coordinated the finances for the 9/11 operation.

Overall, the level of funding given by Al Qaeda for external operations is exaggerated.[15] It could be a result of successful US attempts to block finance to and from Al Qaeda. It is also hard to assess the validity of US government agencies' claims about bin Laden and his financial influence. The following examples support the theory that financial contributions to its operatives are not in fact lavish; sometimes they are inadequate. Several bits of circumstantial evidence lend weight to this suggestion. First, the World Trade Centre 1993 co-bomber Muhammad Salameh had to reclaim his $400 deposit from Ryder truck rental in order to buy a plane ticket to leave the US.[16] This he did by going to DIB Leasing Agency at 1558 Kennedy Boulevard, Jersey City.[17] Second, the Nairobi and Dar es Salaam bombers in August 1998 received little funding. Third, Ahmed Ressam and his associates were arrested in the US and Canada in December 1999 for involvement in credit card fraud or petty theft. Fourth, Al Qaeda operatives who were arrested in Jordan while preparing attacks on the Millennium were mostly self-financed by bank robberies, burglaries and the forging of cheques. Fifth, the 9/11 attacks, Al Qaeda's most expensive operation, cost just under $500,000, but even then the unspent funds were remitted back to the parent organisation. On September 8, 9, and 10, Muhammad Atta, Marwan al-Shehhi and

Waleed al-Shehri wired $15,000 to "Mustafa Ahmed" in the UAE, where it was picked up at the Al Ansari Exchange, Sharjah branch. Also, Muhammad Atta sent two transfers of $2,000 to the UAE from a branch of Mail Boxes Etc., a business service organisation, and a Giant supermarket in Laurel, a suburb of Washington, DC.[18] Two more transfers, both totalling about $5,000, were sent from Boston via Western Union.[19] As its operational commanders, Al Qaeda chose those who were careful with the "organisation's funds" and also trained their members accordingly.[20] For instance, the nineteen 9/11 hijackers lived frugally, staying in budget motels, renting cheap cars and eating in pizza parlours and burger bars. However, Al Qaeda did not compromise its operational effectiveness by penny-pinching. For instance, the hijackers bought business class tickets, costing $4,500 each, on the Boston to Los Angeles flight in order to be as close as possible to the cockpit. From past Al Qaeda operations it is clear that large amounts of cash are not of paramount importance to the success of a major terrorist strike provided the organisation is meticulous and the operatives are committed and brave.

Al Qaeda's financial network in Europe, which is dominated by the Algerians, relies heavily on credit card fraud. Security and intelligence agencies estimate that nearly $1 million a month is raised in this fashion. One Algerian cell in Britain that was unearthed in 1997 had raised nearly $200,000 in six months.[21] More such cells have been detected in Britain since 9/11, these being linked to similar networks in Belgium, Spain, France, and the Netherlands. Those committing the fraud on behalf of Al Qaeda were not the beneficiaries, however. All the money raised was transferred out of Britain to banks in the Middle East and Pakistan and the cell members hardly lived in luxury.[22] Al Qaeda even established a special camp in Afghanistan to train its European members in financial crime including credit card counterfeiting.[23] They were instructed how to read and write credit cards by accessing and copying the information from the magnetic strip.[24] At the request of Al Qaeda Afghanistan, the European network bought equipment for encoding and decoding credit cards from unsuspecting legitimate companies. Despite efforts to find and prosecute terrorist suspects engaging in credit card fraud, Al Qaeda's cadres are continually learning new techniques to evade detection. They have purchased credit card manufacturing machines on which bogus cards have been produced, obtained card details from shops and restaurants, skimmed electronic data from cards bought from petty criminals and surfed the internet for card details using web-search engines. Several computers with credit card numbers and other equipment were recovered from Al Qaeda suspects by police throughout Europe.

Al Qaeda's financial network has suffered significantly since 9/11, but it remains largely intact. Immediately after 9/11, the US issued instructions to domestic and foreign banks to freeze the assets of twenty-seven terrorist and related groups associated with Al Qaeda. On September 24, 2001, President Bush issued a new Executive Order targeting terrorist financing. He stated:

> [...] because of the pervasiveness and expansiveness of the financial foundation of foreign terrorists, financial sanctions may be appropriate for those foreign persons that support or otherwise associate with these foreign terrorists. I also find that a need exists for further consultation and cooperation with, and sharing of information by, United States and foreign financial institutions as an additional tool to enable the United States to combat the financing of terrorism.[25]

In response, the Office of Foreign Assets Control (OFAC) blocked terrorist assets and added new terrorist front, cover and sympathetic organisations to its existing list. The order was made effective at 12:01 a.m. on September 24, 2001. Within a month, US and foreign financial institutions froze nearly $100 million worth of terrorist assets, mostly associated with organisations as well as individuals linked to, or part of, Al Qaeda:

Al Qaida/Islamic Army
Abu Sayyaf Group (Philippines)
Armed Islamic Group (Algeria)
Harkat ul-Mujahidin (Kashmir)
Al Jihad/Egyptian Islamic Jihad
Islamic Movement of Uzbekistan
Asbat al-Ansar
Salafist Group for Call and Combat (Algeria)
Libyan Islamic Fighting Group
Al-Itihaad al-Islamiya
Islamic Army of Aden
Osama bin Laden
Muhamad Atif
Sayf al-Adl
Shaykh Sai'id
Muhammad Atef
Ibn Al-Shaykh al-Libi
Abu Zubaydah
Abd al-Hdi al-Iraqi
Ayman al-Zawahiri
Thirwat Salah Shihata
Tariq Anwar al-Sayyid Ahmad
Muhammad Salah

Makhtab Al Khidamat/Al Kifah
Wafa Humanitarian Organisation
Al Rashid Trust
Mamoun Darkanzanli Import Export Company [26]

The US Office of Foreign Assets Control has also released the names of a further 2,500 companies and individuals whose assets are to be blocked. The list includes individual terrorists, some linked to Al Qaeda, some not. For instance, Imad Fayiz Mughniyeh, the principal head of intelligence and operations of Hezbollah, is listed as a senior intelligence officer, born on December 7, 1962, in Tayr Dibba, Lebanon. But Abu Marzook, the Hamas political leader in Jordan and Syria, who is not linked to Al Qaeda, is included with his Egyptian passport and US Social Security numbers. The list also includes companies run by states designated as sponsors of terrorism and various banks, including several from Sudan: Islamic Cooperative Development Bank of Sudan, Bank e Millie Afghan, Bank of Khartoum, and the Agricultural Bank of Sudan.

What has been largely disrupted is Al Qaeda's formal banking network, including many of its clandestine and feeder accounts. Nonetheless, the group has the capability to generate new sources of finance and build an alternative unregulated banking network. As such, despite a greater willingness to share intelligence and coordinate law enforcement efforts after 9/11, the transfers of funds to Al Qaeda will continue. What remains necessary for the success of the strategy is to strike at the sources of funding and not only the conduits of transfer. By implementing sustained international pressure, income from Gulf-funded Islamic charities and revenue from Al Qaeda front, cover and sympathetic organisations — from commercial enterprises to mosques — can be greatly reduced, if not controlled altogether.

The finance and business committee manages the financial resources necessary to sustain Al Qaeda. In a US trial it emerged that in the early days it was headed by Abu Hammam al-Saudi and Abu Fadhl al-Makkee, the latter being involved in Al Qaeda's relocation from Pakistan to Sudan, where he launched a wide range of commercial enterprises. These included Zirqani; Laden International; Althemar al Mubaraka; Quadrat Transportation, Quadrat Construction, and Bareba Commission. Where possible Al Qaeda preferred to raise funds via legitimate businesses and hence eschewed narcotics or the smuggling of migrants. For example Blessed Fruits exported fruits and vegetables; Al Hijra Construction built roads; International al-Ikhlas manufactured sweetmeats, Bank of Zoological Resources manufactured genes for hybrid cattle; Kasalla produced corn hybrids and other agricultural produce; the Happ Tannery in Khartoum produced leather. Al Qaeda also owned food-processing and furniture-making companies and was heavily involved in import-export, purchasing bicycles from Azerbaijan, Maz trucks from Russia, Zetor tractors from Slovakia and cars from Dubai. Among the goods it imported were heavy machinery, fertiliser, sugar, iron, insecticide and machine tools; its exports included ostriches from Kenya, wood from Turkey, lemons, olives, raisins and nuts from Tajikistan, diamonds from Tanzania, lapis lazuli from Afghanistan, precious stones from Uganda and camels from Sudan.[27]

Al Qaeda also had a worldwide network of investments and small businesses. For instance, it owned boats and had a fishing business in Mombasa; in Sweden it invested in the hospital equipment industry, in Denmark in dairy products and in Norway in paper mills.[28] The finance committee also supervises a special office for procuring passports and entry certificates, whether genuine, forged or adapted. Al Qaeda's immigration and documentation office obtains airline tickets and visas. It was originally located in Pakistan and staffed by Hamzalla al-Liby, Abu Yasser al-Jazairi (*alias* Abu Yasser al-Sirir), from Algeria, and Abu Abd al-Sabbur.

Al Qaeda also generated significant sums by infiltrating Islamic NGOs, a measure that became proportionately more important after Osama's assets were frozen by the Saudi regime in 1994 and most of Al Qaeda's companies in Sudan were running at a loss after the imposition of international sanctions. Its ideological appeal and financial resources allowed Al Qaeda methodically to infiltrate unwitting mosques and charities worldwide, which included the Kuwait-based Mercy International in Kenya and Help Africa People. Mercy International supported orphanages, schools, hospitals, mosques and refugee centres in Somalia, where to win influence Al Qaeda financed a malaria research project. The parent charities in Europe and the Middle East were, however, completely unaware of the Al Qaeda infiltration that was taking place in these African branches.

As well as being fully in control of MAK, Al Qaeda controls some branches of IIRO, thereby offering it two further sources of funds and cover. IIRO Philippines was unwittingly infiltrated by Osama's brother-in-law, Muhammad Jamal Khalifa, and was used to support two terrorist groups. IIRO Tanzania, for example, cooperated with Al Qaeda immediately before the bombing of the US embassy in Dar es Salaam in 1998. Similarly IIRO Pankishi Valley in Georgia unwittingly funnelled nearly $10 million raised in Europe to Chechnya, possibly to the Al Ansar *mujahidin*, led by Osama's protégé, Khattab, in 1999/2000.

Al Qaeda's financial system is complex, but comparing it with other organisations does make the picture a little clearer. Some have likened it to the Ford Foundation, where researchers present projects and after careful consideration some are funded while most are discarded. Others have compared it to a multinational corporation. Al Qaeda can also be conceptualised as a holding company and its associate Islamist groups as its subsidiaries, with Al Qaeda providing the venture capital.[29]

Traditionally terrorists have used reputable Western international banks to move money because they are subject to less suspicion and scrutiny by banking and intelligence authorities, the firms concerned being unwitting conduits for such transfers. Al Qaeda uses secular as well as Islamic banks to receive and transfer funds in complex ways. Most Islamic banks are reputable, highly respected, legally grounded and well regulated and only a small percentage conduct transactions of dubious legality. In addition to Islamic banks located in forty-seven countries, Iran, Pakistan and Sudan have reorganised their entire financial systems to meet the criteria of Islamic banking laws. The top 100 Islamic banks have a global capitalisation of $40 billion. Of these, those in the Arabian Peninsula (three of the top ten banks are from Saudi Arabia) are the wealthiest and they account for two-thirds of the capital value of Islamic banks. The annual turnover of Islamic banks in 2000 is estimated at $100 billion.[30]

As *sharia* law forbids making money on loans, each bank has a religious board that monitors it. There are five ways by which Islamic banks provides money to its customers – *mudabara* (money is provided to an investor and profits and losses are shared), *qard al-hasanah* (a loan free of interest usually given to those in need), *musharaka* (the lender becomes a shareholder by providing capital to a business), *murabaha* (where the bank buys and sells an asset with a mark up), and *ijara* (a leasing contract where the bank buys and rents it to a customer). There are three types of accounts: current deposit accounts where there are no returns on the money and the account can be closed at any time; limited *mudaraba* deposits where the money can be used by the banks for its investments projects (for instance, Al Taqwa bank used Hamas funds in the late 1990s and the group suffered heavy losses[31]); and third, limited *mudaraba* deposits where both the bank and account holder determine the investment project and shares the return.

One Islamic bank used by Al Qaeda "[enabled] private individuals to funnel funds to different Islamic causes around the globe in all anonymity."[32] According to a European intelligence agency, a front associated with Al Qaeda used its London, Berlin and Bonn branches to transfer a total of DM3,450,900 to an Al Qaeda associate terrorist group between 1995-7. In the late 1990s, the same bank was repeatedly used by Algerian Islamists to procure weapons, including one transaction amounting to DM247,000 DM in 1998.[33]

Training

Al Qaeda's success in conducting well-coordinated guerrilla and terrorist attacks is largely due to stringent emphasis on training and retraining. It has produced several training manuals of which its standard reference work is the multi-volume, 7,000-page *Encyclopaedia of the Afghan Jihad*. The first ten volumes cover tactics; security and intelligence; handguns; first aid; explosives; grenades and mines; tanks; manufacturing (of arms and explosives); topography and land surveys; and weapons (general). The cover of each volume shows a belt-fed machine gun standing on a window ledge next to a copy of the Koran. The treatment of terrorist training is extensive: a section on tactics entitled "The effect of desert conditions on operations" is subdivided into the following sections: advance; attack; defence; withdrawal; movement and transport; shortage of water; supplies; and maintenance.[34]

As Al Qaeda operates in a wide range of environments, given its global reach, the encyclopaedia caters for urban, non-urban, mountain, desert and jungle terrains. Similarly the volume on explosives classifies them according to their natural characteristics, usage, velocity of detonation composition and so on. One section illustrates how to booby-trap items such as a camera, a radio, a book, a packet of cigarettes, a bottle of wine, a whistle, electronic equipment, a torch, a cake, a chocolate bar, a toothpaste tube, a hairbrush, furniture, a domestic heater and so on.[35] From tiny objects the encyclopaedia moves up in scale, instructing how to bomb big buildings, statues and bridges and how to shoot down aircraft with Stinger missiles. Throughout it is simply and clearly written and the reader does not need to be highly educated in order to act upon the instructions.

The *Encyclopaedia* was written to train a new generation of *mujahidin* to conduct guerrilla warfare and terrorism. Although its composition began soon after the Soviets withdrew from Afghanistan in 1989, its focus at that time was not on how to target the West. Rather, its primary objective was to collate, record and share the *mujahidin*'s unprecedented knowledge and experience of guerrilla warfare with future generations, above all those planning to fight in conflicts such as Kashmir, Bosnia, Mindanao and Chechnya. As Osama was gradually persuaded by the Egyptian members of MAK to follow the terrorist trajectory, so terrorist techniques were incorporated into the manual. Targets mentioned in this section include the Eiffel Tower and the Statue of Liberty. Volume 11, a later addition, covers chemical and biological warfare, and is presented in a separate CD. The training it describes is to be imparted only to handpicked members of Al Qaeda.

The *Encyclopaedia* was compiled, written, translated and edited over five years by the Egyptian and Saudi elements of Al Qaeda, primarily those who had been educated in America and Britain. Much of the material is culled from US and British military manuals, especially the American F-M (field manual) series. It was published by MAK, having been computer typeset and first printed in Arabic, most probably in Peshawar, in 1996, the CD appearing in 1999. While some Asian and Middle Eastern intelligence agencies had access to incomplete photocopies of the *Encyclopaedia* by 1997, the Belgian secret service was the first to recover one although it lacked the expertise and funds to translate it. It is believed that the CIA received a copy from the Jordanian security service only in 1997. As it was compiled and published over many years, there are several extant versions. All the editions are dedicated, first and above all, to God. The acknowledgements and dedications continue with Abdullah Azzam, Osama bin Laden, unnamed *mujahidin* trainers in Afghanistan, the manual's financiers, the publisher and Pakistan:[36]

> A word of truth with a tear of allegiance To our beloved brother and revered Sheikh 'Abdullah' Azzam Who revived the spirit of jihad in the souls of the youth with the word of God. [...] Who suffered harm from most people except from the faithful. [...] This work is dedicated to Allah, then to you. To the beloved brother Abu Abdallah – Osama bin Laden – who was the faithful helper of Sheikh 'Abdullah' Azzam in his *jihad* and in the creation of the Office of Services [MAK]. Who waged *jihad* in Afghanistan with his person and with everything he owned. Who did not cease to wage *jihad* and incite *jihad* to the present day. Who has been wronged in his *jihad* by most of those who cling to Islam. [...] Let Allah strengthen you and reward you for what you have done. For the sake of Islam, to you, from all Muslims and [especially] those who wage the *jihad*.
>
> To the brothers who participated in the publishing of this *Encyclopaedia* – no one knows [them] except Allah. We ask Him to put this effort into the balance of the Day of Judgement and reward with all the best all those who translated, designed, printed, wrote, collected material, or those who took pictures, sent computers – or anything else that we may have forgotten.
>
> Let Allah weigh these things with all your good deeds on the Day of Judgement.
>
> Allah, be he exalted, says. he who doesn't thank others is not thanked. [...]
> We thank the state of Pakistan, the government and the people for the presence of the Arab brothers on its land (despite the many problems it has endured from the enemies of Allah) and the victory it has given to its brothers, the *mujahidin* of Afghanistan. And we ask Allah to weigh this good deed with their other good deeds for the sake of Islam and the Muslims.

The curriculum in an Al Qaeda training camp naturally varies depending on the mission that has been assigned to the trainee. The three standard courses are basic, advanced, and specialised. Basic training pertains to guerrilla warfare and Islamic law (*sharia*); advanced training involves the use of explosives, assassination techniques, and heavy weapons; and specialised training covers surveillance and counter-surveillance, forging and adapting identity documents, and conducting a maritime or vehicle-borne suicide attacks.

Recruit, basic or general training was the commonest form of instruction provided in Afghanistan. While tens of thousands of young and zealous Muslims graduated from camps run by Al Qaeda, only a few thousand were invited to join Al Qaeda itself. These privileged ones were the best of the best, and often already had specialised language or technical skills. They were continuously assessed and tested for their commitment and dedication before and after joining.

Al Qaeda uses another manual, *Declaration of Jihad against the Country's Tyrants (Military Series),* exclusively for terrorist operations.[37] The cover depicts a globe through which a sword pierces Africa and the Middle East. Dedicated to the "young Muslim men who are pure, believing and fighting for the cause of Allah, the principal author states "It is my contribution towards paving the road that leads to majestic Allah and establishes a caliphate according to the prophecy."[38] The eighteen lessons include a "general introduction", "necessary qualifications and characteristics for the organisation's members", "counterfeit currency and forged documents", "organisation of military bases", "apartments and other places", "concealment, means of communication and transportation", "training", "weapons: measures related to buying and transporting them", "member safety", "security plans", "definition of special operations", "espionage (1): information-gathering using open methods", "espionage (2): information-gathering using covert methods", "assassinations using poisons and cold steel", "torture methods" and "prisons and detention centres". In the wider public interest I have chosen not to discuss the techniques it recommends for perpetrating violence, especially the use of improvised explosive devices, poisons and so on.

The manual was written by an experienced instructor of the Islamic Group of Egypt before it merged with Al Qaeda, after which the former played a key role in Al Qaeda's support and strike operations. The manual was written between 1993-4, drawing largely on the Egyptian Islamic Group's experience of support and terrorist operations in urban Egypt. In the dissemination of information, "need to know" principles and operational security are meticulously followed. Following the dedication page the manual reiterates: "In the name of the Allah, the merciful and compassionate, [this volume] belongs to the guest house. Please do not remove it from the house except with permission."[39] These three lines are followed by an emblem and an illegible signature, perhaps of the person in charge of the safe house.

Al Qaeda puts great stress on the fact that its members should be psychologically trained for war, and it often dispatches instructors to the West to impart to new members religious indoctrination, which is considered far more important than battlefield or terrorist combat-training. The organisation believes that this policy produces fighters with the requisite mental resilience to sacrifice themselves. Most of Al Qaeda's 9/11 pilots and their accomplices did not undergo extensive military training; rather, their psychological conditioning and willingness to die for Allah were considered the operational priorities. Al Qaeda also believes that commitment to the ideology of the organisation frees its members from "conceptual problems".[40] Although the media refer to 9/11 and the USS *Cole* attacks as "suicide" operations, Islamist military groups considers them to be "martyrdom" attacks, given that suicide *per se* is forbidden in Islam. Hence another qualification to join Al Qaeda is a willingness to "do the work and undergo martyrdom for the purpose of achieving the goal and establishing the religion of majestic Allah on earth".[41]

Religious instruction covers Islamic law, Islamic history and contemporary Islamic politics; how to preserve one's faith when interacting with non-believers; Islamic jurisprudence; how to wage *jihad*; the history of Prophet Muhammad; and other information on Islam to be used to defend one's beliefs.[42] Paramilitary training covers all aspects of military instruction, from codes of ethics and behaviour; light and heavy weapons training; setting booby-traps; navigation and the use of a compass and maps; urban warfare, including using buildings for cover and fighting from foxholes and bunkers.[43] Paramilitary training also includes assassination, hand-to-hand combat, knowledge of parts of the body vulnerable to lethal force, the use of knives, guns and rope to kill, poisoning, communications and surveillance techniques. Surveillance detection training is reserved only for *Shura* members.[44]

Common to Al Qaeda and its associate groups are the fourteen mandatory qualifications required before one is admitted as a member of an Islamist military organisation: knowledge of Islam, ideological commitment, maturity, self-sacrifice, discipline, secrecy and concealment of information, good health, patience, unflappability, intelligence and insight, caution and prudence, truthfulness and wisdom, the ability to observe and analyse, and the ability to act.

In the *Declaration of Jihad agains the Country's Tyrants*, the paramount qualification for membership of an Islamist group, including Al Qaeda, is to be Muslim — whether a convert or not is immaterial. To quote from the manual:

> The member of the Organisation must be a Muslim. How can an unbeliever, someone from a revealed religion [Christian, Jew], a secular person, a communist, etc. protect Islam and Muslims and defend their goals and secrets when he

does not believe in that religion [Islam]? The Israeli Army requires that a fighter be of the Jewish religion. Likewise, the command leadership in the Afghan and Russian armies required anyone with an officer's position to be a member of the communist party.[45]

Although all Al Qaeda members are Sunni Muslims, it cooperates with Shia Muslims, and occasionally with non-Muslim terrorists or organised criminals. However, these relationships are not strategic but tactical. Examples include Al Qaeda's ties with Hezbollah and the Liberation Tigers of Tamil Eelam (LTTE) in acquiring a suicide attack capability.

Of the seven tasks of an Islamic military organisation listed in the manual, the first is the "removal of those personalities that block the call's path".[46] Those specified for elimination are "all types of military and civilian intellectuals and thinkers for the state."[47] The remaining six tasks are the "proper ultilisation of the individual's unused capabilities; precision in performing tasks and working collectively to complete a job from all perspectives, not just one; controlling work and not fragmenting it or deviating from it; achieving long-term goals such as the establishment of an Islamic state and short-term goals such as operations against enemy individuals and sectors; establishing the conditions for possible confrontation with regressive regimes and their persistence; and achieving discipline in secrecy and through performing tasks."[48]

As with almost all Islamist movements, Al Qaeda specifically targets young men as recruits. It presents a picture of youths who have ignored the Koran and been led astray by apostate rulers:

They [the apostate rulers] tried, using every means and seduction, to produce a generation of young men that did not know anything except what [the rulers] want, did not say anything except what [the rulers] think about, did not live except according to the rulers' way, and did not dress except in the rulers' clothes. [...]The bitter situation the nation has reached is a result of its divergence from Allah's course and his religious law for all places and times. That bitter situation came about as a result of its children's love for the world, their loathing of death, and their abandonment of *jihad*.[49]

Nonetheless, Al Qaeda also presents a picture of a "large group of those young men" having woken up from "their sleep" returning to "Allah, regretting and repenting"[50]: "The young men returning to Allah realised that Islam is not just a performing ritual but a complete system: religion and government, worship and *jihad*, ethics and dealing with people, and the Koran and the sword."[51] With the aid of the Koran and *hadith* and drawing lessons from the past and the present, Al Qaeda lures and fastens the youth to its fold:

Unbelief is the same. It pushed Abou Jahl – may Allah curse him – and Kureish's valiant infidels to battle the prophet – God bless and keep him – and to torture his companions – may Allah's grace be on them. It is the same unbelief that drove Sadat, Hosni Mubarak, Gadhafi, Hafez Assad, Saleh, Fahed – Allah's curse be upon the non-believing leaders – and all the apostate Arab rulers to torture, kill, imprison and torment Muslims.[52]

Stating that the "young came to prepare themselves for *jihad*, commanded by the majestic Allah's order in the holy Koran", the training manual quotes from the Koran: "Against them, make ready your strength to the utmost of your power, including steeds of war, to strike terror into the [hearts of] the enemies of Allah and your enemies, and others besides whom ye may not know, but whom Allah doth know."[53]

Al Qaeda assigns a high priority to conducting special operations in the belief that they boost Islamic morale and lower that of the enemy. The manual lists their benefits as follows: they build a reserve of fighters by preparing and training new members for future tasks; they serve as a form of necessary punishment, mocking the regime's admiration among the population; they remove the personalities that stand in the way of the Islamic *da'wa* (call); they publicise issues; they help to reject compliance and submission to the regime in its practices; they provide legitimacy to the Islamist group; they spread fear and terror through the regime's ranks; and they attract new members to the organisation.[54] The disadvantages are also set out: special operations restrain the Islamic *da'wa* and preachers; they reveal the structure of the military organisation and financially drain it; they spread terror and fear among the population; they increase the regime's safeguards and precautions against future operations; they cannot precipitate the fall of the regime in power; the failure of an operation increases the regime's credibility; repeated failure lowers the morale of the organisation's members themselves, causing them to lose faith, and boosts that of the regime; and, finally, they can prompt a regime, in retaliation, to try to assassinate the group's leaders.[55]

Another indicator of Al Qaeda's thoroughness is found in the manual, namely that after the execution of an operation at the place and time specified, a full report identifying the strengths and weaknesses of the attack is prepared and sent to the head of Al Qaeda so that its impact can be gauged and the effectiveness of future operations improved. For instance, against his assigned role, the performance of each individual Al Qaeda cadre is evaluated for the purpose of rewarding or reprimanding him for his conduct: "Those deemed weak or lazy were dismissed."

The manual also explains and justifies why the kidnapping for ransom, torture, killing and exchange of hostages are permitted in Islam, especially if the victim is a non-Muslim. Hostage-taking is seen as an effective method of obtaining information and increasing the bargaining power of the group. In this connection an Islamist ideologue is quoted:

> We find permission to interrogate the hostage for the purpose of obtaining information. It is permitted to strike the non-believer who has no covenant until he reveals the news, information, and secrets of his people. [...]The religious scholars have also permitted the killing of a hostage if he insists on withholding information from Muslims. They permitted his killing so that he would not inform his people of what he learnt about the Muslim condition, number [of his captors], and secrets. [...] The scholars have also permitted the exchange of hostages for money, services, expertise and secrets of the enemy's army, plans and numbers.[56]

Tactics

Contemporary terrorist groups have perfected the art of agent handling to generate high grade or high quality intelligence. Unlike the rag-tag terrorist groups of the Cold War period, sophisticated terrorist groups of the post-Cold War period have developed intelligence wings comparable with government intelligence agencies. By running agents into the political establishment, security forces or security and intelligence apparatus, Al Qaeda and Islamist terrorist groups have infiltrated both Middle Eastern and other governments. For instance, several former Middle Eastern especially Egyptian, Pakistani, and Central Asian police officers and military personnel as well as several former European military and at least one US military personnel have served in the ranks of Al Qaeda. Considering the scale of penetration – both ideological and by infiltration – it is likely that there are several dozen serving Al Qaeda supporters and sympathisers. Although one of the most dangerous tasks, where exposure and death are not uncommon, agent-handling whether conducted by a state or by a terrorist group is extremely rewarding.

Al Qaeda's global terrorist network strictly adheres to the cellular (also known as the cluster) model, "composed of many cells whose members do not know one another, so that if a cell member is caught the other cells would not be affected and work would proceed normally".[57] Cell members never meet in one place together; nor do they in fact know each other;[58] nor are they familiar with the means of communication used between the cell leader and each of its members.[59] As Western intelligence agencies rely heavily on technical methods of information-gathering, Al Qaeda employs electronically non-detectable forms of communication, primarily the human courier. Moreover Britain's GCHQ and America's NSA codebreakers have failed to crack Al Qaeda email communications encrypted in the widely available "Pretty Good Privacy" (PGP) encryption software.

Al Qaeda has a sophisticated agent-handling system to manage its global terrorist network. Its two tiers of agent-handlers manage agents outside Afghanistan and in the regional nodes. They also cultivate sub-agents whose primary responsibility is penetrating and infiltrating Muslim migrant communities to recruit, gather intelligence and conduct operations. Al Qaeda attack teams use the cover of migrant communities to plan, prepare and execute operations against Western targets. Al Qaeda supporters from among migrant communities assist Al Qaeda's operatives — providing safe houses, communication, transport, intelligence and finance — in launching attacks against their host countries. The 9/11 attacks were an exception to this general rule, and one can anticipate a similar strategy being adopted for further high prestige attacks. Till recently Al Qaeda's penetration of liberal democracies has been facilitated by the failure to clamp down on the dissemination of terrorist propaganda and fund-raising activities. In Canada, continental Europe, Australia and New Zealand, for example, distribution of terrorist propaganda and related fund-raising continues even after 9/11.

Strategic and tactical direction of the global terrorist network is provided by the leadership of Al Qaeda, including Osama and his deputy al-Zawahiri. Osama directly coordinated important operations such as the September 11 attacks, and while al-Banshiri and his deputy Muhammad Atef worked on the ground in Somalia. Osama provided the strategic leadership for the East African embassy and USS *Cole* attacks and reviewed the plans at every stage, pinpointing on photographs of the targets where the explosives-laden truck and boat respectively should be positioned. Al Qaeda's experienced Egyptian, Algerian and Yemeni terrorists were always involved in planning and conducting such attacks.

In the run up to the Nairobi and Dar es Salaam bombings, Al Qaeda had infiltrators in place who lived normal lives as sleeper agents for several years; some had severed connections with the organisation but their enthusiasm had been rekindled by a fresh approach, and they had been persuaded to help. Western intelligence believes there are layers of deep penetration Al Qaeda sleeper agents in Europe and North America, awaiting activation. These dormant cells are harder to detect than active ones which take more risks when planning attacks, and maintain the tightest of security precautions.

Most Al Qaeda attacks involve three distinct phases. First, intelligence teams mount surveillance, be it on a static or a moving target. Based on the target intelligence obtained, the attack team rehearses its operation in an Al Qaeda camp, often on a scale model of the building or vessel in question. Next an Al Qaeda support team arrives in the target area and organises safe houses and vehicles, bringing with it the necessary weapons and explosives. Lastly, Al Qaeda's strike team arrives and withdraws after completing the mission, unless it is a suicide attack. As the exfiltration of attack teams in a hostile environment is very difficult, suicide is likely to remain Al Qaeda's preferred tactic for the foreseeable future. Considering the range and significance of targets (embassies, a naval destroyer, the Pentagon and World Trade Centre) Al Qaeda has selected, one can safely predict that it will continue to stage spectacular land, sea and air attacks in the future, especially against symbolic or high-profile targets in Europe, North America and elsewhere.

To ensure Al Qaeda's operational effectiveness, the group stresses the need to maintain internal security, dividing its operatives into overt and covert members functioning under a single leader. They are expected to follow certain measures to prevent arrest, some of which are described below.

An overt member should not be curious or inquisitive about matters that do not concern him; he should not discuss with others what he knows or hears; he should not carry on him the names and addresses of members; if his outward appearance is Islamic, he should refrain from visiting known troublespots — especially during times of heightened security and crackdowns by the authorities — and remain at home. He should be extremely guarded in use of the phone and should burn all correspondence after reading it. In addition to the above, covert members — undercover operatives — should also not reveal their true names to other operatives. While his general appearance should not indicate Islamic orientation — beards, long shirts, recognisable Muslim dress codes and carrying copies of the Koran are to be avoided — his behaviour should also eschew traditional practices, such as the greetings "May Allah reward you" or "Peace be on you". False identity documents are to be carried and all the personal information contained therein memorised.

Covert members should not rent or buy property near prominent buildings and must avoid visiting Islamic public spaces — mosques, libraries, bookshops, musical events and so on. To protect covert members, overt members should conduct dry runs of the places and routes where covert members are scheduled to travel. Both covert and overt members should avoid causing trouble at work or in their residential neighbourhoods, maintain familial relationships and refrain from sudden changes in their daily routine, conversation, movements and demeanour. Nor should covert members sever too hastily their previous relationships.

Covert members must avoid attracting unnecessary attention by advocating one thing or denouncing another, or by getting too passionate about their cause, thereby criticising or praising the organisation. Al Qaeda operatives should secure their homes every time they leave and refrain from violating no-parking zones, taking photographs, or sending letters or leaving messages unless absolutely necessary. They are advised not to write anything down that could later be revealed with forensic techniques, such as rubbing paper with lead powder. At all times they must also practise counter-surveillance techniques. Covert members are to contact overt members only when necessary and such contact must be brief. Al Qaeda has both single and married operatives, the latter being enjoined "not to talk with their wives about Jihad work"[60] or to travel with them: "A wife with an Islamic appearance [veil] attracts attention."[61] All such security precautions developed for overt and covert members also apply to Al Qaeda's leaders, to whom significant resources are devoted for their protection. To preserve operational effectiveness at all levels of Al Qaeda compartmentalisation, the "need-to-know" principle and secrecy are paramount. Al Qaeda's support (propaganda, fund-raising, procurement, training) and operational (surveillance/intelligence-gathering and prosecution of attacks) components function semi-independently of each other.

Al Qaeda's global network has survived by its members strictly adhering to the principals of operational security. As of mid-2001, Al Qaeda's permanent or semi- permanent presence had been confirmed in seventy-six countries, including those without discernable Muslim communities but which are suitable for procurement, e.g. Japan, Bulgaria, Slovakia. The basic building blocks of Al Qaeda support and operational cells targeting the US and its allies are safe houses, secure communication and transportation systems. Safe houses are chosen after careful consideration both of their location — avoiding isolated, secluded or deserted locations — and the nature of the operation for which they will be used: e.g. meetings, storage, preparing arms and munitions, hiding fugitives, or planning attacks. The renting of safe houses must be carried out by hand-picked members or supporters using false names and appropriate cover, and who have a non-Muslim appearance. No Al Qaeda operative was to rent more than one safe house in the same area or from the same rental office. Great care is also taken not to rent premises that have hitherto come to the attention of the police or security forces, preference being given to new developments where neighbours do not know each other.[62] Ground floor accommodation is preferred because it facilitates escape options, and all Al Qaeda safe houses must have contingency plans for vacating them at speed in case of a raid. Secure areas are to be prepared in the safe house for hiding documents, arms and other important items, and visitors must be given the necessary cover — as students or employees — and avoid going there at suspicious times. Al Qaeda instructs its operatives, before entering a safe house, to ensure that no surveillance is taking place, the "all clear" to be made known via pre-arranged signals. All locks and keys in safe houses, shops, mosques and other buildings are to be replaced, and safe houses visible from adjacent apartments are to be avoided.

Al Qaeda emphasises the need for perfect cover, to be corroborated by supporting documents — for a physician a medical diploma, membership of a medical union, an official permit — or even rudimentary knowledge of medical procedure. Furthermore, operatives are to blend their cover with local conditions, hence a doctor ought to establish a clinic in a suitable location. If other Al Qaeda members visit the operative, their cover stories must match. Al Qaeda instructors drive home the point by telling trainees that they should not arrange meetings in expensive hotels if their overseas cover is that of an ordinary worker.

Although communication is detectable, it is vital for any sustained activity, and Al Qaeda regards it as the "mainstay of the movement for rapid accomplishment".[63] As the use of satellite communication is limited to Al Qaeda's leadership and its affiliated groups, it does not feature in the basic military training manual from which these and other guidelines have been drawn.

Al Qaeda assigns the highest priority to secure communications, and each cell leader in the field determines how each member will keep in touch, stressing that communication should be quick, explicit and pertinent. After Indian intelligence provided Osama's satellite phone number to its US counterparts,[64] Al Qaeda became increasingly aware of the dangers of this means of communiciation[65] and has since taken measures to reduce the risk of detection, including limiting the duration of transmission to five minutes and positioning the device near a high frequency source, such as a TV station, embassy, or consulate. Voices ought to be disguised, the times, location and frequency of calls altered, and nothing in the conversation should raise suspicion. There are suspicions that Al Qaeda deceived coalition forces in Afghanistan during the Tora Bora campaign by broadcasting pre-recorded tapes indicating that Osama and other leaders were in the area, whereas they had in fact gone elsewhere.

Al Qaeda trains its operatives in every single aspect of communication, its manual stating: "communication should be carried out from public places. One should select telephones that are less suspicious to the security apparatus and are more difficult to monitor. It is preferable to use telephones in booths and on main streets."[66] The manual also explains the need for communication security: "Because of significant technological advances, security measures for monitoring telephone and broadcasting equipment have increased. Monitoring may be done by installing a secondary device on a telephone that relays the calls to a remote location. [...] That is why the Organisation takes security measures among its members who use this means of communication."[67]

By examining a range of manuals from government intelligence agencies, Islamist military groups developed guidelines to help its operatives meet face to face, including the use of disguises. Before two parties meet in public, Al Qaeda predetermines the place and arrival and departure times of both parties; the duration of the meeting; and an alternative date and time in case it should fall through.[68] Al Qaeda guidelines also specify that the shortest possible time should elapse between arranging a meeting and it taking place, primarily to reduce the risk posed by an operative with knowledge of the rendezvous being arrested.[69]

Al Qaeda adopts different guidelines depending on whether the two parties know each other or not.[70] If the individuals recognise each other, a single safety sign suffices, such as the carrying or movement of a particular object — keys, a newspaper, a scarf — indicating that no surveillance is taking place. Using such precautions Al Qaeda cadres can even meet in public. If two individuals are not known to one another, Al Qaeda specifies an elaborate, concurrent, three-stage set of guidelines to establish identification. These involve caution at every stage, emphasising the need to act naturally, to speak quietly, not to write anything down and to have a mutually agreed security plan in case the meeting is compromised. The disadvantages of meeting in person are enumerated to increase awareness of the threat facing Al Qaeda operatives: the risk of capture; the danger of security forces photographing them, recording their conversation and gathering evidence; and the risk of exposing the identity of the cell leader to its members. Using intermediaries to send and receive messages minimises these threats. In non-Islamist terrorist groups even non-members are used as couriers, but Al Qaeda insists on these being dedicated members of the organisation who have met the fourteen entry requirements. Security measures to be adopted by the intermediary include knowing the recipient of the message; familiarity with the meeting's location; agreement on special signals, date and time; selecting a public rendezvous that does not raise suspicion; and travelling by secondary roads (if driving) or bus and train to minimise surveillance.

When letters are used to communicate between group members they should contain only a few pages, they should be mailed from a post office far from the sender's residence, secret information should not be explicitly spelt out, the sender's name and address must be fictitious, the receiver's address must be clearly visible and neither the full postage cost or PO box fees should be overlooked. Letters sent overseas should go to a prearranged, inconspicuous address rather than the agent's home.

Al Qaeda uses three types of secret communication: common, standby and alarm. Common communication between two members should be conducted undercover after inspecting the surveillance situation; standby communication replaces common communication when one of the two parties is unable to communicate; and alarm communication occurs in response to security force penetration.

Al Qaeda members follow different guidelines for the use of public (trains, buses) and private (cars, motorcycles) transport. They should select public transport that is not subject to frequent checking; an operative's cover, including his appearance, should match his mode of transport (tourist bus, first or second class train compartment, etc.); important items should be placed among other passengers' luggage or in a different compartment; night arrivals are to be avoided, so too is speaking to cab drivers, many of whom are informers. When using cars and motorbikes in overt activity, the driver should possess proper registration documents, secure the vehicle to prevent its confiscation or theft, ensure that the model of vehicle used matches the operative's cover, and, unless the organisation has no alternative, ensure that his own vehicle is not used in attacks.

Similarly, in covert operations, discretion in the use of the vehicle should be maintained, traffic rules obeyed, and care taken to avoid being tailed by the police and other agencies. To prevent tracing the driver, vehicles should be purchased using forged/adapted documents, they should be parked securely but with exit routes available, and the vehicle's colour should be changed for an operation and thereafter returned to its original colour, licence plates should be altered and large petrol stations avoided, again to minimise surveillance by CCTV. Finally, all vehicle purchases and sales are to be carried out only by experienced operatives.

Al Qaeda's training program is designed to create self-contained cells that operate independently of a central command. When an Al Qaeda member left Afghanistan on a mission he was not expected to take weapons or explosives with him; instead he was taught to be self-sufficient, to manufacture an explosive device from commercial products, and to procure transport and store munitions near his target. When acquiring weapons in small quantities, Al Qaeda has a four-stage security plan — pre-purchasing, purchasing, transporting and storage.[71] In pre-purchasing, test whether the seller is a security agent, acquire familiarity with the site of the transaction and check for informants and security personnel. While the seller and buyer should not be visible from another location, they should be able to see the surrounding area. The purchaser should be suitably attired to match his cover story and he should practise counter-surveillance techniques. Al Qaeda operatives followed such operational security procedures in Europe and South East Asia in a series of operations the group attempted in late 2001.

During purchasing, verify the weapons, and pay only after inspecting and testing them. Limit the time spent with the seller, depart immediately after the purchase is completed, and exercise extreme caution in the event of any untoward behaviour by the seller or those around him. While transporting weapons, carefully determine the route in advance, avoiding main roads, and choose a suitable time for the operation, with observers travelling ahead of the main vehicle and giving the all clear only after confirming that the storage facility is free of surveillance.

Weapons should not be stored in remote areas or in well-protected localities such as parks or near public buildings. Nor should weapons be stored in rooms used by family members unaware of their father's or husband's role as an Al Qaeda agent. Apartments rented for this purpose should be taken on a long-term basis to avoid suspicion, and arsenals should not be visited frequently or the weapons inspected more than absolutely necessary. A coded record should be kept of all weapons, ammunition and explosives and only the arsenal keeper and the cell's leader should be aware of its location. Bombs and detonators should be protected from extreme heat and humidity, explosives and detonators stored separately, detonators handled cautiously, and weapons lubricated and packed carefully along with ammunition.

Another feature of Al Qaeda's specialised training for commanders and instructors was in how to build and manage camps, and it also taught foreign Islamists how to establish training sites. The guidelines are strict and include seclusion due to the threats posed by police, informants and public curiosity; and availability of day to day necessities, medical facilities, suitable accommodation and other buildings for fitness training, target practice and tactical rehearsal. Such camps must be guarded at all times and have numerous escape routes. Great care has to be taken in moving to and from these facilities: even senior leaders entered or left Al Qaeda camps in Afghanistan at night because of US daylight satellite surveillance. Once again, "need to know" principles are followed.

Security measures for trainees also applied to trainers, including a comprehensive security check before arrival; protection of the location and its personnel; and very careful selection of trainees — in groups of 7-10 for undercover terrorist operations and in larger numbers for guerrilla operations. Trainers did not reveal their identity to trainees or that of the group's leaders; a small ratio of trainees to each trainer was maintained; training team members did not know each other and only those engaged in training were allowed to remain in the training camp.

In the post 9/11 context, such precautions enabled Al Qaeda to establish training camps outside Afghanistan. These were not always large facilities; in Europe urban training camps can be located in private houses where Al Qaeda instructors impart mission-specific training such as firing, dismantling and storing weapons and concealing them about the person or in a safe house.

The media and communications committee disseminates Al Qaeda news or information in support of its political and military activities. Khalid al-Fawwaz, currently awaiting extradition from Britain to the

US, is alleged to have established an Al Qaeda press office for Europe in London in 1994, operating under the cover of the Advice and Reformation Committee (ARC). The committee at Al Qaeda headquarters also published an Arabic daily *Nashrat al-Akhbar* (Newscast) and a weekly report disseminating news about Al Qaeda, Islam in the world, *jihad* and related issues. The newspapers were printed in Hayatabad in Showa City, Afghanistan, and Abu Musab, nicknamed " Reuter" for his effectiveness as a journalist and propagandist, headed the committee.

The role of the *fatwa* and Islamic study committee is to justify Al Qaeda's actions. When a recruit is inducted, he agrees to pursue Al Qaeda's agenda and execute any order provided a *fatwa* justifying the action is cited, and Al Qaeda's religious scholars on the *fatwa* committee issue these Islamic rulings. They also preach and propagate Al Qaeda's model of Islam and ensure periodic indoctrination of the rank and file. According to US court records, the pioneering members of the committee were Abu Saad al-Sharif, Abu Muhammad Saudi, Abu Faraj, Abu Qatada, Abu Ibrahim al-Iraqi Hajer, Dr Fadhl el-Masry and Dr Abdel Omez.[72] In addition to heading the *shura* council, al-Zawahiri ran the *fatwa* committee.

Ideology

To understand the mindset of Al Qaeda's volunteers one must appreciate their belief system and the group's ideology, which is founded on Islamism and the pursuit of *jihad*. Various Islamists, including Al Qaeda, have misinterpreted — or at times reinterpreted — *jihad* as "holy war". Lexically *jihad* is the exertion of one's utmost effort in order to attain a goal or to repel something detestable.[73] According to Ibn Haibban, "The [*mujahid*] is the one who strives against his self."[74] In the *sharia*, *jihad* comprises the supreme personal sacrifice in order to raise the word of Allah, to aid his fight.[75] As Abud Dawud said: "Perform jihad against the pagans with your wealth, yourselves and your tongues."[76] The principal aims of *jihad* are to remove oppression and injustice; to establish justice, well being and prosperity; and to eliminate barriers to the spread of truth.[77]

In the Koran — the Word of God revealed to the Prophet Muhammad — *jihad* is used in several different contexts. These include recognising and loving the Creator; resisting the pressure of parents, peers and society; staying on the straight path steadfastly; striving for religious deeds; having the courage and steadfastness to convey the message of Islam; defending Islam and the community; helping friends who may not be Muslim; removing treacherous rulers from power; defending all of the above through pre-emptive strikes; winning the freedom to inform, educate and convey the message of Islam in an open and free environment, and thus freeing people from tyranny.[78]

In a military context *jihad* can have two roles, either offensive or defensive. The former is performed when the enemy is attacked in his own territory; the latter when an enemy is expelled from the jihadist's homeland. Unlike offensive *jihad*, defensive *jihad* is a compulsory duty. Nonetheless, the Koran declares: "Let there be no compulsion [or coercion] in the religion [Islam]. The right direction is distinctly clear from the error."[79] The six rules of *jihad* are:

1. *Jihad* is for the sake of Allah, not for the sake of wealth, goods, fame, glory or power;
2. Obedience to the *imam*;
3. Avoid misappropriating booty;
4. Respect pledges of protection;
5. Manifest endurance under attack;
6. Avoid corruption.[80]

Terrorism, the deliberate killing of non-combatants, is forbidden in the Koran unless they fall under the category of conspirators: "And fight, in the path of Allah, those who fight you, and do not transgress limits."[81] Ironically, the religious scholar most quoted by Osama, Ibn Taymiyyah, also states:

> As for those who cannot offer resistance or cannot fight, such as women, children, monks, old people, the blind, handicapped and their like, they shall not be killed, unless they actually fight with words and acts. Some [jurists] are of the opinion that all of them may be killed on the mere ground that they are unbelievers, but they make an exception for women and children since for Muslims they constitute property. However, the first opinion is the correct one, because we may only fight those who fight us when we want to make Allah's religion victorious.[82]

Quoting the Sunan, Ibn Taymiyyah states that when a woman was killed the "Messenger of Allah halted and said: 'She was not one who has fought [...] tell him not to kill women, children and serfs.'"[83] In effect, contemporary Islamists such as al-Zuwahiri and Osama are engaged in an unprecedented exercise of corrupting, misinterpreting and misrepresenting the word of God to generate support for their political mission. Or, as Marty and Appleby have described the role of Islamist ideologues:

> By selecting elements of tradition and modernity, fundamentalists seek to remake the world in the service of a dual commitment to the unfolding eschatological drama (by returning all things in submission to the divine) and to self-preservation (by neutralising the threatening Other).[84]

The tradition of *jihad* dates back to the medieval Crusades, when Muslims rallied against the Christian West. Abd el-Kader declared a *jihad* against the French colonial occupiers of Algeria in 1832, while in the aftermath of the Indian Mutiny of 1857 Sir Sayyid Ahmad argued that *jihad* was valid only in "defensive war and could not justify further resistance to British rule as long as the British did not interfere with the practice of Islam."[85] Abdul Ala Maududi (1903-79), the Indian-born Pakistani ideologue, was the first to instrumentalise the concept of *jihad* in a political context. For him its purpose was to establish the rule of the just, religious freedom — even for non-Muslims — and an Islamic government. His writings inspired others such as Hasan al-Banna (1906-49) and Sayyid Qutb (1906-56, the leading ideologue of Egyptian fundamentalists who was executed by Nasser) to develop the idea further in the Middle East, primarily against Israel and the Jews. Middle Eastern Islamist ideologues argued that *jihad* was mandatory, presenting it as an individual duty rather than a communal one. For neglecting his duty of *jihad*, the Egyptian President Anwar Sadat was branded an apostate and assassinated by the Egyptian Islamists. *Jihad* as a political concept returned to Asia with the influx of Arab *mujahidin* to Afghanistan from 1979 onwards.

As mentioned in earlier chapters, Al Qaeda was conceptualised by Azzam, not Osama, and hence the former's imprint is firmly embedded in the psyche of its leadership. To legitimise Al Qaeda's campaign, Osama chose selectively from, and based his arguments on, his mentor's writings. This was borne out after the 9/11 attacks when his deputy, al-Zawahiri, closely echoed Abdullah Azzam's words when describing Spain as belonging to the Islamic world. The fact that Osama used them to lend credence to his narrow political vision as well as to advance his own goals is not widely known. One of the key reasons why he and Azzam parted company in the late 1980s was the latter's firm contention that terrorism was not an acceptable tactic. At that point Egyptian veterans of the Afghan campaign were planning to turn to terrorism on their return home, and having lived in Egypt Azzam understood the implications of their decision.

As an activist as much as an ideologue, Osama and his subsequent mentors (al-Zawahiri, al-Turabi, the Blind Sheikh) developed and broadened the appeal of Al Qaeda's ideology to attract the widest possible support, and in the process it evolved into the broadest terrorist network yet known. The fact that he was not trained as a religious scholar but has a more pragmatic mindset probably accounts for his doctrinal flexibility, hence his willingness to establish links with Shia groups like Lebanese Hezbollah. Most Islamist struggles against non-Muslim governments, even their guerrilla or terrorist groups, did not see eye to eye with his universalistic brand of Islam. They were engaged in territorial campaigns. Nonetheless, Osama has attracted widespread politicised and radicalised Muslim support because of his anti-Western and anti-Israeli rhetoric. It is its very broad ideological disposition and targeting of American, Western and Israeli interests that has made Al Qaeda's support and operational infrastructure global and resilient. Moreover, although Osama is an Arab, he advocates pan-Islamic unity (the rebuilding of the Umma, the community of believers), not pan-Arabism. With the exception of Aum Shinrikyo and Al Qaeda, all the guerrilla and terrorist groups that emerged in the Middle East, Asia and elsewhere since 1968 have been mono-ethnic. For example Hezbollah recruited only Lebanese; the Armed Islamic Group only Algerians; and the Egyptian Islamic Jihad only Egyptians. Again it was Azzam who steered Osama towards creating a multi-national organisation based on the idea of uniting the vanguard of the believers, irrespective of their geographic origin. Nor is there any doubt that the multi-ethnic nature of the Afghan *jihad* and the thinking of Hasan al-Turabi, who was trying to build a pan-Islamic movement from Sudan, influenced Osama. Hence it is both its religious nature and elitist culture (albeit open to anyone provided they demonstrated their will and desire to join before being accepted) that helped Al Qaeda broaden its appeal to both Middle Eastern and non-Middle Eastern Islamist groups.

Osama never interpreted Islam to assist a given political goal. Islam is his political goal, his rhetoric, philanthropy towards the Muslim poor and military support for oppressed Muslims having great resonance among young Muslims the world over, including those living in the West who found it difficult adapting to, and integrating with, their new environments. Osama had no formal training in Islam apart from an understanding gleaned from his own reading (wherever he travelled, his large personal library went with him). He nevertheless learned extensively from his mentors, above all Azzam, who was instrumental in Al Qaeda's articulation of *jihad*. In a seminal document entitled *Join the Caravan*, which was distributed widely, he wrote:

> When the enemy enters that land of the Muslims, *jihad* becomes individually obligatory, according to all the jurists, mufassirin and muhaddithin... When *jihad* becomes obligatory, no permission of parents is required... Donating money does not exempt a person from bodily *jihad*, no matter how great the amount of money given...*jihad* is the obligation of a lifetime... *Jihad* is currently individually obligatory, in person and by wealth, in every place that the disbelievers have occupied. It remains obligatory continuously until every piece of land that was once Islamic is regained... *Jihad* is a collective act of worship, and every group must have a leader. Obedience to the leader is a necessity in *jihad*, and thus a per-

son must condition himself invariably obey the leader, as has been reported in the hadith: "You must hear and obey, whether it is easy or difficult for you, in things which are pleasant for you as well as those which are inconvenient and difficult for you." [86]

Al Qaeda believes that until US troops are ejected from Saudi Arabia, Muslim society will be "living a life of sin". As one fighter put it, "Until the US troops are removed from all lands of the Muslims, no Muslim is absolved from sin except the *mujahidin*."[87] To mobilise the Muslim masses, Osama is likely to make the same argument regarding US troops in Afghanistan and Pakistan.

By constantly referring to Allah, in both his writings and speeches, Osama suggests that he is carrying out Allah's divine wish. He also seeks religious justification for his edicts. In the legal ruling dated February 23, 1998, Osama prefaced his pronouncement as follows:

> Praise be to God, who revealed the Book, controls the clouds, defeats factionalism, and says in His Book: 'But when the forbidden months are past, then fight and slay the pagans wherever ye find them, seize them, beleaguer them, and lie in wait for them in every stratagem (of war)'; and peace be upon our Prophet Muhammad bin-'Abdallah, who said: 'I have been sent with the sword between my hands to ensure that no one but God is worshipped, God who put my livelihood under the shadow of my spear and who inflicts humiliation and scorn on those who disobey my orders.'[88]

Raising awareness among Muslims of the grievances that gave rise to Al Qaeda is essential for recruitment, and therefore the organisation attaches great importance to propaganda, in particular the need for Muslim youths to reflect on the state of their societies. Hence it attributes Muslim societies' greatest misfortune and decadence to their abandonment of *jihad* "due to the love of this world and abhorrence of death. Because of that, tyrants have gained dominance over the Muslims in every aspect and in every land."[89] Eight principal reasons for joining the *jihad* are: first, so that non-believers do not dominate; second, because of the scarcity of manpower; third, fear of hellfire; fourth, fulfilling the duty of *jihad* and responding to the call of Allah; fifth, following in the footsteps of pious predecessors; sixth, establishing a solid foundation as a base for Islam; seventh, protecting those who are oppressed in the land; and eighth, seeking martyrdom.[90] Those who led the *jihad* in Afghanistan were considered the sons of the Islamic movement — the religious scholars and *hafiz* (those who have memorised the Koran). Even those who wished to fight elsewhere were attracted first to serve in Afghanistan and later to return to the regional conflict of their choice.

In terms of leadership qualities, Osama is the model Islamist, the preeminent leader of the pioneering vanguard. He possesses "charismatic and authoritarian leadership, depends upon a disciplined inner core of adherents, and promotes a rigorous socio-moral code for all followers" — the ideal characteristics of an Islamist leader.[91] The Islamist leader should have a calm personality that allows him to endure the psychological traumas of experiencing bloodshed, murder, arrest, imprisonment, and reverse ones such as killing one or all of his organisation's comrades. Amid such conditions, the manual states, "[He should be able] to carry out his work"[92] and "The member should have plenty of patience for enduring afflictions if he is overcome by the enemies. He should not abandon this great path and sell himself and his religion to the enemies of his freedom. He should be patient in performing his work, even if it lasts a long time."[93]

Together with Osama, the *shura majlis* formulates Al Qaeda's policies and strategies, which the leader exhorts everyone to follow to the letter. Like all Islamist groups it has "set the boundaries, the enemy identified, converts sought, institutions created and a sustained strategy developed in pursuit of a comprehensive reconstruction of society."[94] Although its objectives have altered little since it was founded, its strategies have evolved over the years. As defined by Osama, Al Qaeda has short, mid- and long-term strategies. Before 9/11, its immediate goal was the withdrawal of US troops from Saudi Arabia and the creation there of a Caliphate. Its mid-term strategy was the ouster of the "apostate rulers" of the Arabian Peninsula and thereafter the Middle East and the creation of true Islamic states. And the long-term strategy was to build a formidable array of Islamic states — including ones with nuclear capability — to wage war on the US (the "Great Satan") and its allies.

At the outset Al Qaeda supported guerrilla and terrorist campaigns against Muslim and non-Muslim regimes where Muslims were perceived as being victimised. In this connection Osama issued *fatawa* [Islamic decrees] in August 1996, February 1997 and February 1998. No other writings, whether classified or in the public domain, better reflect Al Qaeda's worldview than these three declarations, which urge Muslims to rise against the America. The August 1996 edict, issued by Al Qaeda soon after Osama returned from Sudan to Afghanistan, stated:

> It should not be hidden from you that the people of Islam have suffered from aggression, iniquity and injustices imposed upon them by the Zionist-Crusader alliance and their collaborators to the extent that the Muslims' blood has become the cheapest in the eyes of the "world", and their wealth has become as loot, in the hands of their enemies. Their blood was spilt in Palestine and Iraq, The horrifying pictures of the massacre of Qana, Lebanon, are still fresh in our memories. Massacres in Tajikistan, Burma, Kashmir, Assam, the Philippines, Fatani, Ogaden, Somalia, Eritrea, Chechnya, and Bosnia-Herzegovina have taken place,

massacres that sent shivers through the body, and shake the conscience.

All of this — and the world watched and heard, and not only did they not respond to the atrocities, but also, under a clear conspiracy — between the USA and its allies, under the cover of the iniquitous "United Nations" — the dispossessed people were even prevented from obtaining arms to defend themselves. The people of Islam awakened, and realised that they were the main target for the aggression of the Zionist-Crusader alliance. And all the false claims and propaganda about "Human Rights" were hammered down and exposed for what they were, by the massacres that had taken place against the Muslims in every part of the world.[95]

While continuing with its support for Islamist regimes, groups and parties, Al Qaeda targeted the secular rulers of the Middle East for failing to create Islamic states and for suppressing Islamists. Osama highlighted not only the victimisation of Muslims by non-Muslim regimes but also the persecution of religious scholars and others fighting for the restoration of Islam. Osama also spoke of the efforts by the US and its friends to isolate him and Al Qaeda:

We — myself and my group — have suffered some of these injustices ourselves; we have been prevented from addressing the Muslims. We have been pursued in Pakistan, the Sudan and Afghanistan — hence this long absence on my part. But, by the Grace of Allah, a safe base is now available in the high Hindu Kush mountains in Khrasan.[96]

Beginning in 1987, Osama called for a boycott of American goods in support of the Palestinian intifada. In retaliation for the imposition of us sanctions against Sudan and later Afghanistan, he reiterated this call. In 1996 he called in a *fatwa* for Saudi citizens to wage economic warfare against the US by boycotting its goods. His intention of fomenting rebellion within Saudi Arabia is well illustrated in the interview given to CNN's Peter Arnett.

The first [problem] is their subordination to the US. So our main problem is the US government while the Saudi regime is but a branch or an agent of the US. By being loyal to the US regime, the Saudi regime has committed an act against Islam. And this, based on the ruling of Sharia, casts the regime outside the religious community. Subsequently, it has stopped ruling people according to what Allah has revealed, not to mention many other contradictory acts. When this main foundation was violated, other corrupt acts followed in every aspect of the country, the economic, the social, government services and so on.[97]

Targeting the royal family has never been easy, especially in such a tightly controlled country as Saudi Arabia, although King Faisal was assassinated by his nephew in 1975. However Osama has always been keen to minimise civilian casualties in his homeland and hence eschews operations in the Kingdom that might jeopardise his considerable popularity there. Instead he campaigns against America, believing that if it were defeated the Saudi royal family would ultimately fall:

> [Osama bin Laden] has directed a call to the Muslims throughout the world to declare a *jihad* against the Judaeo-Christian alliance which is occupying Islamic sacred land in Palestine and the Arabian peninsula.[98]

Osama's decision to turn against America resonated among other Islamist groups. For example, in April 2000 a poster circulated in Pakistan's North-West Frontier Province depicting burning US, Indian and Israeli flags and a cocked Kalashnikov poised to fire. The slogan read:

> Our *jihad* will continue until America is expelled from Saudi Arabia and other countries of the world. It is our responsibility to free the world from their [US] control. The non-Muslim world should know it well that a Muslim is always ready to die in the name of God. I am not afraid of America. I will continue my work. No one can stop me.[99]

Osama is a self-acknowledged terrorist and makes no pretence about his strategy of using and justifying terror as an instrument. Unlike the terrorists of the 1960s to the 1990s, who generally avoided high casualty attacks for fear of the negative publicity they would generate, Al Qaeda is not in the least concerned by such matters. Referring to the fight against the Americans in Saudi Arabia, the *fatwa* of February 1998, of which he is the lead signatory, states:

> Terrorizing you while you are carrying arms on our land is a legitimate and morally demanded duty. It is a legitimate right well known to all humans and other creatures. [...] It is a duty now on every tribe in the Arabian Peninsula to fight, jihad, in the cause of Allah and to cleanse the land from those occupiers. Allah knows that their blood is permitted [to be spilled] and their wealth is a booty; their wealth is a booty to those who kill them. [...]These youths know that if one is not to be killed one will die [anyway] and the most honourable death is to be killed in the way of Allah.[100]

Martyrdom is assigned the highest priority by Al Qaeda's volunteers, who have succumbed to the psychological and spiritual influences of Islamist ideologues. Killing and dying for Allah are viewed as the highest form of sacrifice. Although other terrorist groups driven by Islamist ideology, such as Hamas, prepare its fighters to die for the cause, no other group has invested so much time and effort as Al Qaeda in programming its fighters for death. This explains why an unusually high percentage of Al Qaeda attacks are suicide operations. By condemning the target and reiterating the reward of sacrifice, the ideologues reinforce the appeal of death in war. On a tactical level, Al Qaeda uses the willingness of its fighters to die to drive fear into the enemy.

Terrorism is only one of Al Qaeda's tactics. As a multi-dimensional group, it can engage the enemy on several fronts simultaneously. The long-term strategic threat that it poses to international security is the politicisation and radicalisation of Muslims, a phenomenon that has gone unchallenged by the West as well as by Middle Eastern and Asian Muslim countries. Needless to say, if governments and civil society respond only to Al Qaeda's military threat and not to its ideological challenge, in the long run the organisation will have no difficulty in recruiting more terrorists from successive generations of disenchanted Muslim youths.

To instrumentalise his group's pan-Islamic ideology, Osama despatched thousands of Al Qaeda and other terrorist "graduates" to join Islamist groups worldwide, the introduction of these alumni boosting the wider terrorist agenda. These fighters are devout Muslims inspired by Islamic scholars and willing to sacrifice their lives in the name of Islam. Hence the international system has witnessed a marked increase in the number of Islamist groups engaged in suicide operations (originally pioneered by Hezbollah in the 1980s) and Islamic movements emphasising "martyrdom", especially in Kashmir and Chechnya.

Al Qaeda's leadership, its membership and some of its associate groups genuinely believe that they have created a new Islamic Universal Order. Although Al Qaeda has lost its physical base, namely the state within a state it created with the Taliban regime, it has compensated for this loss, which it anticipated, by building a global network. Today it is a truly transnational terrorist group. Since 9/11, however, many Islamist groups, parties and regimes have been cautious about identifying themselves too closely and openly with Al Qaeda for fear of bringing down the wrath of America on their heads. However they support its aims and objectives and Al Qaeda continues to maintain links with many of them.

To understand Al Qaeda's position within the spectrum of Islamist groups one has to examine the four main categories into which the latter fall, although there is usually overlap between them — the revolutionary, the ideological, the utopian, and the apocalyptic. Revolutionary Islamist groups seek to legitimise violence by advocating and practising collective decision-making, drawing selectively on the ideology of Sayyid Qutb. They include Egyptian Islamic Jihad, Palestinian Hamas, Palestinian Islamic Jihad, and Algeria's Armed Front of the Islamic Jihadists (FIDA). Revolutionary Islamists do not generally kill members of their own community with whom they differ. The Armed Islamic Group of Algeria (GIA) was a revolutionary group until it killed another prominent Islamist, Said Akrour, in 1995. After becoming a utopian group, it engaged in large-scale, senseless massacres in the summer of 1996, transforming itself into an apocalyptic group. Like one of these groups, Iran under Ayatollah Khomeni fell into the revolutionary category.

Ideological Islamist groups and leaders have a coherent discourse of political violence. They include Hezbollah, Islamic Group of Egypt and the Moro Islamic Liberation Front. Hasan al-Turabi and Abu Hamza al-Masri (propagating the international version of Salafism) are ideological Islamists. They offer a systematic set of ideas that justify violence, the use of which is highly regulated and controlled from above and carefully tailored to suit political and social contexts while cognizant of its effect on group dynamics and even survival itself. They often have a widespread constituency mutually reinforced by a social services machinery which by extension serves to limit the scale and scope of violence.[101]

Utopian Islamist groups seek to destroy the existing order. They operate at every level, from the local to the global, and do not form alliances with the state, which they always contest. They have no rational political approach or strategy, and endorse no traditional social structure; they are reinventing tradition. Their doctrinal principles include no negotiation, no dialogue and no peacemaking. A few utopian groups that are millenarian cross the threshold and become apocalyptic. Examples include the Salafist Group for Call and Combat of Algeria, Libyan Islamic Fighting Group, the Abu Sayyaf Group and, until the 9/11 attacks, Al Qaeda. The Taliban also belonged to this category.

Apocalyptic Islamist groups use collective violence but are indiscriminate. They firmly believe that they have been divinely ordained to commit violent acts and are most likely to engage in mass-casualty, catastrophic terrorism. Most specialists believe that they lack the patient, systematic, approach needed to develop the elaborate organisation, trained personnel and equipment, by which alone potent chemical, biological, radiological or nuclear (CBRN) agents can be produced. When a specialist on Islamist apocalyptic terrorism was asked how many such groups there were, she replied "Thank God, we only have two."[102] She was referring to Al Qaeda and the Armed Islamic Group of Algeria.

Although Al Qaeda ceased to be a utopian group after the World Trade Centre attacks and joined the apocalyptic category, it retains strong characteristics of other categories. In stage one a utopian group seeks to destroy the existing political order, at which point, in its eyes, it does not kill individuals but only employees of the state. In stage two a utopian group targets the existing social, economic and cultural order. By moving to stage two, the group joins an apocalyptic category. Al Qaeda's suicidal crashing of hijacked passenger aircraft into the World Trade Centre — a non-political, non-military and non-governmental target — was a deliberate attack on human beings and their private economy, also on what had become a potent cultural symbol. Its motives were unambiguous. By its decision to conduct a mass-casualty attack, Al Qaeda moved from being a utopian Islamist group to an apocalyptic one. This shift is likely to set the trend for an increased volume of terrorist violence by Islamist and non-Islamist groups in the foreseeable future. Al Qaeda's move towards being apocalyptic rather than Utopian after 9/11 is due principally to the atomisation of an already fragmented and loosely organised multinational enterprise. Seeking revenge by destroying the West's existing order was already a priority; after 9/11 it became imperative, no matter how long it would take.

Opinion among terrorism specialists remains divided over whether Al Qaeda should be classified as an apocalyptic organisation. A group can be classified as apocalyptic only if it channels its energies into fulfilling an end of time prophecy. While many Jewish, Christian and Islamic groups have an apocalyptic dimension, not all of them are truly apocalyptic. As such, some Islamist groups driven by these theologies tend to become apocalyptic to realise an Islamic apocalypse — the Mahdi of Sudan being one, another being the Saudi Ikhwan, which attacked the Grand Mosque in Mecca in 1979.[103] Contrary to popular belief, however, Al Qaeda has never sought an apocalyptic goal. Closer examination suggests that it is a very practical group, with clear aims and objectives, but one that is capable of chameleon-like manouevring.

3

AL QAEDA'S GLOBAL NETWORK

"We say to our brothers in Palestine, that your children's blood is equal to our children's blood. Blood for blood and destruction for destruction. As the great Allah is my witness, we will not let you down until victory is achieved or we become martyrs." (Commentary from an Al Qaeda recruitment video seized by police in London in the aftermath of 9/11)

Al Qaeda pursues its objectives through a network of cells, associate terrorist and guerrilla groups and other affiliated organisations, and shares expertise, transfers resources, discusses strategy and even conducts joint operations with some or all of them. While Al Qaeda cells mostly operate in the West, its associate groups are more numerous in the South or developing world, while its affiliates operate in Muslim societies or countries with Islamic communities. Al Qaeda's own cadres are better motivated, trained and disciplined than its associate members, and tend to be more mobile and to have a wider reach, whereas Al Qaeda's associates operate on a local level. While associate groups attack tactical targets, strategic targets are Al Qaeda's responsibility. According to the CIA, Al Qaeda can draw on the support of some 6-7 million radical Muslims worldwide, of which 120,000 are willing to take up arms.

Decentralisation

Al Qaeda's global network, as we know it today, was created while it was based in Khartoum, from December 1991 till May 1996. To coordinate its overt and covert operations as Al Qaeda's ambitions and resources increased, it developed a decentralised, regional structure. For instance, the Sudanese, Turkish and, briefly, Spanish nodes ran clandestine military activities in Europe and North America. Except for the London bureau (the Advice and Reformation Committee), which had a global remit for propaganda and coordination, the worldwide nodes have no formal structure and no hierarchy. Assignments are carried out by individuals designated for the purpose as the "person responsible". Nor do the regional nodes have a fixed abode: after Al Qaeda relocated from Sudan to Afghanistan in May 1996, its European and North American bureau moved to Turkey and Yemen, but after the arrest of Mamdouh Mahmud Salim, one of its key figures in Europe, in Germany in September 1998, the responsibilities of the Turkish bureau moved again, this time to Spain. With the increased threat facing Al Qaeda in late 2001, the regional bureau and nodal responsibilities shifted to cells and thereafter to senior members resident in Western Europe who travelled frequently back and forth to Afghanistan. Likewise in 1998, after the Indonesian dictator Suharto fell from power, Al Qaeda's regional bureau chief Abdullah Sungkar and his deputy Abu Bakar Basiyar moved from Malaysia to Indonesia. Nonetheless, the support base created in Malaysia continued to provide both recruits and resources; instead of weakening the organisation, displacement provided fresh opportunities. As these examples testify, Al Qaeda is structured in such a way that it can react very quickly to changing events on the ground. Mobility, flexibility and fluidity will be the guiding principles of its post-Taliban structure.

Organisationally, Al Qaeda is the natural offshoot of the Muslim Brotherhood, a consequence of its political agenda, but unlike the latter it has never compromised its original aims, converting the rhetoric of the Muslim Brotherhood into concrete action. The Muslim Brotherhood's failure to achieve its objectives may also have made certain Islamists receptive to Al Qaeda's message: although the Brotherhood spoke of martyrdom, Al Qaeda actually practised it on a worldwide scale. Nonetheless, it built on the Brotherhood, drawing on its committed followers, its structures and its experience. It is organised along the lines of a broad-based family clan with its constituent multinational members designated as "brothers", a term commonly used by religious Muslims when referring to each other. Hence its North African "family" (exclusively Algerians, Egyptians, Tunisians, Moroccans, Libyans) is responsible for activities in Europe, its Southeast Asian "family" (Malaysians, Indonesians, Filipinos, Singaporeans) for operations in the Far East, and its Central Asian "family" for the region from Turkey across Muslim Central Asia into Xingjiang in China.

As a global multinational, Al Qaeda makes its constituent nationalities and ethnic groups, of which there are several dozen, responsible for a particular geographic region. Although its *modus operandi* is cellular, familial relationships play a key role. As a cultural and social network, Al Qaeda members recruit from among their own nationalities, families and friends. After training is completed, the very best of new recruits are integrated among, and assigned to work within one of these families. For example, Osama bin Laden referred to the head of the 9/11 operation as "Muhammad [Atta] from the Egyptian family".[1] Within the organisation itself, the notion of brotherhood ingrained in Islam helps Al Qaeda cohere. Osama is regarded as the elder brother and no one disputes his leadership of this wider "Islamic family" of the modern era.[2] What gives Al Qaeda its global reach is its ability to appeal to Muslims irrespective of their nationality, giving it unprecedented reach. It can function in East Asia, in Russia, in the heart of Europe, in Sub-Saharan

Africa and throughout Canada and the United States with equal facility. As the world succumbs to the forces of globalisation, becoming more culturally diverse, so have Al Qaeda's reach and depth of penetration increased.

It overcame the problems posed by cultural and linguistic barriers in an innovative fashion: it organised its families regionally but also functionally. Al Qaeda's Libyans managed the documentation and passports office in Afghanistan; its Algerians ran fraudulent credit card operations in Europe; and the Egyptians looked after most of the training facilities worldwide. The organisation into families was socially and culturally compatible too. For example, as a member of the Tunisian family an Al Qaeda Tunisian member living in or posted to Italy kept in touch with Tunisians elsewhere in Europe. Dependent on his responsibilities in Italy, he worked with members of other "families" assigned to his cell. Although most of Al Qaeda's European cells have been based on one nationality, its US operational cells have always been multinational. For instance, only Algerians staffed the British Al Qaeda cell that is suspected of plotting to mount a sarin poison gas attack against the European Parliament in Strasbourg in February 2000. In contrast, there have been no mono-nationality cells in the US, except in the Mid-West, where Al Qaeda's Syrian "family" has a presence in Chicago and Michigan. However it is easier for security forces to track a terrorist cell if all its members are from the same country and speak the same language or dialect, so this practice is likely to change as a direct result of 9/11. The European and US cells are almost certain to develop a multinational character in the near future.

The membership of an Al Qaeda cell varies from two to fifteen, a cellular network that draws heavily on the conspiratorial model of the Islamic Group of Egypt and the Egyptian Islamic Jihad introduced by al-Zawahiri, who had restructured and professionalised the latter after a series of setbacks. Although it has since gone its own way and is considered the most sophisticated of all Islamist terrorist groups, Al Qaeda's structure remains close to that of its Egyptian antecedents. The Islamic Group of Egypt's "different geographical branches [comparable to Al Qaeda's regions] were divided into cells, called '*anquds*', Arabic for a bunch of grapes. [...] each *anqud* was self-contained. If it were plucked, as from a grapevine, its disappearance would not affect the others."[3] Cells assigned for special missions like 9/11 and the Los Angeles airport attack during the millennium celebrations are coordinated through an agent-handling system where a cell leader reports only to his controller or agent-handler. Most agent-handlers live near the target location or in the "hostile zone." — Europe or North America. Some report to a principal agent-handler who never leaves Afghanistan, Pakistan or another "safe zone". Al Qaeda's cellular network also makes it resistant to intelligence service penetration: "When they have a hierarchical system they are much easier for law enforcement to penetrate."[4] By constantly reviewing past failures, Al Qaeda continually strives to improve its agent-handling system. The post-Taliban version is likely to be an improvement on the earlier one: more tightly controlled, more self-contained, more self-reliant and with fewer operatives.

Al Qaeda's *lingua franca* is Arabic, as it is, to a certain extent, for many literate Muslims. As an organisation established and dominated by them, Arabs staff the vital positions and control all the key operations. Interestingly, Al Qaeda refrained from posting non Arabic-speakers to Europe and North America, its two most important assignments. This is in spite of its membership being truly global. Most non-Middle Eastern members, especially the top echelons, learnt Arabic. Even in battle, many carried the Koran and a Chinese-Arabic, Persian-Arabic, Russian-Arabic, Tagalog-Arabic, Bahasa-Arabic or other dictionary. Proficiency in the language was also mandatory for senior command posts.

Although "family" members function regionally, individuals are occasionally handpicked and crossposted outside their region for specialist missions. For instance, the 9/11 operation brought together Saudis, Egyptians, Lebanese, Yemenis, Moroccans and Arabs from UAE. Of the nineteen hijackers who died in the attacks, fifteen were from Al Qaeda's Saudi "family". With the exception of a few members who communicate directly via satellite phones with Al Qaeda leaders in Afghanistan and elsewhere, most members rigorously observe the cellular system. Those at the apex of the cell system and the regional leaders reported to Abu Zubaydah, who was till March 28, 2002 head of Al Qaeda's external operations. In addition to screening recruits from overseas and later assigning them to agent-handlers, he served as "principal agent-handler" managing those who keep in touch with cell leaders

Al Qaeda encouraged its family structure by organising its training camps in Afghanistan accordingly. Those used exclusively to train European and North American Muslims in terrorist tactics that were targeted by the US military immediately after 9/11 were Khalden near Khost, Al Badr I, Al Badr II, Al Katbah, and the Moroccan camp in Derunta, and the Algerian and Tunisian camps in Jalalabad. Where possible, Al Qaeda also tried its best to select and assign trainers by nationality: the Tunisian camp's emir was Ben Hassine, a Tunisian. The establishment of camps and trainers by nationality demonstrates Al Qaeda's reliance on the "family structure" and its desire to preserve it. Although Al Qaeda's headquarters moved from Afghanistan to Peshawar and then to Khartoum, it always retained a substantial training and operational infrastructure in Afghanistan. To quote the British-based Islamist Sheikh

Abu-Hamza al-Masri, it is the "land of *jihad*", the "*jihad* capital" and the "major sign of the Muslim struggle of our times."[5]

Abu Zubaydah is a Saudi national of Palestinian origin who was born in Gaza in 1971. Operating under multiple aliases, especially Egyptian ones, and working for several front organisations, above all MAK, he travelled and communicated regularly with Al Qaeda leaders. Next to Osama, he was the most important functionary in the group, and after the death of Muhammad Atef in November 2001 became even more critical to the organisation. With the loss of its infrastructure in Afghanistan, Al Qaeda increasingly depended on him for organisational and infrastructural management. He was also the most elusive and least photographed senior member of Al Qaeda, and operated clandestinely even as far as its other leaders are concerned. Although Zubaydah was Al Qaeda's most widely-travelled member, there were no charges against him on the record and the US Justice Department has neither issued a public warrant against him nor identified him in a public indictment. He was captured in a joint CIA, FBI, ISI and Pakistan police raid on his operational headquarters in Faisalabad, Pakistan, at 3am on March 28, 2002. Al Qaeda's terrorist charged with bombing Los Angeles airport during the Millennium celebrations, Ressam, said of Abu Zubaydah: "He is the person in charge of the camps. He receives young men from all countries. He accepts you or rejects you. He takes care of the expenses of the camps. He makes arrangements for you when you travel coming in or leaving."[6] When captured Abu Zubaydah was living in a three-storey villa with a high stone wall in the suburb of Faisal Town. During his attempted escape he was shot in the stomach, groin and leg and his Syrian associate, Abu al-Hasnat, was killed. Another Al Qaeda member was injured along with one Pakistani and three American officers.

Al Qaeda's operational network carries out reconnaissance and surveillance of intended targets and conducts assassinations, bombings, ambushes and other attacks. In addition to successfully completing many missions, a significant number of planned bombings and assassinations have been thwarted. At least three to four dozen operations were detected and disrupted by government security and intelligence agencies or called off by Al Qaeda. In 1992 Al Qaeda planned to blow up a plane, according to the CIA. However an Al Qaeda member engaged in the plan was arrested and the operation aborted. In the same year Al Qaeda planned to destroy a target in the US by procuring explosives in Italy and shipping them to America via Cuba. According to the CIA, the operation was also aborted. Al Qaeda also planned an attack on an American building in Karachi in 1993, but the arrest of two of its operatives forced Al Qaeda to abort the plan. These include attempts to bomb the US embassies in Tirana, Sarajevo and Kampala and a plot to assassinate King

Abdullah of Jordan in summer 2000, news of which reached him while he was aboard a cruise ship in the Mediterranean. In other circumstances Al Qaeda has cancelled attacks due to the prevailing political situation, revealing that it is not entirely scornful of public opinion. Echelon (satellite) and other technical monitoring of their communications traffic around April 1996 revealed the postponement of a planned attack against Western targets in Singapore. On the 18th of that month around 108 Lebanese civilians seeking refuge in the UN camp at Qana had been killed by Israeli mortars after a Hezbollah attack against the IDF (Israel Defence Forces). Osama was keen not to dissipate what he envisaged as widespread revulsion against Israel's action and hence called off the strike in South East Asia. Al Qaeda's team in question was very determined to go ahead, having spent years preparing the attack, and according to the intercepts it proved difficult for Osama to convince it otherwise.

Al Qaeda is primarily a Middle Eastern group, based in Asia but with a worldwide network. Its leading lights are all Arabs and they hold all the key positions. Nevertheless Osama realised after moving to Asia in May 1996 that this was one of the organisation's weaknesses and hence rectified the situation by recruiting non-Arabs and forging ties with Islamists outside the Middle East, above all with the Taliban. To enhance diversity — essential to its plans for a global *jihad* — Al Qaeda campaigned on a common Shia-Sunni platform. This unprecedented position gave it a global reach and revealed that, although puritanical, it is a highly pragmatic organisation, willing to adapt and refine its ideology in order to retain operational effectiveness. This trait was critical in establishing and maintaining links with associate and affiliated groups, some of which differ from it doctrinally. Most of these non-Al Qaeda groups adhered to Salafi ideas about Islam. To gain strategic depth in new regions, Al Qaeda propagated this potent ideology beyond the Middle East, and today most groups waging *jihad* — including those in Palestine, Algeria, Kashmir, Bosnia, Chechnya, Afghanistan, Eritrea, Somalia and the Philippines — are inspired by Salafi ideals. As one Al Qaeda member said, "Members of this branch worship and love Allah above all else. They do not even believe or follow the Imams and the Sheikhs. They only pledge their allegiance to Allah and to his Messenger."[7]

Al Qaeda's associate groups in South and Southeast Asia were deeply influenced by Sayed Abdul A'la Maududi, the founder of the Jamaat-i-Islami, and by Sayyid Qutb, both of whom sanctioned the use of violence for the establishment of Islam. They also appealed for Muslims to return to the Koran and the Sunna, with the principles of Islam applied to modern society by the use of rational judgement in religious matters. Maududi and Qutb reaffirmed the place of Islam in politics and society in countries that had suffered from the imposition of secularism and the

Western paradigm of democracy. They both argued against Western political thought, especially the concept of sovereignty, and called for the establishment of a "revolutionary vanguard of true believers" to establish Islamic states.

In addition to ideological training, Al Qaeda provided these associate groups with military expertise, religious-political indoctrination and terrorist-guerrilla training, thereby significantly improving their guerrilla and terrorist capabilities. Furthermore, Al Qaeda's 055 Brigade allowed them the opportunity of becoming battle-hardened, such experience proving invaluable on their return to their home countries, at which point they would become fully-fledged agents of Al Qaeda, imparting its ways of thinking and acting to their fellow-believers. In order to make Al Qaeda's reach and impact better understood, the remainder of this chapter is devoted to describing and explaining Al Qaeda's worldwide network of cells, associate and affiliate organisations.

North America

In the early and mid-1980s Al Qaeda's founder, Abdullah Azzam, visited twenty-six American states and by the late 1980s its precursor organisation, MAK, had thirty functioning offices in the US. At that time Azzam and MAK were regarded as friends and allies of America, and he was not apparently scrutinised or put under surveillance. After Osama split from Azzam and approved of his murder, he sought to gain control of MAK's headquarters at 566 Atlantic Avenue, Brooklyn, in New York's Arab district. Osama also wanted to take charge of MAK's American infrastructure through the Blind Sheikh. After fleeing house arrest in Egypt the Blind Sheikh travelled to Sudan where he obtained a US visa sponsored by a fellow Egyptian, Mustafa Shalabi, the MAK representative in New York. Shalabi's help was repaid in 1991 when the Blind Sheikh had him killed in New York, (he had ordered the assassination the previous year of Rabbi Meir Kahane, founder of the Jewish Defence League). Although the Sheikh's follower and fellow Egyptian El Sayyid A. Nosair was acquitted of the murder charge, he was convicted of possessing illegal firearms, having learned to shoot at the High Rock Gun Club in Naugutuck, Connecticut, from 1989.[8]

Sheikh Umar Abd al-Rahman was the only Islamist scholar of sufficient standing who could take on Azzam's mantle, hence his elevation to leadership of the international *jihadists* was widely welcomed. In addition to his fellow Egyptians and the Muslim Brotherhood, he also had the support of the Algerian, Afghani and Pakistani elements in Al Qaeda. Moreover he and Osama are in their own ways brilliant ideologues and they had known each other for many years.

Born in Egypt in 1938 and blinded by diabetes as a baby, Umar Abd al-Rahman had mastered a Braille copy of the Koran by the age of 11.[9] He was imprisoned in 1970 for describing praying for President Nasser (who had just died) as a sin, and placed under house arrest in 1989 for inciting civil unrest.[10] He is regarded as the spiritual leader of Egypt's Islamist opposition. The Blind Sheikh was living in Brooklyn when he was arrested in 1993 for conspiring to bomb the United Nations building, road tunnels and bridges, the FBI headquarters, government offices, and legislators and officials perceived supportive of Israel. He and his team planned to bomb these targets simultaneously, an operational technique advocated and developed by Osama after he met Imad Mughniyeh, who masterminded the bombings of the US Marine barracks and French paratrooper HQ in Beirut in 1983. Under an FBI entrapment scheme, a court in New York City found him and nine of his followers guilty of seditious conspiracy to wage a "war urban terrorism against the USA". He was found guilty of the murder of Rabbi Kahane; of planning to assassinate President Mubarak of Egypt on a visit to the USA; and of plotting a series of simultaneous attacks on high profile targets.[11] His sons, Muhammad and Abu Asim, fought in Afghanistan and Tajikistan and serve with Al Qaeda. US intelligence community believes that Muhammad was killed in Afghanistan in late 2001.

The Blind Sheikh was only one of many Islamist clerics who advocated violence against their newly adopted hosts. The efficient, swift and harsh American response of arresting him and his followers and extraditing from Egypt, the Philippines, Malaysia and Pakistan several Islamists suspected of taking part in the World Trade Centre bombing, deterred further Al Qaeda attacks in the US in the second half of the 1990s. However, the American government did little to monitor the extremists inside the country who provided the funding and personnel for several *jihad* campaigns. The US was also one of the main centres for Al Qaeda procurement. Operating through a front company, its UK representative, Khalid al-Fauwaz, procured a satellite phone from Ogara Satellite Networks of Deer Park, New York, for $7,500 (the phone number, 00-873-682505331, was used by Osama to communicate with his terrorist network). Another Al Qaeda member, Ziyad Khaleel, bought several batches of 400 minutes of telephone time from the same company, and Essam al-Ridi purchased weapons and a plane which he flew to Khartoum. The US intelligence community never imagined that the satellite phone and aircraft would be used to accumulate resources and plan attacks on US personnel in East Africa and the Horn, but the notion that insulating itself from the rest of the world would protect the country and its citizens abroad had lulled the US into a false sense of security. This isolationist mentality focused on guarding borders, not looking at the strategic threat building within the US. Quantifying the scale of ideological and physical infiltration by Islamist groups, Sheikh Kabbani of the Islamic Council of America said in January 1999:

> We can say that [the Islamists] took over 80% of the mosques in the United States. There are more than 3,000... This means that the ideology of extremism has been spread to 80% of the Muslim population, mostly the youth and the new generation.[12]

Due to the radicalisation of some American Muslims by Islamist preachers and the penetration of Muslim diasporas by foreign terrorists, the FBI infiltrated several American Muslim communities. The prevailing orthodoxy in law enforcement was that as long as American Muslims who supported or participated in terrorism elsewhere did not harm American interests, neither the FBI nor other US agencies would act against them. Al Qaeda was well aware of US intelligence monitoring of Muslim communities and hence relocated the 9/11 operational team away from known Islamic strongholds. It built a completely new network from scratch, one that did not forge links with any of its existing networks in the US, which Osama believed to have been compromised by the FBI. The participants in the 9/11 operation were Middle Eastern members of Al Qaeda who were sent to the US from Europe and Asia to train there and attack prestigious targets. Using US passenger aircraft and crashing them into domestic targets was, according to a former Al Qaeda member, "like me tightly holding your finger, turning it towards you and poking it into your own eye."[13]

Three of the four aircraft reached the target, killing all the passengers and crew and some 3,000 men, women and children on the ground. The novel tactic of using commercial passenger aircraft as improvised guided missiles had succeeded to an extent that could never have been imagined. Because of Al Qaeda's extraordinarily successful operation and security procedures, much concerning the strike and its planning remains unknown. No details are available, for example, of how the Saudi Arabian hijackers were recruited, trained and managed by their agent-handlers. Investigating authorities are not even sure where these cells were based.

After the first plane, flown by Muhammad Atta the operations commander, crashed into the North Tower, Al Qaeda's Emir General — Osama bin Laden — followed the progress of the operation from Afghanistan via radio and satellite television broadcasts. Al Qaeda had originally planned the attack for September 9, but due to unknown operational constraints it was postponed. A videotape subsequently recovered from Afghanistan, showing Osama welcoming a visiting Saudi Arabian Islamist, gives a candid picture of his reaction and that of other

Al Qaeda members to the news of the attack's success:

Osama Bin Laden: "...we calculated in advance the number of casualties from the enemy, who would be killed based on the position of the tower. We calculated that the floors that would be hit would be three or four floors. I was the most optimistic of them all..... due to my experience in this field, I was thinking that the fire from the gas in the plane would melt the iron structure of the building and collapse the area where the plane hit and all the floors above it only. This is all that we had hoped for."

Shaykh: "Allah be praised."

Osama bin Laden: "We were at [inaudible] when the event took place. We had notification since the previous Thursday that the event would take place that day. We had finished our work that day and had the radio on. It was 5:30 p.m. our time. I was sitting with Dr Ahmad Abu-al-Khair. Immediately, we heard the news that a plane had hit the World Trade Center. We turned the radio station to the news from Washington. The news continued and no mention of the attack until the end. At the end of the newscast, they reported that a plane just hit the World Trade Center."

Shaykh: "Allah be praised."

Osama bin Laden: "After a little while, they announced that another plane had hit the World Trade Center. The brothers who heard the news were overjoyed by it."

Shaykh: "I listened to the news and I was sitting. We didn't...we were not thinking about anything, and all of a sudden, Allah willing, we were talking about how come we didn't have anything, and all of a sudden the news came and everyone was overjoyed and everyone until the next day, in the morning, was talking about what was happening and we stayed until four o'clock, listening to the news every time a little bit different, everyone was very joyous and saying 'Allah is great', 'Allah is great', 'We are thankful to Allah', 'Praise Allah'. And I was happy for the happiness of my brothers. That day the congratulations were coming on the phone non-stop. The mother was receiving phone calls continuously. 'Thank Allah. Allah is great, praise be to Allah.' (Quoting the verse from the Quran)

Shaykh: "Fight them, Allah will torture them, with your hands, he will torture them. He will deceive them and he will give you victory. Allah will forgive the believers, he is knowledgeable about everything."[14]

To launch the 9/11 operation Al Qaeda used Germany, the UAE, and Malaysia as launchpads to enter the United States. Cells in each country were established independently of each other. They were secured by strict compartmentalisation but a few select members were permitted to liaise between the compartmentalised cells, each of which separately assisted the 9/11 operation. As its overall operational commander Al

Qaeda chose Atta, a man of unswerving commitment, industry and honesty. The son of an Egyptian lawyer, he arrived in Germany to study architecture and urban planning at the Hamburg Technical University where he completed a thesis in 1999 entitled "Khareg Bab-en-Nasr: An Endangered Ancient Urban District of Aleppo: Urban District Development in an Islamic Oriental Town".[15] The preface contained the words "Say, my prayer and my sacrifice and my life and my death are all for Allah, the Lord of the Worlds."[16] Atta was recruited by the Takfir Wal Hijra, an Egyptian religious organisation, and subsequently by Al Qaeda, some time before his research visit to Egypt in August 1995. In his will, dated April 1996, he wrote that he wanted "to die as a good Muslim" and wished to be buried facing Mecca.[17] One of his two legal witnesses was a Moroccan student of electronics at the same university, Mounir al-Motassadeq. Together they founded an Islamist discussion and prayer group, "Islamic AG", that held meetings in a room provided for the purpose by the university. On his return after undergoing training by Al Qaeda in Afghanistan in 1996-7, Atta recruited two more Arabs studying in Germany, Marwan al-Shehhi from the UAE, and Ziad Jarrah from Lebanon, both from respectable, well off families. Jarrah studied airframe construction and aeronautics and later travelled to Afghanistan for training by Al Qaeda.

The 9/11 attack demonstrated that Al Qaeda could be innovative and that its operational techniques were being constantly refined in the light of previous operations. For example its four attack teams stayed well away from known Arab or Muslim neighbourhoods, and, appreciating the dangers posed by using forged or adapted passports and entry visas for its prized operation, cell members used genuine travel documents to reach their target locations. Al Qaeda's German cell assigned for 9/11 applied for and received new passports while in Germany in order to hide evidence of their trips to Pakistan and Afghanistan.

Throughout the preparatory phase of the operation, the tightest security was maintained. Al Qaeda's principal agent-handlers in Afghanistan were preparing another operational cell in Malaysia, and until Atta arrived at Newark airport on a tourist visa from the Czech Republic on June 3, 2000, he knew only of his role and that of his cell members. To maintain secrecy, the cells communicated with Afghanistan by encrypted email and commercial and human couriers. Although only four pilots were required for the operation, half a dozen Al Qaeda members trained in American flying schools in the eighteen months before the attack. Together with al-Shehhi, Atta attended the Airman Flight School in Norman, Oklahoma, and from July to December 2000 they attended flight-training classes at Huffman Aviation in Venice, Florida, paying $38,000 in fees. The bulk of their expenses were provided by Mustafa

Ahmed al-Hawsawi (*alias* Mustafa Ahmed), an Al Qaeda accountant. Born in Jeddah on August 5, 1968, al-Hawsawi went from Afghanistan to the UAE to manage the financial end of the operation. He wired the bulk of the funds from a moneychanger in Sharjah via Citibank in New York and on to Florida. On June 29 al-Shehhi received $4,790 wired from UAE to Manhattan; and, in Atta's name, they received $109,440 in four wire transfers to their joint account held at SunTrust Bank in Southern Florida, from July to September 2000. Through their flatmate Ramzi bin al-Shibh in Germany (*alias* Ahad Sabet, Ramzi Muhammad Abdelah Omar), al-Shehhi received further transfers of cash. Al-Shibh, born in Yemen on May 1, 1972, was also an Afghanistan-trained Al Qaeda member. After failing to obtain a US visa, he served as a "cut out" (an intermediary chosen to enhance operational security) in Germany, coordinating the finances of the operation along with al-Hawsawi in UAE.

Unlike the unit in Germany, the Al Qaeda cell in Malaysia was under surveillance. Two Al Qaeda members based there, Khalid al-Midhar and Nawaf al-Hazmi, arrived in Los Angeles from Bangkok on January 15, 2001. Although they had come to the attention of the Malaysian Special Branch and the CIA earlier, in keeping with the Cold War tradition of monitoring spies, neither of the agencies made any arrangements for their arrest. Also in Malaysia was Zakarias Moussaoui (*alias* Shaqil, *alias* Abu Khalid al-Sahrawi), another would-be suicide hijacker, of Moroccan origin. Born in Saint-Jean-de-Luz in southwestern France on May 30, 1968, he grew up in a Muslim family headed by a divorced mother who did not regularly practise her religion.[18] A promising student, he attended London's South Bank University in 1995, during which period he attended the Finsbury Park mosque, an Islamist stronghold in the capital. Although born and brought up in France, he became an ardent Islamist. He travelled to Chechnya, where his friend Masood al-Benin was killed in combat, and on several occasions to Afghanistan where in 1998 he received training at Al Qaeda's Khalden camp. After setting up an email account with a Malaysian ISP he contacted Airman Flight School in Norman, Oklahoma. His support cell in Kuala Lumpur led by a former Malaysian army captain turned businessman provided him with letters of introduction from Infocus Tech in October 2000. These stated that he was their marketing consultant in the US, Britain and Europe and would receive a monthly allowance of $2,500. After leaving Malaysia, Moussaoui arrived for a briefing in Afghanistan via Pakistan in December 2000. Before heading for Oklahoma in February 2001 he arrived in London to meet an Al Qaeda contact who was based in Germany. At Chicago airport he declared possession of $35,000 and later opened a bank account in Norman, where, after contacting by email the

Pan Am International Flight Academy in Miami, he began flight training at the Airman Flight School in May 2001. When about to run out of money, he contacted al-Shibh in Düsseldorf on July 29 and August 2, 2001. Using the Al Qaeda name "Ahad Sabet" he received two wire transfers totalling $15,000 from Al Hawsawi using the alias "Hashim Abdulrahman". After retaining $1,000, al-Shibh wired $14,000 in money orders from train stations in Düsseldorf and Hamburg on August 1 and 3 to Moussaoui in Oklahoma. Money transfers were kept just under $10,000 to avoid arousing suspicion.

The operation's financial planning was thus highly sophisticated. All four cells had independent bank accounts and most attack team members had a bankcard with an identical personal identification number common to the cell. For example, Fayed Ahmed, Saeed al-Ghamdi, Hamza al-Ghamdi, Waleed al-Shehri, Ziad Jarrah, Satam al-Suqami, Mohald al-Shehri, Ahmed al-Nami and Ahmed al-Haznawi had opened Florida SunTrust bank accounts with cash deposits.[19] Realising the risk of opening accounts in the US, Mustafa Ahmed al-Hawsawi and Fayez Ahmed travelled to the UAE where they used cash to open checking and savings accounts at a branch of Standard Chartered Bank on June 25, 2001. On July 18, using Fayez Ahmed's power of attorney, al-Hawsawi collected his Visa and ATM cards in the UAE and shipped them to Florida, Fayez Ahmed using his Visa card for the first time in Florida on August 1.

Al Qaeda's codes for general and mission-specific training were followed to the letter; hence the hijackers, being advised to keep physically fit and mentally alert, all joined local gyms.[20] In February 2001, Atta and al-Shehhi attended a health club in Decatur, Georgia; in March 2001 Moussaoui joined a gym in Norman, Oklahoma, and between May and July, 2001, Jarrah did likewise in Florida where he also took martial arts lessons, including kickboxing and knife fighting. Waleed al-Shehri, Marwan al-Shehhi and Satam al-Suqami also joined gyms. Al Qaeda anticipated that passengers might attack them during their operation and the hijackers were ordered to build and maintain their body strength. Until a month before the operation, the hijackers had planned to threaten or if necessary to use knives to gain control of the aircraft. An Al Qaeda associate group, Harkat-ul Mujahidin, had used a knife to stab a passenger, intimidate the crew and gain control of an Indian Airlines aircraft, IC-814, en route from Kathmandu to New Delhi on December 24, 1999. The 9/11 teams realised that their scheme might be compromised if team members were caught trying to smuggle illicit knives on board the planes and so carried box-cutter knives less than four inches long which were permitted by the Federal Aviation Authority. In addition to pepper sprays, these boxcutting knives were the only weapons carried by the hijackers.

All the cells independently acquired flight deck simulation videos, Atta buying those appropriate for Boeing 747, Boeing 200 and Boeing 757 Model 200 and other items from the Ohio Pilot Store in November 2000.[21] The next month he also purchased flight deck videos for the Boeing 767 Model 300 ER and Airbus A320 Model 200 from the same store, as did Nawaf al-Hazmi and Moussaoui. Rehearsing was another central precept of Al Qaeda doctrine and all the cell members took check rides. For instance, Atta and al-Shehhi took a flight check ride around Decatur, Georgia, in February 2001,[22] and Jarrah did likewise at a flight school in Fort Lauderdale. They followed the Al Qaeda precepts of thorough reconnaissance and rehearsal by taking the same flight over and over again to familiarise themselves with airport security and access to the cockpit. Only a month before 9/11 a passenger informed the FBI of suspicious behaviour by passengers of Middle Eastern appearance travelling first class who seldom talked among themselves and only in whispers.

Except for two recruits, Midhar and Hazmi, none of the Al Qaeda suicide squads selected for 9/11 had a past terrorist record, which again diminished the chance of the operation being detected. Although planning was co-ordinated by encrypted email, the cell leaders met at least once. Between April 23 and June 29, 2001, thirteen of the nineteen suicide hijackers who had left the target country returned for their final briefings from different points of the world: Satam al-Suqami, Waleed al-Shehri, Ahmed al-Ghamdi, Majed Moqed, Marwan al-Shehhi, Muhammad Atta, Ahmed al-Nami, Hamza al-Ghamdi, Mohald al-Shehri, Wali al-Shehri, Ahmed al-Haznawi, Fayez Ahmed, and Salem al-Hazmi. Nawaf Al Hazmi was already in Oklahoma to consult with his cell colleagues on April 1, 2001. Atta travelled widely, to Switzerland, the Czech Republic and Spain, to debrief his visiting principal agent-handler in January and July 2001. All the hijackers maintained a low profile and covered their tracks perfectly. For instance, intelligence agencies have no hard evidence that Atta met any member of Al Qaeda while in Spain; as he was heading a special operation, even Al Qaeda's alleged leader in Spain, Abu Dahdah, was kept in the dark about his visit. Spanish intelligence monitored a then unexplained phone call Abu Dahdah received from an Al Qaeda 9/11 trainer, Shakur, nearly a month before the New York and Washington attacks: "At this moment, I am teaching classes. In the classes we are now touching on the subject of aviation, and we have also cut the bird's throat."[23] On his second visit to Spain, Atta rented a car and spent a week in Madrid.

Contrary to the public's perception, not all the hijackers came from overseas for the 9/11 attack. For instance, Al Qaeda recruited and trained

Hani Hanjor, a Saudi, who had entered the US in 1996 on a student visa to study English.[24] Between January and March 2001, Hanjor attended pilot training courses in Arizona and another at the Pan Am International Flight Academy in Minneapolis. Having driven from Oklahoma to Minnesota, the suspected hijacker Moussaoui paid $6,300 in cash on August 10 to the same academy for simulator training on a Boeing 747 Model 400. He proved an inept student and apparently explained to his instructors that he only wanted to learn how to steer an aircraft in flight, not how to take off or land. Naturally this aroused their suspicion and he was apprehended by the FBI on August 16 and held on immigration violations.[25] Moussaoui was found in possession of two knives, fighting gloves, shin guards, flight deck videos for a Boeing 747 Model 400 and Model 200, flight manuals for a Boeing 747 Model 400, a flight simulator computer programme, software that could be used to review pilot procedures for the Boeing 747 Model 400, notes referring to a handheld GPS receiver and a camcorder, a handheld aviation radio, a notebook listing two German phone numbers and the name of Ahad Sabet, letters from Infocus Tech and a computer disk containing information relating to the aerial dispersal of pesticides. However the FBI failed to examine his computer before September 11. On the pretext of launching a crop-spraying company, Moussaoui had inquired in June 2001 about crop-dusting and acquired computer information on the techniques involved. This suggests that Al Qaeda was considering a parallel operation using unconventional weapons to inflict mass casualties.

The arrest of Moussaoui forced bin Laden's organisation to bring forward its operation to strike America's outstanding landmarks. Although Al Qaeda strives to train agents who disclose nothing to their captors, in reality they were well aware of the growing danger to the operation with every day that passed. Moreover Moussaoui was one of the few suspected terrorists who knew about both the Hamburg and the Kuala Lumpur cells. With the imminent threat of being compromised, Al Qaeda's cells stepped up their financial, logistical and administrative preparations within a week of Moussaoui's arrest. On August 22, Fayed Ahmed used his Visa card in Florida to obtain $9,400 in cash, which had been deposited into his Standard Chartered Bank account in UAE the day before. On the same day Jarrah purchased an antenna for a Global Positioning System (GPS), other GPS-related equipment and schematics for 757 cockpit instrument diagrams. (The GPS allows an individual to navigate to a position using coordinates pre-programmed into the units.) From August 25 to August 29, all the hijackers purchased airline tickets with cash or online from airline web sites — except Khalid al-Midhar and Majed Moqued of American Airlines Flight 77.[26] As their Visa card did not match their mailing address, they drove to the Baltimore-

Washington International Airport and paid cash for a one-way airline ticket. The meticulous pre-planning of every aspect of the operation is once again reflected in the timing of Atta's dispatch of a FedEx package from Florida to Dubai in early September. It is likely that it contained his farewell message to the head of his Al Qaeda "family". Al-Hawsawi left for the UAE on September 11, taking Atta's parcel with him, made six ATM withdrawals using the Visa card in Karachi on September 13, and proceeded to Afghanistan via Peshawar. According to the Indian security services and police, Al Qaeda had also prepared a back up team to attack the World Trade Centre[27] and had two other teams of trained pilots and hijackers poised to strike targets in India Britain and Australia, some of whom, it is alleged, had also trained at the Tyler International School of Aviation in Dallas, Texas.[28]

The quality of Al Qaeda's 9/11 operatives was markedly different from those sent to attack US targets in previous years, as were their tactics and targets. Without exception, they were handpicked above all for their unshakeable willingness to kill and die for Allah, as was illustrated in Atta's will. Moreover, even though Moussaoui was arrested three weeks before the operation, he disclosed nothing of the plot, even refusing to enter a plea on charges that could lead to his execution when produced in court on January 2, 2002. If one reviews Al Qaeda's operation to target the continental US on the eve of the millennium celebrations, the qualitative improvement in almost every aspect of terrorist practice becomes apparent. That operation's commander had been 34-year-old Ahmed Ressam, a former member of the Armed Islamic Group of Algeria who had convictions for weapons smuggling in his own country in 1992 and for other offences in Europe in the early 1990s. In 1994 he arrived in Canada, admitting to immigration officials that his French passport was false and claiming asylum, alleging political persecution in Algeria. He lived on petty crime and welfare until the Canadians rejected his asylum application and in 1998 left for Afghanistan via Frankfurt and began training in the Khalden and Jalalabad camps. According to US court proceedings, after discussing the target with Ressam, his alleged Al Qaeda agent-handler, Abu Doha, obtained approval from Osama to plan the bombing of Los Angeles airport. Operating under the cover name of Benni Antoine, Ressam returned to Canada in April 1999. Al Qaeda provided him with $12,000, having told him to generate the rest of his financial resources through crime. After failing to raid a foreign exchange bureau he stole credit cards, burgled hotels and opened a shop in Montreal. Operating as Abu Reda, he recruited members for Al Qaeda without ever referring to the group's name, in keeping with its code. To transmit messages, funds and travel documents to Ressam, Al Qaeda dispatched its veteran Mauritanian member, Ould Slahi, based in Duisburg,

Germany, to Montreal.

In preparation for entering the States Ressam flew to Vancouver, rented a vehicle, checked into a motel and purchased $4,000 worth of fertiliser, the key component of improvised car bombs. After a couple of weeks he left via ferry from Vancouver Island to Port Angeles, near Seattle, on December 14, where he immediately aroused the suspicion of US customs. Inspector Diana Dean said: "He began to rummage in the console of the car and both hands disappeared from sight, which we don't like."[29] When his boot containing the bomb was being searched, he escaped, attempting to hijack a car but was pursued and apprehended by Inspector Michael Chapman. Al Qaeda had promised that after the operation they would arrange fresh identity papers for him to live incognito. After resisting interrogation for several days, during which time the US agencies believed that Al Qaeda's target was either the Space Needle in Seattle or the TransAmerica Building in San Francisco, Ressam began to co-operate in an attempt to secure a lesser sentence. Realising the threat of terrorist infiltration from Canada, with its relatively relaxed immigration policy, the Americans tightened security along their shared border and instigated special security measures to protect key public buildings from car bombs. Al Qaeda responded to these counter-measures by simply getting their operatives into the target country on commercial airlines, carrying correct identity papers and with sound alibis for their presence.

On October 7, 2001, Osama broke with Al Qaeda's tradition of never claiming responsibility for attacks and praised the 9/11 operation, vowing that the United States would never "enjoy security" till "infidel armies leave" the Gulf. Al-Zawahiri called on Muslims everywhere to join in their battle against the United States while his spokesman and confidant, Suleiman Abu Ghaith, announced that Muslims were duty bound to attack US targets worldwide. Although the vast majority of Muslims were appalled by Al Qaeda's strikes, some secretly, and a few openly applauded and admired Osama's organisation for taking on the might of America.

Most American Muslims — both Arab and non-Arab — do not support political violence, especially terrorism, but there is widespread resentment of the perceived influence of the Jewish lobby in shaping US foreign policy and America's role in the Middle East, especially its political, economic and military support for Israel. Thus although there is some degree of sympathy with Al Qaeda's objectives, most Muslims living in the West abhor the tactics adopted to advance its aims. However Al Qaeda's American support base is significant because it is well established and of high calibre. Unlike their Canadian and European counterparts, Al Qaeda's American supporters are mostly wealthy and influential professionals, concentrated largely in New York-New Jersey and to a lesser extent in Chicago. Because many American Muslims are well-educated and goal-oriented, Al Qaeda values them highly. Like Muslim migrants in Europe and Western converts to Islam, they held or continue to hold important positions in Al Qaeda at home or abroad. Furthermore, as US passport-holders they arouse less suspicion when crossing international borders. Al Qaeda's recruitment policy is to accept a national of any country provided he is a committed Muslim or a convert to Islam, but it made extraordinary efforts to recruit Westerners of Muslim Arab origin. There were a few, including retired and serving military personnel, who worked for or supported Al Qaeda. One such was Ali Mohammad, *alias* Abu 'Abdallah, who trained Osama's bodyguards and other Al Qaeda members and planned many of its significant operations. A former member of the Egyptian Islamic Group in New Jersey, Abu 'Abdallah, was part of a 14-man Al Qaeda team consisting of retired US military personnel that entered Bosnia through Croatia to train and arm its *mujahidin*.[30] Another American, Abu Musa, of Palestinian extraction, coordinated the Shia Iranians and the Sunni Arabs who were constantly clashing.[31]

An integral part of the Al Qaeda support network is its affiliate organisations. These, it should be stressed, are NGOs that were not established by Al Qaeda but have been infiltrated by it, of which there are several in the United States. Many of these enjoy charitable status, and since 9/11 the FBI has stepped up surveillance of such bodies, freezing the funds of three US-based Islamic NGOs. Benevolence International Foundation (BIF) and the Global Relief Foundation (GRF), both based in Chicago, are currently under investigation by US authorities for their alleged links with terrorist groups.[32] The BIF has its roots in Lajnat al-Birr al-Islamiyya (LBI-Islamic Benevolence Committee), also known as the Islamic Charity Committee. LBI had its headquarters in Jeddah and offices worldwide, including in Peshawar, Zagreb and Zenica. Adel Batterjee formed LBI in Pakistan to provide humanitarian assistance for Afghan civilians during the anti-Soviet *jihad*. After the governments of Egypt and Algeria complained to Saudi Arabia that LBI was funding Islamists, the Saudi government shut down its Jeddah office in February 1993 and Batterjee resigned. In addition to heading the Al Shamal Bank of Sudan, Batterjee, who knew Osama well, wrote *Al-Arab al-Ansar*, a booklet about the participation of Arabs in the anti-Soviet Afghan *jihad*, where bin Laden's role is described in great detail.

According to the CIA, a former LBI employee in Zagreb was involved in the kidnapping of six Westerners in Kashmir in July 1995.[33] Al-Faran, a faction of Harkat-ul-Ansar (now known as Harkat-ul-Mujahidin), was responsible for the operation, in which several of those abducted were subsequently murdered. At that time, among the Kashmiri groups, Al Qaeda was closest to Harkat-ul Ansar. The LBI employee left Pakistan for the US and thereafter travelled to Bosnia in October 1995.[34] In addition to providing support to at least one commander of an Al Qaeda training camp in Afghanistan, this LBI employee also worked for MAK and the Benevolence International Foundation of Peshawar, Pakistan.[35] According to the CIA, the International Islamic Relief Organisation also maintained close ties with LBI. The latter's office in Zagreb also came under the close scrutiny of the Croatian security service.

In 1992 Batterjee formed Benevolence International Foundation (BIF) in Florida and shortly afterwards relocated it to Chicago, and Emaan Arnaout, *alias* Abu Mahmud, a Syrian-born US citizen, was appointed as its head, a post he continues to hold to date. As part of his mission he travelled widely, visiting conflict zones in the Balkans, the Caucasus and Asia, channelling US-generated humanitarian support. Until it was shut down in December 2001, BIF Chicago supported BIF Peshawar. As of early 2002, BIF Peshawar funds an orphanage in Koti-Ashrot, near Kabul. The patron of the orphanage is Hafeezullah, a former employee of the Taliban Foreign Ministry, with whom Osama and his family stayed six months after returning to Afghanistan. A fluent Arabic-speaker, Hafeezullah also served as Osama's interpreter and visited him regularly when the latter returned to Jalalabad. Although an influential member of the Taliban regime, Hafeezullah became very close to Al Qaeda and, until he fled in October 2001, Arabs, mostly Al Qaeda members, were frequent visitors to his residence.

When the FBI raided BIF's Chicago office the search warrant named "Samir Abdul Motaleb", an alias of a well known MAK employee.[36] From 1995 to 1998, according to US intelligence, another BIF Chicago employee, Suleman Ahmer, specialised in making radical speeches throughout the US in support of *jihad* campaigns in Afghanistan and Chechnya. Before he left for Pakistan, where he now lives, Ahmer founded another charity, Nasr Trust, also registered in Chicago.[37] Although BIF's funds were frozen, its office in Chicago continues to function. BIF (US) raised $3.6 million in 2001.

Another Islamic NGO that had its funds frozen was the GRF. One of its employees, another US citizen of Syrian descent, worked in the mid to late 1980s for MAK and Beit al-Ansar, formed by Osama. He was responsible for processing documents for Arab volunteers who fought the Russians in Afghanistan. In 1992, after the fall of the pro-Soviet regime, he travelled to Kabul and later to Zagreb, Jordan, Yemen, Pakistan and Bangladesh, where he worked for BIF.[38] Another GRF member who worked for MAK until 1995-6 ran the Masadat al-Ansar (Lion's Den) training camp, which had been established jointly by Azzam and

Osama.[39]

Key Al Qaeda leaders have also visited the United States in recent years, including Muhammad Jamal Khalifa. When US immigration arrested him in San Francisco in December 1994, a search of his luggage revealed, *inter alia*, documents setting out the "outline of the institution of *jihad* which includes "the Wisdom of Assassination and Kidnapping, the Wisdom of Assassinating Priests and Christians, the Wisdom of Bombing Christian Churches and Places of Worship, the Wisdom of Martyrdom Operations, the Wisdom of Reconciliation with the Enemy and other various methods".[40] Also found were extensive discussions of assassination, the use of explosives, military training and *jihad* as well as details of Islamist movements such as Hamas and Palestinian Islamic Jihad.[41] Khalifa was held without bail until January 6, 1995 and then charged with visa fraud, furnishing false information and flight to avoid prosecution. He was subsequently extradited to Jordan for allegedly financing the 1994 bombing of a cinema in Jordan, for which he was later tried and acquitted. As Al Qaeda's chief for South East Asia in the early 1990s, Khalifa was responsible for financing *Oplan Bojinka*, but when arrested in San Francisco and until he was acquitted in Jordan, the US intelligence community had no knowledge of his role in it. After the World Trade Centre and Pentagon attacks, intelligence authorities arrested Khalifa in Saudi Arabia.

Notwithstanding increased security measures implemented after 9/11, the US remains a very open and vulnerable society. The threat of terrorism remains high. In the mid to long term the only sure way of protecting America — short of destroying Al Qaeda's entire infrastructure abroad, an objective that is likely to remain unattainable — is for the FBI and other agencies to step up massively their recruitment of agents from migrant Muslim communities in order to penetrate Al Qaeda's core and penultimate leadership. Only this sort of real time intelligence offers the hope of ultimately destroying the terrorist infrastructure and support systems on which Al Qaeda depends.

Europe

Compared with its North American and Asian networks, Al Qaeda's European operation is of fairly recent origin. It established itself by infiltrating four well-established networks — FIS, Takfir Wal Hijra; the GIA and the Salafist Group for Call and Combat (Gamaa Essalafiya lid Da'awa wal Qital; Groupe Salafiste pour la Prédication et le Combat: GSPC) — as well as by setting up its own cells in the by now familiar manner. As European borders are well policed, Osama and al-Zawahiri realised that establishing a network from scratch would not be easy and therefore decided upon ideological infiltration of FIS, GIA, GSPC and Takfir Wal

Hijra networks. Al Qaeda was only partially successful in infiltrating FIS, a moderate Islamist party. It had much more success in penetrating the more radical and secretive Islamist groups, including the Takfir network, of Egyptian origin, which is deeply rooted in North Africa, from Algeria to Egypt. Al-Zawahiri is also the leader of the Takfir Wal Hijra. By cultivating the leadership of two Algerian terrorist groups, Al Qaeda infiltrated the GIA and thereafter the GSPC; hence Algerians form a large proportion of Al Qaeda's European cadres. Most Al Qaeda operatives in Europe are European Muslims, however, above all first- and second-generation migrants from the Middle East and North Africa, mostly Algerians, Moroccans, Tunisians, Libyans and Egyptians. There are also several dozen European converts to Islam that serve and are supportive of Al Qaeda plus a number of British Asians, some of whom have been detained in Camp X-Ray. As of early 2002, international security and intelligence agencies estimate there to be at least 300 active and dormant members of Al Qaeda and Al Qaeda associate Islamist members in Europe.[42] Without exception they are the cream of Al Qaeda's trained members. Although some 150 of their members have been arrested since 9/11, Al Qaeda has more than enough operatives ready for activation in Europe. Components of this terrorist web overlap with their criminal counterparts, sometimes working closely with organised networks run by Chechen, Russian, Ukrainian, Pakistani, Nigerian, Turkish and Kurdish criminals. They do so in order to acquire genuine passports; to forge and adapt identity documents needed to obtain passports; to smuggle people across borders, including Al Qaeda recruiting officers and operatives; to engage in credit card fraud and robbery to raise funds; and to intimidate opponents. Al Qaeda also planned a campaign of assassinations in Europe but in the wider interest of not disrupting the network's "far more important operations" refrained from doing so. In their sights had been the exiled King Zahir Shah of Afghanistan (before his return from Rome to Kabul in April 2002) and other opponents of the Taliban, the strike at Ahmed Shah Masood being a grim example of what they might have achieved.[43] Al Qaeda has also encouraged its European cell members to join the armed forces of their respective countries in order to receive military training that can be put to use in other, terrorist, contexts.

Al Qaeda's European network was constantly under the threat of disruption from host governments and also had to deal with the problems of movement from its European theatre to Afghanistan and back. After the East Africa bombings in August 1998, not all Al Qaeda's European recruits could travel to Afghanistan through Pakistan due to the restrictions imposed by the Pakistan government. Although Al Qaeda developed creative mechanisms to overcome this restriction, many of its recruits travelled to far further afield, to the Philippines, Chechnya or Indonesia for training.

Britain

Of Al Qaeda's network in Europe the French and British arms are the longest established, and the most robust terrorist support infrastructure established by any group in a European country is in Britain, a society and a culture generally tolerant of migrants. However, its hospitality has been abused by terrorists, and six months after 9/11 the key activists of the network remain at large. Despite the legal proscription of foreign terrorist groups in February 2001 under the Terrorism Act 2000, British attempts to neutralise the infrastructure of Al Qaeda and related groups have been gravely inadequate. Without a doubt, London was Al Qaeda's spiritual hub in the Western world.

In 1994 a trusted friend of Osama, Khalid al-Fawwaz, came to London,[44] where he met and liaised with Saudi opposition figures, including an exiled academic whom Osama later phoned personally to thank him for his help.[45] Al-Fawwaz managed Al Qaeda's Advice and Reformation Committee (ARC) office in Beethoven Street, West Kilburn, London, which was equipped with state-of-the-art communications enabling him to talk directly to Osama. ARC provided the perfect cover for advancing Osama's interests. For instance, in March 1997 it arranged a meeting between him and a team of CNN journalists.[46] Despite his denials, Osama was closely involved with the ARC, which disbursed funds, procured equipment and recruited members. On an ARC letterhead "Osama M. bin Laden" signed the ARC's "London Office" resolution which stated: "The consultative assembly of the Advice and Reformation Committee intending to extend its activity and to ease communication resolves this Monday 11 July 1994: (1) to establish an office in London; (2) to appoint Mr Khalid A. al-Fawwaz director of this office."[47] Al-Fawwaz ran the office for five years before his arrest by the British authorities on September 28, 1998.

Another opponent of the Saudi regime, Dr Saad al-Fagih, headed the Movement for Islamic Reform in Arabia (MIRA). A former professor of surgery at the King Saud University, he ran a sophisticated support office with excellent communications. MIRA and similar outfits also reached out to the wider world. For instance, MIRA and the London-based Committee for the Defence of Legitimate Rights (CDLR) disseminated the English translation of the 12-page Arabic *fatwa* issued by Al Qaeda in February 1996. It stated that "the Al Saud and the American occupation are the source of evil, and they are so intertwined and interconnected that they have become organically connected to evil."[48] The

British authorities took no action to restrict the dissemination of this material. Al-Fagih also purchased a satellite phone that was later used by Al Qaeda.[49]

Along with al-Fawwaz, the ARC was staffed by two loyal members of al-Zawahiri's Egyptian Islamic Jihad, Adel Muhammad Abdul Almagid Abdul Bary (*alias* Adel Abdel Bary, Abu Dia), and Ibrahim Hussein Abdelhadi Eidarous (*alias* Ibrahim Eidarous, Daoud, Abu Abdullah, Ibrahim). The latter maintained satellite phone links between the Al Qaeda leadership and its British cell, provided forged and adapted passports for Al Qaeda operatives, and disseminated Al Qaeda literature, including press releases. His colleague, Abdul Bary, born on June 24, 1960, had managed Al Qaeda training camps and guesthouses before arriving in Britain. Egypt had sentenced him to death *in absentia* for terrorism, including the bombing of the Khan el-Khalili, a tourist landmark in Cairo.[50] Nonetheless, the British Special Branch arrested them only in July 1999. Al-Fawwaz is also allegedly linked to the 1998 East Africa bombings, for which he awaits extradition to the USA. Britain bore the costs of his legal aid (£428,000).[51] Once again the weakness of the British criminal justice system in the fight against foreign terrorist support networks had been exposed.

Three Islamist clerics of a radical persuasion are based in Britain — Omar Bakri Muhammad, Omar Mahmud Othman (*alias* Abu Umr al-Takfiri, Abu Qatada) and Moustapha Kamel (*alias* Abu Hamza Al Masri, Abu Hamza). After listening to their sermons, at least 100 British and European Muslims travelled to Afghanistan and some are now held by the Northern Alliance or are in American custody at Camp X-Ray. In addition to preaching in their own mosques, these Islamist clerics attracted youths from other mosques throughout Britain. Richard Reid, the so-called "shoe bomber", and Zacarias Moussaoui, accused of being the twentieth 9/11 hijacker, worshipped at the Brixton mosque in South London headed by Imam Abdul Haqq Baker, a moderate and respected cleric. Thereafter, they were exposed to the sermons of Omar Bakri Muhammad and Abu Qatada, the Palestinian cleric who preached to the Baker Street Prayer Group. Moussaoiu was in London with Richard Reid, a British convert to Islam, who after receiving instruction in Khalden camp in Afghanistan returned to Europe to serve Al Qaeda and undertook surveillance missions to Malaysia, Turkey, Egypt, Israel, the Netherlands, France, and Belgium. Reid's failed attempt to detonate explosives concealed in his shoes on an American Airlines Paris-Miami flight in December 2001 led to his arrest. Although the French and Israeli security services knew that he was a radical Islamist, the British did not.

Britain was also the main meeting place in Europe for those who were later to join Al Qaeda. Two of those who met at the Finsbury Park mosque, at which Abu Hamza preached, were Djamel Beghal and Kamel Daoudi. Beghal, an Algerian who acquired French citizenship by marrying a French woman in 1993, fell under the influence of Egyptian Islamists before being recruited and appointed as Al Qaeda's leader in France. Before that he had lived in London and Leicester where he joined Takfir Wal Hijra. In late 2000, after leaving his family behind in Pakistan, Beghal went to Afghanistan to discuss a plan to strike at American targets in Paris. Although he could not meet Osama in Kandahar in March 2001, he did see Abu Zubaydah, his principal agent-handler, who presented to him as a mark of appreciation gifts from Osama. En route to Europe Beghal was arrested in Dubai in July 2001, where he revealed to his interrogators that Al Qaeda had deposited funds in a Moroccan bank to finance terrorist attacks.[52] He also disclosed Al Qaeda's plans to attack the US Embassy in Paris either by crashing an explosives-laden suicide helicopter on to it or by using an Al Qaeda suicide bomber with explosives strapped to his body. Simultaneously Al Qaeda planned to destroy the American Cultural Centre with a car bomb. A few days after Beghal was extradited to Paris, on September 30, 2001, he retracted the statements given to the UAE authorities and to the French in the hope of exploiting the justice system of a liberal democracy where torture is forbidden.

Beghal's suspected bombmaker was his former flatmate Daoudi, a second-generation North African of French citizenship. Daoudi, who escaped the French police, was arrested in Leicester and deported to France at the end of September 2001. A graduate of Al Qaeda's Afghan training camps, he is thought to have been the group's European encryption specialist for internet communication and the use of codes. Nizar Trabelsi, a former professional footballer, is suspected of being Beghal's suicide bomber. A member of Takfir Wal Hijra, he had trained in Afghanistan and apparently believed that a "martyrdom" operation would cleanse his past sins.

Mounting international pressure after 9/11 finally galvanised the British authorities into action: Abu Qatada's West London home was raided and £180,000 in various currencies seized (till then he had been fraudulently claiming welfare). Abu Qatada, who enjoys political asylum in Britain, was named by the UN as a terrorist suspect and by the Spanish authorities as Al Qaeda's spiritual ambassador in Europe. He is also a leader of Takfir Wal Hijra, currently headed by Ayman al-Zawahiri. Despite intelligence that he had met Osama in the 1980s, Abu Qatada denies ever having done so. However he is wanted by the Jordanian government in connection with a series of bombings in Amman in 1998. When the British authorities enacted special legislation in late 2001 in order to detain the likes of Abu Qatada, he slipped the net, but as of early 2002 he remains in Britain, communicating with a few trusted associates by email. Another Algerian, Abu Doha, who was Ressam's agent-handler is also a key figure in Britain. When police raided his home they found forged and adapted passports and bomb-making instructions.

From January 2002 onwards, British police arrested several Al Qaeda suspects, especially Algerians and other Middle Eastern nationals who have been living in Europe for extended periods. Investigations in January 2002 are believed to have revealed that the arrested Algerian asylum seekers Baghdad Meziane and Brahim Benmerzouga had been using Leicester as an Al Qaeda support base. Despite the arrests in late 2001 and early 2002, the extremist milieu remains in place in London (as an Arab taxi driver in London who served with Osama in Afghanistan said when interviewed, "We fucked the Soviets. Now we are going to fuck the Americans."[53]), although only a tiny minority of British Muslims support the aims of Al Qaeda, most of whose members and supporters entered Britain from the Middle East. However, the reluctance of the authorities to counter this threat decisively is harming the wider reputation of Britain's Muslim community.

One can only presume that the previously unpublished revelation that London was a simultaneous target of the 9/11 attacks has galvanised the British into action. At the planning stage of the New York and Washington attacks, Al Qaeda realised that Britain would most likely support any punitive American action against the organisation and its Afghan hosts, the Taliban, and so planned a simultaneous attempt to destroy the Houses of Parliament by crashing into it a British Airways aircraft hijacked from London's Heathrow airport. Muhammad Afroz, an Indian suicide pilot trained in Melbourne, Australia, Britain and the US was subsequently arrested in Mumbai, India. Afroz's cell was apparently one of three fully trained Al Qaeda teams, the other two having been assigned targets in India and Australia. On the basis of the interrogation of suspected Al Qaeda agents, Indian intelligence believes that Al Qaeda had infiltrated a suicide team into Britain to attack the Houses of Parliament. In addition to striking Westminster in an airborne attack, they also had plans to attack Tower Bridge on the river Thames, but the latter target was dropped in early September. The suicide team was to hijack a British Airways flight bound from London to Mumbai on September 9, 2001 (the original date scheduled for the Washington and New York attacks) but in an encrypted email received at the last moment from their Al Qaeda operational commander in America, the operation was postponed to September 11, 2001. The Al Qaeda cell in Britain chose to hijack a domestic London to Manchester flight, for which they assembled at Heathrow airport around 14.30 on September 11.[52] The flight was scheduled for 17.00, but by then the US strikes had taken place and the authorities at Heathrow had quickly grounded all domestic and international flights.

In addition to Muhammad Afroz, his cell, according to his testimony, consisted of two other pilots, "Mushtaq Ahmed" and "Al Amir", both from Afghanistan. Afroz, however, retracted his confession on 30 April 2002 saying he had made the statement under duress after the police threatened to kill his brother, Farooq Razzak. The court had earlier, on 9 April set him free on bail because the Mumbai police that arrested him had first booked him under the Prevention of Terrorism Act (POTA). The police, subsequently, told the special court that they wanted to drop the charges made under POTA and further press charges under the Indian Penal Code. The court granted him bail on the same day that the police charge sheeted him under sections of the IPC accusing him of waging or attempting to wage war against the government of India.

After the Washington and New York attacks, flying clubs throughout Britain were checked by Special Branch detectives and so Afroz returned to Mumbai on Sept 22, 2001.[55] There he kept switching from hotel to hotel to avoided going home, until he was arrested by the police in Navi Mumbai (New Bombay) on October 2, 2001. During questioning Afroz revealed — but later retracted — that he had taken a six-month simulator-training course at the Tyler International School of Aviation in Dallas, which he completed in October 1999. Two other Pakistani terrorists — Shahid Akhtar Sayeed (*alias* Sandy, 30), and Mistry Zahoor Ibrahim (*alias* Zia, 25), who Afroz said had trained with him in America — were involved in the hijacking of Indian Airlines IC-814 from Nepal to India.

One passenger was killed, but the remainder were freed after the plane flew to Kandahar in Afghanistan, a mission that clearly had the backing of the Taliban authorities.[56] Among the convicted terrorists freed from prison in India as part of the deal to end the hijack was the British-born Omar Saeed Sheikh, who was arrested in February 2002 by police in Karachi investigating the kidnap and murder of the *Wall Street Journal* reporter Daniel Pearl, an operation in which Al Qaeda involvement is strongly suspected.[57] Corroboration of the planned attack on Britain has come in reports of Sheikh's questioning, although there is as yet no evidence of a link between him and Afroz. Sheikh, who is clearly linked to Al Qaeda, admitted complicity in the suicide attacks on the Jammu and Kashmir Assembly in Srinagar in October 2001, the Indian Parliament the following month and the killing of six police officers guarding the US Information Centre in Calcutta in January 2002.[58]

Just after the 9/11 attacks a source suggested to one Western intelligence agency that an Al Qaeda associate group, Lashkar-e-Toiba, had been involved in the US attacks. In hindsight it seems that the intelligence was wrongly attributed and instead referred to an Al Qaeda Asian cell that was planning an attack on Britain. Afroz's testimony is also corroborated by the fact that, away from the glare of publicity, intelligence received by the British security services led to the arrest and deportation of a key member of an Asian terrorist group who had arrived in Britain from America immediately after the 9/11 attacks.

France

Britain is regarded by Al Qaeda as an integral part of its network on the European continent and in terms of operational planning and execution the parent organisation in Afghanistan draws no distinction between them. Before the 9/11 attacks and Prime Minister Blair's immediate willingness to send British forces to aid the Americans in the Afghan campaign, Al Qaeda had always perceived France to be its principal enemy, largely because of how it props up the anti-Islamist governments of North Africa, notably in Algeria, Tunisia and Morocco. Particularly detested was French assistance for the Algerian authorities after they abrogated the 1991 election results that would have brought to power a democratically elected Islamist government. As such, Al Qaeda's strategy was founded on using the rest of Europe as a means of targeting France. Initially, the Islamists were keen to attack foreign, largely American, targets on French soil but later the threat shifted to French objectives. Due to terrorist incidents perpetrated on its soil by North African Islamists, France's security services are among the best informed and most active in their attempts to counter Al Qaeda.[59]

Beginning in the early 1990s, Al Qaeda conducted a massive practical and ideological infiltration of FIS (Islamic Salvation Front) and other Algerian Islamist political parties and terrorist groups with the aim of demonising France among Algerians, including the large émigré community living in Paris, Marseilles and other big cities. The formidable impact of sustained French political and financial support for the Algerian state since 1992 is explained in FIS's publications:

> Crusader France and some of the leaders of unbelief and atheism are working to encircle the FIS leaders who are abroad to impose a political blockade on the voices calling for the right to the Umma and the building of an Islamic state on Algerian soil. [...] Atheist France is not content with its support for the unjust junta, it has even gone so far as supplying it with sophisticated military material such as night combat helicopters and chemical bombs which exterminate living things without destroying buildings.[60]

Al Qaeda successfully infiltrated the leaderships of FIS, the GIA and later the GSPC, and having taken control of their networks built a state-of-the-art organisation in Europe. Via its affiliate GIA and GSPC cells, Al Qaeda has been targeting France since 1994, but the French security services thwarted several dozen operations. Although it is difficult to pinpoint Al Qaeda's role in specific attacks, the French have arrested Al Qaeda-trained and financed GIA and GSPC members since 1995.

The GIA began its long campaign of violence in Algeria after murdering two Frenchmen in September 1993, killing another five foreigners and kidnapping three French consular officials in October 1993; it also killed seven Italian sailors and kidnapped the Oman and Yemeni ambassadors to Algeria in July 1994, whom it released with messages to the Algerian President Zeroual that it would cease its campaign if its leader, Abdelhak Layada were released. The government refused to accede to this request. In August it attacked the French embassy — resulting in the death of five French officials — and in December hijacked an Air France aircraft with the intention of crashing it in the heart of Paris. Within 24 hours of the French security forces storming the plane, the GIA retaliated by killing four Catholic priests in Algeria. A GIA bomb on the Metro at Saint-Michel station near Notre Dame cathedral in Paris killed four and inured eighty-four in July and a nail bomb injured seventeen, including eleven tourists, in Paris in August 1995. A GIA car bomb in Paris killed four in December 1996. Although its campaign in France was of limited success, the GIA drew international attention to Algeria's conflict and was described in the press as one of the most ruthless terrorist groups in history. The GIA also murdered 63 Algerian travellers in August 1996; massacred 120 civilians in villages near Algiers in November; and car bombed and killed ten and injured nearly 200 in two incidents in Algiers in December 1996. The French authorities, who were monitoring its European and North American network, also uncovered a plan to attack Jewish targets in France in November 1994. Between July and October 1995 the GIA detonated a further eight bombs in France, three of which went off in Paris metro stations, killing ten and injuring over 200 people. After a three-day manhunt, Khaled Kelkal, who had planted the bombs, was shot by the French police in Lyon in October 1995. In September 1999, France's special anti-terrorism court sentenced twenty-one GIA terrorists and supporters engaged in these attacks to terms of 6-10 years. Of the three key defendants — Boualem Bensaid, Smain Ait Ali Belkacem and Karim Koussa — Bensaid's lawyer claimed that his client was "a soldier whose actions were dictated by religion."[61] Others said that the charges were unfounded and that they were in a "state of war".[62] The GIA even established a training camp in the Ardeche, but ultimately law enforcement agencies infiltrated and dismantled its organisation in France.

The most spectacular GIA operation that bears the Al Qaeda hallmark was the GIA's hijacking of an Air France Airbus A-300 Flight 8969 in Algiers on December 24, 1994. Of the 227 passengers, forty were French nationals. After the hijackers released some women and children and murdered three of the 227 passengers, the Algerian authorities permitted the aircraft to leave for France. The intention of the GIA cell led by the twenty-five year-old Abdul Abdallah Yahia, *alias* Abou, was to crash a fully fuelled plane on to the Eiffel Tower in the heart of Paris (the French consulate in Oran had received an anonymous warning that the ultimate aim was to blow the plane up in mid air over Paris). Further debriefing of the passengers revealed that the four GIA hijackers were carrying explosives; had requested and received a wristwatch from a passenger; and had discussed "martyrdom".[63] After duping the terrorists into believing the aircraft did not have sufficient fuel to reach Paris, the French authorities diverted it to Marseilles, whereupon, instead of the 10 tons of fuel needed to fly from Marseilles to Paris, the GIA requested 27 tons, threatening to blow up the plane if their demands were not met. In response the élite French anti-terrorist force — the Groupe d'Intervention Gendarmerie Nationale (GIGN) — stormed the plane, led by Commander Denis Favier.[64] All four terrorists were killed and 161 hostages and crew rescued. The success of the anti-hijack operation was a direct result of the then Interior Minister Charles Pasqua refusing to cooperate with the terrorists and risking anti-hijack action. Within twenty-four hours of GIGN storming the plane, the GIA killed four Catholic priests in Algeria. The hijacking of the French airbus with the stated intention of conducting a suicide attack on a landmark target should have alerted the international security and intelligence community to the possibility of this tactic being adopted again. Sadly, it did not.

When its infrastructure came under attack in France, the group relocated to countries perceived to be more tolerant and less willing to hunt it down. For instance, when the French stepped up their operations against the GIA its mobile cells dispersed to Italy, Belgium, Germany, Switzerland and Spain.[65] When Belgium jailed GIA leaders, the group threatened to create a "bloodbath", stating: "The GIA gives Belgium 20 days to reverse its actions against the *mujahidin*. It must stop its torture, free those in jail or under house arrest and secure the return of those extradited abroad."[66] The Belgian court in May and the French court in June 1999 issued judgements against the GIA terrorists and their supporters.[67] However, the cases lasted several years and sentences were lenient. For instance, members of the French "Hotel de l'Harmonie" cell, which was dismantled in March 1995, were sentenced to 2-8 years.[68] The FIS's military wing also had an exiled leadership council based in Germany, headed by Rabah Kebir, and its military cells operating through charities in France and Germany procured weapons in Europe for their campaign in Algeria.[69]

In April 1997 the Spanish police arrested eleven GIA terrorists and supporters in Valencia. The GIA obtained weapons from Italy, Poland and the Czech Republic as well as Germany and Britain.[70] There is evidence too to suggest that its networks have recruited non-Algerians:[71] the Belgian national Marc Muller, who supplied the GIA with arms, was found in possession of eight tonnes of arms and ammunition while two French nationals, David Valat and Joseph Jaime, had shotguns, ammunition and material to make detonators.[72]

Along with Al Qaeda, the FIS, GIA and later GSPC maintained links with other Islamists such as the two Egyptian groups, their Libyan Islamist counterparts, Lebanese Hezbollah and others in the Middle East and Central and South Asia. Hezbollah helped by providing training in Lebanon from Iranian advisers, while Al Qaeda camps in Sudan instructed Algerian terrorists. As a consequence Algeria severed diplomatic ties with Iran and Sudan in March 1993, although this did not disrupt Iranian or Sudanese support for terrorism. The Algerian groups also had well publicised links with Islamist groups in Afghanistan and Pakistan, the beginning of the Algerian campaign having coincided with the end of the anti-Soviet Afghan *jihad* (1979-89). For example, Djaffer el Afghani, the GIA leader from September 1993 to February 1994 was Afghan-trained. A member of Daawa wa Tabligh since 1982, he went to Afghanistan in 1989, returned to Algeria in 1992 and committed several murders and attacks on public buildings. He was only one of several hundred Algerians to follow this route.

After Antar Zouabri assumed leadership of the GIA in 1996, the group engaged in several large-scale massacres of Algerian civilians which were conducted with appalling brutality. Osama, who opposed Muslims killing fellow Muslims though clearly not those working on behalf of state security forces in countries like Algeria, expressed his displeasure and forged a direct relationship with Hassan Hattab, the head of the GIA network in Europe, persuading him to split from the GIA parent organisation because it was targeting more Muslim civilians than Algerian security force personnel. In August 1998 Hattab's followers in Europe linked up with the GSPC, a small Islamist group with an ideology compatible with Al Qaeda's. With extensive Al Qaeda support, Hattab took over the GSPC leadership and by late 1998 had painstakingly built it into the leading Algerian terrorist group. By this manoeuvre Osama gained direct control of the GSPC's European network, giving him access to another fully-fledged structure with which to target his enemies. His influence over GSPC was evident by 1999 and Osama often phoned

Hattab to discuss operations.[73] By the late 1990s, the GSPC was conducting most of Al Qaeda's propaganda and terrorist campaigns in Western Europe, especially in France. Only the persistent and harsh French response led to a de-escalation of its operations. With sustained attrition of its network, the French temporarily crippled the opportunities for the GSPC to operate effectively. Despite this disruption the GSPC managed to generate some new cells among the Algerian diaspora, but in the final phase its activists turned to low level organised crime to compensate for the lack of material support they were receiving from Algerians in France.[74] A Western intelligence agency has also reported that Abdelmajid Dichou, another key GSPC leader, joined Osama in Afghanistan in either 1999 or 2000.

Although the GSPC was and is an Al Qaeda associate, Al Qaeda's *fatwa* did not identify it as one of the signatories, most likely because it believed that exposing the Al Qaeda-GSPC link at that time would be counter-productive. Compared to the groups that did put their names to the *fatwa*, the GSPC had a far greater reach in the West. In contrast to the popularly held view, this demonstrated that Al Qaeda was more pragmatic than dogmatic. Al Qaeda has tried its best to keep its alliance with GSPC clandestine — even Islamist preachers in Europe are cautious about referring to it by name in their writings.[75]

Another semi-autonomous group with links to Al Qaeda was Groupe Roubaix, though this linkage is disputed by some Western intelligence experts. Although Al Qaeda maintain ties with some criminal groups to raise funds and obtain arms, it is wary of the relationship going any further than that. For example, after Janjalani, the leader of the Abu Sayyaf group, was killed in the Philippines in December 1998, the ASG became more criminal in nature, prompting Al Qaeda to strengthen its links with the Moro Islamic Liberation Front.

Lionel Dumont, a French convert to Islam, formed Groupe Roubaix after serving with the French military in Somalia and thereafter in Bosnia where he joined the Takfir Wal Hijra *mujahidin* faction.[76] Although wanted for terrorist offences, Dumont escaped to Bosnia, where he conducted operations and was later arrested but escaped in 1999.[77] Fateh Kamel, the leader of Groupe Roubaix, was arrested in Jordan on December 15, 1999 and extradited to France on February 2001 to stand trial for the Paris Metro bombings. Groupe Roubaix, staffed by GIA and GSPC members, included Ahmed Ressam, the millennium bomber. French intelligence suspects that he was involved in the Paris Metro bombing that killed four and injured ninety-one.[78]

Netherlands, Belgium, Italy, Spain

Through its Algerian network Al Qaeda used neighbouring countries, especially the Netherlands, to mount attacks in France. While there was near perfect coordination between Al Qaeda cells in the Netherlands and France, the Dutch authorities failed to cooperate with the French, a falling out that had a detrimental effect on security, intelligence and judicial co-operation. The Netherlands has also been a favoured location for Al Qaeda banking and investment. Only two Al Qaeda linked accounts at two Dutch banks were detected, and *c.*$500,000 was frozen after 9/11, but there are thought to be many more accounts in existence. In addition to its return on its extensive investments, Al Qaeda Europe raised several million dollars through the efforts of various charities. In addition to having offices in Siegen (Germany), Vienna and elsewhere in Europe, al-Muwaffaq — a charity which was the unwitting victim of Al Qaeda infiltration — operated from the Dutch town of Breda. Funds raised were diverted to support Al Qaeda camps in Afghanistan and its activities in the Balkans. Similarly, al-Haramain Islamic Foundation of Saudi Arabia was represented in the Netherlands by the el-Tawheed Foundation. Al-Haramain Islamic Foundation's Director in Riyadh was represented on el-Tawheed's board. In Balkans and East Africa al-Haramain was heavily infiltrated by Al Qaeda, almost certainly without the knowledge of its principal donors. In addition to its Rotterdam and Amsterdam cells, Al Qaeda established units in other Dutch cities with large migrant populations. This presence enabled Marwan al-Shehhi, a 9/11 pilot, to visit the Netherlands in April 2001 and in December 2001 Ahmed el-Bakiouli and Khalil el-Hassnaoui, Dutch citizens of Moroccan origin, entered India with the intention of fighting with Al Qaeda/Taliban against the Americans, and were killed by Indian security forces on January 13, 2002. In addition to Dutch citizens of Arab origin, there are several native Dutch converts to Islam openly willing to sacrifice their lives for Allah and go to Afghanistan. They included Hassan Barzizaoua, 28, of Moroccan origin; Abdul Jabbar Van de Ven, 24; and Abdullah Bekx, 30, a member of al-Waqf Foundation's Muslim Youth in the Netherlands.[79] What is interesting in this case is that they did not seem deterred by the West's response, both governmental and on a personal level, to the 9/11 attacks and their aftermath, suggesting that a threat may continue to emanate from migrant communities in Europe. The Dutch government had done little to control the spread of Islamist propaganda or fund-raising, hence tacitly facilitating an expansion of Al Qaeda's support base in the country. Osama specifically referred to support from the Netherlands in a remark caught on video:

"Some of them said that in Holland, at one of the centres, the number of people who accepted Islam during the days that followed the operations were more than the people who accepted Islam in the last eleven years. I heard someone on Islamic radio who owns a school in America say: 'We don't have time to keep up with the demands of those who are asking about Islamic books to learn about Islam.' This event made people think [about true Islam] which benefited Islam greatly."[80]

In Belgium and the Netherlands Al Qaeda recruited mostly Moroccans, one of the two largest migrant communities. Until December 2001, it benefited from the reluctance of continental European states, especially Belgium, to extradite its nationals. As many smaller European countries, including Belgium, did not perceive a direct threat to their own interests till the wave of GIA bombings in France in the mid-1990s, their governments sometimes awarded citizenship even to known Islamists and did little or nothing to disrupt terrorist support infrastructures. As the French authorities were successfully targeting the Al Qaeda-trained and financed GIA in Paris, the latter moved its infrastructure to Belgium. For instance, Kamel Nourredine, who participated in the Paris bombings of July 1995, threw a grenade at police in Belgium. He escaped to the Netherlands but was extradited back to Belgium. Belgian police also recovered from a car a CD version of the 7,000-page Al Qaeda manual *The Encyclopaedia of the Afghan Jihad*, suggesting that Al Qaeda was providing non-weapons training to its operatives in the Low Countries.

The exploitation by Al Qaeda members of the freedom of movement within Europe, especially between Belgium and the Netherlands, was demonstrated by Richard Reid, the "shoe bomber". He obtained a fresh UK passport from a British consulate in the Netherlands; he later visited Afghanistan and did not wish to arouse suspicion by travelling on a passport with a Pakistan visa. Reid therefore requested another passport from the British Embassy in Belgium, which he received. Apart from their operational value to Al Qaeda, a European passport, especially a British one, fetches $5-10,000 on the black market.

After September 11, 2001, cooperation and coordination between the European police and security services naturally increased. Nonetheless, tensions remained: the French were especially annoyed by the breaking up by Belgian and Dutch authorities of two interlinked Al Qaeda cells in which cell members were arrested and weapons, identity documents and propaganda material seized on September 13. This was because they had been trying to infiltrate the groups with informers to generate long-term intelligence. Plans to destroy the US Embassy and American Cultural Centre in Paris were recovered from the safe house of Nizar Trabelsi and Abdelcarim el-Hadouti and bomb-making materials found in a snack bar run the latter's brother, Fouzi, in Brussels. Both Hadouti brothers and a third man linked to a terrorist attack escaped, possibly to

Morocco.[81] Jérome Courtailler led the second cell in Rotterdam. His brother David had stayed in Moussaoui's Brixton apartment while in Britain and when the French arrested him on his return from Afghanistan, Jérome moved to the Netherlands. In his apartment Dutch police found twenty-eight passports, bomb-making manuals and *jihad* videos including film of Al Qaeda attacks. Jérome had even provided the Belgian passports used by Ahmed Shah Masood's assassins. These were stolen from the Belgian Embassy in The Hague and from the Belgian consulate in Strasbourg in 1999. For his role in stealing passports an Algerian from Eindhoven was arrested in December 2001 and extradited to Belgium. Al Qaeda cell members in Belgium and the Netherlands also worked with organised criminal groups, notably Algerian and Moroccan, who supported them for both ideological and financial reasons.

Al Qaeda developed its Italian network as a safe haven for operatives who were being hunted elsewhere in Europe, and as a transit base for Islamists going to fight in the Balkans and the Caucasus. Al Qaeda's Italian cell obtained its recruits from mosques, *madrasas* and community centres. Despite Italian police raiding the Milan mosque in 1995, both it and its affiliated Islamic Cultural Centre continued to advance Al Qaeda aims and objectives. The mosque's Imam, Anwar Shaaban, of the Islamic Group of Egypt, was wanted by the Italian authorities but was killed in Bosnia fighting with the *mujahidin*. Ramzi Ahmed Yousef worshipped at the same mosque before the 1993 World Trade Centre bombing and Al Qaeda's North African members dominated its decision-making structures and congregation. Al Qaeda's leader for northern Italy, Essid Sami Ben Khemais headed the Milan-Gallarate cell. An Afghanistan-trained Tunisian, Khemais co-ordinated Al Qaeda's activities in Europe, maintaining perfect cover: he ran a cleaning service. Another member of Al Qaeda's Tunisian family, Tarek Maaroufi, visited Khemais in September 2000 to coordinate Al Qaeda's plans to bomb US targets in Italy. Although Maaroufi was arrested on December 19, 2001 on charges of passport forgery, Belgium has resisted Italian efforts to extradite him (he is a Belgian citizen) for acts of terrorism perpetrated by the GIA.[82] Italian authorities arrested Khemais in April 2001 after he travelled to Al Qaeda's regional bureaux in Spain to finalise preparations for an operation.

The proximity of Spain to North Africa and its large Muslim population made it a natural choice as an Al Qaeda hub, a role that became critical after its Turkish cell was disrupted, at which point Al Qaeda relocated its regional bureau to Spain. Before Ressam, the millennium bomber, flew to North America, he too visited Spain, where he met Al Qaeda's GSPC members.[82] Ressam and other Al Qaeda operatives visited

Alicante and Castellon, both towns with large Algerian migrant populations, while Muhammad Atta went there for briefing in January and July 2001, before the 9/11 attacks. An unemployed Syrian bricklayer based in Spain, Abu Dahdah, headed Al Qaeda's support operations for Europe, including recruitment. He travelled widely, meeting, among others, Osama in Afghanistan, and also went to Indonesia, Malaysia and Turkey. He inspired Al Qaeda operatives with such gratitude and trust that they even shared aspects of the 9/11 operation with him before it was carried out. Abu Dahdah was finally arrested with some of his cell members in November 2001.

Under Spanish surveillance since 1997, Muhammad Boualem Khnouni (*alias* Abdallah) allegedly headed an Al Qaeda support team specialising in forging and adapting documents, obtaining high-tech equipment such as night-vision goggles, and raising funds via credit card fraud. The cell members, who were all Algerians in the GSPC, were arrested only on September 26, 2001. This cell was in touch with another of Afghan-Bosnian- and Chechen-trained members, of Algerian, Syrian and Tunisian origin, operating in Madrid and Granada. Contrary to press reports, however, there were no links between ETA and Al Qaeda. As a former Al Qaeda member who served in Europe said: "ETA has nothing to offer. They can learn from us but there is nothing in the relationship for us." [83]

Germany

For two decades Germany has been a main centre for terrorist propaganda, recruitment, fundraising, investment, procurement and shipping. In addition to infiltrating large Muslim migrant communities, Al Qaeda set up terrorist cells in Hamburg, Frankfurt, Düsseldorf and Duisburg. Laws that restricted security service surveillance and coordination between the different *Länder*, or states, marred the police response.

Al Qaeda has long had a presence in Germany, its importance for the group being reflected in the fact that it was visited half a dozen times by the chief of European operations, the Iraqi Mamdouth Mahmud Salim, until his arrest in Germany on September 16, 1998. Salim was born in Iraq in 1958 and operated under cover as a businessman.

The US had access to high quality Al Qaeda members since 1998, but not all of them have proved cooperative. After seeking an understanding that he would not receive the death penalty, Salim was later extradited from Germany to the US, but while at the Metropolitan Correctional Centre in Manhattan, he, together with a Tanzanian Al Qaeda member, Khalfan Khamis Muhammad (*alias* Zahran Nassor Maulid), stabbed two prison guards, one in the eye, and sprayed irritants on others during a failed escape attempt.[84] Salim was tried, found guilty and sentenced to a further jail term in connection with this incident. This incident shaped American perceptions of the unrelenting behaviour of Al Qaeda prisoners and detainees, a reaction manifested in conditions at Camp X-Ray.

Immediately after 9/11 German intelligence worked closely with its US counterparts to develop a comprehensive picture of Atta's cell in Hamburg. Every Al Qaeda member connected with the attack had left Germany before the operation, including Said Bahaji, a German of Moroccan origin. Bahaji was Al Qaeda's leader in Germany and had received military training in the *Bundeswehr* (army). Until he married in 1999, he lived in the same Marienstrasse apartment as Muhammad Atta, paying the rent, obtaining visas and ensuring that Al Qaeda's operatives were focused on their mission. One week before the suicide attacks he left for Afghanistan.

The German police and intelligence services stepped up their surveillance operations and arrests after 9/11, in the process unearthing the fact that Al Qaeda's European cells were not structured country by country but rather on a free-floating, cross-border basis, some being multinational, others mono-national. The Algerian Muhammad Bensakhria (*alias* Muhammad Ben Aissa, Meliani), headed the Frankfurt cell, which was named after its GSPC leader. Al Qaeda had trained the "Meliani Commando" in Afghanistan and its members were under German surveillance. On December 26, 2000, Al Qaeda agents in Milan and Frankfurt were arrested, thwarting the group's planned bomb and poison gas attacks, in conjunction with London cell members, against Strasbourg's European Parliament building, cathedral and market. Before the Al Qaeda safe house was raided, Bensakhria escaped but was arrested in Spain and extradited to France. His cell included two Iraqis, one Algerian and a French Muslim. The six-member Al Qaeda associate group GSPC in London was detected and disrupted. In their Strasbourg attack the cell was to have used sarin, the nerve agent developed by the Nazis and successfully deployed by Aum Shinrikyo in Japan five years earlier.[85] Toxic gases and poisons were tested by Al Qaeda in several places in preparation for their use against Western targets. Experiments with cyanide gas, with the intention of introducing it through office ventilation systems, took place, and animals, mostly dogs, and several human "guinea pigs" died as a result.[86] Training in the use of chemical agents took place in Afghanistan, and an instruction manual was recovered from the house of a Libyan Al Qaeda member in Manchester, England. Al Qaeda operatives were also overheard discussing unconventional agents over the phone: the German-based Libyan agent, Lased Ben Heni, was monitored discussing the use of poison over the phone with Sami Ben Khemais. They talked of transporting in "tins of tomatoes" an "extremely efficient liquid that suffocates people [...] as soon as you open [the tin]" and using it against French citizens.[87] The intelligence community believes that Heni knew in advance of the 9/11 attacks. He was arrested on October 10, 2001 and extradited to Italy. Khemais, head of the Varesse cell and known as "Commander Varess", dressed in designer clothes, ate in expensive restaurants and lived in an affluent neighbourhood while in Germany. However, while in Spain he played the part of an illegal immigrant, sleeping in a van and dressing in shabby clothes.[88] Several of the German cell members who had volunteered for martyrdom operations were denied US visas. For example, Zakariya Essabar, a Moroccan student who studied at the same college in Germany as the 9/11 hijacker Ziad Jarrah, was assigned to enter America. After arriving in Germany in February 1997, he stayed with Atta until May 2000 and thereafter with Ramzi Bin al-Shibh till early 2001; he left Germany when his visa request was denied. Similarly, Bin al-Shibh arrived in Germany in 1995, shared an apartment with Atta in 1998-9 and worked at the same computer company in Hamburg.[89] On four occasions al-Shibh had his applications to enter the US from Germany and once from Yemen denied, and even after he wired money to a flight training school in Florida on August 14, Jarrah failed in his attempts to enrol him. Although al-Shibh was angry to have missed participating in the martyrdom operation, he remained in Hamburg to coordinate financial transactions between the US and the UAE, the main source of funds for 9/11. The last wire transfer al-Shibh (using the name "Ahad Sabet") received was for $1,500 from al-Hawsawi (using the name "Hashim Ahmed"). On September 3, al-Shibh left Düsseldorf for Madrid and did not return to Germany. Al Qaeda has a reserve of experienced and motivated cadres like Essabar and al-Shibh, would-be-suicide hijackers trained for future operations.

Although no Al Qaeda members have been arrested in Switzerland, several of its key leaders and supporters have lived there at different times. These included al-Zawahiri, who, according to Egyptian intelligence, held Dutch, Egyptian, French and Swiss passports, the latter two in the name "Amin Othman" and his Dutch one as "Sami Mahmoud". Contrary to some reports, al-Zawahiri never applied for political asylum in Switzerland. Atta went there two months before the 9/11 attacks and purchased a knife in Zurich on July 8, 2001.[90] Switzerland is also an important transit point for several Al Qaeda members, and the group has invested heavily in Swiss real estate and in the banking sector.

The Balkans

Al Qaeda infiltration of the Balkans began immediately after war broke out in Bosnia in 1992, also the year in which the Communist regime in Kabul was overthrown. To quote the *mujahidin* commander Abu Abdel

Aziz, who has no connection with Al Qaeda, "Only fifteen days lapsed [after the conquest of Kabul] and the Bosnian crisis began. This confirmed the saying of the Prophet, peace and blessings be upon him, who said, 'Indeed Jihad will continue till the day of Judgment.' A new Jihad started in Bosnia, 'we moved there', and we are with it, if Allah wills."[91] Kateebat al-Mujahideen [*mujahidin* battalion], known as "el-Mudzahidin" in Bosnian, was a part of the seventh battalion (Sedmi Korpus, Armija Republike BH) of the Bosnian Third Army, and up to 4,000 foreign *mujahidin* fought against the Serbs. Although the percentage of Arabs in the *mujahidin* was small, their exploits grabbed the headlines and they were greatly feared, even after the fighting ended in 1995. As one *mujahid* explained why they had come to help: "[Bosnian Muslims] were slaughtered, others were killed, while others were forced to exile. The chastity of their women was infringed upon for the simple reason that they were Muslims. The Christians took advantage of the fact that the Muslims were defenseless with no arms. They recalled their age-old hatred."[92] The ferocity of the retaliatory killings by the Arab *mujahidin* shocked the Bosniaks (Bosnian Muslims), and is still talked of today. Al Qaeda videos showing Arab *mujahidin* playing football with the severed heads of Serbian soldiers were seen by several Western journalists at the time. The *mujahidin* also became heavily involved in welfare organisations bringing relief to the Bosniak population as a whole.

The biggest impact of Al Qaeda and other Islamist groups, however, was felt in their taking control of Islamic NGOs, most of which they infiltrated with Egyptian and Algerian cadres again to the fore. Osama himself is credited with having visited the Balkans in 1993, although there is no firm evidence of his having travelled to Bosnia.[93] NGOs operated mostly in the Muslim areas of northeastern and central Bosnia and as in the Afghan conflict military aid reached the *mujahidin* and humanitarian aid the civilian population. It is even believed that some terrorist groups gained "access to credentials for the UN High Commission for Refugees and other UN staffs in the former Yugoslavia".[94]

In many ways, the Balkan wars triggered the proliferation of Islamic NGOs moving into conflict zones where Muslims were perceived to be under threat. Saudi Arabia, Kuwait and other Gulf states were the major donors, the Saudis alone providing over $600 million to Bosnia.[95]

Role of Islamic NGOs and charities in the Balkans

The al-Haramain Islamic Foundation, also known as Mu'assasat Al-Haramain al-Khayriyya (Charitable Establishment of the Two Holy Mosques; Saudi al-Haramain Foundation) had offices in Macedonia, Sudan, Kenya, Somalia, Zagreb, Rijeka, Osijek, Belikoj, Albania and elsewhere in Europe. Al-Haramayn funded and supported the *mujahidin* battalion in Zenica.[96] Its Zagreb office was raided by the Croatian security services in an effort to curb smuggling, while in Macedonia, the CIA alleged, al-Haramain raised funds through narcotics trafficking and prostitution.[97] Ahmad Ibrahim al-Najjar, a member of Egyptian Islamic Jihad since 1979, joined al-Haramain's Tirana office in 1993, representing his own group and Al Qaeda in Albania. He exemplified the terrorist who travelled and worked overseas under cover of charitable organisations. In June 1998, two days before he left for Kosovo, he was apprehended and extradited from Albania to Egypt, where he had already been sentenced to death *in absentia* for the attempted bombing of the Khan el-Khalili bazaar in Cairo in 1997. Before he received a life sentence with hard labour, he told journalists: "I support the Nairobi operation, because the embassy is the biggest centre for spying and monitoring Islamic movements in the region."[98] In addition to operating in the Balkans under the cover of al-Haramain, al-Najjar also provided Al Qaeda with financial and logistical support.

Under the Dayton Peace Agreement most of the *mujahidin* left Bosnia, but a few hundred who married local women and found employment remained. With the pressure building up against terrorist groups, several Islamic NGOs severed their overt ties with Al Qaeda and other Islamists. However, Al Qaeda had in place Algerian members with Bosnian citizenship who were preparing to attack both the US Embassy and SFOR troops, plans which were disrupted when the Bosnian government arrested Bensayah Belkacem. He and others were tried and acquitted by the Bosnian supreme court in January 2002 of planning attacks against American targets but were later detained by US forces. The Americans had monitored Belkacem communicating with Abu Zubaydah and the latter's cell phone number was retrieved from Belkacem's phone.[99]

Third World Relief Agency (TWRA), with its headquarters in Sudan, had offices in Austria, Turkey, Germany, Switzerland, Zagreb, Tuzla, Sarajevo, and Split. Al Qaeda raised millions of dollars through TWRA for its operations in Bosnia and Croatia. In retaliation for the arrest of a senior Egyptian Islamic Group member, a TWRA employee, a member of the same group, carried out a suicide car bombing against a Croatian police station in Rijeka in mid-October 1995. The Croatian security forces killed the mastermind of that operation, Anwar Shaban, former *mujahidin* leader in Zenica, in December that year. At the time of his death he, together with Egyptian Islamic Group and Al Qaeda, were planning to attack NATO forces about to be deployed in Bosnia. TWRA relocated its office from Zagreb after its weapons smuggling operations were exposed.[100]

Al Qaeda also had a clandestine presence in Albania, and on August 23,

1998, its plot to attack the US Embassy in Tirana was foiled due to sound and timely intelligence: an Albanian gunmen was killed by security guards when he tried to force his way into the already evacuated embassy. The threat remained, however: on July 17, 1999, Albanian authorities arrested two Syrian and one Iraqi Al Qaeda member. Other Al Qaeda members and associate members, especially from the Egyptian groups, continued to be arrested in Albania and in the neighbouring countries, often by their counterpart agencies at the behest of the CIA's Directorate of Clandestine Operations. On August 5, 1999, Al Qaeda, using the cover of Egyptian Islamic Jihad, said it would retaliate against the US for its role in extraditing its members from Albania to Egypt. Although Al Qaeda's plans to attack US targets in Albania and Kosovo have to date failed, their support operations continue apace and they have recruited extensively in the region. In February 2002 the Macedonian authorities killed seven terrorists in an encounter, said to be Afghan or Pakistani *mujahidin* fighting with the UCK, but their identities remain in question.

The Caucasus

After its collapse Al Qaeda made inroads in the former USSR. It established an office in Baku and supported the Azeri *mujahidin* in their war against Christian Armenia for control of the disputed Nagorno-Karabakh enclave, from 1988 till 1994. According to Russian foreign intelligence, 1,500 Afghan veterans entered Azerbaijan in September 1993.[101] The Chechens also cooperated with other Muslims in the former Soviet Union, including the Azeris. For instance, the Chechen *mujahidin* purchased missiles not only for themselves but also for their Azeri counterparts, and they played a key role in the recapture of Goradiz, a town southeast of Nagorno-Karabakh's capital, Stepanakert. By the summer of 1994 their numbers had increased to 2,500. After suffering heavy casualties in battle with the Armenians the Azeri Afghan brigade was dissolved in 1994, but many of its remaining troops participated in other regional conflicts. A few disgruntled and disbanded members of the brigade resorted to terrorism in Baku, mostly bombings of public places and transport infrastructrure.

Al Qaeda's major involvement in Russia began when Jokar Dudayev, a Soviet Air Force general, initiated a campaign for an independent Chechnya. Dudayev was supported by the Chechen branch of the Muslim Brotherhood, the Islamic Path Party.[102] Fighting began in December 1994, after the end of the Azerbaijan-Armenia conflict, freeing several experienced fighters to join the Chechen *mujahidin*. Dudayev's military commander Shamil Basayev, himself Afghan-trained, had a close relationship with Osama. By August 1995 the 6,000 guerrillas fighting the Russians in Chechnya included 300 Afghan Arabs.[103] Experienced *mujahidin* from Bosnia-Herzegovina and Azerbaijan also joined them, and gradually the conflict spilled over into neighbouring Ingushetia, Daghestan and North Ossetia. The intelligence agencies of the governments of Saudi Arabia, Lebanon and Iran directly and indirectly supported the Chechen guerrillas. With this increased backing for the guerrillas Russia proper was affected, and even Moscow witnessed a series of bombings.

Osama maintained a close ideological, technological and financial relationship with Khattab, the military commander of the *mujahidin* in the Caucasus, and resources and personnel were exchanged between the two. As mentioned in an earlier chapter, Al Qaeda's 055 Brigade had an unusually large percentage of Chechens and Central Asian Muslims, and in combat against the Northern Alliance over half of the fighters killed were foreign. Before arriving in Chechnya, Khattab fought in Afghanistan as a "teenager" and thereafter in Tajikistan as a "brilliant commander".[104] In some battles — such as the Lion's Den Operation in 1987 — Osama and Khattab fought side by side under the leadership of Khattab's teacher and mentor, Hassan as-Sarehi. In 1995, as-Sarehi, according to the Saudi government, played a role in the bin-Laden-inspired Riyadh bombing, after which he was extradited to Saudi Arabia from Pakistan. After the civil war in Tajikistan ended, Khattab moved to Chechnya, where as head of foreign *mujahidin*, he was appointed military commander of the operations under the overall commander, Shamil Basayev. To fight the Russians in Chechnya and Daghestan, Khattab mobilised *mujahidin* from Ingushetia, Ossetia, Georgia and Azerbaijan, with the finances provided by Al Qaeda. Russian officials state that Osama provided $25 million to the Chechen *mujahidin*, but this cannot be independently verified.

In addition to the Arabs serving in Chechnya, several hundred Chechens were trained in Al Qaeda's Afghan camps and provided with weapons. In the Caucasus, Al Qaeda's Afghan-trained members were model fighters, who often went on to occupy senior posts, thereby increasing Osama's renown. The Al Qaeda-influenced Al Ansar *mujahidin* — considered the fiercest and best organised of the three major *mujahidin* groups fighting the Russians in Chechnya — were also responsible for most of the Chechen conflict's suicide attacks, previously an unknown tactic. According to a European intelligence agency, Al Qaeda assisted the Al Ansar *mujahidin* in weapons-trafficking *via* Russian, Ukrainian and Chechen criminals. During the first Chechen war, Ukraine, notably Odessa, was a prime transit-point for *mujahidin* fighters and weapons smuggling.

Egypt

As mentioned in an earlier chapter, in only a decade Osama bin Laden created a powerful international terrorist group by co-opting experienced Islamist groups into Al Qaeda, the integration of the two Egyptian groups being pivotal. By 1989 Al Qaeda had established operational cooperation with the Egyptian Islamic Group and with the Egyptian Islamic Jihad and later absorbed them into its structure. Their leaders were co-opted as leaders of Al Qaeda and its umbrella body of Islamists headed by Osama, "The World Islamic Front for the Jihad Against the Jews and the Crusaders".

The Egyptian groups founded in the late 1970s developed an international presence as a means of surviving the Egyptian government's harsh domestic crackdown on their activities. As Sheikh Umar Abd al-Rahman remains in a US prison, the Egyptian Islamic Group's effective leader and operational commander is Rifai Ahmed Taha — he served on a council with Abdelaker Hammad, Muhammad Shawki al-Islambouli, Mustafa Hamza and Osama Rushdi.[105] Egyptian Islamic Jihad is also factionalised: its leader in exile is al-Zawahiri and Abdud al-Zumar commands those in prison. One of its factions, Tala'i al-Fatah (Vanguard of Conquest), led by al-Zawahiri, worked closely with Al Qaeda, as did al-Zumar. Both al-Zawahiri and Osama have a deep affection for the Blind Sheikh, and Al Qaeda has campaigned tirelessly for his release, Osama being particularly incensed on hearing that the Sheikh was being strip-searched daily in prison. For instance, the Vanguard of Islamic Conquest issued several warnings to the US in 1997 to release the Blind Sheikh or face the consequences, threatened to attack US and Israeli targets in 1996, and "regretted" that Americans and Jews were not killed in the Luxor tourist massacre in November 1997.[106] At Al Qaeda's insistence the Abu Sayyaf Group also sought his release in exchange for American tourists kidnapped in the Philippines.

For the two Egyptian groups, working independently and merging with Al Qaeda was a marriage of convenience. Egyptians also held over 60% of the group's key positions and appointments. Socio-economic and political conditions in Egypt had seen the dispersal of Egyptians to the Middle East, Europe and, to a lesser extent, North America, and there is a high percentage of radicalised Egyptian intellectuals, professionals and military who wish to see an Islamic regime in power in Egypt. Unlike the Palestinian diaspora, the Egyptian network was largely dormant, awaiting mobilisation in order to precipitate political change at home. Egypt had also been the fulcrum of the Islamist revival in the Middle East, with many of the movement's pioneers — Muhammad Abduh (1849-1905), Hasan al-Banna and Sayyid Qutb — being Egyptian.[107] In operational terms the Egyptians brought with them long years of experience in guerrilla and terrorist operations and contributed significantly to the anti-Soviet Afghan *jihad*.

Constant disunity between the Egyptian Islamic Group and Egyptian Islamic Jihad had — with a few notable exceptions, namely the assassination of President Anwar Sadat by Egyptian Islamic Jihad in October in 1981 and the attempted assassination of President Hosni Mubarak by the Egyptian Islamic Group in Egypt in December 1992 — plagued the Egyptian Islamists, and their full potential was only harnessed after Osama bridged the gap between them by painstakingly cultivating the leaderships of both groups. Thereafter he also became their principal financier and provided training and non-Egyptian fighters. Al Qaeda played a direct or indirect role in several operations, including the attempt to assassinate Mubarak in Ethiopia in 1995; the suicide bombing of the Egyptian Embassy in Islamabad in 1995; the massacre of fifty-eight tourists in Luxor in 1997; and attacks against Coptic Christians in 1997. The Luxor attack was masterminded by Al Qaeda's number three leader, Rifai Ahmed Taha, the leader of the Islamic Group of Egypt, and praised by al-Zawahiri, suggesting that there now existed closer cooperation between the two groups. On September 18, 1997, a tourist bus was raked with gunfire and petrol bombed outside the Egyptian Museum in Cairo, killing 9 Germans, the bus driver and injuring 26 others. After warning tourists not to travel to Egypt, the Egyptian Islamic Group hailed the attackers as "mujahidin brothers".[108]

Algeria

In terms of Al Qaeda membership, Algerians are most numerous after the Egyptians. Al Qaeda's infiltration of the Algerian Islamists can be explained by the latter's sophisticated underground organisation in Europe. By cultivating their leaders and providing training and finance, Al Qaeda absorbed this ready-made network. Although the campaign for an Islamic state in Algeria was developed and nurtured by the FIS, the Islamist agenda was effectively hijacked by GIA, which Al Qaeda soon infiltrated. The Algerian Islamist Khamareddine Kherbane, an Afghan veteran, was close both to the GIA and Al Qaeda's leaderships. Formed in 1993 and led by Abdelhak Layada, the GIA waged the most brutal terrorist campaign yet seen in the Middle East, against not only the security forces but also ordinary Algerian Muslims.

The GIA constantly changed the nature of its campaign. It began in 1993 by killing diplomats, clergy, industrialists, intellectuals, feminists, journalists, priests, and foreigners but from 1996 murdered tens of thousands of innocent Algerians.[109] The intelligentsia, especially those influenced by Western values, were branded "false Muslims" or "anti-Islamic civilians" and selectively targeted.[110] The GIA's failed in its plan to broaden the political conflict into a religious one, however, and when it realised it could no longer depend on popular support, it became even more brutal and began targeting villages: raiding parties slit the throats of their victims, including children; kidnapped men and women including young girls; and at times they massacred entire village populations by hacking their victims with daggers, swords, axes and knives. Others were beheaded, beaten to death, or cut with chain saws and in these "abominable massacres" the mutilated victims often bled slowly to death.[111] Those who attempted to flee were doused in petrol and set on fire, and during some massacres the terrorists broke for lunch, demonstrating their macabre mindset. To create panic and fear, the GIA issued ultimatums and forced entire villages to evacuate their homes. Their mass casualty attacks included detonating car bombs in public places. Claiming that its actions were driven by *jihad*, the GIA bombed markets, restaurants, hotels, schools, universities, discotheques, cinemas, public beaches and city centres both in Algiers and elsewhere. Trains, school buses and even ambulances were not spared, people were murdered inside mosques, houses were set ablaze when the victims were still inside, and women who failed to cover their heads were killed in the street. This veritable cult of violence shocked Islamists worldwide. At this point Al Qaeda distanced itself from the GIA, reflecting Osama's pragmatism. The massacres prompted four Islamist groups, including the Libyan Islamic Fighting Group and Egyptian Islamic Jihad, to issue communiqués denouncing what was taking place, and by mid-1996 Al Qaeda and other Islamists withdrew support from the GIA leadership. It is noteworthy that anger was directed at the leadership, not at the group or the cause. Through its associate groups, Al Qaeda declared:

> Due to the deviations and legal mistakes committed by its Amir...Jihad in Algeria, which started almost five years ago, faced a major setback following the massacre of a number of leading scholarly and jihadi figures by the current Amir of the GIA, who is believed to be surrounded by regime spies and collaborators.[112]

Osama's displeasure was expressed in public and in private, and prompted him to forge direct links with the head of the GIA's European network, Hassan Hattab, who also disagreed with Muslims killing each other. On September 8, 1997, the GIA issued its infamous declaration justifying the massacres, stating that the Algerian people were "kaffirs, apostates and hypocrites because they did not support the GIA against the government".[113] Claiming responsibility for its excesses, including the forcible use of "temporary marriage" (*sabi*) and rape of women they captured, the GIA claimed that it was all "sacrificing for the cause of Allah."[114] They went on to describe *sabi* as:

> ...holding women as booty and possessions who can be sold, used as permanent

servants, automatically separated from their husbands if they were married, and become the property of those who took them. That includes access to the body willingly or unwillingly, to be inherited unless they become pregnant; they are then called the mother of the child of a possessor. They automatically become free once their possessor dies.[115]

In response Al Qaeda severed all ties with the GIA leadership, denounced Antar Zouabri and encouraged Hassan Hattab to break away and join GSPC, a group formed in May 1998 with several hundred GIA members. Thereafter both Al Qaeda support and the security forces concentrated on undermining the GIA, paving the way for GSPC to emerge, Al Qaeda's large-scale penetration of which was completed between 1998 and 2000. The GSPC's European network came under close scrutiny after one of its procurement cells was disrupted in Britain in 1999.[116] Although a successful trial did not ensue, the early detection of a GSPC cell in Britain was a major blow to the group.

Other than receiving assistance from Sudan until early 2001, the GSPC maintains links with all the main Salafist groups. By 2000 it was the dominant Islamist terrorist group in Algeria and in succeeding years has become more active and more violent than the GIA. As of 2002, GIA and GSPC are the only major terrorist groups active in Algeria, their respective manpower being estimated at 800 and 1,800.[117]

Although the numerical strength declined, the Algerian terrorists have become more professional in the face of the government's increased success, based on widespread, and especially French, support in combating the Islamist insurgency. Moreover, Algeria has also been helped by other governments in North Africa and the Middle East while its dialogue with the Sudanese and the Iranians has persuaded the latter to scale down their assistance to Algerian Islamism.[118]

The GIA was led by nine Emir generals during its first eight years, all of whom were either killed or imprisoned.[119] In February 2002 the then leader, Antar Zouabri, was killed along with two henchmen in his home town of Boufarik, near Algiers. His death is likely to strengthen Al Qaeda's associate group GSPC even further, and the new GIA leader may even depart from the tradition of targeting Algerian civilians and cooperate with Al Qaeda and GSPC.

Yemen

Al Qaeda's Yemeni membership is the third largest after the Egyptians and Algerians. After Al Qaeda was formed, Osama worked closely with the Islamic Army of Aden (Jaish Aden Abin al Islami of Yemen), also known as Al Abyan, and an Al Qaeda training camp was set up in the southern village of Mudiyah.

As an alternative base to either Sudan or Afghanistan, Osama long thought of moving to Yemen. Only some 35% of Yemen is under the permanent influence and control of the government, so its state of lawlessness would have made it an ideal base for Al Qaeda. In its eyes the US was expanding its sphere of influence from the Arabian peninsula into the Horn of Africa by stationing troops in Somalia and later forging close ties with Ethiopia. Hence Yemen had an extremely strategic location. In December 1992 Al Qaeda mounted an attack on US troops billeted in hotels in Aden. They were en route to Somalia, where they were engaged in Operation "Restore Hope", bringing aid relief and, it was hoped at the time, political stability to the country. Al Qaeda detonated bombs in two hotels in Aden. The American troops escaped unscathed but an Austrian tourist and a hotel worker were killed. Al Qaeda had also laid plans to destroy the US embassy in Yemen in 2001 but the operation was detected. Of the Aden strike the CIA stated: "We can confirm from our sources that bin Laden was indeed involved in this operation."[120] Long after the event Osama publicly claimed responsibility for this and the Somalia attack of 1993.

Al Qaeda's network in Yemen grew in importance throughout the 1990s, especially its transit and logistical aspects. Many of the group's operations in Sub-Saharan and North Africa, even those in Egypt, were launched from there. Yemen also housed several Al Qaeda businesses and safe houses which adapted and forged passports as well as entry visas.

Al Qaeda mounted two maritime suicide operations from Yemen, of which one was successful. Unknown to the world's press, an explosives-laden boat attempted to sink the USS *The Sullivans* in Aden on 3 January 2000, timed to coincide with the millennium celebrations. The operation failed because the craft was so overloaded with TNT that it sank before it reached the target. Until much later the US intelligence community had no idea of what had happened because Al Qaeda was a tough target to penetrate.

Al Qaeda had planned simultaneous millennium attacks in three countries. In the first, US and Israeli tourists in Jordan were to be killed; the second was the bombing of Los Angeles international airport; while the third was the plan to sink USS *The Sullivans*. The first and second operations were detected and foiled while the third failed. After extensive sea and land reconnaissance, Al Qaeda mounted two other operations in Yemen in 2000 and in 2001. It had obtained advanced knowledge of the arrival of USS *Cole* on its first-ever voyage to Aden, and Osama was keen to see it sunk or crippled because it was an Arleigh-Burke-class destroyer from which cruise missiles were launched at his home and camps in Afghanistan in 1998. He even allocated funds for the attack to be filmed on video though the assigned cameraman failed to record it as he overslept. This did not endear him to Osama. On October 12, 2000, two men aboard a small craft laden with C4 explosives moored alongside the larger vessel, made a defiant gesture, then blew themselves up. As an Al Qaeda manual, *War Cry of the Mujahidin*, states: "A warship can be immobilised by placing 1.2 kg of plastic explosive on the propeller shaft. A mere 1.3 kg can destroy the engine. [...] 4 kg on the base can sink it." Seventeen American sailors died and thirty-nine others were seriously wounded. Al Qaeda had planned for the two attacks since May 1998, when the USS *Mount Vernon* paid an official visit to Aden, staying three days. The brains behind the operations were Jamal al-Badawi, an Al Qaeda Egyptian member, Tawfiq al-Atash, a Saudi member who lost a leg in Afghanistan, and their agent-handler Muhammad Omar al-Harazi (*alias* Abdul Rehman Hussain Muhammad al-Safani), an Al Qaeda Saudi member of Yemeni origin. Al-Harazi was also responsible for tasking Al Qaeda members to attack US targets in East Africa, in the Indian subcontinent and in Southeast Asia. As he had done in Kenya, he left Yemen a few days before the operation. He purchased the boat in Saudi Arabia and oversaw the assembly of the infrastructure for the operation, which included a trailer, a towing vehicle and an explosive charge. Al-Harazi was operating from Al Qaeda's regional bureau in Malaysia while the 9/11 attacks were being prepared.

Early in 1995 Osama suggested to Shaykh 'Abd-al-Majid al-Zandani of Yemen the need for the creation of a "Gulf Battalion", using Iranian funds and weaponry, for deployment in the Gulf, including the Horn of Africa.[121] The proposal was never implemented, for reasons unknown. However, Al Qaeda developed close relations with Ahmad Muhammad Alia al-Hada, a Yemeni Afghan veteran and close friend of Osama. Of 1,100 phone calls made from Osama's Compact-M portable satellite phone from Afghanistan from May 1996 until 1998, a phone registered in the name of al-Hada received 221 phone calls.[122] Nonetheless, the US intelligence community failed to act decisively and as a result Al Qaeda staged the USS *The Sullivans* and USS *Cole* attacks. Al Hada's son-in-law, Khalid al-Midhar, an Al Qaeda member, participated in two operations, including planning the USS *Cole* attack. He was also commander of the cell that hijacked the aircraft that crashed onto the Pentagon on 9/11. Another son-in-law of al-Hada was tasked to enter the US in late 2001/early 2002 by Al Qaeda to conduct a suicide operation together with a team of thirteen others. The plot was uncovered in mid-February 2002, but the second suicide squad remains undetected as of April 2002. Al-Hada also lost two of his sons fighting for Al Qaeda. One was killed in an explosion in Afghanistan and another blew himself up in Yemen in mid-February 2002 when the authorities came to arrest him.[123]

United Arab Emirates

Over the years, Al Qaeda has used the United Arab Emirates (UAE) as a major centre for its support operations and it was one of three countries to recognise the Taliban regime. After the Taliban captured Kabul and Osama moved to Afghanistan, there were as many as three to four flights a day from Sharjah to Kandahar, via the national airline, Ariana, and charter flights.[124] Among the air cargo, according to Dr Ravan Farhadi, the Afghan permanent representative to the UN, were chemicals and poisons. Citing Afghan and American intelligence reports, Farhadi said cyanide and other toxic substances purchased in Germany, the Czech Republic and Ukraine were "channelled through the United Arab Emirates" and flown out of Sharjah on Ariana cargo runs to Kandahar.[125]

The UAE has also been a major centre for Al Qaeda's financial operations, and it is now well known that most of the funds wired to America before the 9/11 attacks was sent from there. Furthermore Al Barakaat, the Somali bank and remittance facilitator, was based in Dubai. According to US officials, Al Qaeda skimmed off an estimated $25 million a year in handling and money-exchange fees from that bank.[126] The bank, which has strongly protested its innocence, claims it was unaware of such interference by Al Qaeda. Although a number of committed Al Qaeda supporters are based in the UAE, the government has fully cooperated with Washington since September 2001.

Libya

Libya under Gaddafi became the first country in the world to issue a warrant against Osama bin Laden. For the murder of Silvan Becker and his wife, two German nationals, in Surt, Libya by Al Qaeda's Libyan members on March 10, 1994, the judicial authorities of Libya filed a request for the extradition of Osama from any country except Israel. In response to Libya's request dated March 16, 1998, Interpol issued a red notice on Osama and three of his accomplices for murder and possession of illegal firearms. His accomplices were named as al-Chalabi Faraj, born in 1966; al-Warfali Faez Abu Zeid Muftah, born in 1968; and al-Alwan Faraj Mikhail Abdul-Fadeel Jibril, born in 1969.[127] According to the German secret service, Becker was their Arabist and his untimely death gravely affected Germany's ability to effectively monitor the growing Al Qaeda infrastructure in Germany. As the request for Osama's arrest came from Interpol's Tripoli branch, other governments did not take it seriously. The group responsible for the murder of the Germans was al-Jama al-Islamiya al-Muqatila, popularly known as the Libyan Islamic Fighting Group, of which several hundred Libyans who fought against the Soviets in the 1980s were part. In addition to conducting sporadic attacks against the Gaddafi regime they also attempted to assassinate the Libyan leader, sometimes with the help of Western intelligence agencies. The Libyan Islamic Fighting Group, with an office in the UK, was working closely with Al Qaeda, of which it is an associate group. It has been designated as such by the US authorities in the wake of 9/11.

Saudi Arabia

Unlike in Egypt, Algeria and Yemen, no well-defined group engaged in sustained terrorism has emerged in Saudi Arabia. Nonetheless, fifteen of the nineteen 9/11 hijackers were Saudis, demonstrating an overwhelming antipathy towards the Saudi royal family, especially among Saudi exiles. Although it was and is difficult to conduct operations inside such a tightly policed state as Saudi Arabia, Al Qaeda has created a large support base there. By establishing small cells it inspired and supported Saudi Islamists to conduct several small-scale operations and one major attack against American targets to date. A large amount of anti-royal propaganda is also smuggled in and disseminated by Al Qaeda.

On the northern perimeter of the King Abdul Aziz airbase, Khobar Towers, Dhahran, a truck bomb exploded, killing nineteen US servicemen and injuring several hundred on June 25, 1996. The facility housed both US and allied forces engaged in Operation Southern Watch, the air coalition over Iraq. The Canadian authorities arrested Hani Abdel Rahim al-Sayegy, a suspect in the bombing, in March 1997, extradited him to the United States, who in turn extradited him to Saudi Arabia, where he remains in custody. On May 22, 1998, however, Saudi officials concluded that an indigenous group was responsible for the attack. Although Al Qaeda's involvement was suspected, today the Saudi security services attribute it to Saudi Hezbollah, an Iranian-supported Shia group.

In November 1996 a massive car bomb caused extensive damage to the Office of the Programme Manager, Saudi Arabian National Guard (OPM/SANG) in al-Olaia, Riyadh. The Saudi security service apprehended four terrorists who were subsequently beheaded. Before being convicted by the Saudi regime, they claimed that they were inspired by Osama's writings. All were Saudi nationals, three of whom had fought in Afghanistan and one in Bosnia. They were also in receipt of pamphlets and faxes from the Advice and Reformation Committee in London. Of the explosion's seven victims, four were Americans, while forty-two were injured in the bombing of the American-run training school. In keeping with its policy, it is very likely that Al Qaeda concealed its role in this operation. After the bombing, the Saudis successfully sought the extradition from Pakistan of Hassan As-Sarehi, the mastermind of the Lion's Den Operation in 1987. Al Qaeda's role is further substantiated by the provision of both training and explosives to the Saudi terrorists and its close relationship with both the Lebanese Hezbollah and Iran.

By June 1998 US federal agencies complained that the enquiry into the bombing of its military facilities had reached an impasse and withdrew, leaving behind only one field officer in Saudi Arabia. Clearly the Saudi regime did not want to credit Osama with the attack, boosting his reputation even further, and hence chose not to share its findings with the Americans. The two bombings, Osama said, were aimed at dislodging the "US occupation" of Saudi Arabia. Calling the perpetrators "heroes", he added that he had great respect for those who committed the acts. "I also say that what they did is a great job and a big honor that I missed participating in."[128] Al Qaeda had no special expertise in bombing big buildings and had turned to Hezbollah for assistance, receiving help from the Lebanese group and its Iranian backers. Al Qaeda's base in Sudan provided training and explosives and transported the attack team to Saudi Arabia.

Al Qaeda raises most of its funding from Saudi Arabia via investments and charities, with various individuals donating an estimated $1.6 million a day to Islamic causes.[129] Even a fraction of this sum would underwrite its budget in the region. As Colonel Gaddafi told the Americans in the wake of 9/11, "if you want to combat terrorism, bomb London and Riyadh." For once Gaddafi was right; London was the unwitting host to several Islamist terrorist groups, and Saudi Arabia was tacitly providing the finance. Contrary to media speculation, there is no direct financial link between the Saudi Bin Laden Group, a huge family business, and Al Qaeda.[130] Several investigations by the US, French, Swiss and British governments have failed to unearth any proof that one supports the other.

The only relation of Osama's who worked with Al Qaeda was his brother-in-law, Muhammad Jamal Khalifa, a Saudi national of Jordanian origin. Born in Medina on November 3, 1956, Khalifa served in Pakistan and Afghanistan during the anti-Soviet campaign.[131] Operating under the cover of an Islamic missionary, he travelled worldwide advancing Al Qaeda's aims and objectives. Since 1988, the year Al Qaeda was founded, he has used the Philippines as a base, serving as director of the Philippines branch of the International Islamic Relief Organisation.[132] As a reputable worldwide organisation providing relief for Islamic causes, IIRO unwittingly provided Khalifa with the perfect cover to develop Al Qaeda's NGO network. On the pretext of offering humanitarian assistance, he attracted vast legitimate donations, especially from the Gulf, but in reality the funds raised assisted both humanitarian and terrorist projects. Most NGOs in Khalifa's well-entrenched network, some of which enjoyed charitable status, were purpose-built to funnel funds for terrorism. His operations in the Philippines, where he spent many years, are well documented.[133] According to the Philippines police and intelligence community, after incorporating International Relief and Information Centre (IRIC) in the Philippines as a parent organisation on June 28, 1994, Khalifa founded, bought or linked the following organisations to it without there being aware of what was happening:

Islamic Presentation Committee (IPC);
Islamic Studies, Call and Guidance (ISCAG);
Islamic World Committee Foundation (IWCF), incorporated in September 1993;
Islamic World Wisdom Worldwide Mission (IWWWM) incorporated in September 1994;
International Islamic Efforts of the Philippines (IIEP), based in Davao City and incorporated in March 1993;
Darul Ehsan Orphanage and Hifsul Qur'an Centre (DEHQC), based in Davao City and incorporated in February 1993;
Islamic Da'wah Council of the Philippines (IDCP), incorporated in October 1989;
Islamic Da'wah and Guidance International (IDGI), incorporated in March 1994; and
Daw'l Imam Al-Shafee (DIAS), based in Zamboanga City and incorporated in March 1994.[134]

Khalifa and his trusted accomplices incorporated these affiliates into IRIC. For instance he, his wife Yabo and two of his colleagues incorporated DIAS. In addition to receiving funds from IIRO, the Muslim World League in Rabita and Al Qaeda channelled money to Khalifa. Among the NGOs associated with him were Jamiat al-Makhudum al-Islamiah (now known as Islamic Institute of the Philippines) in Zamboanga City, Lanao Del Notre Islamic Foundation and Guidance Centre in Iligan City, and the Organisation of Islamic Efforts in Marawi City. Khalifa was owner or part owner of Benevolence International Corporation, Jobs Worldwide, Inc., E.T. Dizon Travel, Dizon Realty and Khalifa Trading Industries. He also shipped goods between Malaysia, the Philippines, the Netherlands and Saudi Arabia, the revenues thus generated being diverted to fund Islamist projects.[135]

In June 1994 Khalifa left the Philippines but returned in October and opened a branch of the Muwafaq Foundation in Manila. Although he ceased to work for IIRO, Philippines, he maintained relations with its staff, mostly Hamas members, including its coordinator in the Philippines.[136] In the late 1990s Khalifa spent time in Saudi Arabia, where he was kept under surveillance. As he enjoyed the patronage of several prominent figures in the Philippines he thought the government would not obstruct his plan to return there.

A Philippines police report also revealed that, in addition to maintaining contact with Ibrahim Mata, the head of Islamic Studies, Call and Guidance (ISCAG), Khalifa remained in touch with Jack M. Jikiri, President, Philippine Al-Amin Society, Inc., and with two Iraqis, Dr Majeed M. Faizal and Abdul Salam Zubair, both of whom were working for Khalifa Trading Industries in Metro Manila.[137] Khalifa continued to maintain a relationship with ASG and MILF leaders and Abdul Raneim al-Taihi, the suspect in the bombing of San Pedro Cathedral, Davao City, in December 1993. Khalifa also supported Sabab in the Philippines, a chapter of the International Muslim Brotherhood. After 9/11, he was arrested by the Saudi government but subsequently released.

Iran, Lebanon, Hezbollah

Another previously undisclosed fact about Al Qaeda concerns the ties it forged with both Iran and Lebanon as well as with Hezbollah, the feared and resourceful resistance movement of Lebanese Shias supported by these two states and Syria. In addition to uniting the two most powerful Egyptian terrorist groups, Osama's other achievement was to forge a working relationship between Shia and Sunni terrorist groups in keeping with his goal-oriented rather than rule-oriented doctrine. By virtue of this strategic partnership, he united the Middle East's two most dangerous terrorist groups, Al Qaeda and Hezbollah; the latter had long been regarded as the region's most technically advanced outfit, one that Hamas, Palestinian Islamic Jihad and the GIA sought to emulate. Iran received nearly 10% of Osama's outgoing calls from Afghanistan from mid 1996 to 1998, suggesting that Iran was maintaining a relationship with Al Qaeda even after he developed close ties with the Taliban in Afghanistan, a regime unfriendly towards Tehran.

Osama was closely supported in this enterprise by Mamdouh Mahmud Salim, Abu Fadhl al-Makkee and Abu Fadhl al-Iraqi, who persuaded other Al Qaeda members of the need to overcome sectarianism. According to the US court record, Osama was living in Khartoum when the renowned Sudanese religious scholar Ahmed Abdel Rahman Hamadabi brought with him to meet the Al Qaeda leadership Sheikh Nomani, representing the Iranian Shias, who occupied an Iranian government-maintained office in Khartoum, and had access to the highest echelons of power in Tehran. This meeting, chaired by Osama, was the first in a series between Al Qaeda and Iran on the one hand and Hezbollah on the other. Al Qaeda was keen to invest time and effort in the relationship from a technical point of view too. As mentioned above it had difficulties bombing big buildings, having failed in February 1993 in its plan to collapse one tower of the World Trade Centre on to the other, which it hoped would result in an estimated 250,000 casualties. Within a few weeks of the Khartoum meeting, however, Iran consulted Hezbollah and Al Qaeda was invited to send a contingent to Lebanon. The Al Qaeda team included Abu Talha al-Sudani, Saif al-Islam el-Masry, Salem el-Masry, Saif al-Adel and other trainers, including Abu Jaffer el-Masry, the explosives expert who ran the Jihad Wal camp in Afghanistan. In addition to developing this capability with Iranian assistance, Al Qaeda also received a large amount of explosives from Iran that were used in the bombing of the East African targets. The training team brought Hezbollah training and propaganda videos with the intention of passing on their knowledge to other Al Qaeda members and Islamist groups.

The cooperation did not end with Al Qaeda members receiving training in Lebanon. According to the testimony of Ali Muhammad before the court of the Southern District of New York on October 20, 2000, he set up a meeting between Osama and the Hezbollah leadership, represented by Imad Mughniyeh, Hezbollah's best known expert in security, formerly a specialist with the PLO's élite Force 17 as well as its Islamic wing — Khomeini's Fatah Islamites. He joined Hezbollah as a bodyguard to its spiritual leader Sheikh Fadlalah and later became head of external operations.[138] He is credited with the operation that forced the withdrawal of the US-led Multinational Forces (MNF) that came to oversee the evacuation of the PLO from Beirut in August 1982. Mughniyeh is suspected of having planned and supervised the simultaneous suicide bombing of both the US marine barracks and the French paratrooper HQ in Beirut on April 18, 1983. The Americans lost 241 Marines, their heaviest military defeat since Vietnam. Twenty seconds later a second suicide truck hit the paratrooper HQ 4 miles away, killing 58 soldiers, France's highest military loss of life since the Algerian war. Mughniyeh had also planned simultaneously to destroy the Italian HQ but the Italian troops were billetted in tents, not in a building, thereby nullifying the purpose of a suicide attack.[139] In response to this appalling loss of life the multinational peacekeeping force withdrew from Lebanon.

It was Mughniyeh who inspired Osama to develop coordinated, simultaneous attacks as a regular *modus operandi*, and this has been the hallmark of most subsequent Al Qaeda operations, including 9/11 and the East Africa bombings. The CIA's nightmare was that Osama, the leading Sunni terrorist, and Mughniyeh, the leading Shia terrorist, would combine their forces. Mughniyeh, who was especially close to the Iranians, helped Al Qaeda to develop its agent-handling systems, having specialised in conducting long-range operations — including the suicide bombing of the Jewish community centre and the Israeli consulate in

Buenos Aires in 1992 and 1994 respectively. Both Hezbollah trainers and experts from Iran's Ministry of Information and Security trained Al Qaeda fighters in Sudan (in existing Al Qaeda facilities), Lebanon (in Hezbollah camps) and Iran (in officially run bases).[140] Thereafter Al Qaeda's *modus operandi* came to resemble closely that of Hezbollah. The latter kept the Marine barracks in Beirut under surveillance for months,[141] while Al Qaeda learned in some cases to keep its targets under surveillance. for years before mounting an attack. Although they came from two different traditions, the motivation of the Hezbollah suicide bomber was little different from that of his Al Qaeda counterpart. After a final briefing and blessings, the Hezbollah bomber

> ...knew from all the preachings and talks he had received that the instant he died he would be met by Hour al-Ayn, a nymph of unimaginable beauty and serenity. She would tend to his wounds, wipe away the blood and escort him to heaven. He would die the most sublime death of martyrdom, and paradise was certainly his reward.[142]

Similarly, Hezbollah constantly denied responsibility for bombing the US Marine barracks and French paratroop HQ in 1983. Although the US was privy to Hezbollah-Al Qaeda cooperation as far back as late 1998, it did not take decisive steps to criminalise the Hezbollah leadership, even though the group had killed and kidnapped many Americans. This was interpreted by Hezbollah as a sign of weakness, prompting it and Al Qaeda to think they could attack the USA with impunity. This feeling was reinforced by their realisation that, after the debacle in Somalia, American politicians were loathe to risk the lives of their armed forces by deploying them in high-risk overseas operations. It was only a month after the September 11 bombings that the FBI placed Mughniyeh, now thought to be living in Iran, on its list of twenty-two persons designated as "wanted terrorists leaders". Despite Iran having been responsible for the deaths of over 1,500 Americans and being the world's most active state sponsor of terrorism,[143] the US has failed to bring key leaders such as Mughniyeh to justice. US intelligence suffered two major losses that depleted their strategic capability in the Middle East: the CIA's Beirut station chief, Robert Armes, was killed in the Embassy bombing of April 23, 1983, while William Buckley was kidnapped in March 1994 and killed soon afterwards. Moreover the Iranian intelligence services shielded Hezbollah from US intelligence penetration.Mughniyeh operated for Hezbollah and Iran, depending on either's political or security interests at the time.[144]

The Hezbollah-Al Qaeda relationship was a strategic partnership, indicative of a major shift in terrorist thinking. Throughout the 1990s, ethnonationalist Muslim groups were supplanted by, or fell under the influence of, Islamist groups, thereby paving the way for further ideological tolerance and inter-group cohesion as a means of confronting a common enemy. This interesting development was not confined to the Middle East: Shia and Sunni groups also cooperated in Asia, the first signs of this being seen in links between Hezbollah and Al Qaeda associate groups such as the Moro Islamic Liberation Front (MILF), which facilitated and supported Hezbollah's operations in the Asia-Pacific in the late 1990s. The disruption of a Hezbollah cell in Singapore in 1998 and arrest of Hezbollah operatives in 1999 and 2000 in the Philippines is compelling evidence of this new cooperation. The arrest of Pandu Yudhawinata, an Indonesian Hezbollah operative, at Manila's domestic airport was a direct result of monitoring the MILF liaison officer Abdul Nasser Nooh's communication with Islamic charities connected with Hezbollah in the Philippines. Furthermore, Hezbollah's plans to recruit Malaysians and Indonesians to conduct terrorist attacks in Australia and Israel have been detected. Trilateral cooperation between the US, Israel and the Philippines, also led to the arrest of the Malaysian-based Hezbollah leader, Hisham (*alias* Jaafar), who was planning terrorist attacks in South East Asia.

Hezbollah and Al Qaeda networks in South East Asia also use the same NGO infrastructure to advance their aims and objectives. Legitimate international Islamic organisations, including charities funded by respectable governments, were penetrated and exploited by Al Qaeda and Hezbollah via the MILF to advance their objectives. Abdul Nasser Nooh, based in Makati City, Manila, facilitated Al Qaeda and Hezbollah operations. He worked with the Philippines-based Muslim World League (MWL), International Islamic Relief Organisation (IIRO), Darul Hijra Foundation (DHF), International Islamic Conference (IIC) and other international Islamic organisations. Through him both Al Qaeda and Hezbollah infiltrated unwitting domestic Islamic non-governmental organisation such as the Islamic Dawah Council of the Philippines (IDCP), whose purpose was to propagate Islamic principles and knowledge.

Iraq

Iraq is a secular regime. Although its intelligence agencies have aided Islamist terrorist groups that target Western interests, there is no evidenc to indicate that Iraq has supported Al Qaeda. Iraq's support for Islamist and other, secular, terrorists as well as criminal organisations increased during and after the Gulf War. Through their various intelligence agencies, using diplomatic facilities such as the DPL mailbag, they moved money, arms, ammunition and explosives to countries ranging from Thailand to the Philippines and Sri Lanka with the intention of attacking US and allied targets. It is believed that Osama approached the Iraqi government twice, in Turkey and in Egypt, before Baghdad responded. Although it was suspected that meetings between Al Qaeda and Iraqi intelligence operatives took place in Prague (between Muhammad Atta and Ahmad Ibrahim Samir al-Ani, a veteran espionage practitioner, who operated under diplomatic cover), this has now been denied by the Czech authorities. Atta's last departure point for the US before 9/11 was Prague, which he left on June 3, 2000. After failing to enter the Czech Republic through Prague's Ruzyne airport on May 30, 2000, due to inadequate documentation, he entered by bus, this time with correct papers, on June 2.[145] A year later, in June 2001, the Czechs expelled al-Ani for keeping in regular contact and perhaps sponsoring Islamists planning to blow up the Prague headquarters of Radio Free Europe/Radio Liberty.

Unlike the Iranian-Al Qaeda relationship, the extent of Iraqi-Al Qaeda cooperation is purely a matter of speculation and as of March 2002 there is no evidence to link Iraq either to 9/11 or to the anthrax attacks in the United States

Israel/The Occupied Territories

Al Qaeda has forged ties with Hamas and Palestinian Islamic Jihad, given the many Palestinians who went to Afghanistan and rose to important positions in the organisation. While Azzam was neither a member of Fatah or Hamas, he funded the latter during its formative years. However, according to a leading specialist on Al Qaeda, Palestinian groups were reluctant to cooperate with Al Qaeda because of its habit of absorbing any organisation that "gets too close to it".[146] He added: "Look at how the Egyptian groups were absorbed and Osama gained virtual control of them."[147] There are several charities based in Sudan and Pakistan which are close to Al Qaeda that also fund Hamas and Palestinian Islamic Jihad. For example, the intelligence community has monitored one such charity in Islamabad in order to determine whether funds were being transferred from it to Hamas.[148]

The Israeli security and intelligence services — Shin Bet and Mossad — believe that Al Qaeda has infiltrated the Occupied Territories and that it is only a matter of time before it mounts an operation against Israel.[149] A number of Palestinians, mostly from Jordan (including, untill his detention in March 2002, its chief of operations, Abu Zubaydah), serve in Al Qaeda, and records seized in Afghanistan in late 2001 reveal that it has been training Palestinians till very recently. However, up till now only Hindawi, a Palestinian whose family comes from Halhul, and Nabil Ukal, a 27 year-old Palestinian from the Jabaliya refugee camp in the Gaza Strip, have been arrested on suspicion of being members of Al

Qaeda. Hindawi, allegedly trained by Al Qaeda in the Durante camp in 1998, was recruited when he was living in Lebanon. At the time of his arrest in February 2000, his father was the chief of police of the Palestinian Authority in Hebron.[150] While trying to recruit members for his cell, Ukal was detained in Rafah in the southern Gaza Strip on June 1, 2000. Investigations revealed that he had gone to Pakistan in October 1997 for a course in religious study but was recruited by an Al Qaeda associate group there and trained in Afghanistan. Ukal's Al Qaeda agent-handler asked him to establish a support infrastructure via recruitment, including of Israeli Arabs.[151] Upon his return to the Gaza Strip in 1998, Al Qaeda handlers in Jordan and Britain kept in touch with him by email.[152] Ukal also met the spiritual leader of Hamas, Sheikh Ahmed Yassin.[153] Ukal was indicted by the military court at the Erez Crossing in the Gaza Strip and charged with "planning a large-scale attack in the center of the country, recruiting suicide bombers, and planning attacks on Israel Defence Forces soldiers."[154]

These arrests did not deter Al Qaeda. Instead of infiltrating an operative from the Occupied Territories into Israel, Al Qaeda dispatched Richard Reid, the "shoe bomber", to Tel Aviv to reconnoitre targets with the intention of striking inside Israel. From July to December 2001, his travel schedule included London, Amsterdam, Tel Aviv, Cairo, Pakistan, Afghanistan, Amsterdam, Brussels and Paris.[155] His visit to Israel was exposed by accident when, in January 2002, *Wall Street Journal* reporters purchased a computer in Kabul containing several thousand files, one of which referred to various journeys by Abdul Ra'uff, Al Qaeda's *alias* for Reid. The explosive he used also links him to cooperation with Palestinian groups: each of his shoes contained 4oz. of Pentaerythritol Tetranitrate (PETN) and Triacetone Triperoxide (TATP),[156] the latter being an explosive used extensively by Palestinian Islamic Jihad/Hamas.[157]

Africa

About one third of Africa's 700 million inhabitants are Muslim, and Islamists see Black Africa as their newest theatre. Apart from North Africa, Al Qaeda's influence in the continent is primarily concentrated in East Africa. Abul Bara' Hassan Salman, Deputy Emir, Jamaat-e-Jihad Eritrea (Eritrean Islamic Jihad Movement), an Al Qaeda associate group, expressed Islamist thinking about the strategic relevance of the Horn:

> Politically, the African Horn refers to all the countries of East Africa. It includes Somalia, Djibouti, Eritrea, Ethiopia, and Kenya. The area is of particular strategic importance as it links the East with the West through the Red Sea, that is between the agrarian and industrial societies. The region is also an oil producer and has great mineral deposits in the Red Sea. The Horn's strategic security sig-

nificance increased since the establishment of a Jewish nation in Palestine. These catalysts, along with some others, made the region a highly sought-after place particularly by the colonialists and imperialists, both past and at present.[158]

While in Khartoum, Osama reportedly developed a close working relationship with Sheikh Arafa, the leader of the political wing of the Eritrean Islamic Jihad Movement, who was living in a guesthouse in Khartoum. In the by now familiar pattern, Al Qaeda went on to train several hundred of the Movement's members in its Sudanese and Afghan camps and provided money to further the group's operations against the Eritrean government; while in Sudan, Al Qaeda donated $100,000 specifically to improve its military activities. For liaison between the two groups the Eritrean Islamic Jihad Movement appointed Muhammad al-Kheir, one of its leaders who was close to Abu Ubadiah al-Banshiri. Within Al Qaeda, the Eritrean Islamic Jihad Movement is also known as Jamal Jihad. Islamists in the region believe strongly that the Horn of Africa is facing a furious Christian onslaught, and Al Qaeda's response to events in Yemen, Somalia, Kenya and Tanzania is triggered by this perception. Abul Bara' Hassan Salman adds:

"As for the latest Christian onslaught being led by America, its scenario is being executed by the puppet regimes in the region. This onslaught is also an attempt to impose the sovereignty of the Christian minorities in the region in order to ascertain the strategic security and economic needs of the imperialists. As a result, and following the fall of the Mengistu regime in Ethiopia and the Siyad Barre regime in Somalia, notwithstanding that these regimes followed the Eastern bloc, America arranged the scene in the following manner: (a) Giving the rule to two Christian rebel groups in both Eritrea and Ethiopia; (b) Splintering of Somalia and inciting tribal wars therein in order to create the opportunity for both Eritrea and Ethiopia to take advantage of the battles to fulfil their own designs in the absence of the Islamic balance in the African Horn, which Somalia represents in one respect; (c) declaration of economic and diplomatic siege along with media misinformation about Sudan so that the balance can break up completely in all the extremities in the region."[159]

The Horn of Africa and the Red Sea, regarded by the Islamists as 'their' regions, are likely to witness increased activity in coming years as Islamists seek to counter external influences.

The catalyst for the five-fold Islamist strategy is (a) the effective effort on the part of the Islamic jihad and da'wa tides in the African Horn; (b) the education of the Muslim population and their awareness of the extent of the conspiracy and plotting of the Christians both regionally and internationally; (c) the possibility of establishing a Somalian government capable of maintaining a political balance; (d) the alertness of some of the Arabic countries to the danger of the Jewish presence in the region — this will help to review their position with respect to providing support to the people of the region; and (e) the efforts of the Palestinian jihad will also Insha'Allah play a role in upsetting the security of the Jewish government and to confine its external influence.[160]

The NIF supported nearly a dozen Eritrean Islamist and other opposition forces beginning in the 1990s, including the Eritrean Islamic Jihad Movement, Eritrean Liberation Front, Eritrea Kunama Movement and the Red Sea Democratic Organisation. In retaliation, Asmara severed diplomatic relations with Khartoum and permitted the Sudanese opposition, the National Democratic Alliance, to open an office in the former Sudanese embassy in Asmara. Al Qaeda also sought to establish links with other African Islamist political parties and armed groups, especially in 1992-6. The plight of the Muslims of the Ogaden, an area situated southeast of Ethiopia, with Kenya to the south, Somalia to the east, and Djibouti to the north, came to the attention of Osama soon after he established himself in Khartoum in December 1991. It is an exclusively Muslim area with a long history of hostility to outsiders, where Arabic and Somali are spoken. Because it is a lawless zone beyond the reach of government agencies Al Qaeda was quick to establish a presence there. Al Qaeda operatives made several visits to Ogaden and met representatives of Jama'at-ul I'tisam Bilkitab Wassuna (Islamic Union of the Mujahideen of Ogaden). Since the Ethiopian army conducted operations there in 1992, 1993 and 1995, the people of Ogaden have increasingly looked to Islamism to defend themselves. To mobilise the local population, the Islamic Union of the Mujahideen of Ogaden claimed that the US and Israel were behind the Ethiopian government attacks:

[In 1994] the Ethiopian Christian government requested other Christian countries to interfere militarily in Ogaden, and to attempt to completely wipe out the mujahideen. So America and Eritrea became directly involved in the battle. [...] This stage saw the American jets take off from the Indian Ocean bombing the mujahideen positions for hours at a time, whilst the Eritrean soldiers were firing their fixed cannons and tanks at the domicile of the mujahideen.[161] [...] We planned to use the militia war strategy and to avoid large-scale confrontations with the enemy, particularly as the Ethiopian forces along with their American and Israeli allies had staged a broad attack on the *mujahidin* both through land and sea during 1994. [...] There are also hundreds of American and Israeli experts who are training the Ethiopian army in all aspects.[162]

Although Al Qaeda had no hand in establishing the Islamic Union of the Mujahideen of Ogaden, it supported the group, which is today largely based in Western Somalia. Gradually the *mujahidin*'s capabilities increased and they even struck in the Ethiopian capital, Addis Ababa. On July 8,

1996, they attempted to assassinate both the transportation minister and Abdul Majeed Hassan, the Ethiopian government's representative in the Ogaden.[163] In mid-1997, the various Islamist groups formed a five-member alliance — Oromo-Somali-Afar Liberation Alliance (OSALA) — also the Islamic Union of the Mujahideen of Ogaden — which brought together the Islamist groups of Somalia, Western Somalia, and Ethiopia. Its stated aim was to "replace the present minority rule with a government of the majority, putting an end to centuries of Christian domination and Judaeo-Christian ideological hegemony."[164] The OSALA chairman, Bushra Hussein, added: "since the majority of the people in this region are Muslim, the future constitution must draw heavily from the tenets of Islam."[165] The success of these groups has been limited, however, because they are largely tribal in structure and as such there is little prospect of long-term unity.

As well as supporting these Islamist groups, Al Qaeda fostered cooperation between them. The closest to Al Qaeda is the Eritrean Islamic Jihad Movement, through which the former spearheaded its unification attempts:

> The external front...is a very sensitive front from the aspect of our strategic security. In this respect we (a) liaise and exchange our experience and expertise with other Muslim organisations which also work to challenge the various corrupt regimes in the region; (b) concentrate our activities amongst Muslims through means which will enable them to see the conspiracies of the enemies and their plots to uproot Islam and Muslims; (c) strive to generate suitable opportunities to support our jihad through Islamic means; (d) move around neighbouring countries and expose the corruption of the Eritrean regime and its danger over the entire region on the religious, security and political fronts.[166]

Somalia, a "failed state", has no official government and is divided into three parts, each "ruled" by local warlords. Despite denials from Somali political leaders, Al Qaeda has been transporting men and material through its vast, unguarded coastline for many years. It was also suspected that Al Qaeda had established an operational base on the remote island of Ras Komboni. Reports that Somalia might offer a hiding place for Osama prompted the American government to consider searching for Al Qaeda bases there in the wake of 9/11.

As the Islamist vanguard it was incumbent on Al Qaeda to manifest Muslim displeasure at the US intervention in the Horn of Africa. Beginning in early 1992 Al Qaeda established a network in Somalia. Al Qaeda's then deputy Emir for military operations, Muhammad Atef, was entrusted with the mission, and frequently visited Somalia in 1992 and 1993. In early 1993 Al Qaeda's chief instructor, Ali Muhammad, came to train the attack team drawn from al-Itihaad al-Islamiya (Islamic Unity), formerly known as the Muslim Brotherhood, an associate group of Al Qaeda. On October 3-4, Al Qaeda-trained al-Itihaad al-Islamiya fighters attacked US forces in Mogadishu, killing eighteen US personnel. The blame focused on General Muhammad Farah Aideed, but Osama was in fact behind this key operation. Although the world's attention was drawn to the deaths of American soldiers and the subsequent humiliating US withdrawal, Al Qaeda-trained Somalis killed Belgian and Pakistani peacekeepers too. On the Somalia operation, referring to Osama's role in the attacks, the CIA later stated: "Information from our sources confirms his involvement."[167]

According to Indian intelligence interrogation of Maulana Masood Azhar, the then general secretary of Harkat-ul-Ansar, now head of Jayash-e-Muhammad (both Al Qaeda associate groups in Pakistan), a number of Arab *mujahidin* who trained and fought in Afghanistan moved to Somalia. In the early 1990s international concern at *muhajidin* involvement in terrorism forced Pakistan to expel many foreign fighters from its soil. As Arab countries were hardly keen to accept them, some 400 went to Sudan and thereafter to Somalia, where they joined al-Itihaad al-Islamiya in 1993. Some of their number kept in touch with Azhar and with Maulana Fazal-ur-Rehman, leader of Harkat-ul-Mujahidin, another Al Qaeda associate group in Pakistan. As Azhar explained:

> The Pakistani troops under the UN have been placed at central trouble spots, while Indian troops were placed near borders where mostly the non-Muslim populations lived. This placed the Pakistani troops in vulnerable positions guarding the life and property of Americans. When an American vehicle moved, it was guarded by the Pakistanis. The muhajidin wanted to engage the Americans, the biggest enemies of Islam, but due to the presence of the Pakistani troops the mujahidin faced a dilemma. In the attack against Aideed's radio station, many Pakistan troops lost their lives. The Pakistanis who till now were the champions of Islam found the tide turned against them and found themselves unwelcomed.[168]

To increase the pressure on Pakistan to withdraw its contingent of UN-commanded troops from Somalia, Azhar published some of these letters in Arabic and in Urdu translation in *Sadah-e-Mujahid*, a magazine he had established in Karachi in 1991 at the request of Maulana Fazal-ur-Rehman. Furthermore, Masood Azhar visited Nairobi in December 1992 where he met al-Itihaad al-Islamiya leaders and two *mujahidin* from UAE who urged him to keep up the pressure on the Pakistani government. A week later, as agreed, Masood Azhar returned to Nairobi with journalists from *Weekly Zindagi*, *Jang* and *Urdu Digest* and a representative of the All Pakistan Newspaper Malikan Association.[169] On their return home the Pakistani press condemned the role of Pakistani troops in Somalia, and Masood Azhar printed 5,000 copies of a booklet on the same theme.

As of early 2002, al-Itihaad al-Islamiya had withdrawn from the ports of Merka and Kismayo and the inland center of L'uuq, which its 3,000 armed fighters had dominated, using it as a staging-post till the mid-1990s for sorties into Ethiopia and Kenya.[170] Ethiopian military intervention since August 1996 had in the mean time depleted its strength, but al-Itihaad al-Islamiya has established a presence in northeastern Somalia, operating from the semi-autonomous region known as Puntland. Through its port, Bosaso, al-Itihaad al-Islamiya is also reported to have sent volunteers to fight with Al Qaeda in Afghanistan.[171]

As mentioned above, the US government froze the funds of the Somali banking network, Al-Barakaat. Although Ahmed Nur Ali Jim'ale, the company's founder, denies links with Al Qaeda, US officials state that he is a "member of the kitchen cabinet" of Osama.[172] Jim'ale, a former Somali warlord, had long opposed the presence of American troops in his homeland.

Al Qaeda's role in expelling US troops from Somalia is acknowledged by local Islamists. Abu Yaser, a media spokesperson for the Islamic Union of Mujahidin in Ogaden was reported as saying: "The team of Shaykh Osama bin Laden had an effective role in repelling the American invaders from Somalia, that is because they participated in that battle with some explosives and in launching attacks against the army of the alliance."[173] On June 8, 1998, the US Attorney General indicted Osama for his role in training the tribesmen who killed eighteen US soldiers in Somalia in 1993. The indictment was sealed until a month after the East Africa bombings in 1998. The Al Qaeda team that trained the Somali Islamists for this operation escaped in a Cessna aircraft normally used for smuggling *qat*, a mildly narcotic leaf chewed by most Somali men.

Sudan

Sudan was Al Qaeda's home from December 1991 to May 1996, a base from which it could seek to extend its influence throughout Africa. Sudan's President Omar al-Beshir and the nation's spiritual leader Dr Hasan al-Turabi steadfastly supported Al Qaeda for many years before they were forced by international pressure, especially sanctions, to expel the group. Although Osama and his cohorts left on a chartered C-130 from Khartoum to Afghanistan on May 18, 1996, the links between the Sudanese regime and Osama continued and the disposition of the Sudanese government to Al Qaeda and Islamists remained unchanged. But in early 2001 the relationship between General Omar al-Beshir and Dr Hasan al-Turabi deteriorated; al-Beshir got wind of Turabi's plans to oust him and placed him under house arrest. Al-Beshir also secretly approached the Clinton administration with an offer to extradite Osama to the US, but his suggestion was spurned (after 9/11 Clinton admitted that the refusal to accept the offer was his biggest mistake). Seeing the writing on the wall, al-Beshir decided to cooperate fully with the Americans after the 9/11 attacks. From October 2001 he provided invaluable information to the CIA and European intelligence agencies on Al Qaeda. However the threat posed by Islamists has not diminished in the Sudan and is likely to re-surface from time to time. Parallels are often drawn between Osama and his Sudanese precursor, the Mahdi, who fought a *jihad* against the British in the late nineteenth century.

The information in the following section on Sudan was revealed in the course of the New York trial of those involved in the East Africa embassy bombings of 1998. When Al Qaeda's headquarters moved to Khartoum in late 1990, Osama was warmly received. With the connivance of the regime, Al Qaeda diversified its financial and terrorist network. Although its links with the political establishment are known, those with the Sudanese security and military organisations have not been widely discussed. To influence the state, Al Qaeda gradually infiltrated the intelligence organs of the Islamic party structure — Islamic Security (IS-SOR: external, ideological and strategic); Al Amn Al Sawri (AAS: internal and counter-intelligence) and the Militia People's Defence Force (PDF: internal) Internal Surveillance Wing. Al Qaeda also tried to infiltrate several ministries including the Interior and Security Ministry (Internal Security: AAD), the Ministry of Foreign Affairs (External Security Service: AKK); and the Ministry of Defence and Chief of General Staff (Ministry Intelligence Directorate). For instance, Jamal Fadl of Al Qaeda also worked for AAS, also known as the Delegation Office and the Revolutionary Security Service.

In addition to establishing state-of-the-art training infrastructure, official patronage enabled Al Qaeda to conduct CBRN weapons research and run a weapons shipping network in Sudan. Al Qaeda used the Hilat Koko military facility to test a container of uranium from South Africa purchased for $1.5 million in 1994. This was obtained, via high-ranking Sudanese official intermediaries, by Jamal Fadl, for which he received a $10,000 reward. At the Hilat Koko centre "viability tests for chemical artillery shells, apparently made from anti-riot paralysing agents," were carried out.[174] Based on a source close to Al Qaeda, Western intelligence agencies have reported that Al Qaeda's interest in building a so-called "dirty bomb" was precipitated by the Chechen *mujahidin*, who left a caesium-filled canister in a Moscow park in the hope of spreading harmful radiation. Osama also authorised research into instant contact poisons such as ricin,[175] one of those discussed in Al Qaeda training manuals recovered in Europe and Afghanistan.

Using Sudan as a transit point, Al Qaeda transferred weapons it procured from Russian and Ukrainian criminal gangs and from Iran to its associate groups. For example, a 60 metre freighter captained by Habib al-Pakistani and Abu Muhammad al-Yemeni shipped weapons from a protected quay in Port Sudan's armoured/mechanised infantry barracks to the Saif Islam Jannubi Movement in Saana, Yemen, and to Saudi Arabia to target US military facilities in 1993. The importance of Sudan was such that Al Qaeda's shipping network ceased to function after 1996 when the organisation moved to landlocked Afghanistan. However, Al Qaeda chartered vessels and used others belonging to at least one other terrorist group to transfer weapons and personnel to associate groups via Karachi Port.

Al Qaeda enjoyed the patronage of the Sudanese state until the rift between the Islamists (led by al-Turabi) and al-Beshir's military widened in the mid-1990s. It is very likely that elements in the military envisaged the disaster Osama would bring upon Sudan. Senior members of the regime, such as General Abdullah Hassan al-Hadi, head of internal security, and Lt.-General Bakri Hassan Salih, an aide to the President, were particularly mistrustful of Osama. But there were others in the military, some still serving, who furnished Al Qaeda with documents, supervised transfer of weapons to it, maintained the link to Iran and held advisory meetings with Al Qaeda members regarding tactics used against the Soviets in Afghanistan. The late Brigadier Ali Mukhtar Kamal, deputy head of military intelligence and later head of Islamic Relief in Jeddah, was a key Al Qaeda contact.

The funding the Islamist regime in Khartoum received from the Middle East, ranging from Saudi Arabia to Iran, was used to influence the socio-religious, cultural and political spheres not only in Sudan but also in the rest of Africa. Under the banner of Islam, Khartoum assisted Islamists in Kenya, Uganda, Tanzania, Somalia and Ethiopia. By early 1995, Iranian funding enabled the National Islamic Front and Al Qaeda to establish twenty-three training camps throughout Sudan. Although most were dismantled after Osama's departure to Afghanistan in May 1996, Sudanese Islamists maintained a dozen facilities for ideological and practical instruction. They included two camps for Arabs in Merkhiyat; one camp for Eritrean, Ethiopian, Ugandan, Somali and occasionally Palestinian Islamists in Al-Qutanynah; one camp for training Palestinian, Libyan, Iranian, Iraqi, Yemeni, Chinese and Fillipino Islamists in Jabel al-Awliya; one for training Egyptians, Algerians and Tunisians in Shendi, near Port Sudan; one for treating casualties in Soba; while one in Sejara near Omdurman controlled training throughout Sudan. There is evidence to indicate Sudanese government military facilities and instructors trained foreign Islamists even after Osama's departure. However, with the arrest of al-Turabi in 2001, all the camps were shut down.

Al Turabi's greatest contribution to Islamism was to bring together forty Islamist political parties and terrorist groups under the banner of the Popular Arab and Islamic Conference. During the day delegates gathered openly in the conference venue, talking politics and religion, while at night small groups got together privately to discuss how to wage war against the US, Israel and their allies. Osama attended some annual meetings of the PAIC, which were partially funded by Al Qaeda and on one occasion he was photographed with other delegates by a Western intelligence agency.

In retaliation for Khartoum's support for Egyptian Islamists, Cairo permitted the Sudanese opposition the National Democratic Alliance, to open an office and host a meeting in August 1998. In March 2000, Egypt re-established relations with Sudan, a relationship that had been gravely damaged by Khartoum's involvement with Al Qaeda.

Sub-Saharan Africa

Al Qaeda has also established links with a dozen or so Islamic parties and Islamist groups in Central and Southern Africa. While some of these are with key individuals, others are with political parties and terrorist groups. The CIA managed to thwart the Al Qaeda bombing of the US embassy in Kampala, Uganda, on September 18, 1998 and twenty suspects were arrested.[176] Al Qaeda's influence also extends to South Africa, where it is in touch with Islamists and criminal organisations and supported the violent anti-American protests at the US Embassy in Cape Town in May 1996. Two Islamist movements in the city, People Against Gangsterism and Drugs (PAGAD) and its associate, Qibla, have been designated by the US as terrorist organisations. PAGAD launched a bombing campaign in Cape Town in 1998 that included American targets. Al Qaeda's East Africa bomber, Khalfan Khamis Muhammad, was arrested in Cape Town in October 1999 and subsequently convicted and jailed for life.

Al Qaeda's most ambitious African operation was its coordinated attacks against the US Embassies in Nairobi and Dar es Salaam on August 7, 1998, which had been planned since 1994, when Al Qaeda first established a presence in Nairobi and Mombasa. Until his death, Abu Ubadiah al-Banshiri, and thereafter his deputy and successor, Muhammad Atef, spearheaded the operation together with Ali Muhammad. The latter surveyed the US embassy in Nairobi as a possible target, taking photographs and making reconnaissance sketches. When these were shown to Osama in Khartoum, he applied his knowledge of civil engineering to identify the path of entry of the explosives-laden vehicle into the embassy compound. The operation was originally planned for 1996 but was delayed on three counts. First, international sanctions imposed on Sudan shortly after Al Qaeda's attempted assassination of President Mubarak in Ethiopia in June 1995 precipitated intense domestic pressure on Al Qaeda from the Sudanese authorities, and Al Qaeda's investments, businesses and trade in Sudan suffered accordingly. With the threat of increased US military assistance to Khartoum's hostile neighbours looming, the Sudanese President Brigadier Omar al-Beshir put pressure on Al Qaeda to cease its military activities. Second, Abu Ubadiah al Banshiri's death was a major setback. And third, as international sanctions began to bite, the influence of Sudan's Islamist leader Dr Hasan al-Turabi, who was very close to Osama, diminished. As al-Beshir had earlier handed over the notorious international terrorist Ilich Ramirez Sanchez — known as Carlos the Jackal — to the French, Osama believed he was planning to arrest and extradite him to the US. When Osama got wind of this secret protocol he decided to leave for Afghanistan in May 1996. With this, Al Qaeda had to abandon Sudan, relocate its training infrastructure to Afghanistan and use Yemen as a launch-pad for future operations in East Africa.

Unlike the Somalia operation, the East Africa operation was a suicide mission and the attack teams comprised volunteers from Al Qaeda's Saudi and Egyptian families. They had either approached Osama personally or written to the Al Qaeda leader and made an explicit request to participate in a martyrdom operation. After arriving in Kenya the Al Qaeda members Fahid Muhammad, Ali Msalam and Sheik Ahmed Salim Swedan purchased a Toyota truck which they altered in order to position and transport their bomb. In early August 1998, the Al Qaeda team gathered in 43, New Runda Estates, Nairobi to execute the bombing of the U.S. Embassy in Nairobi. On August 7, 1998, Al Qaeda Saudi members Assam and Muhammad Rashed Daoud Al 'Owali, drove the explosives laden Toyota truck to the US embassy. Assam was the suicide bomber while his accomplice Al 'Owali was to protect him and the truck until it reached the target. Al'Owali, who was born in Liverpool, had been trained by Al Qaeda in explosives, hijacking, kidnapping, assassination and intelligence techniques and had fought alongside the Taliban against the Northern Alliance. He had met Osama in 1996 and asked to be selected for a martyrdom operation. As Assam drove the explosives-laden vehicle into the rear of the embassy, Al 'Owali, who also expected to perish, jumped out and threw a stun grenade at a security guard. The detonation of the truck demolished a multi-story secretarial college, severely damaged the U.S. embassy, and the co-operative bank building, and killed 213 people and injured 4,500. Although Assam was killed in the explosion, Al 'Owali somehow survived. Rather than commit suicide, which is forbidden in Islam, he decided to escape. Although he had no money, passport or escape plan, he phoned an Al Qaeda safe house in Yemen to have money transferred to him in Kenya. According to the British government: "The number he rang in Yemen was contacted by Osama bin Laden's phone on the same day as Al 'Owali was arranging to get the money".[177]

In Dar es Salaam at about the same time another Al-Qaeda suicide bomber struck the US embassy, killing eleven people. The bomb was carried in a Nissan Atlas truck, which Al Qaeda members Ahmed Khfaklan Ghailani and Sheikh Ahmed Salim Swedan had purchased in Dar es Salaam in July 1998. The operatives involved included Mustafa Muhammad Fadhil and Khaflan Khamis Muhammad. On their arrests, Khalfan Khamis Muhammad divulged his role and that of his accomplices. The death toll would have been higher had not security guards prevented the truck from entering the area immediately adjacent to the Embassy. Osama attributed the success of the operation to al-Banshiri. On 7 and 8 August 1998, the London based Advice and Reconciliation Committee faxed media organisations in Paris, Doha in Qatar, and Dubai in the UAE claiming responsibility for the attacks on behalf of Al Qaeda. Al Qaeda also filmed Al-'Owhali saying on camera that he was from the "Third Martyr Barracks First Squad of the El bara bin Malik division of the Army for Liberating the Islamic Holy Lands", although it did not release the video. British intelligence traced an ARC telephone number which had been in contact with Osama's satellite phone immediately before the attack. Demonstrating the close relationship between Al Qaeda's leadership and the ARC, Al Qaeda Afghanistan had provided the London office with information about the attack before it occurred. Because the Al Qaeda leadership assumed that Al'Owali would die in the operation, the press releases issued by the ARC claimed that two Saudis in Nairobi and one Egyptian in Dar es Salaam had perished in the bombings. Although a small minority of those killed and injured were Americans, many Islamists rejoiced at the attacks, claiming that collateral damage was inevitable. Al Qaeda tried to minimise the mounting worldwide criticism over the non-American deaths. Its front organisation, which used the *nom de guerre* of the Islamic Liberation Army of the People of Kenya, stated:

> Attack of the brigade of the martyr Khaled al-Saad was only aimed at the US. The Americans humiliate our people, they have occupied the Arabian Peninsular, they extract our richness, they enforce a blockade, and, in addition, they support the Israeli Jews, our arch enemies, who occupy the Al Aqsa mosque.[178]

This communiqué, dated August 11, 1998, further declared:

the attack was justified because the Government of Kenya admitted the Americans to have used their land to fight Muslim neighbours especially Somalia. Furthermore, Kenya collaborated with Israel. In this country you find the most anti-Islam Jewish centres in the whole of East Africa. From Kenya, the Americans supported the war of separation in Southern Sudan led by the fighters of John Garang.[179]

In an attempt to diffuse responsibility and further confuse public opinion, Al Qaeda issued another communiqué, on August 12, using another front organisation, the Islamic Liberation Army:

Because the Americans and the Jews occupy the surroundings of the Al Aqsa mosque, because of what the Jews do in Palestine such as destroy their homes, because one million Iraqis died and religious leaders in America and other countries are subservient to America, because of the fortunes gained by oil revenues that belong to the Muslims, we are forced to wage jihad anywhere in the world at any given moment. The fight against the US and its allies, the Jews of Israel, is a fight between life and death. Before the Nairobi bombing we warned Muslims not to visit anything that is American and we repeated this warning. We are forced to wage a jihad anywhere in the world at any given moment."[180]

The East African attacks wrecked the lives of thousands of Africans and many Americans. The US Foreign Service officer, Howard Kavaler, who lost his wife in the Nairobi bombing, alluded to the impact of the 9/11 attacks on those who had already suffered:

"For the past three years, two months and eleven days, I have had to live with recurring flashbacks of the bombing and my vain attempts to locate my wife's remains. The clouds of dust, the dangling wires, the invisible cries for help that were muffled by mounds of concrete and twisted steel are still front and center in my mind with a degree of clarity that has not attenuated with the passage of time. In fact, the carnage of the 11th of September has only served to exacerbate these nightmarish memories.[181]

Kavaler also described the impact of the bombing on his young family:

"There was no one to assist me as I comforted Maya, my eight-year-old daughter, who cried all night last spring because her mother would not be present the next day to hear her sing at a school talent show. Tara, my thirteen-year-old, went to her first coed party without the loving encouragement and maternal advice that only Prabhi could have provided. [...] You may recall that Tara wrote about her mother, and I quote: 'I miss the time we spent together, I miss that she loved me like no one else could, and I miss her helping me with things that were hard. My heart hurts everyday. I hope it will go away. A kid's heart shouldn't hurt every day. A kid shouldn't have to miss her mother every day.' As much as I try to be both a father and a mother, I will always, no matter how hard I try, come out more than a tad bit short in fulfilling the latter role. In fact, balancing the demands of working full-time as a Foreign Service Officer with the needs of my daughters became too overwhelming. In August, I retired [...] having decided to dedicate myself solely to ensuring my girls' welfare and happiness."[182]

Thirteen days after the East Africa bombings the US responded by attacking Al Qaeda infrastructure in Afghanistan and Sudan, the Americans securing from Pakistan the first news that Osama was alive. Half an hour after the attacks al-Zawahiri had phoned the Pakistani journalist Rahimullah Yusufzai saying Osama was "safe and sound".[183] Osama immediately suspected Pakistan's connivance in the attempt to kill him, though no evidence for this has emerged.

Immediately after the attacks, the US suspended diplomatic and business operations in some other African countries where Al Qaeda was known to have a presence: Somalia, Sudan, Congo, and Guinea-Bissau. Osama was thinking beyond his traditional African base, the Horn, wishing to make inroads among the Muslims of Central and West Africa. Plans were set in motion for further attacks against US embassies as a means of politicising and radicalising African Muslims, in the hope of provoking anti-Muslim backlashes in the countries concerned. However the National Security Agency's monitoring of satellite phone conversations between Afghanistan and sub-Saharan Africa alerted it to, and helped thwart, Al Qaeda's plans to bomb at least twelve US embassies, including the US mission in Abidjan, capital of the Ivory Coast. Since 9/11 the CIA has withdrawn some of its best operatives from Asia and elsewhere who are familiar with monitoring Islamist movements. They have now been deployed in many African countries where previously this issue was not regarded as a priority. There is also strong circumstantial evidence of the growing popularity of Osama and Al Qaeda in Northern Nigeria, a predominantly Muslim area, and other parts of West Africa's Sudanic belt. While in Sudan, Al Qaeda and the National Islamic Front (NIF) played an important role in supporting Ugandan Islamists directly and through NGOs. In 1994, Salafi Foundation of Uganda was supported by Al Qaeda/NIF to develop the Ugandan Mujahidin Freedom Fighters (UMFF). In addition to training in Juba, Nesitu, Jebellin in the south of Sudan, camps were established in Buseruka, Hoima, near Lake Albert. Sheikh Jamil moved to Kenya where he coordinated UMFF activities. By joining other opposition forces, UMFF evolved into the Allied Democratic Forces (ADF), which relocated to the Democratic Republic of Congo to challenge the Kampala government. After Al Qaeda moved to Afghanistan in 1996, handpicked ADF members were trained in Afghanistan as explosives experts. While Sudan supported the Lord's Resistance Army, Uganda aided the Sudanese People's Liberation Army. In 1995, when Uganda closed down the Sudanese embassy in Kampala, the Sudanese intelligence officers were transferred to Kenya to continue their work. Even after Osama's departure from Sudan, Khartoum supported the Ugandan Islamists including the West Nile Bank Front operating from Zaire along the Zaire-Ugandan border. According to a Canadian intelligence source, Al Qaeda planned to assassinate President Museveni and another African leader visiting Kampala in 1999.[184] Khartoum's support for Ugandan Islamists did not cease until the signing of a peace agreement between Sudan and Uganda in December 1999.

Al Qaeda and the NIF of Sudan also launched long term plans to penetrate Muslim communities in Sub-Saharan Africa by infiltrating NGOs. According to intelligence sources, "90% of the International Islamic NGOs operating in Uganda were either established or operated" by Arabs with funding from the Middle East.[185] Often the funders and managers of these NGOs in their parent countries did not know what was happening in the outreach offices. For instance, the Islamists in Sudan infiltrated, or attempted to infiltrate, in Uganda the Islamic African Relief Agency, Islamic Call Society, International Islamic Relief Organisation, Hassan Turabi Memorial School, Al Mutada al-Islamia, Concorp International Company (construction business), Africa Charitable Society for Mother and Child Care, Cof-Tea Company, Pan Africa Commodities, and the Gar Al Nabi Free School.[186] The Sudanese Islamists in Uganda also infiltrated the Justice Forum (JEEMA) of the former Presidential candidate Kibirige Mayanja. Another organisation, Munadhamat Al Dawa Al Islamia, also based in Nairobi, Kenya, was reportedly behind guerrrillas of the Allied Democratic Forces of Western Uganda in their attempt to destabilise the Museveni government.

Latin America

Considering Al Qaeda's robust infrastructure elsewhere in the world, it enjoys a rudimentary presence in Latin America. Communication and human intelligence coupled with the arrests of suspects since late 1998 suggest that it is active in the region. For nearly a decade, the presence of Hezbollah, Hamas, Islamic Group of Egypt and other Islamist groups have converged with organised crime groups in the triple-border area of Puerto Iguazu, Argentina; Foz do Iguazu, Brazil; and Ciudad del Este, Paraguay. Although Al Qaeda's regional network is supposed to be based in the triple border, no Latin American or other intelligence agency has yet presented concrete proof of an Al Qaeda presence.

The arrest and interrogation of an Afghanistan-trained member of the Islamic Group of Egypt in Uruguay on February 27, 1999 was the first suggestion of a possible Al Qaeda presence in the region. There have been further arrests up to early 2002. The Islamic Group of Egypt has merged with Al Qaeda at strategic, operational, and tactical levels and functions almost as one organisation. The five Egyptians are being investigated in connection with two attacks — a failed attempt to assassinate President Mubarak in Addis Ababa and the massacre of tourists in Luxor in 1997. Both these operations were mounted by Egyptian terrorists trained by Al Qaeda in Sudan and Afghanistan respectively. Al Qaeda's Egyptian members are also thought to be operating in Ecuador, one of them having been arrested and extradited to Egypt. Based on the Uruguay arrests and other intelligence, Argentinian intelligence submitted a report in 1999 confirming that "agents of the Al Qaeda organisation headed by Osama bin Laden had been identified in the triple border area."[187] An official Argentine report added that Muslims politicised and radicalised by Hezbollah were providing finance to Al Qaeda.[188] On April 6, 2001, the US closed its diplomatic missions in Paraguay, Uruguay and Ecuador following intelligence that an Al Qaeda attack was likely.

Latin America has suffered for many years from high levels of domestic and international terrorism. Argentina witnessed two mass casualty attacks by elements of Hezbollah, a group that had mostly refrained from terrorists operations outside Lebanon. The first was a Hezbollah suicide attack against the Israeli diplomatic mission on March 17, 1992, while the target of the second suicide attack was a Jewish community centre (July 17, 1994). The investigation into the bombings, which killed 125 people, is still in progress but the Argentine authorities indicted Mughniyeh. As the attack on the Israeli diplomatic mission occurred within a month of Israel's assassination of the Hezbollah Secretary-General Abbas Musawi, Mossad believes that Hezbollah drew on its existing infrastructure in the triple border areas to launch the attacks.[189] But Hezbollah's network extends far beyond the triple border area and it is has been closely watched by several intelligence services since 1992, thereby restricting its ability to plan complex operations. Since then Paraguay police have recovered Hezbollah propaganda material in raids and found evidence of large financial transfers from US-based charities diverted through the triple border area to Iran and Lebanon.[190] The Islamist terrorist threat to Latin America and beyond will depend to a large extent on post-9/11 Al Qaeda-Hezbollah decision-making, two groups that hitherto have cooperated to advance common aims and objectives.

Islamist groups active in Latin America are also establishing links with organised crime groups in East Asia and the former Soviet Union.[191] Drugs from Latin America have been exchanged for weapons from the former Soviet Union.[192] Furthermore, the Paraguayan Cartel of Pedro Juan Caballero, the Japanese-Brazilian cartel, the Turkish cartel, and the Chinese mafia (14-K Triad, Pak Lung Fu) have also been detected in the triple border area.[193] Cooperation with organised criminals is bound to improve the terrorist capability of domestic and foreign groups in the region. Islamist groups in Latin America also cooperate across the Shia and Sunni divide. Argentinian State Intelligence Service's (SIDE) Sala Patria or Department for International Terrorism filmed meetings and monitored communication between Shia and Sunni groups and more importantly monitored their links with the Middle East and elsewhere. In the light of Shia-Sunni cooperation, Al Qaeda could always use or draw on Hezbollah's infrastructure. Due to geographical remoteness many in government believed that Latin America was the only continent where Al Qaeda would find it difficult to establish and maintain a presence.[194] Distance is not a factor that safeguarded the victims of other Al Qaeda attacks. Hence Latin American governments could do much to reduce the threat of international terrorism by improving bilateral and regional cooperation and strengthening monitoring of shared borders.

ASIA: AL QAEDA'S NEW THEATRE

"Bin Laden does not exist at the moment. But he dominates everything. He may have gone off our screens. [...] But he is everywhere. [...] That is his greatest achievement." (Jason Burke, "Evil's Advocate", *India Today*, New Delhi, January 7, 2002, p. 39.)

Al Qaeda's network in the Asia-Pacific region

As many as three dozen Middle Eastern, Asian and European terrorist groups trained in the Syrian-controlled Bekaa valley in Lebanon in the 1970s and 1980s. In the early 1990s Afghanistan replaced Lebanon as the major centre of international terrorist training, and by October 2001, forty foreign terrorist groups were operating there. The lack of a far-reaching US policy in Asia led the US to abandon war-ravaged Afghanistan after the *mujahidin* defeated the Soviet forces. As mentioned previously, instead of working with Pakistan to demobilise Afghan *jihad* veterans that had won them the Cold War, the US turned its back on Afghanistan and Pakistan in 1989. By 1993 it was even threatening to designate its erstwhile anti-Soviet ally, Pakistan, as a sponsor of terrorism, largely because many former *mujahidin* had been persuaded by Islamabad to fight the Indian security forces in Kashmir. Successive Pakistani governments used the *jihadi* training and operational infrastructure on the Pakistan-Afghanistan border to arm, train and finance up to two dozen Kashmiri groups. Although there is no evidence that the Pakistani intelligence establishment directly supported Al Qaeda, they did help its associate Pakistani and Kashmiri groups for the specific purpose of using them as proxy military forces to undermine Indian control of Kashmir. (It has long been customary for South Asia's intelligence agencies — including India's RAW — to support terrorist groups for short-term political gain, often compromising long-term security goals.)

Whenever Al Qaeda interacted with a terrorist group or a government, its potent Islamist ideology and the irresistible financial rewards it offered saw them either become fully absorbed into the wider Al Qaeda network or fall within its sphere of influence. It was a only a matter of time therefore before the Taliban began to succumb to Al Qaeda's broader strategic plan. Within a year of Osama arriving in Afghanistan in May 1996, they too had turned against the West and the government in Kabul was offering a safe haven for terrorists. It was a nexus that would have tragic consequences for the people of Afghanistan.

The Asian counterparts of Al Qaeda were not as highly motivated, well trained or well led in the early stages as their Arab allies, but with indoctrination, training and leadership they have improved. At the time of writing, Asian members of Al Qaeda account for one fifth of the organisation's strength. Their leaders are handpicked, mostly educated in the Middle East, speak Arabic, unlike the vast majority of Asian Muslims, and were already of a radical bent. Al Qaeda's Asian core is handpicked from several hundred *jihadi* volunteers who fought in Afghanistan, including, *inter alia,* Central Asian, Chinese, Pakistanis, Bangladeshis, Indonesians, Malaysians, Singaporeans and Filipinos. Since the early 1990s, a few thousand Muslims from Central Asia, China and South and South East Asia either trained in Afghanistan or received in-country training in Al Qaeda or Al Qaeda-associate camps. The latter were mostly in the Philippines, Malaysia and Indonesia, and some of those trained in them later travelled to Afghanistan for advanced instruction. On their return home they did not immediately initiate violent political campaigns; instead Al Qaeda retained them as a strategic reserve for future deployment, even establishing a database of their biographical data for the purpose.

Central Asia and Xinjiang (Western China)

With its base in Afghanistan Al Qaeda did not find it difficult to recruit several hundred Soviet Central Asians — Uzbeks, Kazakhs, Kyrghyz, Tajiks and Turkmens — into its ranks. This process was both a symptom of the growth of Islamic movements in Uzbekistan, Kazakhstan, Kyrghyzstan, Tajikistan, and Turkmenistan and a reason for their reassertiveness. Muslims in these countries had expected the successor states of the USSR to restore Islam as the guiding principle of politics, but the area's regimes have remained secular in outlook. The Islamic Renaissance Party (IRP), started by Tajik intellectuals in Astrakhan, Russia, in June 1990, which campaigned for the introduction of *shariah* in Muslim areas, inspired the formation of IRP, Tauba (Repentance), Islam Lashkarlary (Fighters of Islam) and Adolat (Justice) in the Ferghana Valley. Of the 20 million or so Central Asians, 10 million live in the Valley, of whom some 60% are Uzbeks.[1] It is a region of high unemployment and fertile ground for Islamic revivalism. With Moscow's influence diminishing after 1989, Islamic organisations and preachers, especially from the Gulf, arrived to establish *madrasas* and mosques.

Soon after Uzbekistan became independent in 1991, IRP radicals protested government corruption and demanded land to build a mosque. When the authorities refused, they seized the Communist Party headquarters and declared Namangan in the Ferghana valley an Islamic state. The leaders of the rebellion was Juma Namangani, a twenty-two year old former Russian army paratrooper who had served in Afghanistan in 1987; Tahir Yuldash, *alias* Tohirjon Yuldeashev, 24, a *mullah*, and Abdul Ahad, 33, a Saudi-trained Wahhabi. Disillusioned with the IRP, they founded Adolat, built a mosque and a *madrasa* with Saudi funds and also developed a rudimentary weapons capability. As their popularity grew, the Uzbek President, Islam Karimov, who was consolidating his presidency, negotiated a settlement. In return for limited autonomy, Namangani's party disarmed, after which the government arrested twenty-seven Adolat activists, banned the group in March 1992 and began hunting down the remainder. Namangani fled to Tavildara in the Garm Valley of Tajikistan with thirty of his supporters and joined forces with Tajik Islamists who were fighting in order to gain political power in their own country.

Al Qaeda supported the Tajik Islamists' struggle to topple the Russian-backed Communist government. Osama's protégé Khattab and others fought in the ensuing Tajik civil war, and after the conflict ended in a negotiated settlement Al Qaeda's front companies began trading with Tajikistan. The spillover from the civil war also affected Uzbekistan and its neighbours: Adolat was inspired by the Islamic Movement of Tajikistan (IMT) to transform itself into the Islamic Movement of Uzbekistan (IMU). Islamist groups in Afghanistan, including that of Ahmed Shah Masood, the former Northern Alliance commander, and Osama bin Laden, assisted the IMT. Ideologically IMT was the creation of Muhammad Rustamov Hindustani, who studied in Deoband, India, and opened a clandestine *madrasa* in the 1970s; although this was later shut down by the Soviets, who jailed him and his followers for fifteen years, he had introduced his students to Islamic revolution.[2] Abdullah Saidov (*alias* Sayed Abdullah Nuri Masood) headed the political wing of the organisation, and Muhammad Sharif Himmatzade the military wing. Both were his protégés. They established Hizb-i-Nehzat-i-Islami (HNI), a branch of the IRP, Moscow, the former later evolving into the IMT, which established bases in Garm and Northern Afghanistan. Finally, the IMT and other opposition forces joined forces as the United Tajik Opposition (UTO), a partner in the coalition government since 1997. Ahmed Shah Masood, an Afghan Tajik who actively supported the UTO, later joined Russia and Iran in ending the Tajik civil war. Although a few radical Tajik Islamists continue their struggle, Qazi Akbar Turadzhon Zoda, a Soviet-era *mufti* acceptable to both the UTO and the government, has established an official Islam that is broadly accepted.

After the UTO joined the Tajikistan government, some of its members clandestinely assisted the IMU. The UTO "emergency situations minister", Mirzo Ziyeyev, became the IMU's strongest ally. While Namangani remained in Tavildara working with the UTO, Yuldeashev moved to

Kabul and Peshawar from 1996-8, building close links with the Taliban and Al Qaeda. In 1997, with the signing of the peace accord in Tajikistan, most IMU fighters moved to Afghanistan. Although Namangani maintained links with the UTO, he was disillusioned by its compromise with the government. The IMU leadership met with several anti-Karimov political parties both in Turkey and in Afghanistan in 1997 and 1998, when Al Qaeda also had a presence in Turkey. The Uzbek parties opposed the IMU's principle of using force to topple Karimov and hence decided to pursue democratic means, thereby rejecting the IMU's offer of collaboration. The IMU, formally established in Kabul in 1998, gradually came under the influence of the Taliban and Al Qaeda, the former rejecting the Uzbekistan government's request for Namangani's extradition in June 1999. When Uzbekistan's foreign minister Abdulaziz Kamilov met the Taliban ambassador to Pakistan Abdul Salam Zaif to reiterate the extradition request, Zaif announced that Afghanistan had formally granted Namangani asylum.[3] After giving the IMU the right to set up bases and collect funds, the Taliban invited its units to fight with it against the Northern Alliance.

The IMU used its infrastructure in Tavildara (170 km southeast of Dushanbe), Tajikistan and in Afghanistan to conduct guerrilla raids into Uzbekistan and terrorist operations within it. After Kyrghyzstan forces were deployed against the IMU under Uzbek pressure, the IMU also declared war on Kyrghyzstan. The IMU tried to assassinate President Karimov and attack the government in Tashkent in February 15 1999. Six car bombs exploded, killing sixteen people and wounding about 100. After this campaign, Afghan-trained IMU units led by Namangani moved from Tajikistan into Uzbekistan through Kyrghyzstan. They also took three Kyrghyz military personnel and four Japanese geologists hostage in southern Kyrghyzstan in August and September 1999 respectively. After the Kyrghyz were kidnapped in Osh, Namangani demanded $1 million and a helicopter to fly him to Afghanistan. As the response was negative, he moved with his men to Batken, kidnapped the Japanese and continued fighting till October 25, 1999. The IMU demanded the release of tens of thousands of Muslims imprisoned in Uzbekistan in exchange for freeing the hostages, and insisted that the Kyrghyz leadership allow IMU units to cross unimpeded into Uzbekistan. The Uzbek National Security Council Secretary, Mirakbar Rakhmankulov, claimed with good reason that the guerrillas' aim was to destabilise the whole of Central Asia and establish an Islamic state, adding that the Taliban movement and others, namely Al Qaeda, supported them. To secure the release of the hostages the Japanese government sent a delegation to Tajikistan, and although it denied paying a ransom it is likely that Japanese business interests paid the $2 million demanded to free their colleagues.[4] Tajikistan persuaded Namangani and the IMU members in Tavildara to leave for Afghanistan, the Islamist leader arriving in Mazar-e-Sharif in early November with his family and 600 fighters. Thereafter Namangani and Osama became very close and the IMU were given the full run of Al Qaeda facilities, being trained in infiltration, demolition and kidnapping, tactics valuable for their struggle.

With the ransom the IMU procured better weapons and recruited more members. In August 2000 a heavily-armed IMU group attacked Ferghana, once again demanding the release of Islamic prisoners, the reopening of mosques and the establishment of an Islamic state. The IMU forces claimed that they had control of the strategic town of Kamchik, and clashes continued throughout August. The propensity of guerrillas to encroach upon the territory of surrounding states increased in September 2000, leading the US to place the IMU on their list of foreign terrorist organisations. Fortunately, a group of Americans kidnapped by the IMU managed to escape after pushing a sentry off a cliff. In 1999 and 2000, Kyrghyzstan lost fifty-five soldiers in combating the IMU, spent $16 million on defence and increased its defence budget by 250%.[5] IMU incursions had become annual events and their new recruits were still training in Al Qaeda camps in Mazar-e-Sharif and Kunduz. In December 2000, under international pressure, Tajikistan cracked down on the IMU's activities.[6] In a bid to strengthen its relations with the West, Tajikistan applied in May 2001 for NATO PfP membership, and the World Bank pledged it $430 million.[7] With the melting of snow in the mountain passes in August 2001, the IMU launched another incursion — which, however, petered out after 9/11. Russia was planning to deploy 50,000 troops on the Central Asian borders separating Afghanistan in 2003.[8]

The IMU threat was exaggerated by Central Asian states to secure more funding from Western donors, the Uzbek government estimating IMU strength at 5,000 fighters,[9] whereas in fact it was closer to 2,000. For the IMU to maintain that many combatants it needed to raise $2.4 million a year,[10] and hence it became increasingly dependent on the Taliban and Al Qaeda. In keeping with Al Qaeda's outlook, the IMU forged a common front with the Taliban, Al Qaeda, and Chechen and Uighur separatists, increasingly campaigning on a pan-Islamic platform. It was rapidly developing into a Central Asian regional force when the US intervened in Afghanistan in October 2001. Although the Taliban were decimated and Namangani may have been killed in the US bombing, the IMU is unlikely to fade away. With the sharp depletion of its strength in Afghanistan from October 2001 onwards, the group that is likely to pose a significant threat is Hez but Tehrir (HT). Founded by Taki-a-Din Nabkhani Filastyni in Jordan and Saudi Arabia in 1952, it is a non-violent Islamist party organised in the form of clandestine cells; its members recruit from relatives and friends to build mass support for an Islamic state. The religious and political nature of HT as well as its non-military, non-confrontational character, make it very resilient. In many ways the IMU has been following the military, and the HT the political, path towards the common goal of creating an Islamic state. Although banned in the Middle East and Soviet Central Asia the group has an extensive presence. and also raises significant funds in Britain and Germany. Both the level of activity and support for it have grown in Soviet Central Asia because of the failure of the newly independent states to alleviate poverty, provide adequate educational and employment opportunities, and raise the standard of living. There has also been a general failure on the part of the Muslim Central Asian countries to break the increasing momentum of support for the creation of Islamic states in the region, and till recently the Taliban-Al Qaeda models of Deobandi-Wahhabi-Salafist teachings went unchallenged.

Wherever Al Qaeda cannot physically make its presence felt, it relies on ideological penetration to spread its influence, a feat it has already accomplished in Muslim Central Asia. Some Al Qaeda members in Afghanistan are likely to retreat to Central Asia, where they may team up with Al Qaeda-trained associate members active in the Ferghana Valley, thereby leading to an improvement in the fighting capabilities of the Ferghana Islamists. Thus Ferghana's role as an axis linking the Islamist pockets of Tajikistan, Uzbekistan and Kyrghyzstan will likely see it emerge as a base for a new wave of post-Taliban Islamism.

China

At the height of the Cold War, the People's Republic of China trained Muslim Uighurs from the country's far western province of Xinjiang to fight the Russians in Afghanistan, fearing that the "old silk route along the Karakoram highway built across Kashmir's northernmost extremity could, in time, come under Moscow's domination if the Soviet Union was not dislodged from Kabul."[11] The fallout of this strategy was the return of "victorious Uighur *jihadi*s to Xinjiang, where some of them fuelled the simmering insurgency" for an independent Uighuristan.[12] Until October 2001 Al Qaeda camps also trained Uighurs, to fight not the Russians but the Chinese Communist rulers of the Muslim-majority province of Xinjiang.

The origins of the struggle for an independent Eastern Turkestan (Xinjiang) date back to the secret establishment of the Eastern Turkestan People's Party during the Cultural Revolution. The group was known first as the "Uighurstan People's Party" until its name was changed to the "Eastern Turkestan People's Party" and thereafter to the "Eastern

Turkistan Islamic Party". As the number of religious schools and mosques increased, so the idea of fighting for the establishment of an Eastern Turkistan Republic in Xinjiang gathered momentum. Uighur discontent rumbled on for many years but the acknowledged turning point was the Barin uprising of 1990, when Afghan-trained Islamists set up loudspeakers in mosques in the villages of Barin and Turand and broadcast speeches praising *jihad*.[13] The local police were attacked and their weapons seized, at which point the Chinese government responded decisively. Its over-reaction to the Barin uprising only served to attract more Uighurs to the separatist Islamist banner:

In May and June 1991, there were also armed [clashes] in the cities of Bole and Dacheng in the north-western part of Xinjiang. Bomb attacks on buses in the Xinjiang capital Urumqi in February 1992 injured many, and there are reports of bombings in many other towns in Xinjiang in March the same year. In June 1993, a bomb exploded at government buildings in Kashgar killing at least 10 people, and others were reported. In April 1995, there were serious disturbances in the area around the town of Yining/Ghulja near to the border with Kazakhstan, and some demonstrators demanded that the Yining area be incorporated into Kazakhstan. Nearly two years later in February 1997, the most serious [clashes] in Xinjiang since the foundation of the PRC took place in Yining/Ghulja. It cost many lives although the precise number is disputed by the Chinese and sympathisers of the local Uighurs. Many more were injured and thousands were arrested in the mass repression that followed.[14]

Today there are several Islamist groups in Xinjiang fighting for independence, and others have developed an extensive presence in Pakistan, Kazakhstan, Kyrghyzstan and Germany, where funds are raised. Gradually, however, the ethnonationalist character of the Uighurs' struggle has been overshadowed by pan-Turkism and pan-Islamism. The Islamist threat in Xinjiang manifested itself in a series of terrorist attacks against official targets there and even in Beijing, thus conforming to Al Qaeda's doctrine of striking the centre instead of fighting in the periphery. Chinese officials investigating the Islamist terrorist support network in Kazakhstan and Kyrghysztan have also been targeted.[15]

Despite massive Han Chinese inward migration, the *Altishahr* region in the south of Xinjiang, bordering Pakistan and Afghanistan, is home to 80 per cent of Uighurs. Through a co-ordinated network, the influx of Chinese Muslims to Pakistan and Afghanistan for indoctrination and training has been frequent in the 1990s. One such fighter was Noor Muhammad, born in Perkin Shaghen in China, who joined the Islamic Party of Turkestan in Kashgar. The party obtained a passport for him and he then went to Pakistan where he linked up with an Islamic Party cell and attended the Jamaat Uloom Abu Hanifa *madrasa*. Sheikh Serajuddin, the principal of the *madrasa*, encouraged him to participate in the Afghan *jihad* and after training for a month in the Rishkhor military base in Kabul he was deployed to Jabal os Seraj as part of an attack against the Panshir Valley, where he was injured and captured. When interrogated he said that, along with his colleagues, he would "continue to fight and liberate his country from Chinese control and will establish an Islamic government."[16]

Of the two strategies adopted by the Chinese government to counter the spread of Islamism, one is to facilitate migration to Kyrgyzstan, but Kyrgyz of Chinese origin who served in Al Qaeda and the Taliban only became more determined to return to China to establish an Islamic state. For instance, Abdul Jalil, from the Aghesto area of Xinjiang, went to Kyrgyzstan but after a while left for Pakistan and later Kabul.[17] While studying at the Dar ul Uloom Sharia, along with other Chinese Muslims, he was recruited to fight for the Taliban. He was captured by Northern Alliance soldiers in 1999, having killed two of their comrades and while in custody revealed that if released he would resume his religious training and participate in the "liberation war for his country [Xinjiang] for non-Muslims."[18] The spirit and determination of the Chinese Muslims remain undimmed and there are clear signs of the conflict escalating: in January 2002, an Uighur terrorist carried out another suicide mission in China, a tactic that was very likely motivated by Al Qaeda indoctrination and training. Largely due to arrests in Xinjiang, the Chinese secret service has developed reasonably good intelligence on Al Qaeda, in particular its use of Hong Kong as a source of logistical procurement. The contest between the two is likely to be protracted, bloody and inconclusive.

South East Asia (Singapore, Malaysia, Indonesia)

Except for Singapore and, to a lesser extent, Malaysia and the Philippines, Al Qaeda's network in the Asia-Pacific has remained virtually intact in the wake of 9/11. It first made inroads with the visit of Muhammad Jamal Khalifa to the region in 1988. After Ramzi Ahmed Yousef bombed the World Trade Centre in February 1993, Osama dispatched him to the Philippines for a second time to infiltrate Filipino Islamist groups. Financially backed by Khalifa, he was to train the Abu Sayyaf Group (ASG) in terrorist techniques. Osama personally forged the link with Abdurajak Janjalani, the founder and leader of ASG and introduced Yousef to him in Peshawar. ASG's organisation, ideology, target selection and tactics are deeply influenced by Al Qaeda: it has conducted mass casualty attacks, bombed churches, murdered missionaries and foreign priests and kidnapped foreigners, especially Americans. The extent of the Al Qaeda-Philippines link was such that by integrating a few hundred Moros from Mindanao, in the southern Philippines, first to wage *jihad* and thereafter to secure Al Qaeda's assistance in their fight for an independent Islamic state, it established a special Moro sub-brigade in Afghanistan. Khalifa, operating through Mercy International, the International Islamic Relief Organisation (IIRO) and other unwittingly infiltrated Islamic NGOs, also funded many domestic Islamic NGOs and even an Islamic university in the Philippines. Al Qaeda's links with two groups — ASG and the Moro Islamic Liberation Front (MILF) — prompted the Americans to give the Philippines armed forces intelligence and training assistance after 9/11, and two hundred advisers were despatched from the US in February 2002.

As envisaged by bin Laden, Al Qaeda's influence spread from the Philippines to the rest of South East Asia, where its network is longstanding, well-entrenched and extensive. After establishing a logistics network in the Philippines from 1988-93, Al Qaeda launched *Oplan Bojinka* in 1994, under Yousuf's direction, the details of which emerged in the US trial of Ramzi Ahmed Yousef. Its principal elements were to assassinate Pope John Paul II and President Clinton during their visits to Manila; to assassinate President Fidel V. Ramos, two senior government officials, several foreign ambassadors to the Philippines and other diplomats, military and police officials and private individuals; to bomb commercial centres, department stores, the US Embassy, an international school, Catholic churches and vital government installations; to kidnap prominent personalities for ransom, hold up banks and financial institutions and rob commercial establishments such as SM department stores; to assassinate miscellaneous US and Israeli nationals; to bomb eleven US passenger aircraft flying over the Asia-Pacific region.

As a test run, Yousef boarded a Philippine Airlines (PAL) flight from Manila via Cebu to Tokyo on December 11, 1994. When it touched down in Cebu he disembarked after having left on board an improvised explosive device (IED) containing nitro-glycerine, which is virtually undetectable at airport controls. In the resulting explosion, one Japanese national, Haruki Ikegami, a 24 year old, died and eleven other passengers were injured. Although the explosion blew a hole in the fuselage, the pilot, in a brilliant feat of flying, managed to make an emergency landing at Naha airport in Okinawa. Although the name "Al Qaeda" was not used, Yousef phoned the Associated Press in Manila and claimed responsibility for the attack. After this partly successful rehearsal, Al Qaeda continued with its plan to attack eleven American aircraft simultaneously. Coded files found in Yousuf's computer listed five bombers with their responsibilities:

"Mirqas" plants a bomb on a United Airlines flight from Manila to Seoul. The plane continues toward San Francisco from Seoul but would explode in mid air. He plants a second bomb on a Delta flight from Seoul to Taipei, which would explode on the continuation of the flight to Bangkok. He leaves the plane in Taipei and flies to Singapore, then home to Karachi.

"Markoa" plants a bomb on a Northwest flight from Manila to Tokyo. It continues toward Chicago but would explode over the Pacific. He boards a Northwest flight from Tokyo to Hong Kong and plants a bomb that is set to explode a day later over the Pacific on the way to New York. He disembarks in Hong Kong and plants a bomb set to explode a day later over the Pacific on the way to New York. He later flies to Singapore and then back to Pakistan.

"Obald" plants a bomb on a United flight from Singapore to Hong Kong, set to detonate in mid flight on the next leg of its journey to Los Angeles. He meanwhile boards a United flight from Hong Kong to Singapore, plants a bomb that is set to go off on the return leg to Hong Kong, and directly from Singapore to Pakistan.

"Malbos" flies from Taipei to Tokyo on United and plants a bomb set to go off as the plane heads to Los Angeles. He flies from Tokyo to Hong Kong and places a bomb aboard another United flight set to go off 24 hours later as the plane flies from Tokyo to New York.

"Zyod" flies from Bangkok to Tokyo on a United flight, placing a bomb set to explode over the Pacific as the flight nears Los Angeles. He flies to Taipei via Seoul and places a bomb on a second United flight before flying back to Bangkok on a United flight and placing a third bomb. He escapes to Karachi while the second and third planes are set to explode on their way to the US.

US prosecutors said the bombing in rapid succession over a 48-hour period of United, Northwest and Delta airlines jets bound for America's West Coast from cities throughout Asia would have killed as many as 4,000 Americans.[19] When mixing explosives a fire broke out in Yousef's flat and the authorities were alerted to the detailed Al Qaeda plans that it contained, many of which pointed towards the group's future terrorist agenda. However, following the arrest of the core of the Yousef cell, American investigators erroneously believed that the threat from Al Qaeda would diminish. No effort whatever was made to penetrate it, let alone understand the group's motivation, despite the knowledge that it had been responsible for the planning and partial execution of three operations – the bombing of the World Trade Centre (1993), New York landmarks (1993) and an aircraft over Japan (1994). Although Osama was in Sudan during *Oplan Bojinka* and denied having any links to Yousef, circumstantial and other evidence points to Yousef being indeed an Al Qaeda operative. First, Yousef lived in Al Qaeda safe houses before and after the World Trade Centre Bombing of 1993 and immediately before travelling to the Philippines to launch *Oplan Bojinka*; second, he trained in Afghanistan in an Al Qaeda camp; third, Muhammad Jamal Khalifa provided his cell with financial and logistical support; fourth, Yousef's

Arab companions were all known to Osama, trained in Al Qaeda camps or lived in Al Qaeda guest houses; fifth, Wali Khan Amin Shah, Yousef and Khalifa visited an ASG base in Tabuk on January 29, 1992, and gave Janjalani P160,000 for terrorist operations in Mindanao[20] (Janjalani bombed Basilan public market on July 11, 1992, to protest at the conduct of the province's elections, and assassinated an Italian priest, Father Salvatore Carceda, on May 20, 1992[21]); sixth, Khalifa's torn business card was recovered from the Paranaque residence of Wali Khan Amin Shah, a co-conspirator of Yousef in the plot; seventh, Yousef's laptop computer seized from the Dona Josefa apartment had a photograph of Wali Khan Amin Shah; and lastly, in two interviews broadcast on US television in 1997 and 1998, Osama referred to those who carried out the earlier attack on the World Trade Centre in 1993 as "role models."[22]

Although Osama denied ever having met Yousef, he praised him publicly, and in private conceded he was Al Qaeda's best operative. Yousef was Al Qaeda's most celebrated deep undercover operative, and his career provides insights into the Al Qaeda mindset.[23] Abdul Basit Mahmoud Abdul Karim, *alias* Yousef, was born in Kuwait on April 27, 1968. His father Muhammad Abdul Karim, from Pakistan, moved there during the boom years of the oil trade and worked as an engineer for Kuwait Airlines; his Kuwaiti mother's family were Palestinian refugees. Along with other expatriates, he felt that the Kuwaitis were treating him and his family as second-class citizens, a dissatisfaction that turned to radicalism when Yousef came under the influence of Sunni Wahhabi and Salafi preachers. Yousef was an above-average student and popular in school, excelling in all subjects, including chemistry. In 1986, Karim brought his entire family to Turbat, a village in the remote and almost unpoliced Pakistani province of Baluchistan, near the border with Iran and Afghanistan, where local tribesmen roamed unhindered, smuggling drugs and weapons, and occasionally attacking Soviet units alongside the *mujahidin* or moving into Iran.

That year Karim sent Yousef to Britain for further education. He spent several months in Oxford studying English as a foreign language and went again to Britain in August 1987, obtaining a degree in computer-aided electrical engineering from the West Glamorgan Institute of Higher Education. His major project was applying computer design to geometric Islamic patterns, but he also took a course in micro-electronics, which the FBI believe almost certainly helped him to build his miniature nitro-glycerine bombs later. In Swansea, he mixed freely with locals and students, because although he despised the West he did not despise the pleasures of the West. Yousef joined the Swansea branch of the proscribed Egyptian branch of the Muslim Brotherhood (Ikhwan al-Muslimin) but decided that it was not sufficiently committed to the

Islamic revolutionary cause. In the summer of 1988 he returned to Pakistan and spent several months in training camps at Peshawar funded by Al Qaeda, learning bomb-making and teaching electronics to other terrorists. There he was also reunited with his maternal uncle Zahid al-Shaikh, who had a senior post in Mercy International (a branch of which was established in Manila by Osama's brother-in-law Khalifa), a Saudi-funded charity providing assistance to Afghan veterans and refugees. He also met and befriended Mahmud Abouhalima, an Afghan war veteran who was among those convicted for the World Trade Center bombing in 1993. Yousef was in Kuwait when Iraq forces invaded in August 1990, and his antipathy towards its regime prompted him, like many Palestinians, to aid the invaders; Kuwaiti Interior Minister Sheikh Ali al-Sabah al-Salim al-Sabah described Yousef as a "collaborator" with the Iraqi forces.[24] There is no record of Yousef's activities in the first half of 1991 but later in the year he was back in Pakistan, forging ties with militants including the Sunni Sipah-e-Sahaba (Army of the Companions of the Prophet), of which his father was a member, a group founded in Punjab which believed that it has a holy duty to eradicate Shia Muslims. Yousef married a quiet, pretty girl in her twenties and bought a house in Quetta, the capital of Baluchistan, in 1991. His wife had two daughters while he was on the run from the FBI.

In Peshawar he also met Abdurajak Abubakar Janjalani, the founder leader of the Abu Sayyaf Group. At bin Laden's request he went with Janjalani on his first visit to the Philippines from December 1991 to May 1992, where he acquired from his ASG hosts the nickname "the Chemist", such were his bomb-making skills. Together with his fellow cell members Abdul Hakim Murad and Wali Khan Amin Shah, also close allies of Osama, he trained ASG terrorists in the Madin camp in Basilan.[25] Using documents forged by a member of the Liberation Tigers of Tamil Eelam (LTTE) in the Philippines,[26] he returned to Pakistan, re-emerging some months later at New York's John F. Kennedy Airport on September 1, 1992, using the name Ramzi Ahmed Yousef. He claimed political and religious asylum, saying that he had been persecuted by the Iraqi army. Yousef was accompanied by Ahmad Ajaj, a Palestinian who worked for MAK in Peshawar. Of the six bomb-making instruction booklets found in his luggage, at least one was an Al Qaeda manual.

While in New York he maintained links with Mahmud Abouhalima, whom he had met in Peshawar; an Egyptian, Muhammad Salameh; a Kuwaiti, Nidal Ayyad; a Palestinian American, an Egyptian and the Blind Sheikh. In New Jersey the Yousef group — Salameh, Ayyad and he himself — started their "Bomb Project", using mainly chemicals. Yousef placed the bomb they produced, comprising four canisters of nitro-glycerine, in the basement parking lot of the World Trade Center on February 26, 1993. The resulting explosion was intended to kill 250,000 people but in the event six people died, over one thousand were injured and millions of dollars worth of damage were caused. While Muhammad Salameh, Mahmud Abouhalima and Alah Jobrony were arrested, Yousef escaped to Pakistan, where he lived in his home in Quetta and in Al Qaeda's safe house in Peshawar. Osama had by then departed for Khartoum but Yousef kept in touch with the Al Qaeda leadership. Together with Abdul Hakim Murad and Abdul Shakur, both from Kuwait, he tried to assassinate Benazir Bhutto, then running for election as Prime Minister, but the bomb exploded prematurely, injuring Yousef's left eye. With Murad's help Yousef returned to the Philippines in 1994 to launch *Oplan Bojinka*, which some claimed to be in retaliation for the arrests of Yousef's co-suspects in the WTC bombing.

Al Qaeda members Yousef, Murad and Wali Khan Amin Shah rented an apartment in Manila, where they prepared the plan to assassinate Pope John Paul II, who was due to arrive in January 1995. If the pipe bomb attack failed, Al Qaeda planned for an operative disguised as a priest to shoot the Pope. On January 6, 1995, as Yousef was preparing a device from the chemicals he had purchased, a fire broke out in his apartment, prompting a police raid. The encrypted data on his personal computer was so complex that even when the FBI mirrored his hard-drive they took several months to decode his data. Ultimately this revealed the plans for *Bojinka*, and Murad and Shah were arrested. After saying goodbye to his girlfriend in Manila, Yousef slipped the net, escaping to Peshawar where he stayed in Osama's Beit-Ashuhada (House of Martyrs). Indefatigable in his determination to stage fresh attacks, he tried in February 1995 to get to Thailand in order to bomb the US Embassy in Bangkok. Yousef was also involved in the bombing of a Shia mosque in Iran.

While staying in Islamabad in February 1995, however, he was betrayed by a former accomplice to the Pakistan authorities and extradited to the US to face eleven charges relating to the WTC attack and his plans to destroy American aircraft.[27] After months of evidence, the verdicts were pronounced on February 12, 1997, proclaiming him guilty on all counts. He is serving a 240-year sentence in America's most secure prison. In retaliation for his extradition, Al Qaeda killed four American oil workers in Pakistan.

During his interrogation Yousef never compromised Al Qaeda or divulged his ties to Osama, and his silence allowed both to survive. As a cell leader and mastermind of many operations he shielded his true identity by operating under forty aliases. To Osama and others in Al Qaeda he is the model terrorist, one to admire and emulate. At the time of his arrest, a letter found in his hotel room in Islamabad provides us with clues as to the future trajectory of Al Qaeda. In an attempt to secure the release of Abdul Hakim Murad from Philippine custody, Yousef wrote:

> We are going to take the harshest of measures in order that all Filipino interests inside and outside the Philippines will be subject to destruction. [...] Our measures will include assassinating some prominent figures, foremost among them the Filipino president. They will also include hitting numerous aerial targets. [. . .] We also have the ability to make and use chemicals and poisonous gas for use against vital institutions and residential populations and drinking water sources and others....and if our request is not answered positively, in addition to everything we have mentioned, we shall train the Muslims in the south [of the Philippines] to do this. These gases and poisons are made from the simplest ingredients. We could smuggle them from one country to another if needed." [28]

If Al Qaeda's Emir General did not receive a copy of this historic letter, Osama was certain to have read it from the publicly available transcription of Yousef's trial. Whenever an opportunity arose, Osama requested ASG to demand the release of Yousef, Murad, Shah, the Blind Sheikh and others jailed by the US government in connection with the New York and airliner bombings. In response ASG continues to kidnap or kill foreigners, including Americans, periodically demanding the release of these Al Qaeda terrorist pioneers.

Yousef's deputy was Abdul Hakim Ali Hashim Murad (*alias* Hakim, *alias* Abdul Hakim), who can be described more accurately as Al Qaeda's first would-be suicide pilot, a man whose career eerily predicted that of the 9/11 attack teams. It was he who identified and suggested the World Trade Centre as a target since "it is one of the tallest buildings and the most famous commercial center in the world."[29] A Pakistani by nationality, Murad was born in Kuwait on April 1, 1968 and was single. At that time, his father Ali Hashim Murad, was a crane operator in Kuwait. He came from a large family and spoke Arabic, English, Urdu and Baluchi. Murad took all his studies in Kuwait. After graduating from high school, he obtained a private commercial licence from the Air Continental Flying School, Kuwait, and thereafter continued with pilot ground training at the Continental Aeronautical Flying School at Pasay City in the Philippines. Some time before his journeys to and from Manila he met Yousef in Karachi.[30] He obtained a commercial pilot's licence in August 1991 after taking a technical course at the Emirates Flying School in Dubai after six months of training. He then went on to the US, where he trained at two flying schools: Alpha Tango (A.T.) Flying School, San Antonio, Texas; and Richmore Aviation Flying School, Albany, New York; A.T. Flying School, where he completed the required 275 flying hours for a commercial pilot; and he obtained a commercial pilot's

ASG mirrored Al Qaeda in its actions, the latter gradually developed closer relations with MILF because of the vast overt and covert network it had built both in the Philippines and in the region. ASG, a smaller group, was more radical, but unlike MILF lacked the robust organisation to influence several million Muslims in Mindanao and elsewhere in the Philippines, including Manila. In spite of being in negotiations with the Philippine government since 2000, MILF continued its relationship with Al Qaeda, considered so important that its special operations group teamed up with Al Qaeda to conduct several terrorist attacks, including the unclaimed bombings in Manila at the turn of the millennium. In keeping with MILF policy, its officials always denied having links with Al Qaeda, especially after 9/11. The MILF vice-chairman went to the extent of stating that he had not heard of the name Al Qaeda before 9/11.[42] However, there has been one public acknowledgement of Al Qaeda-MILF links. In a rare interview, the MILF chairman Hashim Salamat acknowledged to the BBC in London that Osama had given financial support to Muslim guerrillas in the country but claimed that the money was used to build mosques and help poor Muslim communities.[43] Al Qaeda operated at multiple levels of which provision of secret training to foreign Islamists by facilitating training with its associate groups was only one element. Helping newly co-opted as well as associate groups to conduct terrorist operations was another element of its agenda. It was also Al Qaeda policy to maintain links with many organisations because it did not wish to be tied down to one particular group; perhaps it was aware of the risk of ASG being eliminated or MILF joining the political mainstream. Al Qaeda also compartmentalised its dealings, including assistance to Filipino Islamists: one Islamist group might not know what Al Qaeda did with another group unless it was absolutely necessary. In addition to breakaway factions of MNLF (Moro National Liberation Front), MILF and ASG, Al Qaeda was in contact with several other small Islamist groups in Metro Manila.[44]

On November 23, 2001, prompted by 9/11,the Philippines intelligence community, which had developed considerable intelligence on Al Qaeda in the Philippines since 1998, launched an operation to disrupt the Al Qaeda network in the country. Using the Philippines as a base, Al Qaeda penetrated several Islamist groups in Malaysia, Indonesia and Singapore. After *Oplan Bojinka* was disrupted in 1995, it decentralised its regional operational and support activities to the rest of the region, notably to Malaysia. Until democracy returned, the political environment in Indonesia was not conducive for Al Qaeda to establish a base in that country. However it worked closely with Indonesian Islamists living in exile in Malaysia during the 1990s, setting up an arrangement with MILF to train them. With the spilling over of the activities of Islamist groups in Malaysia to Singapore, it was able to establish a foothold in both countries. As with its networks in Europe and North America, and in Central Asia, it built a pan-Islamic network linking the key Islamist groups in the region; this was accomplished by infiltrating Jemaah Islamiyyah or Islamic Group (JI), initially an Indonesian Islamist group, in the early 1990s. Thereafter it developed Jemaah Islamiyyah into a pan-Asian network extending from Malaysia to Japan in the north and to Australia in the South. Although the national intelligence agencies in South East Asia knew of an Al Qaeda presence in the region and of coordination between the country cells since the mid 1990s, the existence of a well-coordinated regional network has been a closely guarded secret. The initial breakthrough was achieved by the Internal Security Department (ISD) of Singapore, an agency respected within and outside the region for its professionalism.

ISD's investigations into Jemaah Islamiyyah started soon after 9/11. Muhammad Aslam bin Yar Ali Khan, a Singaporean of Pakistani origin, was tracked down following ISD's suspicions of his Al Qaeda links. Aslam left suddenly for Pakistan on October 4, 2001, and at the end of November, ISD learnt that be had been captured by the Northern Alliance in Afghanistan. It went on to arrest fifteen suspects, of whom eight had been trained in Al Qaeda camps in Afghanistan. However it did not publicise the December 2001 arrests until January 11, 2002, because it wanted to disrupt the entire network in Singapore, thereby providing valuable information for its foreign intelligence counterparts. Thirteen of the fifteen suspects arrested for terrorism-related activities were served with detention orders for two years under Section 8(1)(a) of the Internal Security Act on January 6, 2002.

Recruitment and training of Jemaah Islamiyyah members in Singapore began in 1993, the recruits being psychologically indoctrinated and given practical training in Negri Sembilan, Malaysia, before they were sent to Afghanistan for the much tougher experience of being put through their paces by Al Qaeda. JI's leader in Malaysia, Riduan Isamuddin (*alias* Hambali, Nurjaman), a Malaysian permanent resident of Indonesian nationality, made the arrangements for their entry into Afghanistan via Pakistan, including false documentation purporting to show that a *madrasa* had accepted them as students. Their training in the Al-Qaeda camps included the use of AK47s and mortars, and the study of military tactics. One of the Singaporeans had gone to Afghanistan for training on three separate occasions between 1991 and 2000. Among the documents recovered by IT Forensic Investigation (ITFI) from Muhammad Khalim bin Jaffar's encrypted diskette was a letter nominating Muhammad Ellias and Muhammad Nazir for special training in one of three areas: ambush/assassination, sniping and "field engineering" such as bomb construction.[45] Four of JI's Singapore's cell members were trained by an Afghanistan-trained Indonesian Al Qaeda member in an MILF camp in Mindanao.[46] On their return in 1997 the trained JI members strengthened the organisation ideologically and financially and began surveillance of Western targets. It should be reiterated in connection with Al Qaeda's wider practices that they were quite willing to spend five years preparing one attack against American interests.

The JI organisation in Singapore reports to a Malaysia-based *shura*. After the arrest and detention of Muhammad Iqbal A. Rahman (*alias* Abu Jibril), by Malaysian authorities in June 2001, the acting head of the *shura* is now Hanbali, who is wanted by all the countries in the region and remains on the run.

The spiritual leader of the JI is Abu Bakar Bashiyar, who lives in Indonesia. JI was founded by Abdullah Sungkar and after his death in Indonesia Bashiyar, his closest friend, took over. Both Sungkar and Bashiyar had been Islamists for several decades and JI was formed by Sungkar after meeting Osama in Afghanistan. In Singapore it is headed by a leader with the title "*Qaid wakalah*" and organised into compartmentalized cells, or *fiahs*, which are responsible for fund-raising, religious work, security and operations. Haji Ibrahim bin Haji Maidin, a condominium manager in Singapore, was the leader of JI there till his arrest. He had gone to Afghanistan for Al Qaeda military training in 1993. Faiz bin Abu Bakar Bafana, a businessman, was another leading figure in JI's regional *shura* in Malaysia until his arrest. The rest of those detained were mostly members of the security unit or of one of the three operations cells. The *fiahs* are assigned for terrorist support or operational activities.[47] In keeping with Al Qaeda's code, JI members shunned mainstream Muslim organisations and activities, thus evading detection for nearly eight years by maintaining tight operational secrecy using code-names and encrypted communication.

JI had its own peculiarities: it recruited women, the only Islamist terrorist organisation to do so, anywhere in the world (however there are women serving in Asian Muslim guerrilla and terrorist groups that are secular in ideology, such as MNLF). All the arrested JI members had studied in national schools in Singapore and six had completed full-time National Service (NS) and were reservists. Although Al Qaeda stresses that its members and associate members should join the military and police in their own countries before coming to Afghanistan, it appears that the JI's Singapore cell members did not fall into this category. In Singapore national service is designed to inculcate discipline and patriotism and is open to its citizenry. Most Singaporean Muslims are well travelled and widely read and tend to have moderate views. Extremist Islamism is not popular, to say the least. In contrast, JI Singapore was dominated by foreign extremist ideologues mainly from Malaysia and especially Indonesia and subscribed to an anti-American, anti-Western agenda. Hence its growth in Singapore has been incremental, influenced mainly from elsewhere in the region.

JI established three cells. The first operational one, *Fiah Ayub*, began investigating targets in 1997 and conducted surveillance, including video-tapes, of locations frequented by Americans in Singapore. It formulated two well-developed plans. The first plan was to bomb a regular shuttle bus service conveying US personnel between Sembawang Wharf and the Yishun. When the cell leader went to Afghanistan for training between August 1999 and April 2000, he briefed Al Qaeda leaders on it. Al-Qaeda evinced some interest in it but kept the operation on hold, given that it usually maintains a reserve of at least 100 such targets worldwide. As a predominantly Arab organisation, Al Qaeda wanted its Arab planners to review JI's plan. By the time the JI cell was neutralised in December 2001, preparations were fully developed and the plot was ready for execution. By coincidence, the JI videotape and some handwritten debriefing notes in Arabic were found in the rubble of Mohammad Atef's house in Afghanistan, and the Singaporean authorities quickly obtained a copy. Contrary to some media speculation, ISD initiated its investigation into Al Qaeda alone, only later receiving the cooperation of external security and intelligence agencies. The transcript of a JI videotape had this commentary spoken by its Singapore member, Hashim bin Abas:

"This is the place where US military personnel will be dropped off from a bus and they will walk towards the MRT station, and this is one of the regular buses that carry the military personnel from Senabawang to Yishun MRT station. [...] Now being zoomed in is a bicycle bay where the train commuters parked their bicycles in the morning. [...] This is a bicycle bay. There are some motorcycles being parked there also, this is the pickup point or the drop off point, where people were dropped from their vehicles or being picked up and this is where the American military personnel will line up to board their bus. [...] This is the bicycle bay as viewed from the footpath that leads towards the MRT station. You will notice that some of the boxes that are placed on the motorcycles, these are the same type of boxes that we intend to use. [...] This is the traffic junction where the bus normally stops before it turns right, turns left towards Sembawang. [...] That is a temple with about 1.5 metre high wall. That is the entrance of the temple where many vehicles parked there, so it will not be suspicious to have a motorcycle or a bicycle there. The pillars of the MRT track are very solid. You will notice that there is a drainage hole. It might be useful. Another drainage hole is right at the junction. [...] This is the road along Admiralty Road East, from here you can see the residential area of the US military. On the right side, beyond this, are the Sembawang wharfs where the ships normally anchored for the test, now you can see the residential area of the US military personnel. [...] Now beyond this fence is a playground where normally US military personnel will gather for recreation. [...] This is the residential area. Eagle's Club is a mess for military personnel. This area is privately owned, owned by the US government."[48]

The hand-written notes in Arabic recovered from Afghanistan provide a brief description of Singapore's Yishun MRT station and nearby facilities, based on the JI reconnaissance.

The JI also had another plan, to bomb a US naval vessel in Singapore waters. Found among Khalim's possessions was a Singapore Ministry of Defence map with markings indicating observation posts and a "kill zone" in the channel between Changi and Pulau Tekong. Also found was a list of over 200 US companies in Singapore, three of which were highlighted as potential targets because their staff included prominent members of the American community in Singapore. Other items included two doctored Singapore passports, fifteen forged Malaysian and Philippines immigration stamps, night vision binoculars, and literature on bomb-making and survival techniques.

The second operational cell, *Fiah Musa*, comprised four Asians and an especially valuable member, a European Roman Catholic convert to Islam who was instructed to photograph Paya Lebar airbase, US aircraft and the movement of US personnel, all potential targets. He took more than fifty digital photos of the airbase and aircraft as instructed and handed them over to the cell members. These were recovered from among the possessions of Khalim bin Jaffar, the JI liaison with Al Qaeda.

In September and October 2001 the second cell was approached by JI leaders and Al Qaeda operatives to assist in a plan for terrorist bombings of specific targets in Singapore. The Al Qaeda operatives were known to the local cell members only by codenames. Assisted by cell members, they conducted surveillance of the US Embassy, the Australian High Commission, the British High Commission, the Israeli Embassy, commercial buildings with American tenants and the Ministry of Defence complex at Bukit Gombak. They video-recorded what they surveyed for use in their planning. A copy of the video-recording was found in the office of one of their members. At least six Al Qaeda suicide bombers were scheduled to arrive from overseas to conduct the truck bombings of the strategic targets.

Two of the accused operated according to Al Qaeda's strict operational guidelines. As directing figures, they informed the cell that they needed 21 tonnes of ammonium nitrate to construct several huge truck bombs and a suitable warehouse or secure location where the work could be carried out. One cell member subsequently attempted to purchase 17 tonnes through a contact from a local vendor but he was arrested by ISD before he could follow up and complete the transaction. This demonstrates the imminent nature of the threat that was neutralised. The third cell, *Fiah Ismail*, was formed immediately after 9/11. It conducted preliminary surveillance and observation of a few targets including US companies, but stopped when it got wind of the ISD arrests.[49]

The following profile, taken from court testimony, of one of the terrorists, Fathur Rohman al-Ghozi (*alias* Mike), provides insight into the background, motivation and *modus operandi* of Al Qaeda in the region. He was arrested on January 15, 2002, in Manila just before flying to Bangkok; at that time he was known to the Filipino authorities only as "Abu Sa'ad" and "Freedom Fighter".[50] He has subsequently admitted to his role in Al Qaeda's operations and is cooperating with the authorities.

Born in Kebonzar, Madium, Java Timur, Indonesia on February 17, 1971, al-Ghozi is of Javanese origin, and his parents, two brothers and one sister live in Indonesia. After education at Sekolah Dasar (1978-84) he joined Ma'had Al Mukmin (1984-90) a radical Islamic boys' boarding school established by Abu Bakar Bashiyar, the spiritual leader of JI in Java. After graduating he went to Lahore for further instruction in Islamic studies at Ma'had al-Maududi (1990-5),and during that time was recruited to JI by Usaid and Jamaludin, both Indonesians. He went on to Turkum, Pakistan, and the Afghanistan borders for basic and advanced training in an Al Qaeda camp in 1993 and 1994; with him was Abu Hisyam, another trainee from the Philippines.[51] After qualifying as an Al Qaeda instructor in firearms and explosives, al-Ghozi was placed under Faiz bin Abu Bakar Bafana of JI's regional *shura* who also paid him $500 per month. In addition to serving as a trainer and bombmaking and demolition expert, he recruited South East Asians to Al Qaeda. In time he also functioned as the technical liaison officer between JI's cells in the region, travelling frequently.

Accompanied by an Indonesian JI member, Solaiman, al-Ghozi made his first familiarisation visit to the Philippines by entering General Santos City in a fishing boat from Manado, Indonesia, in December 1996. [52] They went on by jeep to Camp Abubakar where they met Salahudin and Habib, both MILF members who had befriended them in Lahore. In March 1998 al-Ghozi was again ordered to the Philippines via General Santos City to learn Tagalog and establish further contacts there.[53] To secure a Filipino identity, essential for unhindered travel, he applied in Cagayan de Oro City for a Philippine passport under the name of Edris Anwar Rodin. During his travels, his Tagalog and Malay improved; he also spoke English and Arabic. On this second visit he conducted a six-month instruction program for JI, training Indonesians, Malaysians and Singaporeans in the MILF camp complex in Mindanao.[54] Four of the Singaporeans arrested in December 2001 revealed that he had been their demolition instructor. Al Qaeda continued to fund him — for instance, in addition to his initial allowance of P20,000, his escort Solaiman gave him P10,000 during his second trip.[55]

After spending more time in the Philippines recruiting and building up Al Qaeda's network, al-Ghozi returned to Marawi City to Muklis's group to purchase explosives and later went to Indonesia: there, in July 2000, he met a Malaysian woman studying in Indonesia, and the question of marriage arose, but he remained committed to waging *jihad*.[56] He returned to the Philippines through the same route in October 2000 with $1,000 and an undetermined amount of Philippine money as an allowance. In Marawi City he was put in touch with the Special Operations Group of the 3rd Field Division of the military wing of the MILF who told him of their plan to bomb a target in Metro Manila in December 2000.[57] Al-Ghozi's Al Qaeda contacts financed the procurement of 80 kilos of explosives, sending P250,000 to his ATM account as payment. On November 2000, together with others, al-Ghozi went to Cebu to test the feasibility of obtaining explosives. Between 50-80 kilos were purchased, at a cost of P2,400 per kilo, and transported by the group to Manila via the Super Ferry in early December. Then, in a coordinated attack on December 30, 2000, five bombs were exploded in crowded locations in Manila, killing twenty-two and injuring over 100 people. As a crowded train pulled in to a railway station, the first explosion occurred, followed by a second in a park near the American Embassy. Within minutes three other blasts followed — at a bus terminal, an airport and a downtown gas station. Using the term "Freedom Fighter", al-Ghozi phoned the Philippines National Police in Manila and claimed responsibility.[58] He also called the *Inquirer*, a local newspaper, with the same claim.[59]

Tracing his mobile phone revealed that al-Ghozi had received and made calls from and to Malaysia before the bombings.[60] Although the calls were soon traced to al-Ghozi's accomplice, Faiz, the Malaysian authorities could not arrest the latter for nearly a year.[61] Nor was he properly monitored, enabling him to direct an even more deadly operation. Since the millennium bombings, the Philippine intelligence community had been trying to trace al-Ghozi, known as "Freedom Fighter". In January 2001 he went to Zamboanga City via Philippine Airlines to obtain a passport, applying under the name of Randy Andam Alih. His multiple identities initially deceived the security services in the region into believing that he was Filipino. When he got his passport, he went to Malaysia where he was given another $3,000 to buy more explosives in addition to those stored in the house in Cebu.

Accompanied by "Mansor", an Al Qaeda member of Middle Eastern extraction, al-Ghozi arrived in Singapore in October 2001 to help prepare the JI cell for its long-planned attack against Western targets. He was then instructed to go to Kota Kinabalu, Malaysia, where he was given $18,000 to procure 5,000 to 7,000 kilos of explosives. With two others in the Philippines he purchased fifty boxes of TNT (about 1,000 kg) and explosives boosters weighing one metric ton, six rolls of detonating cords, 300 blasting caps and 100 kilos of chemical powder. The transaction was completed in the last week of December 2001 and the explosives were stored at a house in Cabingal, General Santos City, from where JI planned to ship them to Singapore (via Sulawesi, where Al Qaeda has a significant support base). JI had also purchased seventeen M16 assault rifles and fourteen short magazines as well as two rifle grenades intended for its operations in Indonesia; these would be transported in the same ship. On January 12, 2002, al-Ghozi arrived in Manila, the journey being part of the wider JI plot focused on Singapore, and stayed at the City State Hotel in Quiapo. It was here that he was arrested. He was found in possession of a fraudulent Philippine passport, an electronic Bahasa–English dictionary and assorted explosive components. His testimony has revealed in far greater detail than had ever been imagined before a huge network of trained Al Qaeda operatives and sympathisers at work in South East Asia, about which more will doubtless be learned in the months and years ahead.

The recovery of al-Ghozi's arsenal for use in Indonesia and Singapore and the temporary disruption of the Islamist terror network in Malaysia and the Philippines exemplifies the regional linkages that characterise Al Qaeda's presence in South East Asia. It also illustrates the group's propensity to move quickly within and between parts of the world likely to afford it a haven, especially in geographically remote, and hence poorly policed, regions such as the islands of South East Asia.

Congruent with its pattern of infiltrating certain Islamist groups as a springboard for regional penetration and the conduct of terrorist campaigns, Al Qaeda relied on the MILF (Moro Islamic Liberation Front) to nurture small to medium Islamist groups in the region. In the 1980s and 1990s, when some Malaysian religious and political leaders were supportive of, and sympathetic to, the MNLF and MILF, these groups were able to establish a significant presence in Malaysia. Key Al Qaeda leaders and members lived in or periodically visited Malaysia despite frequent denials by the government of Malaysia and persistent disruption by its efficient Police Special Branch respectively. Using Malaysia as its operational base (regional *shura*), Al Qaeda's Asian arm — Jemaah Islamiyyah (JI: Islamic Group) — aims to establish an Islamic republic unifying Malaysia, Indonesia, Brunei, southern Thailand and Mindanao in the Philippines. Originally an Indonesian group, under Al Qaeda's influence JI established cells throughout the region, its plan being to carve out smaller Islamic states from within the existing state borders and later unify them in an Islamic republic.

To this end JI's regional *shura* coordinated its support and operational activities with four groups — Kumpulan Militan Malaysia (KMM), Jemaah Islamiyyah Singapore, the Indonesian Mujahidin Movement and the MILF in the Philippines. With common denominators established, they are suspected of being part of a regional terrorist network operating under the aegis of Al Qaeda. JI is conceivably Al Qaeda's instrument connecting mainstream and renegade terrorist and guerrilla elements in the region.

The Singapore arrests were the first evidence that Al Qaeda is actively fostering connections between domestic groups and planning to use them for something more than logistics. The subsequent multiple arrests in Malaysia and the Philippines uncovered a large and relatively unknown network of sleeper cells — both support and operational — in South East Asia. JI's regional *shura* in Malaysia handled training and operational planning not only in JI Malaysia but also in other JI country cells. For instance, after initial ideological and physical instruction in Negri Sembilan, Malaysia, JI Malaysia and Singapore used Afghanistan and Philippines as its main centres for terrorist training. On occasions, Indonesia was also used. Since the early 1990s, JI's regional *shura* in Malaysia dispatched at least 100 JI recruits from the region to train in the use of firearms and explosives in Al Qaeda's Afghan training camps at Khalden, Derunta, Khost, Siddiq and Jihad Wal. In the late 1990s, operational planning to select targets for attack began, and as well as obtaining fertiliser for making off-the-shelf truck bombs, JI also used the Philippines and Thailand to procure weapons and explosives.

JI's regional structure appears closely to resemble that of Al Qaeda's vertical and horizontal organization — with an Emir as the head and *shuras* in various countries integrated in a regional *shura* in Malaysia. The 13 people arrested in Singapore all reported to a regional *shura* in Kuala Lumpur. The units under the regional *shura* also mirror the worldwide Al Qaeda units in both structure and *modus operandi*. As in earlier cases, the cells had painstakingly studied potential targets over many years; they planned to conduct coordinated, simultaneous and multiple attacks on symbolic targets; and the profiles of those arrested are remarkably similar to the 9/11 perpetrators — middle class, well educated, trained in Afghanistan, totally committed and methodical in their plans to bomb Western targets. The common denominator among those arrested is neither poverty nor lack of education but a shared religious ideology that depicts the United States as the enemy of Islam and a belief that Allah will reward them for waging a global *jihad*.

The investigation also demonstrated how patiently and quietly Al Qaeda had extended its reach in each country. Despite its recruiting and training of members, raising funds and maintaining links with foreign groups, there was little or no previous evidence of a terrorist support and operational network for the police or intelligence community to detect and disrupt.

Despite valiant efforts by the Malaysian Special Branch to identify and arrest suspected international terrorists, key Al Qaeda cadres assigned to the Singapore, 9/11, USS *Cole* and *Bojinka* operations have used the country as a base, demonstrating beyond reasonable doubt that it is a key part of Al Qaeda's worldwide web. It is now known that to launch the 9/11 attacks Al Qaeda prepared two launch-pads: Hamburg and Kuala Lumpur.

The Malaysian case reiterates how, despite periodic disruption, Al Qaeda operatives can survive in South East Asia's current political and security climate. South East Asian security and intelligence agencies realise that JI has a very high capacity to regenerate new cells rapidly and operate under extremely hostile conditions. After the arrest and detention of Mahamad Iqbal B. A. Rahman (*alias* Abu Jibril), an Indonesian cleric, by the Malaysian authorities in April 2001, Hambali, another Indonesian but with Malaysian permanent residence, was appointed the operational head of JI's *shura*. Since December 2001 he has been evading arrest.

In many ways Malaysia is a victim of its geopolitics. The tightly regulated political and security environment in Indonesia under Suharto forced Indonesian Islamists who supported the anti-Soviet Afghan campaign to relocate to Malaysia in 1985. Reminiscent of the crackdown on Egyptian Islamists, Indonesian Islamists too found in Malaysia a tacit host. After JI's founder, Emir Sheikh Abdullah Sungkar, met Osama in Afghanistan in the early 1990s, JI was incorporated as an associate group of Al Qaeda, one of the earliest in Asia to do so, the other being ASG. Over time Al Qaeda gradually absorbed JI into its wider structure, just as it had absorbed Egyptian Islamic Jihad and the Islamic Group of Egypt. And just as the Algerian Islamist groups — GIA and GSPC — were co-opted to work for Al Qaeda in Europe, JI members were similarly co-opted in South East Asia. The integration of JI into Al Qaeda's orbit was perhaps due to the doctrinal compatibility of the two. In a rare interview, Sungkar said that the methodology of JI is to realise an Islamic community by the materialisation of *Quwwatul Aqidah* (faith's strength), *Quwwatul Ukhuwwah* (brotherhood's strength) and *Quwwatul Musallaha* (military strength).[62] More important, Sungkar regarded these strengths as essential to establish Dawlah Islamiyya (an Islamic state) by means of *jihad*.[63] "These, among others, form points deemed vital by Jama'a Islamiyya, whereas other Jama'ah [groups] ignore and generally disregard these strengths," he added.[64]

Although the circumstances of the departure of Bashiyar, Sungkar and others from Indonesia in the 1980s and 1990s were well known to the Malaysian government, they received residence permits and were free to travel around the country, rallying people to their "radical brand of Islam".[65] They initially settled in different parts of Malaysia, but by 1992 Hambali and Muhammad Iqbal had "moved into ramshackle wooden houses next to each other in the town of Sungai Manggis, about 50 miles southwest of Kuala Lumpur."[66] Sungai Manggis is less than 10 miles from the Strait of Malacca, where boats regularly move people in and out of Indonesia without immigration formalities.[67] In 1997 Bashiyar moved into Iqbal's house after Iqbal relocated to another property nearby.[68]After the return to democracy in Indonesia in 1998, Sungkar and Bashiyar returned home. Sungkar died in 1999, and Bashiyar, his lifelong friend and fellow Islamist, assumed the mantle of JI's leadership. Of the clerics Bashiyar was the most vocal, always exhorting the people to join the *jihad*. Like most radical Asian Islamists, he is of Arab descent, but born in Jombang, Indonesia. He is utterly opposed to compromise: in an interview he expressed his thinking when he said "Islam must be sterilized from other ideologies. The specific characteristics differentiate it from other beliefs — although in fact Islam cannot be compared with others because it is perfect. At the same time, there is not a single ideology, apart from Islam, which is sterilised from *shirk* [the ultimate sin in Islam, of associating God with another or suggesting God has divine partners]."[69] Arguing that there is no Islamic socialism, and that Islam is Islam and socialism is socialism, he states: "Islam cannot be democratised. Islam is Islam, democracy is democracy. Each has its own characteristics, and they cannot be amalgamated."[70]

Of the clerics, Hambali was the strategist — he spoke little, stressed secrecy, emphasised training and planned for the long-term war. Although Hambali's name surfaced for the first time in connection with the help he gave the 9/11 hijackers, he had also played a key role in operation Bojinka. In June 1994, Hambali had founded an Al Qaeda front — Konsojaya Trading Company — in Malaysia together with Wali Khan Amin Shah, a member of the *Oplan Bojinka* cell led by Ramzi Ahmed Yousef.[71] According to the Malaysian registry of companies Konsojaya directors included another Afghan, Mehdat Abdul Salam Shabana, who owned the other half of the company's shares, and Hemeid H. Algamdi, described as a 30-year-old Saudi from Jeddah.[72] When Shah escaped from Philippine custody, Hambali provided him a new identity and cover in Malaysia, where he lived on the resort island of Langkawi using the name Osama Turkestani.[73] Furthermore, Hambali was in regular contact with Khalifa, Osama's brother-in-law.[74] Hambali's name surfaced once again as the mastermind of the operation to destroy multiple targets in Singapore in December 2001/January 2002.

On January 5, 2000, Al Qaeda's Malaysian cell hosted Khalid al-Midhar and Nawaq al-Hazmi, two of the 9/11 hijackers, and Ramzi bin al-Shibh, another such who failed to gain entrance to the US. The same cell also hosted Tawfiq Bin Atash and Fahad al-Quso, planners of the USS *Cole* bombing in October 2000. With the arrest of Yazid Suffat, a US educated Malaysian Army captain turned businessman by the Malaysian Special Branch on December 9, 2001, the role of JI's support for Zakarias Moussaoui, the twentieth would-be-hijacker, became known.

Malaysia's Al Qaeda experience is instructive. Although it did not tolerate Al Qaeda as such, the government failed to take pre-emptive action against its known members and supporters living in Malaysia. Had the Malaysian authorities disrupted Al Qaeda's Kuala Lumpur cell, the USS *Cole* attack as well as the carnage of 9/11 might have been prevented. The cell hosting those responsible for planning the USS *Cole* and 9/11 attacks were being monitored by police, even being videotaped by a Malaysian surveillance team on January 5, 2000. The information was turned over to the CIA but both governments failed to make arrests. Malaysian Special Branch believed that by continuing to monitor the cell members they would ultimately learn more about their associates in Malaysia. By the time the US Immigration and Naturalisation Service put two of the hijackers on its list of wanted persons on August 21, 2001, they had already gained entry to the country

KMM also poses a threat to Malaysian and regional security. Although it is an independent group, like MILF or ASG, Al Qaeda works via KMM, another of its associates. Some members of KMM also hold dual memberships of both it and JI. Nik Adli Nik Aziz, son of the Parti Islam Se Malaysia (PAS) spiritual leader Nik Aziz Nik Mat, has been named by the Malaysian government as the leader of the KMM. He served in Afghanistan in 1990-6. On August 4, 2001, he was arrested by the Malaysian authorities. KMM was founded by another Afghan veteran, Zainon Ismail, on October 12, 1995,[75] and has ties with both terrorist groups and political parties in the region. In addition to its links in Malaysia and Indonesia, KMM cooperates with ASG and MILF. Some forty-five of KMM's estimated sixty-eight members trained in camps in Afghanistan.[76] In addition, KMM trained in Mindanao and procured weapons from Thailand and from the Philippines, most likely from ASG and MILF. KMM members are said to have assassinated a state assemblyman, bombed churches and Hindu temples, attacked a police station and robbed banks.[77] KMM's support and operational infrastructure has suffered extensively as a result of its practical and ideological commitment to Al Qaeda's aims and objectives.

To build its military capability, the KMM engaged in a series of robberies and in May 2001, two of its members were killed and six captured during an attempted bank robbery near the capital. The intelligence community is divided whether the KMM leadership was unaware of this particular cell's plans to rob banks.[78] In addition to supporting anti-Christian violence in the Moluccas (Muluku), KMM members allegedly conducted terrorist operations in Jakarta. For instance, in September 2001 the Indonesian authorities arrested KMM member Zid Sharani along with twelve other Indonesians and another Malaysian for two bombings in Indonesia. At the time of the arrest, they were undergoing military training at a village in Padeglang, West Java. Zid is an associate of the Malaysian bomber Taufik Abdul Halim, who was seriously injured when the bomb he planted at a Jakarta shopping mall in August 2001 detonated accidentally. After Taufik Abdul Halim was arrested in Indonesia, a second round of arrests of KMM members in Malaysia followed. The Malaysian Foreign Minister said the KMM was planning to attack a US naval vessel during a rest stop in Malaysia but that the plot was uncovered before 9/11. In December 2001 and January 2002 Malaysia arrested a total of 47 suspects linked to Al Qaeda and more are believed to remain at large.

As in Indonesia, Malaysia is home to many Islamist parties and groups, some of which support Al Qaeda's aims and objectives. However, unlike in Indonesia, the Malaysian government clamped down on pro-Al Qaeda-Taliban demonstrations, especially after 9/11. If the Islamist milieu is not challenged, more violent groups like Al Maunah will emerge. Al Maunah was a Muslim cult dedicated to overturning the Malaysian government through *jihad* whose followers believed its leader Muhammad Amin Razali had mystical powers that would protect them from harm; it was smashed by the Malaysian government and later designated as a "terrorist" group by the US government.

MILF nurtures and maintains links with several individual members of political parties in Malaysia.[79] With the exception of military co-operation with JI and KMM, MILF's links are ideological and political, e.g. with the Movement of the Islamic Unity (APU);Islamic Youth Movement of Malaysia (ABIM); Islamic Front of Malaysia (IFM); Front Malaysian Islamic Council (FMIC); Kongress Indian Muslim Malaysia (KIMM); Malaysian Islamic Youth Movement (MIYM), Barisan Nasional (BN), and PAS (Parti Islam Se Malaysia).

The government of Prime Minister Mahathir Mohamad has alleged that JI is affiliated with PAS, a charge it denies.[80] As Islamist ideology is gathering momentum in Malaysia, so PAS's popularity has grown and it poses a political challenge to other secular parties. In Malaysia, the HQ of PAS displayed two large posters of Osama before 9/11. When asked about them, PAS Central Committee Member Subky Abdul Latiff replied: "Bin Laden sacrificed all his wealth to fight against communists in Afghanistan, so we are very proud of his commitment. Unlike other people with that kind of riches, he went fighting. So we are proud of him, just for that."[81] The poster's caption read: "We declare *jihad* on the American government, because they are a country of criminals, ruthless and unjust. If our effort to liberate the Islamic people is regarded as a terrorist act, then to us it is an honour."[82] After the World Trade Centre attacks, PAS disassociated itself from Al Qaeda, the vast majority of Malaysian Muslims being horrified by what had occurred.

Indonesia

As the world's fourth largest country and the most populous Muslim nation on earth, Indonesia hosts an array of Muslim groups ranging from Islamist to highly liberal. The vast majority of Indonesian Muslims are moderate and tolerant, but several radical groups have emerged. Although the international spotlight is on Abu Bakar Bashiyar, the leader of JI, the man who introduced Al Qaeda to the region is Abdullah Sungkar.[83] Until December 1971 he worked as a *da'i* (preacher), and in 1975 the government banned the Islamic boarding school he had opened. On November 19, 1978, he was jailed for three and a half years for "trying to establish an Islamic state of Indonesia whilst denigrating the nation based on Pancasila".[84] During his appeal against the sentence he escaped to Malaysia in 1985 and later met Osama bin Laden in Afghanistan. Thereafter he worked tirelessly on behalf of JI in Malaysia and throughout South East Asia. He identified three types of Islamic movement in Indonesia. First, political parties in parliament: "If these political parties are based on Islam and desire to establish Dawlah Islamiyya, they will be...categorised as criminal."[85] Second, Islamic organisations active in education and social activities: "These organisations are forbidden by President Suharto if they are based upon Islam."[86] And third, Jama'a Islamiyya, which has the purpose of establishing Dawlah Islamiyya by applying the "strategies of *iman* [faith], *hijra* [migration] and *jihad* [to exert the utmost in one's cause]."[87] After President Suharto stepped down Sungkar returned to Indonesia with Bashiyar, who took control over Pesantren al-Mukmir and established the Indonesian Mujahidin Council with the intention of launching an Indonesian *mujahidin* movement.

To galvanise the public behind his Indonesian *mujahidin* movement Bashiyar began agitating for the implementation of Islamic laws. Of his "Indonesian Mujahidin Council" Indonesian intelligence reported: "About 100 members or mujahidin warriors have been entangled in the conflict between members of the religious communities in Maluku. A number of Jundullah warriors under the coordination of the Preparation

Committee for the Implementation of the Islamic Law Organisation (KPPSI) of South Sulawesi have been involved in similar conflict at Poso, Southeast Sulawesi."[88] At a meeting of 5,000 people called by Tablik Akbar Muktamar II of the Muslim Youth Front of Surakarta on September 16, 2001,[89] Abu Bakar Bashiyar was reported to have stated that "[the President] Megawati, [Vice President] Hamzah Haz, and the military should thank Osama bin Ladin because Allah has released our burden since his struggle is based on Islamic law and not politics."[90]

While the Indonesian Mujahidin Movement and Pasantren Ngruki (an activist religious school in central Java) operate overtly, JI does so covertly. The first indications of Al Qaeda's plans to infiltrate Indonesia became known to Indonesian intelligence in 1998, a few months before Sungkar and Bashiyar left Malaysia and returned to Indonesia. Letters sent by those two to prominent Islamic figures in Indonesia were intercepted. They contained a message from Osama bin Laden: "that the most important obligation for Muslims nowadays was to work hard in order to free Arabian lands from the grip of the enemy of Allah, specially pointing to American Christians and Jews."[91] Reflecting their relationship to the Al Qaeda leader, Sungkar and Bashiyar also stated in the letter that "they were willing to show the most secure way to visit Osama whenever the Islamic prominent figures would like to do so." [92] In response, Al Qaeda dispatched a high-powered delegation to the region to enhance ideological influence and operational commitment between Islamist parties and groups. Foreign intelligence agencies reported that Ayman al-Zawahiri and Muhammad Atef visited the Moluccas and Irian Jaya in 2000, both areas affected by long-running conflicts, thus conforming with Al Qaeda's preference for regrouping in areas where the rule of law is weak.

Of the many operations conducted by Al Qaeda in Indonesia, the millennium bombings on Christmas Eve 2000 are very instructive of their tactics. The campaign of bombings against thirty churches in Jakarta, West Java, North Sumatra, Riau, Bandung, East Java and West Nusatenggara was coordinated with Al Qaeda's Manila attacks and investigations revealed they were authorised from Malaysia and Afghanistan. The operation was compartmentalised with each cell being responsible for a church or cluster of churches and each unit having access to one bomb factory. The latter were supplied with detonators purchased from Malaysia, which is where their instructions emanated from. Eighteen people were killed and eighty-two injured in the attacks, though had all the bombs exploded the casualties would have been much higher.[93] Because the operations were so well planned the Indonesians at first suggested it had been a military operation. Three Afghan-trained Indonesians — Dedi Muyani, Kolis and Enjang (*alias* Jabir) — were arrested. Due to an overall lack of Indonesian action to disrupt Al Qaeda's infrastructure (a state of affairs criticised by the US government in March 2002) the group expanded its influence in Indonesia throughout 2001. As of February 2002, JI had established cells in Surakarta (Solo), Central Java and Jakarta.[94]

The intelligence agencies of both the Philippines and Spain have reported independently the existence of an Al Qaeda training camp in Indonesia. Al Qaeda-MILF interaction led to 400-600 Indonesians being trained in 1996-2001. Within the MILF they referred to these Indonesians as the "Indonesian Islamic Liberation Front" (IILF), a name based on its Philippines counterpart, the MILF. Initially the Indonesians received extensive training in the Philippines, and thereafter they built their own camps in Indonesia. In addition to instruction conducted in Camp Bushra and Camp Abubakar, the establishment of Camp Hudaibie inside Camp Abubakar, exclusively for training foreigners, enabled specialised training to be carried out. The presence of "barracks, administrative offices, a mess hall and a training centre" has been confirmed.[95] Panthbharat, an as yet unidentified island, was where Al Qaeda's first training camp in Indonesia was set up, but Jakarta's law enforcement authorities have yet to make any arrests despite intelligence from many sources that there are Indonesians serving with Hezbollah, JI, Al Qaeda, and other international terrorist groups.

The Indonesian authorities came under intense international pressure when telephone transcripts of Al Qaeda's cell in Spain revealed in November 2001 the existence of an Al Qaeda camp in Indonesia. After a large-scale investigation the security forces of both countries identified a "connection between the Spanish Al Qaeda network and the activity of military training in Poso, Central Sulawesi in July 2001".[96] Indonesian intelligence reported: "The training camp led by Omar Bandon consisted of 8-10 small villages located side by side on the beach, equipped with light weapons, explosives and firing range. Participants of the training are not only from local people but also from overseas. The instructor of the physical training in the camp is Parlindugan Siregar, a member of Al Qaeda's network in Spain."[97]

The CIA and other European agencies have been privy to Al Qaeda operatives moving in and out of Indonesia. In August 2001, the US and British governments issued warnings to its missions in the Asia-Pacific that they were at risk of terrorist attack. Their concerns were specifically focused on Indonesia. There was intelligence at that time of an Al Qaeda attack team entering Indonesia, but despite sound and timely intelligence provided by counterpart agencies, the fragile nature of Indonesia's coalition government prevented a crackdown, which might have polarised and perhaps destabilised the elements of the coalition.

Immediately after 9/11, a European intelligence agency, based on communication monitoring, reported that a prominent member of President Megawathi's government was in close touch with Al Qaeda, and although the Indonesian authorities constantly claim that they are investigating the flow of funds from Afghanistan, Pakistan and the Gulf to Indonesian Islamist groups, no funds have been frozen. On January 23, 2002, under international pressure, the Indonesian police at last interviewed Bashiyar, but he rejected all charges against him other than of praising Osama.

The real danger to Indonesia's long term stability stems not from Al Qaeda — which has only a few cells in place — but from other Islamist parties and groups that continue aggressively to campaign for the enforcement of Islamic law — *sharia.* Many of these are directly and indirectly politicising and radicalising Indonesian Muslims to support Al Qaeda's aims and objectives. Although there are about sixty radical Islamic political groups in Indonesia, only half a dozen are significant:[98] Laskar Jandullah; Ikhwanul Muslimin Indonesia; Gerakan Mujahidin Indonesia; Front Pembela Islam; Ponpes Ngruki; and Laskar Jihad. These groups often link up with their less well known counterparts. For example, in order to deter a US attack on Afghanistan in September 2001, several radical Islamic groups combined their strengths throughout Indonesia, calling themselves "Anti-American Terrorist Soldiers."[99] In its stronghold of Surakarta, Central Java, hundreds of members of radical Islamic groups stormed five-star hotels and the Adi Sumarmo international airport in September 2001. Insisting that its citizens should leave Indonesia if the US attacked Afghanistan, they distributed posters saying: "Once Afghanistan is attacked, people from America and its allies have to get out of Solo [Surakarta]."[100] An Al Qaeda associate group, the MILF, has also tried to establish links with various Indonesian political parties and groups that it feels might be sympathetic to its wider aims. Among those they have targeted are Free Aceh Movement (Aceh Merdeka), Council of Indonesian Muslim Associations (MASYUMI), Nahdlatul Ulema (NU), Muhammadiya, Development Unity Party (PPP) and Dewan Dakwa (Preaching Bureau).[101] However most of these groups have successfully resisted Al Qaeda penetration.

Laskar Jihad Ahlus Sunnah Wal Jamaah (Jihad Force: LJ) is perceived as the most radical of all the Islamist movements in Indonesia. It was established in early 1999 as a reaction to the long-running Christian-Muslim animosity in the Moluccas, its leader Ustad (Muslim scholar) Ja'far Umar Talib having participated in the communal fighting that claimed 8,000 lives and prompted close to 2 million to flee their homes between 1999 and 2000.[102] LJ wishes to establish an Islamic state in Mulaku, the group claiming it has a *fatwa* from Sheikh Rabea bin Hadi al-Madkhali from

Saudi Arabia and Sheikh Migbal bin Hadi al-Wadea from Yemen to wage *jihad* in Ambon

Talib received a scholarship to study in the Institute of Dakwah in Lahore, Pakistan, in 1986 after which he joined the Al-Khairiyah Foundation in Peshawar. Although he has admitted meeting Osama, he has criticised him ideologically in the media. In private his views differ: the chairman of the Islamic Student Movement in Jakarta said: "Jaffar told us that if there is a request from Osama, he is prepared to send Indonesians to fight for Al Qaeda."[103] The Indonesian press too has been intimidated by LJ. When the *Jakarta Post* referred to the foreign *mujahidin* in Afghanistan as "soldiers of fortune" in an editorial in January 2001, a busload of Lashkar Jihad members arrived at its office and protested. Stating that it is an insult to Muslims in general and to former Indonesian volunteers of the Afghan conflict, in particular, an LJ representative said: "This piece is a vulgar, direct attack against the *mujahidin* of Afghanistan. It is also slanderous of us, as if the mercenaries gave birth to Lashkar Jihad."[104]

The Laskar Jundullah (Legion of the Jundullah), another Islamist group is led by M. Kolono. In one of its major campaigns, in October 2000, 150 members of Brigade Hizbullah and Laskar Jundullah performed an "act of sweeping". In this case, "sweeping", which meant searching for Americans. The Novotel, Sahid Raya, Agas, Quality, and Lor Inn hotels were "swept", the objective being to force US citizens out of Indonesia, replace the US ambassador and warn the US military against international intervention and cease its support for Israel. If the proposed conditions were ignored, they would attack all US interests in Indonesia. Some of these larger groups are setting the trends for the smaller ones. For instance, members of Front Hizbullah (FH) all wore black outfits bearing the group's name and attacked businesses considered "sinful", notably entertainment centres and nightspots.

Such radical groups are led and their positions staffed by Indonesians of Arab origin who tend to be more committed to Islamic radicalism. There are also many Indonesians working in the Gulf, some of whom return home with a more rigid interpretation of Islamic belief and practice. Islamic radicalism is also being engendered by Middle Eastern migrants to Indonesia, mainly from Iraq and Afghanistan.[105] For instance, when a LJ leader was arrested by the police in May 2001, the LJ members who visited him communicated only in Arabic.[106] In September 2001 the US Assistant Secretary of State for East Asia and Pacific Affairs, James Kelly, warned of the threat of terrorism to Indonesia from illegal immigrants from the Middle East.[107]

Instead of turning towards the Middle East for inspiration, progressive Muslim leaders in Indonesia have articulated that "moderate Muslims must explore Indonesia's vibrant and indigenous Islamic traditions. The country's rich vein of Islamic scholarship has embraced new ideas and sought to interpret the Holy Koran in a manner that reveals its compatibility with democracy, human rights, gender equality and social justice."[108] Traditionally, South East Asian Muslims have been more moderate and syncretistic in outlook than some of their Middle Eastern counterparts so there is certainly a possibility that local responses to Indonesia's Islamist resurgence will prevail. This has been the case in elections, where the three main Islamic parties won only 14 per cent of the total vote in 1999. However government inaction is creating a greater public space in which Islamism can flourish, the Indonesian élite being divided about how to respond. Six months after September 11, Indonesia was the only country where demonstrations in support of Osama bin Laden are being sustained. The Indonesian élite is divided on how it should tackle these groups. On an international scale, pro-Osama and anti-US demonstrations have been largest and most vociferous in Indonesia.

Thailand

The Pattani United Liberation Organisation (PULO) and New PULO are waging a separatist struggle in southern Thailand, the Islamic character of which has grown dramatically, though they are not in any way Islamist movements and there is no intelligence to indicate that they are linked to Al Qaeda. Moreover the MILF has failed in its attempt to infiltrate several political parties and groups in Thailand.[109] The regional intelligence community agrees, however, that instability in Southern Thailand has been exploited by Islamists in northern Malaysia, including to procure weapons. Pattani United Liberation Army (PULA) has claimed responsibility for several bomb and arson attacks against government establishments in the south and[110] perceived symbols of Thai cultural dominance have also been periodically targeted, including schools and Buddhist temples.[111]

In addition to attempts by Hezbollah, Shia groups originating in Pakistan with possible links to Al Qaeda have been planning attacks against US and Israeli interests in Bangkok. The US Embassy there was closed in November 1998 after the CIA warned that US institutions in Thailand were at risk from attack.[112] The very fact that al-Ghozi and other JI members arrested in the Philippines were planning to travel through Thailand suggests their familiarity with Bangkok and the possible existence of a support cell. For over a decade, Thailand has been a safe haven, logistics base and procurement centre for several foreign terrorist groups, largely due to corruption among segments of the military.

Myanmar

The Islamic Party (Mahaz-e Islami) of Myanmar is thought to have connections with Al Qaeda, and through Harkat-ul Mujahidin, an associate group of the latter, Rohingya Muslims from Myanmar, Bangladesh and Pakistan have joined Al Qaeda. As many as 200,000 Muslim Rohingya refugees fled Myanmar for Bangladesh in 1992 after suffering persecution for their beliefs from the authorities. Their living conditions are poor and they are therefore vulnerable to recruitment by Islamist groups, including Al Qaeda. Although Mahaz-e Islami has only a small presence inside Myanmar, it has a significant following in Pakistan and Afghanistan; in Pakistan it is led by Noor Alem and Abdul Halim.[113] The group also fought with the Taliban and Al Qaeda against the Northern Alliance in Afghanistan with the intention of gaining combat experience before returning to Myanmar. Along with other compatriots from Myanmar, Abdullah Yunus was captured in Daresh Suf on June 8, 1999.[114] He said that if pardoned and released, he would "continue his Islamic political studies and military training and then return to his country and try to free it and implement *sharia*."[115]

Indian intelligence reported that two Pakistani nuclear scientists under investigation by the US for their links with Al Qaeda arrived in Myanmar in early November 2001.[116] This may be linked to Pakistan's interest in protecting protect its scientists working on strategic weapons development programmes from being interviewed by foreigners, especially US federal agents.

Japan and Korea

Although Al Qaeda has no permanent presence in South Korea or Japan, their operatives have visited both countries on procurement and surveillance missions. It aborted a planned operation in Japan and in South Korea in late August/early September 2001.[117] The absence of a sizeable Muslim diaspora in northeast Asia has hindered Al Qaeda in establishing a presence in these countries. Osama's personal pilot Essam al-Ridi visited Japan's Al Qaeda support cell in the first half of the 1990s and with its help procured communication technologies and equipment. The Al Qaeda-financed terrorist Ramzi Ahmed Yousef was behind the bombing of the Cebu-Tokyo Philippines Airways flight in December 1994.

Australia

Through its supporters Al Qaeda has a rudimentary presence in Australia. In Sydney, Melbourne and Adelaide, several Al Qaeda money-raising support cells were established in the late 1990s. Investigations into the JI network in Singapore revealed a significant JI presence in Australia. The Islamic Youth Movement in Australia has also given bin Laden a platform via an exclusive interview he gave to *Nida'ul Islam* (Call of Islam).[118] With relative ease Al Qaeda could mount an operation in Australia, given its Muslim diaspora population, though counter-measures ought to reduce the likelihood of this occuring.

According to Indian intelligence, several members of a Melbourne mosque were trained to fly with the specific intention of attacking high profile targets in the US, Britain, India and Australia,[119] where Melbourne's Rialto Towers skyscraper was on their list.[120] The first and only of the would-be hijackers to be arrested was Muhammad Afroz, son of Abdul Razak from Trombay, Mumbai, India, a member of Al Qaeda's associate group, Student Islamic Movement of India (SIMI). During his court testimony he said he was recruited in 1994, and was ideologically indoctrinated by SIMI, whose vice-president, Khalid Ansari, asked him to learn internet and email procedures. SIMI later sent him to Melbourne, where he too learned to fly, from August 1997 to July 1998, SIMI paying all his expenses via his bank account in Melbourne. While in Australia, Afroz teamed up with other Islamists from Pakistan, Bangladesh, Afghanistan and the Middle East. At the time of writing Afroz's startling revelations about himself were being treated with some scepticism in Australia although the security services there wish to interview him. But the question remains, how did the son of a poor tailor in Mumbai afford flying courses in Australia and another in Britain that alone cost £50,000?

Australia's relative isolation has offered it natural protection, but with improved communications this advantage will diminish and with terrorism shifting to Asia, Australia is likely to become vulnerable, especially if the threat from Al Qaeda associate groups in Indonesia, Philippines, Singapore and Malaysia increases. Both Australia and New Zealand are liberal democracies where terrorists can operate with relative ease. Just as the terrorist threat in the Middle East in the 1970s and 1980s spilled over into Western Europe, so Australia is likely to be affected unless it acts proactively in conjunction with its neighbours to reduce the escalating threat in South East Asia. With the exception of Alexander Downer, its foreign minister, who has done much for Australia and the international community to build support for a global coalition to fight terrorism, Australia's political establishment has been slow in responding to the threat.

India and Pakistan

Al Qaeda's presence in South Asia (India, Bangladesh, Nepal and Pakistan) is well entrenched, the last named being its single most important refuge other than Afghanistan, before and after 9/11. Al Qaeda enjoys a large support base in Pakistan, even though that country's

Islamists remain a small minority, electorally and numerically. Before 9/11, Osama was a popular political figure in Pakistan with a near-mythical status for his role in fighting the Soviets in Afghanistan, supporting the Kashmiris against India and resisting America. Pakistan is one of only two states founded on an avowedly religious principle, the other being Israel, but bin Laden is not regarded as in any sense a religious leader. For instance, when the thirty-three-year old Pakistani Mir Aimal Kansi assassinated two and maimed three CIA officers outside their HQ in Langley, Virginia, on January 5,1993, Osama called on Muslims to retaliate against the US prosecutor in Kansi's trial for disparaging comments he made about Pakistanis.[121] Following Kansi's extradition to the United States, Osama warned that if the US attempted his capture, he would "teach them a lesson similar to the lesson they were taught in Somalia".[122]

At the request of the Taliban Al Qaeda financed and trained several Islamist, notably anti-Shia, groups in Pakistan and Bangladesh, its assistance being motivated by animosity towards Iran. The armed Sunni organisation, Sipah-e-Sahaba Pakistan (SSP: Army of the Prophet's Companions), and its underground splinter Lashkar-e-Jhangvi openly advocate attacks on Shia mosques and Shias in general, several hundred of whom have been killed since the mid-1980s. With the rise of the Taliban, the attacks increased in intensity. SSP leaders accused of involvement in assassinating leaders and conducting attacks against civilians took refuge in Afghanistan and continue to operate from Afghanistan-Pakistan border. In response the Shias established their own armed group - the Sipah-e-Muhammad (SM: Army of Muhammad), which has carried out retaliatory attacks against Sunni preachers, including the murder of the SSP's founder. From being a fringe group, Sipah-e-Sahaba has grown in mainstream popularity, in part due to its help in fighting Indian security forces in Kashmir. In addition to assisting the Islamic Movement of Uzbekistan, the Sunni parties fought alongside Al Qaeda's 055 Brigade. They also continued to kill Shias in Afghanistan, Lashkar's entire leadership being based in Kabul till the American intervention.

Of some two-dozen Kashmiri and Pakistani groups active in Kashmir during the 1990s, Al Qaeda has penetrated several, in particular Harkat-ul Mujahidin (HuM), Jayash-e-Muhammad (JeM: Army of Muhammad), Hezb-ul-Mujahidin (Hezb) and Lashkar-e-Toiba (LeT: the military wing of Markaz-e-Dawa-Al Irshad). As associate groups, their cadres have received sustained training in Al Qaeda camps, especially in kidnapping and infiltration for the benefit of those fighting in India. Furthermore, Al Qaeda influenced their strategy by encouraging and assisting them to strike at the heart of India — New Delhi and the major cities rather than in the periphery, Jammu or Kashmir. Intelligence agencies also reveal that Al Qaeda is working with organised crime groups, including that led by Dawood Ibrahim in Dubai, which is suspected of involvement in a series of simultaneous bomb blasts in Mumbai on March 12, 1993 that killed over 200 people and injured 700.

After regaining control of Bamiyan from the Northern Alliance in June 1999, the Taliban dispatched nearly 200 guerrillas of Al Qaeda's 055 Brigade to fight in Kashmir. This single incident led India, China, Russia and some Central Asian countries to step up assistance to the Northern Alliance, worried that if the Taliban defeated the Northern Alliance, it would gravitate to other regional conflicts.[123]

As Al Qaeda handpicked the best trainers from the anti-Soviet Afghan war it wielded significant influence over non-Arab groups. Immediately after the Soviet withdrawal, it provided combat trainers and explosives experts to impart specialised training in camps of Harkat-u-Jehad-e-Islami and other Pakistani groups that participated in that war. After the Soviet withdrawal the *mujahidin* from Afghanistan were diverted to the Kashmir theatre, which exploded from late 1989. Compared to the native Kashmiri groups, the Afghan Arabs were highly motivated and "fanatical" and came to Kashmir with the single agenda of "liberating their oppressed Muslim brethren from the clutches of Infidels".[124] "They worked in tandem with Al Qaeda and Taliban to achieve their objective of ultimately establishing 'Nizam-e-Mustafa' (Rule of Allah) after freeing Muslims from the subjugation of 'Kafirs'," added a counter-insurgency expert with long years of experience in Kashmir.[125] After the Soviets withdrew, the training camps established for Afghan *mujahidin* in Pakistan, Azad Kashmir and Afghanistan were made available to Kashmiri groups, and simultaneously training camps run by these groups were established inside Kashmir. One such in Kapran, Anantnag run by Harkat-ul-Jehad-e-Islam where Afghan *mujahidin* were training Kashmiris was detected in 1993. Muhammad Yusuf of Pakistan, Muhammad Sayeed of Azad Kashmir, Muhammad Ismail of Jammu and Kashmir, Waqar Shah of Pakistan and others informed Indian interrogators about training at Yawar camp, Afghanistan.[126] This was run by Jalaluddin Haqqani of Hizb-e-Islami; he and its leader Yunus Khalis were both close associates of Osama. With US intervention in Afghanistan in October 2001, Haqqani was appointed commander in chief of Taliban forces in Afghanistan and teamed up with Osama.[127] He was reportedly injured in the fighting in late 2001. Osama personally visited a number of camps and inspired the recruits. For instance, Tariq Mehmood Zargar, arrested in June 1999, Muhammad Akbar Bhat, arrested in August 1999 and Javed Akhtar Abbasi, arrested in May 2000 disclosed that during their military training at various training camps in Afghanistan, they were addressed by *Osama* on the "virtues of '*jihad*' and asked to remain prepared for the protracted war against the infidels in

Kashmir and elsewhere".[128] Javed Akhtar Abbasi further disclosed that he had met the Taliban ministers for power and defence at Jalalabad along with his trainer Amin Abdul Sattar to obtain military hardware. This emphasised the close relationship between Al Qaeda and its host, the Taliban.

Immediately after the US cruise missile attacks on Sudan and Afghanistan, Osama's popularity among the Islamists reached a peak, but Islamabad and some in Kabul realised that it was a question of time before he would bring disaster on the Pakistani and Afghan people. Nonetheless, several Asian Islamist groups pledged support for Al Qaeda and condemned the US. The degree of support from Pakistani Islamists was reflected by numerous pronouncements made in support of Osama. Umer Farooq, leader of Lashkar-i-Toiba, said that "Mujahideen would sacrifice their lives to defend the hero of Islam."[129] Stating that his "Arab guards would frustrate any attempt to harm him", Tariq Madani, leader of Sipah-e-Sahaba Pakistan, threatened that "if the Taliban regime bowed to US demands out of a desire to break out of international isolation, it could split the Taliban ranks."[130] Ghafoor Ahmed, deputy chief of Pakistan's main Islamist party Jamaat-i-Islami, said "The US should stop dictating to Muslim countries, especially to the Taliban," and Mehmood Khan, leader of its youth wing, the Pasban group, urged the Taliban to resist outside pressures.[131] Among the leaders and parties that condemned the US attack and supported Osama were the Pakistan Awami Itehad (PAI) leader Dr Tahirul Qadri and a former head of the ISI, General Hamid Gul. By responding to the Al Qaeda threat unsuccessfully, the US increased support for Osama, Al Qaeda and its associate groups.

Al Qaeda deepened its influence in a number of ways, but Osama was selective in the groups it assisted militarily. Other than the three Harkat groups, he also assisted Hezb-ul-Mujahidin, which used Al Qaeda trainers and training infrastructure as well as Al Qaeda finance to maintain its rank and file. Interrogation of Hezb members arrested throughout India revealed that during their training at various camps in Afghanistan, they were addressed by Osama.[132] They circulated audiocassettes of his speeches in Hezb camps, which were regularly played to motivate the rank and file. Another allurement was the promise of a meeting with Mullah Omar and Osama. For instance the Pakistani Hezb member Muhammad Iqhlaque was sent on a reconnaissance mission to assess security measures in major Indian cities, and when he was arrested in India in August 2000 he confessed that he had been promised a reward of Rs. 30,000 and an audience with the two leaders.[133]

Of the Pakistan based groups engaged in fighting in Kashmir, the three Harkat groups are ideologically and operationally intertwined with Al

Qaeda. In October 1993, Harkat-ul Mujahidin merged with Harkat-ul-Jihad al-Islami (HUJI) to form Harkat-ul-Ansar (HuA). Its alliance leader Maulana Saadatullah Khan stated that the objective of the group is to continue the armed struggle against the USA, non-believers and anti-Islamic forces. Proscribed by the US in 1997, Britain in 2001 and Pakistan in 2002, the strength of HuM is estimated at 5,000.[134] Although the Harkat family of groups were independent at the beginning, they gradually came under the influence of Al Qaeda. When the US launched a cruise missile attack on Afghanistan, twenty-one members of HuM engaged in training and providing security for Osama were killed in Khost. The Harkat leader Fazl-ur-Rehman Khalil is a member of the "World Islamic Front for the Jihad Against the Jews and the Crusaders", led by Osama, his long-time friend. In addition to the February 1998 *fatwa*, they have remained joint signatories of a number of statements issued against the US, India and Israel. On July 18, 1999, Harkat warned that if the US attacked Osama or the Taliban, a war would break out against it,[135] and on May 2, 2001, it threatened to attack New York, Washington and the White House if the US did not change its attitude towards the Kashmir and Chechnya issues.[136] In addition to numerous attacks against the Indian military in Kashmir, Harkat has conducted kidnappings, a hijacking and suicide attacks, and Indian police have arrested several Assamese Muslims trained in HuM camps in Afghanistan. At the behest of Al Qaeda, HuM provided weapons to ASG in the Philippines.

A breakaway faction of Harkat, Jayash-e-Muhammad (JeM), has a strength of 2,000 members.[137] Harkat's leader Fazl-ur-Rehman Khalil was the mentor of Maulana Masood Azhar, Jayash's leader, an alumnus of the Binori town seminary, the largest Sunni Deobandi educational institution in Pakistan. Its alumni consist of virtually the entire Taliban upper echelon, and its head Mufti Nizamuddin Shamzai is both the brain behind the Taliban, its spiritual leader, and the mentor of Mullah Omar. Allama Yusuf Binori and Maulana Mufti Muhammad, the then head of the Jamaat Ulema-e-Islam, established the seminary in 1954. Osama, Mullah Omar and Mufti Shamzai support Maulana Masood Azhar, who made headlines in January 2000 when he declared a *jihad* against both India and the US at the Binori town mosque. JeM recruited widely, including in India, in an effort to increase its operational reach and widen the struggle, and has since turned to suicide attacks, the hallmark of Al Qaeda. One near the main gate of 15 Corps HQ on April 19, 2000, in which five army personnel were injured, and the other in the precincts of Srinagar's Jammu and Kashmir State Assembly on October 1, 2001, in which thirty-eight persons were killed and seventy injured were staged by JeM members trained by Al Qaeda. The JeM claimed responsibility for the attacks and under Pakistani government pressure then withdrew them. On December 13, 2001, five suicide terrorists attacked the Indian Parliament with small arms and bombs, leaving nine people dead and precipitating a general mobilisation by the armies of both India and Pakistan that nearly led to war. Two Pakistan-based groups, JeM and LeT, the latter led by Muhammad Saeed, are suspected of complicity. The US added HuM, JeM and LeT to its list of terrorist groups that operate against India.

To understand the mindset of a Harkat member who avowedly sees himself as a member of Al Qaeda and JeM, we now turn to the life and terrorist career of British-born Ahmad Omar Saeed Sheikh, who gained international notoriety in 2002 for his role in the kidnap and murder of the *Wall Street Journal* reporter Daniel Pearl. Though not as experienced as Ramzi Ahmed Yousef, Omar Sheikh's mental make up is very similar to that of the former: ruthlessly deceptive, cunning, fearless and unpredictably dangerous.

Omar Sheikh's parents, Saeed Ahmed Sheikh and Qaissia, both Pakistanis, migrated to Britain in 1968, and by 1991 had established a garment business, "Perfect Fashions", with an annual turnover of £500,000 ($800,000).[138] In 1991, Omar Sheikh visited Lahore, where he first made contact with Islamist groups, and the following year was admitted to the London School of Economics (LSE) to read Mathematics and Statistics.[139] While a student he set up a business dealing shares and equities, earning up to £1,000 pounds ($1,500) on some days.[140] As a member of the LSE's Islamic Society, he organised a conference on Bosnia in 1993 after being moved by a television documentary on the situation in the Balkans, "Destruction of a Nation". Many students attended, as did representatives of the Al-Muhajiroun organisation, which targets universities and schools for recruitment.

Omar Sheikh's views were hardening, to such an extent that he argued "Muslims can never be friends with Christians and Jews."[141] He visited Pakistan briefly in March 1993 with his father on a business trip where he met the Jammat-e-Islami communications secretary Amir-ul-Azim and exchanged materials on the plight of Muslims worldwide.[142] Omar Sheikh suddenly dropped out of LSE in 1993 and went to Bosnia with the "Convoy of Mercy" providing relief to displaced Muslims. As he explained: "The Bosnian experience left a profound impression on me and reaffirmed my decision to take up arms against the enemies of Islam." [143]

In July 1993 Omar Sheikh arrived in Pakistan, formally joined HuM, and with twenty other recruits went to a HuM training camp in Afghanistan where he began a rigorous training programme led by visiting Al Qaeda instructors. He claimed that he was trained by serving members of the Special Services Group of Pakistan (SSG), but this is highly unlikely. Aware that *mujahidin* are occasionally captured by Indian securit forces, the Pakistani ISI has been careful not to involve the SSG, an élite organisation respected worldwide for its professionalism, in the training of *mujahidin*. Omar Sheikh was probably trained by former members of SSG, who serve as instructors in training camps, including those in Afghanistan. The gap between serving and non-serving officers in this context is of course a fine one and may explain why the Pakistani authorities may be loath to extradite Omar Sheikh to the US because of the complicity of the Pakistani state in his training. Omar Sheikh told his interrogators that he was trained in the following: surveillance/counter surveillance; the art of disguise; interrogation; cell structure; secret rendezvous techniques; hidden writing techniques; cryptology and codes; unarmed combat; and moving (how to enter a room by kicking open the door, falling to the floor and shooting targets. He was also trained in how to plan and conduct operations, including reconnaissance; checking of equipment; selecting personnel; approaching the target; methods of attack; use of signals for withdrawing; communications systems; indoctrination; urban warfare, use of assault rifles, light machine guns and rocket launchers; and night movement, raids and ambushes. Maulana Abdullah then urged Omar Sheikh to undertake a mission to India, but he was refused a visa by the Indian Consulate in Karachi. Maulana Masood Azhar visited Britain to meet with supporters and then went to Delhi, *via* Bangladesh, on an adapted Portuguese passport. His intention was to reach Kashmir to unify two separatist factions — HuA and HuM — fighting the Indian military, but he was arrested. Although Masood Azar is linked with Al-Qaeda's attack in Somalia when eighteen US soldiers are killed, his true role was to act as an emissary of Osama to unite the various Islamist factions. Massood Azar's mission to India was no different and is likely to have received the blessings of Osama.

Maulana Abdullah informed Omar Sheikh that he was planning to host a conference of renowned Muslim scholars and leaders in Pakistan to impress upon Amnesty International the importance of securing the release of Maulana Masood Azhar.[144] While in the UK, Omar Sheikh renewed his British passport, dropping his dual nationality in order to obtain an Indian visa. After being issued with one he went again to Afghanistan via Pakistan for a refresher course. After the course was completed, Maulana Abdullah praised Omar Sheikh as "Britannia Jindabad" and urged him to kidnap British or American nationals or Indian VIPs to seek the release of HuM members in custody. In revenge for the destruction of the Babri mosque in Ayodhya, the option of kidnapping BJP leaders was also discussed. Omar Sheikh then went to Delhi with another operative, "Shahji", who served as his operational controller, and began familiarising himself with the city's layout.

"I visited Deoband, Aligarh, Hapur and Ludhiana just to assess the Muslim feelings about *jihad* in August 1994. I exchanged views from various points of view as a future conqueror — as I fondly imagined myself — a social scientist, a traveller, noting down the intricacies of a new country. I went to many mosques and *madrasas* either talking to them about my ideas pertaining to *jihad* and revolution or asking about them, assessing views and thoughts, comparing them with other Muslims and non-Muslims. Among the *madrasa* students I felt that there was great potential for an Islamic movement to emerge."[145] Shahji met with Omar Sheikh only on September 2, and instructed him to proceed to Agra to start the mission.

During the second week of September, Omar Sheikh visited the diplomatic enclave at Chanakyapuri, the American Centre in Kasturba Gandhi Marg, the British Council Library and the American School near the US embassy with the intention of kidnapping a foreigner "in the protection of the Government of India",[146] having failed in an attempt to kidnap several Israelis after one of them became suspicious of his over-friendly behaviour. Thereafter he scouted for targets at Delhi University and Jawaharlal Nehru University (JNU). Shahji had by now given Omar Sheikh an ultimatum of four days to kidnap a foreigner without violence, otherwise they would have to use other means. He had previously visited Dehra Dun and there, at the Hare Ram Hare Krishna guesthouse, he asked two Britons, Christopher Myles and Paul Rideout, to come sightseeing with him. He picked them up the next day, took them to his safe house, left the room and ushered in three other operatives armed with pistols and an AK47.

The next morning Omar Sheikh left for New Delhi, where he met Shahji, telling him that everything had gone off smoothly. Shahji insisted that one more foreigner — an American — should be abducted. On October 20, Omar Sheikh befriended an American of Hungarian origin, Bela Nuss, in a cafe opposite the Anoop Guesthouse, where Omar Sheikh had registered under a false identity. After talking with Nuss for several hours, Omar Sheikh went off with him by auto-rickshaw on the pretext of taking him for dinner with an Indian family. Instead he was taken to a rendezvous with a van driven by another accomplice of Omar Sheikh. On the way Shahji got into the vehicle and after a while pulled out a pistol with a silencer, telling Nuss not to make a noise and that he would not be harmed; negotiations would take place with the government for his release. A black *burka* (veil) was put over his face to conceal his identity and he was taken to another safe house in Mussoori.

On October 25, 1994, Omar informed Shahji about the developments and prepared a ransom note addressed to the Prime Minister of India demanding the release of Maulana Masood Azar, Sajjad Afghani, and Nasarullah Khan saying that "they must be sent to Ahmad Shah Masjid in Afghanistan" within the stipulated time of 48-72 hours or else the kidnapped persons would be executed.[147] To substantiate his demands, Omar Sheikh purchased a polaroid camera and the newspaper of the day and photographed the victims. He remained confined to his safe house in New Delhi where he and Shahji listened to Pakistani radio for news of the release of their "compatriots."[148] After the expiry of their deadline on October 29, having received no news, Omar Sheikh wrote letters to the British and US Embassies and to the BBC and VOA and mailed them from Kashmir Gate. The following day he went to the *Hindustan Times* and handed over another letter. That evening, when Omar Sheikh, Siddiq and Shahji arrived at the safe house, two policemen ambushed them, asking what they were up to. In the ensuing gunfight Omar Sheikh was shot and captured, being transferred to the high security Tihar jail in New Delhi, after the Uttar Pradesh State Police categorised him as "dreaded".[149] The 400 acre jail, the largest lockup in South Asia, hosts 11,000 prisoners in 2,500 10 x by 8-foot cells. Here Omar Sheikh struck up friendships with both Aftab Ansari from Calcutta, who had studied law and journalism in Varanasi before breaking into organised crime, and his chief of Indian operations Asif Reza Khan.

This failure prompted Harkat to stage a brutal kidnapping. To secure the release of Omar Sheikh, Maulana Masood Azhar and others in Indian custody, it kidnapped six Western tourists in the hill resort of Pahalgam in southern Kashmir, India, on July 4, 1995: John Childs, 41 (American), Donald Hutchings, 42 (American), Paul Wells, 23 (British), Keith Mangan, 33 (British), Dirk Hasert, 36 (German) and Hans Christian Ostro, 27 (Norwegian). A few core military leaders of HuA, trained in Afghanistan by Al Qaeda, participated in the operation. Hitherto the Kashmiri *mujahidin* had refrained from killing civilians (except those labelled as traitors), especially foreigners, but Al Qaeda's influence changed this. Al Faran, the core group that executed the operation, did not reveal its plan even to the Harkat leadership. The ISI was also kept in the dark. When India accused Pakistan of complicity in the kidnapping, the ISI claimed that India's foreign intelligence agency — the Research and Analysis Wing (RAW) — was behind it.[150] Of the kidnapped victims only Childs escaped. He gave valuable evidence to US investigators, especially of the instructions in Urdu his kidnappers received. Despite significant pressure on Pakistan from the American, British and German governments, Islamabad failed to compel Harkat to release the remaining victims, clearly demonstrating that Harkat was out of control. The severed head of Ostro was discovered on a mountain path in August 1995 with a note demanding the release within two days of fifteen jailed Islamists, including Omar Sheikh and Maulana Masood Azhar. Indian intelligence confirmed that the remaining four hostages were killed in December 1995. Harkat continues to operate in Kashmir primarily against the Indian security forces, although its members have also fought overseas, in the Philippines, Bosnia and Chechnya.

Western governments failed to respond decisively to the kidnappings, the Americans designating HuA and Al Faran as terrorist groups only in October 1997, a move that bin Laden responded to by praising HuA.[151] In response to the US designation, HuA reverted to its original name of Harkat-ul-Mujahidin. To the surprise of the British security service, Harkat was busy disseminating propaganda, recruiting members and raising money as well as operating a printing press in Britain. It was not until the enforcement of the Terrorism Act, 2000, however, that the British could legally proscribe JeM and the two other Pakistan-based groups — HuM and LeT.

Harkat remained determined to secure its leaders' release and on December 24, 1999, five of the group hijacked an Indian Airlines Airbus, Flight IC-814, from Kathmandu, Nepal, to New Delhi. The chief hijacker was Ibrahim Azhar, Maulana Masood Azhar's brother. A passenger, Rupin Katyal, was stabbed to death when the plane landed at Amritsar and after refuelling in Lahore the plane headed for Kabul where Afghanistan refused landing. After releasing twenty-six women and children in Dubai the plane touched down in Kandahar where the hijackers demanded the release of thirty-five terrorists from Indian custody and $200 million.[152] On December 31, in return for 155 passengers and crew, the Government of India released Maulana Masood Azhar, Mustaq Ahmed Zargar, a Kashmiri, and Omar Sheikh.

For the benefit of the international media, Taliban soldiers, some armed with Stinger missiles, had surrounded the aircraft to give the impression that it wished to free the hostages, but their true motive was to protect the hijackers. US Special Forces and the CIA later discovered boarding passes for the hijacked IC-814, and other evidence of Al Qaeda/Taliban links to HuM and JeM during their searches of abandoned Afghan terrorist camps.

The freed terrorists later surfaced in Pakistan, and while Maulana Masood Azhar appointed himself as leader of JeM, Omar Sheikh was named as his deputy. Moreover Mufti Azhar Abdul Rashid, the patron of al-Rashid Trust, a Pakistani charity designated by the US after 9/11 as "supporting terrorism", disclosed that Masood Azhar has been appointed the Taliban's Emir in Jammu and Kashmir.[153] The latter continued making fiery speeches to large crowds throughout Pakistan calling for a *jihad* against the US, Israel, and India, without any action by the government. Meanwhile various intelligence agencies reported that Omar Sheikh fell out with Maulana Masood Azhar over his support for the avowedly sectarian Sipah-e-Muhammad, which continued its persecution of Shia Muslims, and joined Al Qaeda. Based in Karachi, he reported to Abu Zubaydah, chief of external operations, and soon became a key figure, especially in terms of fund-raising. The intelligence community believes that he provided $100,000 — generated from a kidnapping in India — to Muhammad Atta. His relationship forged in Tihar jail with Ansari — who fled to UAE when released on bail — enabled him to establish a second base in Dubai. On August 8, 2001, Ansari asked Asif Reza Khan in New Delhi in an email whether he agreed to part with $100,000 for a "noble cause" as requested by Sheikh, and the next day, Khan responded by e-mail that he had no objections.[154] On August 11, Ansari emailed Khan and said that the amount mentioned had been sent, while eight days later Omar Sheikh emailed Ansari to say that: "The money that was sent has been passed on."[155] A Pakistani, Muhammad Aslam, trained at an LeT camp in Khost, Afghanistan, was arrested with Asif Reza Khan in New Delhi in October 2001, charged with the abduction of Calcutta shoe tycoon Partha Roy Burman. After eight days in captivity, Burman was released after his family paid an $830,000 ransom. Khan was shot dead by police in Rajkot, Gujarat, on December 7, 2001, while Aslam remains in custody.

It was via email that Omar Sheikh lured his final victim, Daniel Pearl, to his death. The reporter had been promised an interview with Sheikh Mubarik Ali Gilani, of the Islamic Jamaat ul-Fuqra, an Islamist group, believing that Gilani had ties to the "shoe bomber", Richard Reid. With no prospect of the kidnappers' demand — the release of Al Qaeda prisoners from Camp X-Ray — being met, Pearl was brutally killed by his captors, his death being captured on video. With the mounting American pressure to find Pearl after his capture, Omar Sheikh's relatives in Pakistan were taken into custody by the authorities on February 5, 2001. A week or so later Omar Sheikh was arrested in Lahore.

The Harkat triad forms part of Al Qaeda's support base in Pakistan. Although President Musharraf banned HuM in an attempt to limit its influence, the group wields significant influence. The extent of Al Qaeda's influence was evident too in its former training camp in Afghanistan, at the Rishkhor military garrison, south-west of Kabul, which was converted to a HuM training complex and staffed by Al Qaeda and retired Pakistani military personnel.[156] A 1086-page Al Qaeda training manual in Arabic entitled *Mujahideen ki Lalkaar* (War Cry of the Mujahidin), recovered from the site, now in ruins after US bombing, contains the following: "We saw Russia disintegrate. Now we will see India fall apart. In the flames of *jihad* we will see America ablaze."[157]

Among items recovered were notebooks on Indian political parties and their leaders. Qari Muhammad Irfan from Bahawalpur, Pakistan, had written two pages on extremist Hindu organisations and their leaders, while in a letter home Maulavi Izzatullah Wakif of the Chauhar-Asiya *madrasa* had written in Pushto, "I'm in the *jihad*. I'm happy here."

Organisations like Harkat that have both legitimate political and underground military infrastructures will be critical for Al Qaeda's continued survival. In Pakistan at least, there remains widespread support among all segments of society for Osama's ideas, even after 9/11. This is mediated through his associate parties in Pakistan. In response to the Pakistani government's crackdown on Islamists in Karachi, bin Laden wrote an open letter dated September 24, 2001, addressed "To our Muslim brothers in Pakistan". It reflects the force of his rhetoric, understanding of the Pakistani psyche, and skillful use of religion to build support to fight the US-led anti-terrorist coalition:

I heard with much regret the news of the murder of some of our Muslim brothers in Karachi while they were expressing their rejection of the aggression by America's crusader forces and its allies on Muslim soil in Pakistan and Afghanistan. We ask God to receive them as martyrs and to place them among prophets and the righteous and martyrs and the pious who are the best of company, and to grant their families solace and bless their children and property and reward them for being good Muslims. The children that they left behind are my children and I will care for them, God willing. No wonder the Muslim nation in Pakistan should rise in defence of Islam, for it is considered Islam's first line of defence in this region, as Afghanistan was the first line of defence for itself and for Pakistan against the Russian invasion more than 20 years ago. We hope those brothers are the first martyrs in the battle of Islam in this age. The new Jewish crusader campaign is led by the biggest crusader Bush under the banner of the cross. This battle is considered one of the battles of Islam. We incite our Muslim brothers in Pakistan to deter with all their capabilities the American crusaders from invading Pakistan and Afghanistan.[158]

Al Qaeda, the Taliban and their associate organisations continue to manipulate Islam as a weapon of politics. In an open letter to the people of Pakistan, Osama uses implicit religious coercion to direct and sustain his fight against the US and its allies. As usual, he quotes selectively from the ruling of the Prophet and thereafter appeals to all Pakistanis.

The Prophet [...] said: "He who did not fight or prepare a fighter or take responsibility for the family of the martyr fighter, God will punish him before judgment day — cited by Abu Daoud [a disciple of the Prophet Muhammad]." *Osama* wrote: I assure you, dear brothers, that we are firm on the road of jihad for the sake of God inspired by His Prophet, may peace be upon him, and with the heroic faithful Afghani people under the leadership of the emir of the faithful Mullah Muhammad Omar and to make him triumph over the infidel forces and the forces of tyranny and to destroy the new Jewish Crusade campaign on the soil of Pakistan and Afghanistan. If God helps you, none can overcome you. If He forsakes you, who is there after that, that can help you? In God, then, let believers put their trust.[159]

This widely disseminated letter was signed "Your brother in Islam Osama bin Muhammad bin Laden". Today Osama and other Islamists view Pakistan as the natural launchpad for their attempt to free Afghanistan from foreign rule, eerily echoing Pakistan's role as a front-line state in ejecting the Russians. Al Qaeda continues methodically to work with Islamist groups and parties in Pakistan to build the right milieu to sustain a protracted guerrilla campaign. As the symbol of opposition to Al Qaeda is President Musharraf, Al Qaeda is certain to mount or support an operation by an associate group to assassinate him. It will also continue to mount sporadic operations against Western targets, such as kidnappings and the grenade attack against a Christian church in Islamabad's diplomatic quarter which occurred on March 17, 2002.

The steps taken by Musharraf to reduce the threat of terrorism included: a ban on the carrying of weapons in public (March 2000); a ban on the issuing of new arms licences (February 2001); a ban on terrorist fund-raising (June 2001) and an arms amnesty (June 2001). At a different level there were bans on Lashkar-e-Jhangvi and Sipha-e-Muhammad and a watch notice on Sipha-e-Sehaba Pakistan and Tehrik-e-Jaffria Pakistan (August 14, 2001).[160] He went on to ban LeT, JeM, TNSM, TJP and SSP and placed Sunni Tehrik under watch (January 12, 2002).[161] As Musharraf addressed the nation on in January 12, nearly 400 members of these groups were rounded up and detained.[162] By the end of February 2002 a total of 2,010 members of Islamists groups had been arrested and 624 offices sealed.[163]

The success of Musharraf's efforts will depend on his ability to sustain his actions against domestic Islamists and the level of overseas support — political, economic and military — he receives in doing so. Most Pakistanis perceive Musharraf, who came to power in a military coup in October 1999, as an honest, strong and pragmatic leader who has the country's interests at heart, and they will most likely support his crack-down on extremism provided it benefits the population at large. Al Qaeda's strategy of relocating to Pakistan's tribal areas straddling Afghanistan in based on two assumptions. The first is the hope of repeating history by driving the American and allied forces from Afghanistan in a protracted guerrilla war, just as the international *jihadi* fighters forced the Soviets to withdraw more than a decade ago. The second is that they and the remnants of the Taliban will radicalise Pakistan society, in the process mobilising a widespread revolt against Musharraf that will lead to the installation of an Islamist government in Islamabad. Hence Musharraf's willingness and ability to oppose Al Qaeda, the Taliban and domestic Islamist terrorists will determine the future of the long, rugged and porous Pakistan-Afghanistan border area as well as of Pakistan itself. And this cannot be achieved without his survival of attempts by his enemies to get rid of him.

The Islamist threat to India, Pakistan's arch-enemy, has steadfastly escalated during the last decade. In the fight against India, Al Qaeda's role has been both covert and overt. On December 21, 1999, the Voice of America in Washington received a fax sent on behalf of Nazeer Ahmed Mujjaid, military adviser to Al Qaeda, containing threats to America, Russia and India:

> Americans, Indians and Russians are the leading terrorists. As soon as the snow melts, India will have to face another trial like Kargil. [...] Infidels can not stop Jihad from conspiracies. [...] While the people in Afghanistan, Kashmir and Chechnia are dying of hunger and Americans celebrate Christmas, how is it possible? Mujahideens will continue their efforts against Americans, Russians and Indians. [...] Inshallah, Islam will spread over the entire world.[164]

After 9/11, such pronouncements referred frequently to India. In an Al Qaeda video released on October 14, 2001, Sulaiman Abu Ghaith said:

> Powell and other members of the US administration know that when AI Qaeda promises, it delivers, and the information is what we see not what we hear. The storm of airplanes will not be calmed, if it is God's will. The storm will not calm, especially as long as you do not end your support for the Jews in Palestine, lift your embargo from around the Iraqi people and have left the Arabian Peninsula, and stop your support of the Hindu against the Muslims in Kashmir.[165]

On October 26, 2001, Mullah Muhammad Omar was reported as saying: "The true terrorists are Islam's enemies — the United States, India, Russia and Israel."[166]

In keeping with Osama's doctrine, Al Qaeda dispatched operatives to strike Indian targets while assisting anti-Indian Pakistani and Kashmiri groups. In early 2001 an Al Qaeda Sudanese member, Abdel Rauf Hawash, was infiltrated to New Delhi to plan an attack on the US Embassy. He was arrested in April that year, whereupon he admitted to membership of Al Qaeda and divulged that he had attended three meetings addressed by Osama. His failed attack had been planned by Muhammad Omar Al-Harazi.

The US Information Service Centre (USIS) in Calcutta, India, was attacked by unknown terrorists on January 22, 2002. Four policemen guarding the building were killed by terrorists firing from the backs of motorcycles. Aftab Ansari in Dubai telephoned Indian newspapers and claimed responsibility for the attack, stating that the attack was in protest against "the evil empire of America". As such, the Indian authorities linked this attack to Omar Sheikh. Ansari, who had identified himself as a representative of Harkat-ul Jehad-ul Islami, was arrested by police in Dubai and deported to India on February 9, 2002.

Muhammad Afroz's interrogation also revealed that one of the trained teams of hijackers had as its target the Indian Parliament in Delhi, on which a plane was to be crashed.[167] This plan was aborted, for reasons unknown, if indeed it is true, but Afroz's interrogators in India were told that Parliament was an Al Qaeda target well before the commando-style attack in January 2001. In their eyes, this lends credibility to his testimony, as does the fact that he has since repeated the accusations in court, in camera, having been given a chance to rethink his confession.

The threat from passenger aircraft being used as impromptu missiles is likely to persist. In addition to the arrest of Al Qaeda suspects of Middle Eastern origin learning to fly in Peshawar in March 2002, intelligence sources reported that Al Qaeda was planning to hijack an Indian Airlines (IA), Pakistan International Airlines (PIA) or Sri Lankan Airlines (UL) aircraft and crash it on to a US warship in the Indian Ocean in February 2002.[168] The Indian Police also detected a plan by an Al Qaeda cell in Mumbai tasked to assassinate visiting Vice Admiral V.J. Metzger, commander-in-chief of the US Seventh Fleet. Three Al Qaeda operatives, led by a Chechen, were thought to have slipped into the city unnoticed. Metzger's scheduled visit was subsequently cancelled.[169]

Bangladesh

One of the six signatories of the *fatwa* issued by the "World Islamic Front for the Jihad Against the Jews and Crusaders" in February 1998 was Abdul Salam Muhammad (*alias* Fazlur Rahman), of the Harkat-ul-Jihad-al-Islam of Bangladesh. It was formed in 1992 to recruit volunteers to fight in Kashmir and Afghanistan, but the Bangladeshi authorities now believe that Al Qaeda has funded it. The group also operates in north-eastern India in tandem with several small Islamist groupings. Osama was said to have sent his private secretary to attend a meeting of Harkat-ul-Jihad-al-Islam in Bangladesh to draft a strategy to intensify their violent campaign in that region.[170] Al Qaeda's connections with Bangladesh include a new organisation, known as Servants of Suffering Humanity International, launched in Dhaka. Indian intelligence believes that a 25-member team of Al Qaeda/Taliban fighters arrived in Bangladesh in June 2001 to give arms training to Harkat-ul-Jihad-al-Islam. The group reportedly receives financial assistance from Pakistan, Saudi Arabia and

Afghanistan through Muslim NGOs in Bangladesh.[171]

The media and intellectuals in Bangladesh, as in most Muslim countries in Asia, take an active role against Islamic fundamentalism, and Harkat-ul-Jihad-al-Islam and other Islamist organisations do not enjoy mass support. A few Al Qaeda-trained Bangladeshis are active in the country, actively spreading Islamist ideas in the hope of building support for fundamentalism.[172] In the late 1990s Islamists planned to assassinate the then Prime Minister Sheikh Hasina and to target secular-minded intellectuals. In addition to Harkat-ul-Jihad-al-Islamia, both Bangladeshi and other security and intelligence agencies are investigating alleged Al Qaeda links with other Islamist organisations.[173] With intelligence indicating an impending Al Qaeda operation to assassinate President Clinton during his visit to Bangladesh, which had been planned for the final months of his term in office, his trip was cancelled.

5

THE AL QAEDA THREAT AND THE INTERNATIONAL RESPONSE

"Our next victory, God willing, is going to be in Hejaz and Najd. We will make America suffer a defeat worse than she suffered in Lebanon and Vietnam." (Commentary from an Al Qaeda recruitment video seized by police in London in the aftermath of 9/11)

The context

The global fight against Al Qaeda will be the defining conflict of the early 21st century. Osama bin Laden has built an organisation that functions both operationally and ideologically at local, national, regional and global levels. Defeating Al Qaeda and its associate groups will be the single biggest challenge confronting the international security and intelligence community, law enforcement authorities and national militaries in the foreseeable future.

To terrorise Western governments, their societies and their friends in the Muslim world Al Qaeda recruited and generated support from territorial and migrant Muslim communities worldwide. Today it poses an unprecedented terrorist threat to international peace and security. As its leader, Osama bin Laden inspires and instigates and, through Al Qaeda, provides direct support to his followers to oppose the "enemies of Islam". To challenge Al Qaeda and its associate groups successfully, the international community must develop a multi-pronged, multi-agency, multi-dimensional and multi-national response.

The international outrage following Al Qaeda's multiple attacks on America's outstanding landmarks on September 11, 2001 provided the community of nations with a framework for fighting this terrorist hydra. Since the East African bombings of August 1998, the threat of a mass casualty attack in the US had been apparent, but Washington lacked domestic and international support to intervene in Afghanistan. With the Soviet withdrawal in February 1989, Afghanistan replaced the Syrian-controlled Bekaa Valley in Lebanon as the world's premier terrorist training centre for about forty guerrilla and terrorist groups. With no vital interests at stake in a remote corner of Asia, the West was impervious to the suffering of the Afghan people, who had endured death and destruction for two decades. Like a looming shadow the conflicts the West neglected and ignored are returning to haunt it with a vengeance.

Many factors contributed to 9/11, including America's disengagement from world affairs; the Western myth that controlling its borders will protect a nation from the rest of the world; and international neglect of protracted conflicts. Traditionally, the development of counter-measures has always been a reaction to a breach of security. European governments developed elite forces to combat terrorism in response to Germany's failure to prevent the PLO's massacre of Israeli athletes at the Munich Olympic Games on September 5, 1972.[1] Thirty years later, the gravity of international terrorism had shifted from the Middle East to Asia, but terrorist groups can still conduct long-range, deep penetration operations to strike at the West. The horror, fear and anger that 9/11 unleashed precipitated unprecedented worldwide security, intelligence and judicial cooperation.

To combat Osama's alliance, the World Islamic Front for the Jihad Against Jews and Crusaders (*al-Jabha al-Islaamiyya lil-Jihad Dudda al-Yahood wal-Saliibiyeen*), the international community has formed an anti-terrorist coalition. At the core of Osama's alliance is Al Qaeda, while at the core of the coalition are the Western and Asian liberal democracies – North America, Europe, Australia and Japan, the wealthiest and the most powerful governments that can sustain a protracted campaign against terrorism.

As long as its operational and support infrastructure remains intact, Al Qaeda will threaten both the Muslim and the Western world. Al Qaeda is not invincible, nor is it infallible. Through understanding its operational and ideological techniques, counter-measures can be developed to disrupt, degrade and destroy it. By painstakingly detecting its worldwide physical infrastructure and human network, the organisation can be dismantled and its leadership neutralised.

Understanding the threat

In the past Islamist organisations fizzled out because of a lack of battle-hardened and tested structures. They relied on village, clan and tribe and built organisations based on traditional loyalties. As such, they lacked a modern, robust and resilient organisation. By adapting and seamlessly grafting pre-existing models, Al Qaeda has built an Islamist organisation full of vitality. Its politically clandestine structure is built on the idea of internationalism. Using techniques drawn from Leninism and operating on the Marxist militant model, it uses *noms de guerre*, adheres strictly to a cell structure, follows the idea of a cadre party, maintains tight discipline, promotes self-sacrifice and reverence for the leadership and is guided by a programme of action. Al Qaeda is self-reproducing and therefore hard to defeat.

Because there is no historical precedent for Al Qaeda, the past offers very little guidance. The success and failure of the US-led anti-terrorist campaign will depend on the ability and willingness of America, its allies and its coalition partners to learn as they progress. In an ever-changing, fluid and dynamic environment, only by minimising failures and maximising successes can they prevail against a determined enemy willing to kill and die.

Although heavy bombing detected, disrupted and degraded the physical infrastructure of Al Qaeda and the Taliban in Afghanistan, their fighting cadres are intact. The Muslim territorial and migrant communities from Australia to the Middle East and Canada will continue to provide recruits and finance. Al Qaeda's future survival will depend on the continuing appeal of its radical ideology that sustains a fledgling global support network. In the virtual absence of counter-propaganda, many literate and illiterate Muslims view its ideology as compatible with Islamic theology. To counter its non-military capability and capacity, the anti-terrorist coalition needs both a strategic vision and tactical direction. There is no opposite number in the anti-terrorist coalition to counter Al Qaeda's broad strategy as formulated by Dr Ayman Al-Zawahiri, Osama's principal strategist. Moreover specialists in counter-revolutionary warfare and counter-terrorism lack a model to fight Al Qaeda — both its guerrilla arm, 055 Brigade, and its global terrorist network.

Al Qaeda's strategy

With the US building its multinational coalition and deploying its troops in Afghanistan, the Philippines, Yemen and in Georgia, Al Qaeda is responding by building a multinational alliance of terrorist groups. Advancing the concept of the universality of the battle, it is seeking to widen the conflict from the territorial to the global, countering US initiatives by expanding its existing alliance made up of the "*jihad* movements in the various lands of Islam" as well as "the bases of *jihad* [Afghanistan and Chechnya] liberated in the name of *jihad* for the sake of God".[2] To quote al-Zawahiri, the alliance represents

> a growing power that is rallying under the banner of jihad for the sake of God and operating outside the scope of the new world order. It is free of the servitude for the dominating western empire. It promises destruction and ruin for the new Crusades against the lands of Islam. It is ready for revenge against the heads of the world's gathering of infidels, the United States, Russia and Israel. It is anxious to seek retribution for the blood of the martyrs, the grief of the mothers, the deprivation of the orphans, the suffering of the detainees, and the sores of the tortured people throughout the land of Islam, from Eastern Turkestan to Andalusia.[3]

Seeking to mobilise the "Muslim nation", Al Qaeda projected the confrontation in Afghanistan as a battle of "Islam against infidelity". Reviewing the lack of support by Islamist movements immediately after 9/11, Al Qaeda emphasised the need for perseverance, patience, steadfastness and adherence to a firm set of principles. In keeping with the belief that the key to victory is the example set by the leadership, it placed the responsibility for the campaign on the leadership and the responsibility for the quality of leadership on the membership. Quoting the Koran — "O ye who believe, endure, outdo all others in endurance, be ready, and observe your duty to Allah, in order that ye may succeed" — al-Zawahiri adds:

If signs of relaxation and retreat start to show in the leadership, the movement must find ways to straighten it out and not permit it to deviate from the line of jihad. The loyalty to the leadership and the acknowledgement of its precedence and merit represent a duty that must be emphasized and a value that must be consolidated. But if loyalty to the leadership reaches the point of declaring it holy and if the acknowledgement of its precedence and merit leads to infallibility, the movement will suffer from methodological blindness. Any leadership flaw could lead to a historic catastrophe, not only for the movement but also for the entire nation. Hence comes the importance of the issue of leadership in Islamic action in general and jihad action in particular, and the nation's need for a scientific, struggling and rational leadership that could guide the nation, amidst the mighty storms and hurricanes, toward its goal with awareness and prudence, without losing sight of its path, stumbling aimlessly, or reversing its course.[4]

In his post-9/11 book, *Knights Under the Prophet's Banner — Meditations on the Jihadist Movement*, al-Zawahiri justifies an escalation of terrorist techniques and tactics:

(1) The need to inflict the maximum casualties against the opponent, for this is the language understood by the West, no matter how much time and effort such operations take.

(2) The need to concentrate on the method of martyrdom operations as the most successful way of inflicting damage against the opponent and the least costly to the *mujahidin* in terms of casualties.

(3) The targets as well as the type and method of weapons used must be chosen to have an impact on the structure of the enemy and deter it enough to stop its brutality, arrogance and disregard for all taboos and customs. It must restore the struggle to its real size.

(4) To re-emphasise what we have already explained, we reiterate that focusing on the domestic enemy alone will not be feasible at this stage.[5]

Considering the limitations imposed on Al Qaeda, its post-Taliban exhortations have urged other Islamist groups to engage in mass casualty terrorism. Aware of the depletion of its resources, Al Qaeda has called for a change in *modus operandi* and choice of targets against the superior coalition forces to "keep up with the tremendous increase in the number of its enemies, the quality of their weapons, their destructive powers, their disregard for all taboos, and disrespect for the customs of wars and conflicts."[6] Al Qaeda has also instigated Islamist terrorist groups to strike at foreign targets on their own soil as well as overseas. In a pre-recorded Al Qaeda video, the UA93 hijacker Ahmed Ibrahim Al Haznawi, who planned to target the White House, said: "The time of humiliation and subjugation is over...but, today we are killing them in the midst of their homes. It's time to kill Americans in their heartland."[7] As most Islamist groups are territorially bound, they are unlikely to follow Al Qaeda's request. Nonetheless, Al Qaeda's sleeper cells in Europe and the US, its newly-formed cells and its pre-existing cells introduced from overseas are likely to strike targets on Western soil. As a priority, Al Qaeda has called for the campaign to focus on the continental US. The state of alertness of European and North American countries will not deter it from mounting an operation to strike the West. Nor will conventional methods of deterrence — capture, arrest, trial, imprisonment, or humiliation, injury or death — protect the West from suicide terrorism.

In many respects Al Qaeda is ahead of its opponents. Immediately after US troops entered Afghanistan, it anticipated how the US would use intergovernmental, governmental and non-governmental actors to strengthen its position in Afghanistan, especially in order to alleviate the suffering of the Afghan people. To justify targeting them, al-Zawahiri established six categories of actors who are Western "tools to fight Islam". They are the United Nations, Muslim regimes that work with the west, multinational corporations, international communications and data exchange systems, international news agencies and satellite media channels, and international relief agencies.[8] Al-Zawahiri also stated that in face of the anti-terrorist coalition, an alliance made up of the *jihad* movements in the various lands of Islam is taking place. This implies that the threat to these agencies will come not only from Al Qaeda but also from its associate groups.

Unlike most terrorist groups, Al Qaeda is mindful of the social and the economic costs of its attacks. An insight into Osama's thinking on the impact of 9/11 is likely to inform us of their next wave of strikes:

> I say the events that happened on Tuesday 11 September in New York and Washington, that is truly a great event in all measures, and its claims until this moment are not over and are still continuing.... According to their own admissions, the share of the losses on the Wall Street market reached 16%. They said that this number is a record, which has never happened since the opening of the

market more than 230 years ago. This large collapse has never happened. The gross amount that is traded in that market reaches $4 trillion. So if we multiply 16% by $4 trillion to find out the loss that affected the stocks, it reaches $640 billion of losses from stocks, by Allah's grace. So this amount, for example, is the budget of Sudan for 640 years. They have lost this, due to an attack that happened with the success of Allah lasting one hour only. The daily income of the American nation is $20 billion. The first week they didn't work at all due to the psychological shock of the attack, and even until today some don't work due to the attack. So if you multiply $20 billion by 1 week, it comes out to $140 billion, and it is even bigger than this. If you add it to the $640 billion, we've reached how much? Approximately $800 billion. The cost of the building losses and construction losses? Let us say more than $30 billion. Then they have fired or liquidated until today ... from the airline companies more than 170,000 employees. That includes cargo plane companies, and commercial airlines, and American studies and analysis have mentioned that 70% of the American people even until today still suffer from depression and psychological trauma after the incident of the two towers, and the attack on the Defense Ministry, the Pentagon — thanks to Allah's grace. One of the well-known American hotel companies, Intercontinental, has fired 20,000 employees — thanks to Allah's grace. Those claims cannot be calculated by anyone due to their very large scale, multitude and complexity — and it is increasing thanks to Allah's grace — so watch as the amount reaches no less than $1 trillion by the lowest estimate — thanks to Allah's grace — due to these successful and blessed attacks. We implore Allah to accept those brothers within the ranks of the martyrs, and to admit them to the highest levels of Paradise.[9]

Given the increased threat to Islamist terrorist groups, Al Qaeda is enlisting the support of underground groups as well as legitimate political parties. Instead of Islamist terrorist groups shouldering the burden of politicising, radicalising and mobilising Muslims, Al Qaeda has called upon Islamist political parties to shoulder the duties of propaganda, recruitment and fundraising, thus freeing Islamist terrorist groups to concentrate on planning, preparing and conducting attacks. Al Qaeda calls upon them to "expose" the "rulers" who fight Islam; highlight the "importance of loyalty to the faithful and relinquishing of the infidels in the Muslim creed"; hold "every Muslim responsible for defending Islam, its sanctities, nation, and homeland"; caution against the "ulema of the sultan and reminding the nation of the virtues of the ulema of jihad and the imams of sacrifice and the need for the nation to defend, protect, honor, and follow them" and expose "the extent of aggression against our creed and sanctities and the plundering of our wealth".[10] Among Muslim migrant communities in North America, Europe, and Australia, preventing Islamists from advancing their political aims and objectives non-violently is well nigh impossible. To operate amid tight security and vigilance, Al Qaeda's post 9/11 strategy is designed for Islamist parties hiding behind the political veil to produce a generation of recruits and supporters to sustain the fight in Afghanistan and elsewhere. Until favourable conditions emerge, Al Qaeda will operate through mosques, *madrasas*, community centres and, as best it can, charities in Western Europe and North America.

Damage assessment

With the Taliban leader Mullah Muhammad Omar joining forces with Osama in October 2001, Al Qaeda's force multiplied. Compared to Al Qaeda, a foreign force, the Taliban enjoyed vast support in Afghanistan. It is a dangerous alliance, but one that could have been disrupted had the US given Pakistan more time to negotiate with the Islamic Emirate of Afghanistan to hand Osama over to Islamabad immediately after 9/11. The US-led anti-terrorist coalition initiated its campaign by denying an opportunity for diplomatic efforts by Pakistan to drive a wedge between the Taliban and Al Qaeda. Although the two combined forces in combat against the Northern Alliance, the relationship had its ups and downs. At the request of the ISI, the Taliban imposed restrictions on Osama's activities, especially terrorist operations and press interviews, after the East Africa bombings. Although not strictly enforced, these measures led to significant tension, creating pro- and anti-Osama divisions within the Taliban. Under the leadership of Mullah Omar the Taliban would not have handed over Osama for trial to a non-Islamic court, but the Pakistanis could have prevented the formation of the Taliban-Al Qaeda alliance. Had the US intelligence community developed an accurate assessment of the numerical strengths of Al Qaeda and the Taliban and understood the implications of unity between a relatively unpopular Al Qaeda and a relatively popular Taliban, it could have postponed the US strikes. Today, Al Qaeda, essentially an Arab force, can infiltrate, probe and strike targets because of the links it has developed with the Afghan community through its alliance with the Taliban. The situation would have been very different had Pakistan prevented the Taliban, a regime closer to it than to Al Qaeda, from joining forces with the latter.

Despite this initial drawback, the anti-Al Qaeda/Taliban campaign has witnessed some significant successes. Within the first six months, Al Qaeda lost 16 of its 25 key leaders and the Taliban 21 of its 27 top people on the Pentagon's most wanted list. The group has begun to adapt to the new threat and to replace its losses, but it has suffered two catastrophes. In the first, Al Qaeda's Emir and military commander, Muhammad Atef, was killed by a US airstrike in Kabul, on November 14, 2001.[11] A founder member, Atef had responsibility for both Al Qaeda's domestic Afghan operations as well as the day-to-day running of the organisation. In addition to being Osama's brother-in-law, he planned all the major Al

Qaeda guerrilla and terrorist operations after the death of his predecessor al-Banshiri in April 1996. Atef was deputy commander of the Somalia operation and immediately before his death conceptualised the broad contours of the anti-coalition campaign in Afghanistan in 2001. In the second catastrophe Al Qaeda's director of external operations, Abu Zubaydah, was captured by a joint Pakistani police, FBI and CIA team during raids in Faisalabad, Pakistan, on March 28, 2002. The most elusive member of Al Qaeda, Zubaydah is a Palestinian with Saudi citizenship who managed the terrorist support and operational network worldwide. In addition to serving as the Emir of Khalden, a camp exclusively for terrorist training, Zubaydah was responsible for liaison with foreign terrorist groups and Islamic NGOs. He also organised the passage of Osama's family members back and forth between Pakistan-Afghanistan and Saudi Arabia and oversaw all terrorist operations outside Afghanistan after Osama's return from Sudan in May 1996, including 9/11.

Key Al Qaeda leaders have been captured since September 1998, but its global network suffered its single biggest loss with the arrest of Zubaydah. US officials described him accurately as an "important cog" in the Al Qaeda machinery, especially in the regrouping process, and as the "encyclopaedia of Al Qaeda — its money, its overseas cells, attack plans and identities of its agents are inside his head." Zubaydah usually operated out of Peshawar, and relocated to Punjab after the US intervention in Afghanistan. The grenade attack on the Protestant church in Islamabad on March 17, 2002, in which five people were killed including the wife and daughter of a US official, prompted US-Pakistan agencies to cooperate on the ground. The resulting operation, mounted after interrogation of seven individuals — Pakistani, Ugandan, Mauritanian and Sudanese — captured along the Afghan-Pakistan border,[12] also led to the arrest of 60 Arabs (Syrians, Egyptians, Yemenis), Afghans and Pakistanis. Both Atef and Zubaydah enjoyed the total confidence of the Al Qaeda rank and file.

Other Al Qaeda losses include Ibn Al-Shaykh al-Libi, who was captured in Pakistan, and Abdul Rahim al-Sharqawi and Abd Al-Hadi al-Iraqi who were detained near Khost on January 8. In addition to Atef, the dead include Mohammad Salah and Tariq Anwar al-Sayyid Ahmad, killed during US air strikes near Khost in early November; Abu Salah al-Yemeni, Abu Jafar al-Jaziri and Abu Hafs, killed on January 8 near Khost; and, according to unverified accounts, Mohammad Omar Abdel Rahman. Among the Taliban leaders, its chief of intelligence, Qari Ahmadullah, was killed in a US air strike on December 27. According to the Pentagon an ally of Osama, Juma Namangani, leader of the Islamic Movement of Uzbekistan/Islamic Party of Turkestan (IMU/IPT), who commanded the Taliban forces in Taloqan, was also killed.[13] It will take time for Al Qaeda to replace these experienced leaders, whose expertise, knowledge and contacts were indispensable to the organisation.

In the first six months of the US-led anti-terrorist campaign, there are no indications of Al Qaeda deserting Afghanistan. In contrast, the heavy losses through capture, death and injury suffered by Al Qaeda leaders demonstrate that they are leading from the front. In addition to Osama, Zawahiri, and Rifai Ahmed Taha, the Al Qaeda leadership that survived the first six months of operations included Abd al-Rahim al-Nashiri, Abu Masab Zarqari and Zubair al-Haili, the guerrilla and terrorist operational commanders; Saif al-Adil (Egyptian) and Amin al-Haq (Afghan), bodyguard commanders; and Midhat Mursi (Egyptian), head of weapons research.

Al Qaeda's mindset

Al Qaeda did not anticipate the US induction of ground troops to Afghanistan in the wake of 9/11. Its thinking was influenced by the withdrawal of US troops from three theatres: Beirut after the Hezbollah bombings in October 1983; Aden after the Al Qaeda bombings in December 1992; and Somalia after the Al Qaeda-trained Al-Ittihad attacks in October 1993. When Osama — accompanied by his sons Hamza, Muhammad, Khaled and Laden — visited the site where the first US helicopter crashed in Afghanistan, one of his sons remarked to an Al Qaeda member: "You see? They are commandos. They are a superpower only in Hollywood and in films. Their heroes are only mythical like Rambo and they won't come to Afghanistan. And if they do come here, they will end up in pieces like this."[14]

Al Qaeda's leadership, membership and supporters firmly believe that everything happens according to God's will. Its members state that because God wanted to split the Soviet empire into small states, God sent the Soviet military to the *mujahidin* for the purpose of defeating the Soviets. Osama claimed

> The One who prolonged us with one of His helping hands and stabilised us to defeat the Soviet empire, is capable of prolonging us again and allowing us to defeat America on the same land, and with the same sayings, and that is the grace of Allah. So we believe that the defeat of America is something achievable — with the permission of Allah — and it is easier for us — with the permission of Allah — than the defeat of the Soviet empire previously."[15] Similarly, al-Zawahiri claimed: "Those 19 hijackers who went out and worked and sacrificed their lives for God, God granted their conquest that we enjoy today. The great victory that was achieved was because of God's help and not because of our efficiency or power."[16]

The message "You are carrying out God's wish" makes an Al Qaeda member relentlessly pursue *jihad*. Thus the state of mind of an average Al Qaeda member prepares him psychologically and physically to struggle against all odds, suffer heavy losses yet continue fighting to the death. All Islamic and Islamist movements, including Al Qaeda, think and plan for years, if not for decades. In the mindset of an Al Qaeda member or supporter, whether in Afghanistan, Palestine, Iraq, or elsewhere, the fight is between God's warriors — the *mujahidin* — and Satanic forces — the US troops. As a Muslim's duty is *jihad*, all Muslims are expected to participate, if not support, the *mujahidin* fighting the US.

Will Al Qaeda, like some Islamist groups in the past that compromised with their opponents, be prepared to give and take? No. Al Qaeda was founded on the premise that it will not compromise, however long it takes, however hard the fight and whatever the losses it suffers. As long as Osama is Emir General and al-Zawahiri is the principal strategist, it will not compromise. Post-Osama, its psyche will commit its members to his dream and al-Zawahiri's strategy — until or unless Osama's legacy fades away.

Islamists place their faith in God, but they are also practical. Al-Zawahiri accepts that, and states: "All movements go through a cycle of erosion and renewal, but it is the ultimate result that determines the fate of a movement: either extinction or growth."[17] Until the US intervention in Afghanistan, Al Qaeda was firmly of the view that an Islamic state must be built in the Middle East, the heart of the Islamic world. To build a critical mass, it believes that a sufficient number of recruits must be trained and resources generated in existing arenas of *jihad* such as Afghanistan and Chechnya. By the dispersal of Islamists and the patient building of their organisations outside the Arabian Peninsula and North Africa, Al Qaeda avoids the arrest of its operatives, the seizure of its resources and the detection of its future plans.

With the growing threat to the Al Qaeda leadership in Afghanistan, a difference of opinion separates al-Zawahiri from Osama. Based on his experience of many years in prison, al-Zawahiri believes that when under siege in any theatre Islamists must move out to "safety of a shelter without hesitation, reluctance or reliance on illusions. The most serious dilemma facing someone under siege is the escape decision. It is the hardest thing to leave the family, the position, the job, and the steady style of life and proceed to the unknown, uncertainties, and the uneasy life. But as soon as the door of the cell closes behind the prisoner he wishes that he had spent his entire life displaced without a shelter rather than facing the humiliating experience of captivity."[18] While Osama has vowed to attain "martyrdom" in Afghanistan, al-Zawahiri's wish is for the *mujahidin* to withdraw to other theatres in order to fight another day. Through the first six months since the US intervention in October

2001, the view of Osama prevailed. Except to widen the theatre of battle, there is no indication whatever that Al Qaeda members from Afghanistan are withdrawing to neighbouring areas in large numbers. If Osama is killed, al-Zawahiri is likely to withdraw and return if and when conditions are favourable. Once again, the disagreement between the two leaders concerns al-Zawahiri's desire for a very practical solution to preserve and protect the leadership of Al Qaeda.

Threat trajectory

Al Qaeda's trajectory is no different from that of most terrorist groups. Terrorist initiation, escalation, de-escalation and termination are determined by three factors: the leadership's intent; a group's capability (resources and expertise); and opportunities presented by the enemy for attack. In the first wave, Al Qaeda and its associate groups attacked secular and moderate Muslim countries like Egypt, Saudi Arabia, Jordan and Pakistan. The brutal response of the Middle Eastern and Asian security services led Al Qaeda and its associate members, collaborators and supporters to be detained, tortured and killed and their safe houses, vehicles and finances seized. As a result of these setbacks, Al Qaeda decided to target its distant enemy — the West — that was supporting the near enemy: friendly Muslim rulers and their regimes.

There has been an underestimation of the Islamist threat by the West because until recently it was was largely directed at Muslim rulers, regimes and populations. Western Liberal democracies failed to understand the nature of the multiple *modus operandi* of the Islamists, and provided political asylum, access to banks, passports, social security, legal assistance, and dual technologies to several Al Qaeda members and charitable and non-profit status to their front, cover and sympathetic organisations. As long as Islamists did not target the West, liberal democracies tacitly permitted Al Qaeda and its associate groups to operate — to disseminate propaganda, recruit, raise funds and procure and ship goods. Even today, liberal democracies are against regulating terrorist propaganda, including the internet, a favoured Al Qaeda tool. Al Qaeda and its associate groups raised more funds from liberal democracies than they received from their state sponsors. When the time was ripe, it used Europe, its forward operational base, to strike the US. Moreover, the Western intelligence community, suffering from the Cold War legacy of "monitoring spies" as opposed to disrupting terrorist support operations, had little knowledge of what went on in their backyards. They failed to understand that watching post-Cold War terrorists was different from monitoring Cold War spies. As such, the intelligence community failed miserably to deter Al Qaeda from mounting operations from the West. Until some 2,900 American and other lives were lost on 9/11, Western governments and their security services were reticent about sharing intelligence, and judicial authorities rarely entertained requests for extradition from the rest of the world.

Liberal democracies have limited experience in managing the Islamist threat, but Al Qaeda poses a more serious threat to Muslims. This is not apparent or easily quantifiable. Unlike Western countries that have been physically and psychologically affected by its terrorist attacks, Muslim territorial and migrant communities are susceptible to its ideological penetration. Upon successful penetration, some of their number serve as an extended arm of Al Qaeda, first as sympathisers, then as supporters, thereafter as collaborators, and finally as members. Middle Eastern, Central Asian and South East Asian countries have by and large controlled the contemporary wave of Islamism that began in 1979. After the Syrian military responded to an uprising by Islamists in Hama in 1982, 25,000 civilians were massacred or "disappeared", while 15,000 alleged Islamists were detained by the authorities in Uzbekistan. Every Muslim country from Indonesia to Tunisia has to counter the Islamist threat. In non-Muslim countries hosting Muslim communities, China has managed the Uighurs in Xinjiang and Myanmar the Rohingiya Muslims. However, torture, mass imprisonment without trial and expulsion have not deterred the Islamists. Nor is the range of counter-measures applied in the Global South compatible with the standard of human rights and civil liberties as well as the criminal justice system of the West.

As long as Al Qaeda and its associate groups can appeal to Muslims worldwide to share its ideals, aims and objectives, its support and operational cells will regenerate and multiply. To this end the international community should develop punitive and prophylactic measures aimed at targeting the demand and supply side of Al Qaeda. Equally, sanctions and penalties must be imposed on their sponsors and hosts, whether governments or, more importantly, organisations; a relentless global, regional and national hunt and harsh sentences for Al Qaeda leaders, members, collaborators and supporters; irresistible incentives for Al Qaeda defectors; and attractive rewards for information leading to the arrest of Al Qaeda operatives or disruption of Al Qaeda plans and preparations. But of equal importance are resolving Kashmir, Palestine, and other international conflicts where Muslims are affected; redressing grievances and meeting the legitimate aspiration of Muslims; and helping Arab and Muslim states to improve the quality of life of their citizens. Above all, Al Qaeda's ideology must be countered, in order to deflect and lessen its appeal to serving members, fresh recruits and actual or potential supporters.

As Islamist groups have repeatedly demonstrated in the recent past, a military solution is only one part of a wider strategy of implementing socio-economic and political reforms. Otherwise, the threat will diminish in the short term but re-emerge in the midterm. As Al Qaeda is an uncompromising group, the military option will remain the most effective one in the immediate, mid and long term. As such, state actors, their elite forces and intelligence communities will play the prime role in the fight against terrorism. Nonetheless, governments must work in partnership with other actors. Widespread consensus and sustained support to target Al Qaeda can be built as a priority on the basis of countering its commitment to mass casualty terrorism, including the use of CBRN weapons, and function as a pioneering vanguard inspiring, instigating and providing direct support to other groups. Instead of addressing the threat at a tactical level, the West and other countries must develop a strategic framework for managing the Islamist threat.

Although Al Qaeda threatens both Western and Muslim countries, the West — primarily the US — has the diplomatic, political, economic and military means to set the agenda against terrorism. In order to win, the West and the Muslim world must embark on a new relationship, one that counters the *status quo ante* that gave rise to Al Qaeda. To a large extent, the attitude of the West and the Muslim world has created the current situation. The West must work with the Muslim world — governments *and* people; working only with governments is not enough. Sharing intelligence with Muslim rulers and regimes that proves that Al Qaeda was responsible for 9/11 did little to convince Muslim societies. Therefore, public diplomacy should be an integral feature in the campaign against terrorism.

Active measures against the group should include the military (direct) and non-military (indirect), which can be issue- and region-specific.[19] Military methods will provide the security and political conditions to implement the far reaching socio-economic, welfare and political programs that will have a lasting impact. As the past offers little guidance, both counter-terrorist (offensive) and anti-terrorist (protective) measures against Al Qaeda and its associates in the short-term should be continuously assessed for their successes and failures. Hence the mid-term response depends very much on the outcome of the short-term battle.

Short-term Response

The destruction of Al Qaeda and Taliban infrastructure in Afghanistan has been pivotal to threat reduction. In the first six months of this campaign, the US achieved this feat with minimal losses. Al Qaeda, having merged its forces with the Taliban under Mullah Omar, it tactically repositioned its cadres on the Afghan-Pakistan border and is preparing to wage a protracted guerrilla campaign that might last at least a decade.[20]

In the first six months after 9/11 the global network of Al Qaeda and its associate groups staged attacks against two churches in Pakistan, the kidnapping and murder of Daniel Pearl, a suicide attack against a synagogue in Tunisia, another against a bus carrying French nationals in Karachi, and bombings in Yemen. Al Qaeda's *modus operandi* has changed since 9/11. To make its presence felt, it will now stage attacks against both strategic and tactical targets worldwide.

In the Islamist mindset, Chechnya and Afghanistan are grounds already tested by *jihad*. Islamists claim that the erstwhile Soviet superpower was first defeated by them in Afghanistan and then its successor Russia was also defeated by Islamists in the first Chechen war. However long it takes, Islamists worldwide will support the twin campaigns to defeat the US in Afghanistan and Russia in Chechnya. Pankishi valley in Georgia is also a transit base for Chechen guerrillas seeking to enter Afghanistan. By astute diplomacy, the US has denied the Islamists two critical rear bases — Pakistan and Georgia — that have traditionally supplied Afghanistan and Chechnya. As long as these two frontline states remain friendly to the US, the Islamists cannot win either in Afghanistan or in Chechnya. However, they will wage a protracted campaign until their leaders are killed, supplies are exhausted and recruitment is disrupted.

Pakistan will remain the pivotal state in the fight against terrorism, at least in the mid term. Despite the restrictions placed on Islamabad by the US after the nuclear tests in 1998, General Pervez Musharraf extended vital cooperation. After 9/11 the US lifted the restrictions on Pakistan's trade allowing for up to $426 million in new imports to the US [21] — and pledged to mediate in the Kashmir conflict. The key to ending Pakistani covert military, and overt political and diplomatic, support for the Kashmiri *mujahidin* is for the US to mediate in that conflict with all possible despatch.

Further strangling of terrorist finances; tighter control over the manufacturing and supply of weapons; exchange of personnel; sharing of expertise; and building common terrorist databases are essential in the Global South. Outside Afghanistan, Al Qaeda employs a full range of active measures against its opponents — information infrastructure attack, financial fraud, economic warfare, psychological operations, mass casualty terrorism. To address the threat of catastrophic terrorism, governments must develop new vaccines, medicines and diagnostic tests, stockpile vaccines and antidotes, strengthen health systems by enhancing medical communication and disease surveillance capabilities, improve controls on storage and transfer of pathogens, and impose controls on related equipment. Similarly, protection of nuclear facilities should be greatly enhanced. As Al Qaeda has access to skilled Middle Eastern, Asian and former Soviet scientists, attempts by the group to develop a CBRN capability should be frustrated by the monitoring of rogue scientists and technicians.

Until it decentralises its structure and becomes even more clandestine, Al Qaeda will rely heavily on the infrastructure of its associate groups. Although the US has deployed troops in Mindanao in the Philippines, Yemen, and the Pankishi valley in Georgia, Al Qaeda will survive in Indonesia, Kashmir, Somalia, Chechnya and other theatres. It is seeking to transform the associate groups ideologically and operationally from a territorial *jihad* approach to a universal *jihad* mindset. The JI network in South East Asia, the Harakat network in South Asia, IMU and IPT networks in Central Asia, Takfir and GSPC networks in Europe and North America reflect this new mindset. Since October 2001, the threat has rapidly shifted away from Al Qaeda to other Islamist terrorist groups. To facilitate this diffusion of responsibility, Osama distanced himself from the frontline and spoke for the first time about "Al Qaeda". "I say that the battle isn't between the Al Qaeda organisation and the world Crusaders. The battle is between Muslims — the people of Islam — and the world Crusaders."[22] In many ways his renewed position symbolised the limitations imposed on Al Qaeda and his role as a leader.

Nonetheless, Osama will remain the central rallying point in the fight of the *jihadists* against the "Jews and Christians". As the icon of the international *jihadists*, he has articulated a populist doctrine that "Jihad is the foreign policy of Islamic states" and "Jihad is the Muslim's duty", challenging Muslim rulers and their regimes. Even in the face of adversity, Osama will not relent. The doctrinal principles he articulates will continue to resonate among Muslims worldwide, especially those with grievances against the West. Osama is hailed throughout the Muslim world as the symbol of resistance to the "enemies of Islam". Al Qaeda is driven by a religious ideology, but Osama is a secular leader with no religious authority. Just as Nazism effectively died with Hitler, Islamism of the Al Qaeda brand is likely to die with Osama. His death will break the momentum of the campaign. But, in addition to him, the central targets of the anti-terrorist coalition should include al-Zawahiri and Mullah Muhammad Omar, its conduit to the dispersed Taliban forces and their dormant supporters. As opposed to highly visible actions, such as bombings, which often generate negative reactions, invisible "black operations" such as assassination of terrorist leaders and directing figures should be given priority.

The inability to neutralise the core leadership within the first six months of the anti-terrorist effort is clearly the campaign's single biggest failure. It stems from the traditional inability of Western governments to procure high-grade counter-terrorist intelligence, which is usually developed by cultivating and managing live agents holding membership of terrorist organisations. With the exception of the French, Western operational agencies are unlikely to develop high-grade counter-terrorist intelligence in the short term. After a suicide attack on the US Marine barracks killed 241 US personnel in Beirut on October 23, 1983, it took the CIA five years to penetrate Hezbollah.[23] In the short term, the quality of intelligence and elite forces will determine the outcome of the battle. Initiatives by the US intelligence community immediately following 9/11 have sought to remedy this flaw.[24] Although it presents high risks, recruiting both agent handlers and agents from migrant communities, as well as sharing the intelligence generated with the wider decision- and policy-making community, is essential to be able to respond effectively to the threat in the immediate term.

Mid-term response

While the response to the immediate threat posed by Al Qaeda and its associate groups is largely military, the response to the mid-term threat should be both military and non-military. The key to fighting Al Qaeda effectively is to engage both the military organisation and the support base. Attrition of Al Qaeda's military organisation is the easiest, and can be achieved using the superior military organisation of the West. But the key to strategically weakening the group is to erode its fledgling support base — to wean away its supporters and potential supporters.

As long as Al Qaeda appears legitimate, influential and to be winning, its membership and alliance — the World Islamic Front for the Jihad Against Jews and Crusaders — will grow. To nullify its attractiveness in Muslim eyes its ideology must be discredited. Like other extremist ideologies, such as Nazism and Fascism, violent Islamism will always find modest support. However, the widespread support it enjoys today is driven by the strong belief among Muslims that the West has persistently wronged them. It is international neglect of the Muslim interest in the Palestine and Kashmir conflicts, the presence of US troops on Saudi soil and the frequent double standards of the big players that have legitimised the use of violence.

The US has succeeded in creating a fragile international coalition to fight Al Qaeda by painstakingly building an international consensus against a common threat. If, in order to oust Saddam Hussein, the US unilaterally targets Iraq, where already over a million innocent Iraqis have died, the victor will be Al Qaeda. In addition to dividing and possibly splitting the coalition, it will create the conditions for a fresh wave of support for Islamists. Iran, not Iraq, remains the main sponsor of both Shia and Sunni terrorism — including Al Qaeda and several of its associate groups. There are many other methods of replacing Saddam other than invading Iraq. A skewed US foreign policy aimed at securing

Middle Eastern oil for American industry as well as guaranteeing the security of Israel (a recurring electoral issue) leads the US to support authoritarian Middle Eastern regimes — and Israel — without observing checks and balances. To develop and sustain a broad-based consensus on issues that affect international security, the US must replace unilateralism with multilateralism wherever and whenever possible. The UN, the US, the EU and other credible and powerful actors must develop far-reaching policies to grapple with the protracted conflicts and contentious issues fuelling anti-Western sentiments. There must be a concerted plan by the international community to redress the perceived and actual grievances of moderate Muslims and frustrate the current wave of open and clandestine support for the Islamist agenda. There has been no such plan hitherto.

During the last decade, Islamism has been moving from the margins to the centre stage in Muslim politics and society, and Muslim regimes and societies as well as the rest of the world have failed to check this shift by challenging the ideological underpinnings of Islamism. On the final Friday of Ramadan, 1.5 million worshippers at the Great Mosque of Mecca, and tens of millions more listening around the world, heard a rousing sermon by Sheikh Abdel Rahman al-Sudeis that lambasted "the state terrorism of international Zionism". "Are we incapable", he demanded, "of finding just solutions to stop the flow of Muslim blood, and to revive the Islamic nations' security, greatness and prestige?" [25] Islam's holiest place, where spirituality and charity are promoted, had been converted into a political platform. The pilgrims who usually depart for their homes refreshed with feelings of peace and solace returned disturbed and agitated, and hence vulnerable to the propaganda of Al Qaeda and its associate groups purportedly trying to stop the "flow of Muslim blood". While the anti-terrorist coalition is neutralising Al Qaeda members in Afghanistan, is the situation in Saudi Arabia producing more of them?

Just as during the Cold War, the fight is against an ideology and not against a physical force. The collapse of the Soviet empire demonstrated that Communism was not viable, and it is entirely possible that the defeat of Al Qaeda will evoke a similar response. Osama comes from the richest non-royal Saudi family and al-Zawahiri from one of the most highly educated families in Egypt. These men of violence wearing the cloak of religion advance their aims and objectives by corrupting and misrepresenting religious texts. The question must be posed: is Al Qaeda Koranic or heretical? Although Al Qaeda claims that all its inspiration is from Islam, its massacring of innocent men, women and children (believers and non-believers alike) is contrary to God's word. In addition to several thousand Afghan Muslims massacred by the Taliban and Al Qaeda's

055 Brigade in Afghanistan in the second half of the 1990s, the US failed adequately to highlight over 300 non-American — mostly African and Muslim — deaths that resulted from Al Qaeda's East Africa bombings in August 1998 and the 9/11 operation. Unfortunately, there has been no tradition, security or incentive for credible community or religious leaders to stand up and say that Osama and Zawahiri are not God's men but power-hungry politicians. Like co-ethnic policing, co-religious security cooperation must be developed where religious elders set the standards and ensure that religion is not abused or distorted by those with ulterior political agendas. A vital component of the US-led anti-terrorist strategy must be the discrediting of Al Qaeda's leadership, ideology, strategies and tactics in the very countries where Muslims live and work.

Long-term response

Al Qaeda's new trajectory of targeting the West won it significant support among the Muslim masses. Leaving aside the Muslim elite, ordinary Muslims worldwide view the West through the prism of anti-Americanism. 61% of Muslims polled in nine countries — Indonesia, Iran, Jordan, Kuwait, Lebanon, Morocco, Pakistan, Saudi Arabia and Turkey — denied that Arabs were involved in the September 11 attacks.[26] The corresponding statistics were 89% in Kuwait, 86% in Pakistan, 74% in Indonesia, 59% in Iran, 58% in Lebanon, and 43% in Turkey.[27] Only 18% of those polled in six Islamic countries said they believed Arabs carried out the attacks and just 9% said they thought US military action in Afghanistan was morally justified.[28] In Kuwait, a country liberated by the US from Iraqi aggression in 1991, 36% said that the 9/11 attacks were justifiable.[29] Just 7% said Western nations are fair in their perceptions of Muslim countries.[30] In perception and in reality there are two worlds, the Western and the Muslim. When President George W. Bush said "You are either with us, or with the terrorists", Al Qaeda interpreted it as an American admission of the existence of two worlds,[31] and to build further support it misinterpreted Bush's infamous phrase "waging a crusade against terrorism" as "a crusade against Islam".[32] Clearly the US has no public support from the Muslim world either to fight terrorism or to remain in Afghanistan. However, the US, its allies and its coalition partners would be taking an incalculable risk if they withdrew from Afghanistan without creating the security, socio-economic and political conditions for a modern system of government to function.

Every terrorist group has a lifespan. Al Qaeda's lifespan will be determined by the ability and the willingness of the anti-terrorist coalition to destroy its leadership, counter its ideology, marginalise its support and disrupt its recruitment. Unlike most terrorist groups of the 20th century, Al Qaeda is multi-dimensional. In the lexicon of modern international terrorism, a multi-dimensional group challenges the enemy on the military, political, and socio-economic fronts. Therefore, the key to overcoming Al Qaeda is to interlock and engage with it on all its critical fronts. Although the West can help Muslim rulers and regimes to fight Al Qaeda on the military plane, there is little it can actually do to isolate it politically and win over its support base. As Al Qaeda poses a durable long-term threat to Muslims worldwide, it is the Muslim elite who must stand up and fight the threat it represents. The West can help, but it is a battle that can best be fought and won by Muslims against Muslims.

Islamists are resilient. They move rapidly in search of new opportunities. To influence, control and build support, they step in wherever there is a space. Arab, Muslim and other countries that host Muslim territorial and migrant populations have neglected their welfare for decades, and Islamist parties and groups have filled the vacuum by establishing socio-economic and welfare organisations. The interaction with Muslim communities has given these organisations an opportunity to politicise and radicalise the Muslim masses into supporting their aims and objectives. By their selfless actions and intense ideological indoctrination, the Islamic movements actively recruit members and increase support. Their projects and plans appear much better and worthier of support than the corrupt, unjust and unholy governments that attempt to rule them.

In addition to providing welfare, Islamists formed non-governmental organisations (NGOs) to provide employment and Islamic education. They have mobilised the poor, the illiterate and the needy. Until Muslim rulers and regimes compete with these Islamist-infiltrated NGOs and provide an alternative, groups like Al Qaeda and its associates will always find recruits and financial backers. Those educated in some of the *madrasas* — some, ironically, funded by taxpayers in the West — are especially militant. Although the West remains the principal engine of growth, Islamists educated in the *madrasas* firmly believe that Western civilisation is in decline. To build anti-Western support, Islamists selectively retrieve and present a mixture of fact and fiction as truth. Arguing convincingly that it is only a question of time before the West is overwhelmed, they record that the Western population has declined relatively from 25% of the world total at the beginning of the 20th century to 15% a century later. With the Koran in one hand and a Kalashnikov in the other, the *madrasa*-educated Islamist lives a life of anger and hope. Western governments and NGOs should seek to work with Muslim regimes and societies and help build schools and community centres that impart a modern education and instill humane, non-sectarian values. Among the priorities of the international community should be, as well as reforming education, fostering truly independent media and building criminal justice and prison systems that are truly just.

The increased threat of terrorism in the post-Cold War era is explained by the dramatic changes that have shaped the new strategic environment. Worldwide terrorist behaviour has changed in order to survive and operate in a new international climate. Instead of resisting globalisation, post-Cold War terrorist groups, including Al Qaeda and a variety of Islamist groups, are harnessing its forces. The 1990s saw the end of the East-West confrontation; a prodigious growth in inexpensive international travel; increased porosity of borders; widespread availability of global communication; the resurgence of ethnicity and religiosity; a saturated arms market; privatisation of security; proliferation of NGOs; and other parameters that enhance the resilience of contemporary terrorist groups, almost all of which have developed an external presence. Due to the development of external linkages, terrorist groups of the 21st century will operate both on the domestic and the international scene, and with the formation of global networks it has become more difficult for governments bound by territorial jurisdictions to fight terrorism successfully. More than ever before, post-Cold War terrorist groups share ideologies, transfer technologies, exchange personnel and conduct joint operations. Considering the evolving nature of the threat, no one country will be able to protect its national security alone. If terrorism is to be halted in its tracks, there must be security, intelligence, operational and judicial cooperation between the target and host countries.

The threat posed by Al Qaeda will test the international community, its institutions, its resources and its will to the limit. Like other terrorist groups, it is also an armed political party. Although it cloaks itself in a religious garb, its goal, like that of all other terrorist groups, is political. The difference between Al Qaeda and other terrorist groups is its global reach, motivation and capacity to inflict mass casualties. These call for an unprecedented response.

In the three decades of modern terrorism, Al Qaeda is an aberration. Since 1969, 3,500 civilians and combatants have been killed in Northern Ireland. Terrorists had killed no more than 1,000 Americans, either at home or abroad, over the same period.[33] Only fourteen terrorist attacks killed more than 100 people in the entire 20th century.[34] Until 9/11 the deadliest terrorist attack was a fire started in a cinema in Abadan, Iran, in 1978, which killed 440 people.[35] Al Qaeda's mindset is clearly reflected in the enormity of the numbers killed on 9/11 and its stated determination to kill more.[36] Had it been successful in launching *Oplan Bojinka* in 1995, it would have killed a comparable number of people. Of over 100 Islamist movements that have emerged since the early 1980s, Al

Qaeda is the most deadly. Therefore, the international community's response to it will determine the threat trajectory of existing and emerging terrorist groups — both Islamist and non-Islamist. If Al Qaeda is discredited and destroyed, it will signal to other terrorist groups the consequences of conducting a mass casualty attack. If it survives and succeeds, more groups will emulate its model of political behaviour.

Theorists have long argued that terrorism does not work, but the sad fact is that it does. Western, Middle Eastern and Asian governments were forced to the negotiating table and either devolved power or agreed to devolve power because of the protracted terrorist campaigns by the Irish Republican Army, Euskadi ta Askatasuna (the Basque nationalist movement in Spain), the PLO, the Shanthi Bahini Movement (in Northeast India), the Liberation Tigers of Tamil Eelam and several Kashmiri factions. If terrorism is to fall from favour, a societal norm must be built against its deployment. As the world has moved away (to differing degrees) from slavery, colonialism, Fascism, Nazism, sexism and racism, so humankind can move away from terrorism as a mode of expressing political protest, provided institutions can be created in which people with genuine grievances and legitimate aspirations can express them and find redress without resorting to violence.

When a politically motivated group attacks civilians – irrespective of country, nationality and cause – the only proper response is uncompromising condemnation. Those who kill or maim defenceless people should never be entitled to the honour of being regarded as freedom fighters. Irrespective of the legitimacy of the struggle, the politically motivated killing of civilians is terrorism. Governments, academia, media and civil society organisations can play a central role in formally and informally educating government officials and politicians as well as the public about terrorism as a tactic abhorrent to humankind. The success of instilling such values will depend on the willingness of the international community to resolve genuine grievances and meet legitimate aspirations while enforcing the law against those who practise, support and condone terrorism. Despite commendable efforts by the Malaysian Prime Minister Mahathir bin Mohamad when the foreign ministers of the Organisation of Islamic States (OIC) met in Malaysia in April 2002, the OIC failed to condemn the tactic of suicide terrorism,[37] fearing that condemnation of Palestinian suicide bombings against Israeli civilian targets would criminalise the Palestinian struggle. This immoral response by the OIC was its reaction to the failure of the West adequately to condemn incursions by the Israel Defence Forces into Palestinian territory.

Compared to all other terrorist categories, Islamists have the greatest capacity to attract new recruits and resources because their recruitment and fund-raising infrastructure is enmeshed with the welfare, socio-economic and political fabric of Muslim communities. Therefore, wider support from Muslim societies is imperative if the fight against Al Qaeda and its brand of Islamist terrorism is to be won. Without public support, battles may be won but not the war. For the West to secure the steadfast support of Muslim leaders in the fight against terrorism it must be equally steadfast in grappling with the fundamental issues in the Palestine, Kashmir and other conflicts, which hitherto the international community has shirked. The vast majority of Muslims, like people of other faiths, want to live in peace and harmony. But they will only support the global campaign against terrorism and their leaders' participation in it if the rest of the world is seen to concentrate its attack on the whole range of relevant issues, not just the weapon of terror alone.

May 2002

NOTES

INTRODUCTION

[1] Abdullah Azzam, "Al-Qa'idah al-Sulbah," *Al-Jihad*, 41, April 1988, p. 46. The author is grateful to Reuven Paz, Academic Director, International Policy Institute for Counter-Terrorism, Israel, for translating the original text in Arabic into English.
[2] Ibid., p. 46.
[3] Ibid.
[4] *Declaration of Jihad against the Country's Tyrants, Military Series, Al Qaeda Training Manual*, n.d., n.p., recovered from Manchester, UK Government Exhibit 1677 T, p. UK/BM.
[5] Interview with an intelligence officer, based on communication intercepts between Osama and Salamat, monitored in mid-Feb. 1999.
[6] *A Declaration of War by Osama bin Laden, together with leaders of the World Islamic Front for the Jihad Against the Jews and the Crusaders* (Al-Jabhah Al-Islamiyyah Al-'Alamiyyah Li-Qital Al-Yahud Wal-Salibiyyin), Afghanistan, February 23, 1998
[7] *Background on Osama Bin Laden and Al-Qa'ida*, CIA, Washington DC, 1998, p. 11.
[8] Ulrich Kersten, head of Germany's Federal Criminal Agency, the BKA, estimates the number at 70,000 while the CIA's figure is 110,000. Other, less well informed, Western agencies estimated the number of recruits trained at 10,000.
[9] *A Declaration of War Against the Americans Occupying the Land of the Two Holy Places: A Message from Osama bin Muhammad bin Laden unto his Muslim brethren all over the world generally, and toward the Muslims of the Arabian Peninsula in particular*, Aug. 1996.
[10] Interview with a US intelligence officer, January 2002.
[11] Interview with an Islamist leader, Jakarta, November 2001.
[12] *Background on Osama Bin Laden and Al-Qa'ida*, p. 9.
[13] Confidential source, communications monitoring agency, Western Europe, 2001.
[14] Mark Hosenball and Daniel Klaidman, "Periscope – Calling Al Qaeda: Questions about Iran", *Newsweek*, February 25, 2002, p. 6
[15] Ibid.
[16] Ibid.
[17] Interview with Albrecht Jongman and Alex Schmid. Research conducted by PIOOM (*Programma voor Interdisciplinair Onderzoek naar Oorzaken van Mensenrechtenschendingen*), Netherlands, October 2000.
[18] Karen Armstrong, "Was it Inevitable — Islam Through History", in James F. Hoge, Jr., and Gidon Rose (eds), *How did this Happen? Terrorism and the New War*, New York, Public Affairs, 2001, p. 56
[19] Ibid.
[20] *A Declaration of War by Osama bin Laden*, op. cit.

CH. 1: WHO IS OSAMA BIN LADEN?

[1] "Europe: We Are Still at the Beginning of Jihad in This Region", Ibn-ul-Khattab, Military Commander of the Mujahideen in the Caucasus, Azzam Publications, September 27, 1999.
[2] As it was not compulsory to register births at that time in Saudi Arabia, Osama's exact

date of birth is in dispute. However, most reports state that he was born in 1957. *Background on Osama Bin Laden and Al-Qa'ida*, CIA, Washington DC, 1998, p. 1. According to Yeslem Bin Laden, Osama's half-brother, Osama was born in either 1952 or 1953. Nick Fielding's interview with Yeslem Bin Laden for *The Sunday Times*, London, January 2002.

[3] Khalifa's role in the Philippines is well documented in reports produced by the Philippines intelligence community. See also Simon Reeve, *The New Jackals: Ramzi Yousef, Osama bin Laden and the Future of Terrorism*, London: André Deutsch, 1999, p. 157.

[4] *Mujtahid: A Biography of the Freedom Fighter Osama Bin Laden*, translated by British government, n.d, n.p., p. 3.

[5] Peter L. Bergen, *Inside the Secret World of Osama bin Laden*, London, Weidenfeld & Nicolson, 2001, p. 55.

[6] Biography of Sheikh Abdullah Azzam (*Shaheed*), reproduced in *The Jihad Fixation*, p. 82.

[7] Bergen, *Inside the Secret World of Osama bin Laden*, p. 61. Bergen bases this account on an interview with Essam Deraz, a film maker who covered Osama in the late 1980s.

[8] Ibid.

[9] Author's interview with an Afghan veteran, November 2001.

[10] Bergen, *Inside the Secret World of Osama bin Laden*, p. 61. Abdullah's visit is also based on Bergen's interview with Essam Deraz.

[11] Interview with a European intelligence analyst, August 2000.

[12] Interview with Alexander Downer, Foreign Minister of Australia, Adelaide, October 2001.

[13] Interview with a member of British intelligence, January 2001.

[14] Bruce B. Auster, "The Recruiter for Hate", *US News & World Report*, August 31, 1998, p. 49.

[15] Rohan Gunaratna, "Blowback: Cutting Al Qaeda Down to Size", *Jane's Intelligence Review*, vol. 13, no. 8, August 2001, p. 45.

[16] *The Jihad Fixation*, p. 256.

[17] Ibid., p. 329.

[18] Bergen, *Inside the Secret World of Osama bin Laden*, pp. 59-60.

[19] Abdullah Azzam, *Fi al Jihad, Adab Wa Ahkam* (Guidelines and Rules of *Jihad*) members.tripod.com/~Suhayab.

[20] Ed Blanche, "The Egyptians Around Bin Laden", *Jane's Intelligence Review*, December 2001, p. 20.

[21] Interview with Frank Anderson, former CIA Chief for the Near East and Middle East, February, 1999.

[22] Muhammad Barakat, "Egyptian Terrorism", *Al-Watan Al-Arabi*, Paris, January 22, 1999, p. 4.

[23] Fayzah Sa'd, "After the Death Sentence for Ayman al-Zawahiri and Jail Term for 78 Terrorists and the International War Against Them: Is the al-Jihad Terrorist Organisation Finished?", Cairo, *Rose al-Yusuf*, 24-30 April 1995, p. 5.

[24] Hamdi Rizq, "Jihad unilaterally won bin Laden over, while the Islamic Group was content with financial support", Cairo, *Al-Sharq al-Awsat*, April 20, 1999, p. 3.

[25] "Bin Laden Took Advantage of the Situation of the Egyptian al-Jihad and Islamic Group's Organisations to impose His Control on them and Form a World Front for Liberating Holy Places", Cairo, *Al-Sharq al-Awsat*, April 20, 1999, p. 3.

[26] Muhammed Salah, "Secret Relationship between al-Zawahiri and bin Laden: The Jihad Leader Turned bin Laden into a Mujahid", Cairo, *Al-Hayat*, June 24, 1998, p. 6.

[27] Muhammed Salah, "Ali al-Rashidi, The Egyptian Policemen Who Paved the Way for 'Afghan Arabs' in Africa and Prepared Them to Take Revenge Against the Americans" Cairo, *Al-Hayat*, Septemher 30, 1998, p. 1. Panjsher is pronounced Banshiri in Arabic.

[28] *Osama Bin Laden: His Links to the Egyptian Terrorist Groups*, European Intelligence Agency, 2000, pp. 21-2.

[29] Interview with a former Al Qaeda member, India, November 2001.
[30] *A Declaration of War Against the Americans Occupying the Land of the Two Holy Places: A Message from Osama bin Muhammed bin Laden unto his Muslim Brethren all over the World Generally, and Toward the Muslims of the Arabian Peninsula in Particular,* August 1996.
[31] Reeve, *The New Jackals*, op. cit., pp. 50-5, 188-9.
[32] United States of America *v.* Osama Bin Laden *et al.* Southern District of New York., February 6, 2001.
[33] Ibid.
[34] Ibid.
[35] Ibid.
[36] Ibid.
[37] Ibid.
[38] Ibid.
[39] Ibid.
[40] Ibid.
[41] Ibid.
[42] Ibid.
[43] Ibid.
[44] Ibid.
[45] Exclusive interview with Osama bin Laden, *Nida'ul Islam*, Sydney, October-November, 1996.
[46] "Bin Ladin's Life in Sudan", London, *Al-Quds al-Arabi*, November 24, 2001.
[47] Ibid.
[48] Interview with an Al Qaeda member, October 2001.
[49] Peter Arnett, CNN interview with Osama bin Laden, May 1997.
[50] Rahimullah Yusufzai, *The News*, Pakistan, December 8, 1995.
[51] Interview, Craig Pyes, *New York Times*, January 2001.
[52] *Characteristics of Transnational Sunni Islamic Terrorism*, Washington, DC, CIA, n.d., p. 2.
[53] *Background on Osama Bin Laden and Al-Qa'ida*, Washington, DC, CIA, 1998, p. 9.
[54] *Osama Bin Laden: His Links to the Egyptian Terrorist Groups*, p. 19.
[55] United States of America *v.* Usama bin Laden, *et al.*, United States District Court, Southern District of New York, February 14, 2001.
[56] Ibid.
[57] Ibid.
[58] Ibid.
[59] Ibid.
[60] Muhammed Salah, "Secret Relationship Between Al-Zawahiri and bin Laden", p. 6.
[61] *Nida'ul Islam*, February-March 1997.
[62] Interview, serving ISI officer, May 2000.
[63] Ahmed Rashid, *Taliban: The Story of the Afghan Warlords*, London, Pan Books, 2001, pp. 89-92.
[64] Ibid., pp. 27-9.
[65] "Afghanistan — An Overview of the Year 1996", *Intelligence Review*, Directorate General, Inter-Services-Intelligence, vol. 49, January 1997, p.3.
[66] Bergen, *Inside the Secret World of Osama bin Laden*, p. 102. Based on an interview by Bergen with Saad al-Fagih, head, Movement for Islamic Reform in Saudi Arabia, September 1998.
[67] Osama bin Laden's second *fatwa*, February 1997.
[68] Tim McGirk, "Afghanistan", *Time*, August 31, 1998.
[69] Ibid.
[70] Interview with George Fernandes, Minister of Defence, New Delhi, November 2001.
[71] Interview with a serving ISI officer, May 2000.
[72] Hafeez Malik, "Taliban's Islamic Emirates", Lahore, *The Nation on Sunday*, April 11,

1999.

73 Sreedhar and Mahendra Ved, *Afghan Buzkashi: Power Games and Gamesmen*, Delhi, Wordsmiths, 2000, p. 46.

74 *A Declaration of War by Osama bin Laden*, op. cit.

75 Interview with a European intelligence officer, August 2000.

76 *A Declaration of War by Osama bin Laden*, op. cit.

77 Bergen, *Inside the Secret World of Osama bin Laden*, pp. 108-9.

78 Peter Bergen collection, translated from Arabic to English by Ferial Demy.

79 Bergen, *Inside the Secret World of Osama bin Laden*, p. 109. Bergen bases his account on an interview with Hamid Mir in September 1998.

80 Interview, Finsbury Park mosque, London, September 1998.

81 Interview, Dept. of Defence, Canberra, Australia, September 2001

82 Rahimullah Yusufzai, "Conversation with Terror", January 11, 1999, *Time* <http://cgi.pathfinder.com/time.mgazine/articles/0,3266,17676,00.html> Of the journalists Osama has met since the early 1980s he was closest to the Pakistani journalist Yusufzai, who was the first reporter to meet him after September 11.

83 Bergen, *Inside the Secret World of Laden bin Laden*, p 109.

84 Interview with an Al Qaeda member, September 2001.

85 "Bin Laden Verses Honor *Cole* Attack", Reuters, *Seattle Times*, March 2, 2001.

86 Interview, New Scotland Yard, March 2002.

87 Philip Smucker, *Christian Science Monitor*, March 4, 2002.

88 Ibid.

89 Author's collection at the Centre for the Study of Terrorism and Political Violence (*hereafter* CSTPV), St Andrews University, Scotland.

90 Interview, Jakarta, October 2001

91 Ibid.

92 Kate Noble, "What's in the Name"?, *Time*, January 14, 2002, p. 11, quoting the newspaper *Vanguard*.

CH. 2: AL QAEDA'S ORGANISATION, IDEOLOGY AND STRATEGY

1 United States of America *v.* Osama Bin Laden *et al.* Southern District of New York, February 6, 2001.

2 Author's copy, provided by Tony Davis, the first journalist to enter Kabul after the defeat of the Taliban in 2001. Also see Tony Davis, "The Afghan Files: Al Qaeda Documents from Kabul", *Jane's Intelligence Review*, vol. 14, no. 2, February 2001.

3 Rohan Gunaratna, "The Lifeblood of Terrorist Organisations: Evolving Terrorist Financing Strategies" in Alex Schmid (ed.), *Countering Terrorism Through International Cooperation*, Rome, International Scientific and Professional Advisory Council of the UN and the UN Terrorism Prevention Branch, 2001, pp.180-205.

4 "Saudi Executives Give Funds to Osama bin Ladin", *USA Today*, October 29, 1999. The newspaper quoted from senior US intelligence sources.

5 Ibid.

6 William F. Wechsler, "Strangling the Hydra: Targeting Al Qaeda's Finances" in James F. Hoge, Jr. and Gideon Rose, *How Did This Happen? Terrorism and the New War*, New York, Public Affairs, 2001, p. 137.

7 US State Department Fact Sheet on Bin Ladin entitled "Osama Bin Ladin: Islamic Extremist Financier", August 14, 1996, p. 2.

8 For al-Fawwaz's role, see Simon Reeve, *The New Jackals: Ramzi Yousef, Osama bin Laden and the Future of Terrorism*, London: André Deutsch, 1999, pp. 180, 192, 211, 212.

[9] United States of America *v.* Osama Bin Laden *et al.* Southern District of New York, February 6, 2001.
[10] "Declaration of Jihad Against the Country's Tyrants, Military Series", recovered by Manchester Police from home of Nazihal Wadih Raghie, May 10, 2000, hereafter referred to as UK/BM translation.
[11] UK/BM.
[12] William F. Wechsler, "Strangling the Hydra: Targettting Al Qaeda's Finances", in *How Did This Happen? Terrorism and the New War*, p. 135.
[13] Ibid.
[14] Daniel Klaidman and Melinda Liu, "Malaysia: A Good Place to Lie Low", *Newsweek*, February 4, 2002, p. 17.
[15] Roger Davis, formerly of the UK Defence Intelligence Staff, January 2001.
[16] Mark Huband, "Bankrolling Bin Laden", *Financial Times*, November 28, 2001.
[17] Ibid.
[18] Victoria Griffith, Peter Speigel, and Hugo Williamson, "How the Hijackers Went Unnoticed", *Financial Times*, November 29, 2001.
[19] Ibid.
[20] Interview, Former Al Qaeda member, January 2001.
[21] Interview, New Scotland Yard, March 2002.
[22] Interview, New Scotland Yard, March 2002.
[23] Interview, Terrorism Specialist, Direction de la Surveillance du Territoire (DST), 2000-2002.
[24] Interview, former Al Qaeda member, Europe, 2001.
[25] The White House, Washington DC, September 2001.
[26] United States Foreign Assets Control, Washington DC, September 24, 2001.
[27] *Al Qaeda Infrastructure in Sudan*, European Intelligence Agency, 2001, p. 5
[28] See also, Roland Jacqard, *In the Name of Osama Bin Laden: Global Terror and the Bin Laden Brotherhood*, London and Durham, Duke University Press, 2002, p. 128.
[29] Interview, Ian Synge, Jane's Information Group, London, March 2002.
[30] *Islamic Radicalism: The Financial and European Network of Usama Bin Ladin*, European Intelligence Agency, p. 1.
[31] Interviews, European Security and Intelligence Agency, March 2002.
[32] *Islamic Radicalism: The Financial and European Network of Usama Bin Ladin*, p. 3.
[33] Ibid., p. 4.
[34] *Encyclopedia of the Afghan Jihad, Tactics*, Maktab-al Khidamat, p. 66
[35] *Encyclopedia of the Afghan Jihad, Explosives*, Maktab-al Khidamat, p. 35.
[36] Reuel Marc Gerecht, "Afghanistan: Two Visits to the North – The Terrorists' Encyclopaedia", *Middle East Quarterly*, Transnational Periodicals Consortium – Rutgers University, summer 2001, vol. VIII, no. 3, pp. 79-80
[37] UK/BM translation.
[38] UK/BM translation.
[39] UK/BM translation.
[40] UK/BM translation.
[41] UK/BM translation.
[42] *Background on Usama Bin Ladin and Al-Qa'ida*, CIA, Washington DC, 1998, p. 7.
[43] Ibid., p. 7.
[44] Ibid., pp. 7-8.
[45] UK/BM translation.
[46] UK/BM translation.
[47] UK/BM translation.
[48] UK/BM translation.
[49] UK/BM translation.
[50] UK/BM translation.

51 UK/BM translation.
52 UK/BM translation.
53 UK/BM translation.
54 UK/BM translation.
55 UK/BM translation.
56 UK/BM translation.
57 UK/BM translation.
58 UK/BM translation.
59 UK/BM translation.
60 UK/BM translation.
61 UK/BM translation.
62 "Usually, in old quarters people know know one another and strangers are easily identified, especially since those quarters have many informants." The situation referred to here is most likely that of urban Egypt. UK/BM translation
63 UK/BM translation.
64 Author's interview with an Indian intelligence officer, New Delhi, November 2001.
65 Author's interview with an Echelon project member, Sydney, September 2001.
66 UK/BM translation.
67 UK/BM translation.
68 UK/BM translation.
69 UK/BM translation.
70 UK/BM translation.
71 UK/BM translation.
72 United States of America *v.* Osama Bin Laden *et al.* Southern District of New York., February 6, 2001.
73 members.Tripod.com/~Suhayb.
74 *The Jihad Fixation*, p. 31.
75 members.Tripod.com/~Suhayb.
76 *The Jihad Fixation*, p. 31.
77 Ibid, p. 31.
78 M. Amir Ali, *Jihad Explained*, ict.org.il.
79 Koran, 2:256.
80 *The Jihad Fixation*, p. 31.
81 Koran, 2:190/.
82 Ibn Taymiyyah, *The Religious and Moral Doctrine on Jihad*, members.Tripod.com/~Suhayb.
83 Ibid.
84 Martin E. Marty and R. Scott Appleby, foreword to James Piscatori (ed.), *Islamic Fundamentalisms and the Gulf Crisis*, University of Chicago Press for the Fundamentalisms Project of the American Academy of Arts and Sciences, 1991, p. xii.
85 Douglas E. Streusand, "What does Jihad Mean?", *Middle East Quarterly*, September 1997.
86 Abdullah Azzam, *Join the Caravan*, n.d., n.p., (author's copy).
87 Author's interview with an Al Qaeda member, November 2001.
88 "Declaration of War Against the Americans Occupying the Land of the Two Holy Places: A message from Osama bin Muhammed bin Laden unto his Muslim brethren all over the world generally, and toward the Muslims of the Arabian Peninsula in particular", August 1996.
89 *Reasons for Jihad*, Al Qaeda recruitment document, n.d., n.p., author's copy.
90 Ibid.
91 *Islamic Fundamentalisms and the Gulf Crisis*, p. xiii.
92 UK/BM translation.
93 Ibid.
94 *Islamic Fundamentalisms and the Gulf Crisis*, p. xii.
95 "Declaration of War Against the Americans", August 1996.

96 Ibid.
97 Peter Arnett, interview with Osama bin Laden, CNN, March 1997. Questions were submitted in advance with no follow-up permitted.
98 *Nida'ul Islam*, October-November 1996.
99 *The Jihad Fixation*, p. 267-9.
100 *A Declaration of War by Osama bin Laden*, op. cit.
101 Interview, Magnus Ranstorp, Deputy Director, CSTPV, St Andrews University, April, 2002.
102 Interview, Selma Belaala, Institudes des Etudes Politiques, Paris, January 2002.
103 Interview, Angus Muir, terrorism specialist, CSTPV, St Andrews University, March 2002.

CH. 3: AL QAEDA'S GLOBAL NETWORK

1 Transcript of Osama Bin Laden videotape, mid-November 2001, independently prepared by George Michael, translator, Diplomatic Language Services, and Kassem M. Wahba, Arabic language program coordinator, School of Advanced International Studies, Johns Hopkins University. They collaborated on their translation and compared it with translations done by the US government for consistency. There were no inconsistencies in the translations.
2 Interview, former Al Qaeda member, London, July 2001.
3 John K. Cooley, *Unholy Wars: Afghanistan, America and International Terrorism*, London, Pluto Press, 1999, p. 40.
4 Hugo Williamson, Jimmy Burns, Stephen Fidler and Mark Huband, "A Catastrophic Failure of Intelligence", *Financial Times*, November 29, 2001.
5 Shaikh Abu Hamza, *Al-Misri, Khawaraij and Jihad* (including a full chapter about the massacre in Algeria), Ibn Umar (ed.), Birmingham, Makhtabah Al-Ansar, 2000, p. 105.
6 "Bin Laden's Martyrs for the Cause", *Financial Times*, November 28, 2001
7 Interview, Al Qaeda member, India November 2001
8 John K. Cooley, *Unholy Wars*, p. 41, and Mary Anne Weaver, *A Portrait of Egypt*, New York: Farrar, Straus, Giroux, 1999, p. 90.
9 Ibid.
10 *Jane's World Insurgency and Terrorism* (January-April 2000),.p 290.
11 Ibid.
12 Muhhammad Hisham Kabbani, "Islamic Extremism: A Viable Threat to US National Security", an Open Forum at the US Department of State, January 7, 1999. <http://www.islamicsupremecouncil.org/radicalmovements/islamic_extremism.htm.>
13 Interview, former Al Qaeda member, London, September 2001.
14 Transcript of Osama Bin Laden videotape, mid-November 2001.
15 Christa Denso, "Der dritte Terror-Pilot. Er studierte bei Uns", *Hamburger Abendlatt*, September 17, 2001.
16 John Hooper, "The Shy, Caring, Deadly Fanatic", *The Guardian*, September 23, 2001.
17 For full text of Atta's last will see *Der Spiegel*, October 1, 2001, pp. 32-3. Translated into English by Emerson Vermaat.
18 Ben Fenton, "'Hijacker' Defies US Court with Cry to Allah", *Daily Telegraph*, January 3, 2002, p. 14.
19 USA *v.* Zacarias Moussaoui, US District Court for the Eastern District of Virginia, Alexandria, December 2001.
20 Ibid.
21 Ibid.

22 Ibid.

23 Jose Yoldi, "Garzon Vincula La Red De Bin Laden En Espnana A Con Los Atentados De EE UU," *El Pais*, November 19, 2001

24 Victoria Griffith, Peter Speigel, and Hugo Williamson, "How the Hijackers Went Unnoticed", *Financial Times*, November 29, 2001.

25 Andrew Buncombe, "Man Alleged to be the Twentiech Hijacker Defies Court 'in the name of Allah,'" *The Independent*, January 3, 2002. p. 1.

26 "How the Hijackers Went Unnoticed", *Financial Times*, November 29, 2001.

27 Tactical Interrogation. Report of Muhammed Afroz, arrested on October 2, 2001, Intelligence Bureau, New Delhi, India, p.1.

28 Ibid., p. 2.

29 "Chance Find that Averted Airport Bombing", *Financial Times*, November 28, 2001.

30 Abd-al-Latif al-Minawi, "Egyptian Report: Terrorist Links", Cairo, *Al-Sharq Al-Awsat*, November 8, 1998 p. 4.

31 Ibid., p. 3.

32 "Local charity sent donations to Taliban home", *Chicago Tribune*, March 10, 2002; "Bosnia decides to ban two Islamic charities for financial misconduct", Paris, AFP, March 8, 2002; and "INS holds president of charity suspected of links to Al Qaeda", *Los Angeles Times*, December 18, 2001.

33 *Non-Governmental Charitable Organisations*, CIA, Washington DC, 1996, p. 9, citing multiple sources.

34 Ibid., p. 9

35 Ibid., pp. 9-10.

36 Rohan Gunaratna, "Blowback - Special Report: Al Qaeda", *Jane's Intelligence Report*, vol. 13, no. 8, August 2001, p. 42.

37 Interview, journalist, *Chicago Tribune*, February 2002.

38 Ibid.

39 Yossef Bodansky, *Bin Laden: The Man who Declared War on America*, CA, Forum, 1999, p. 12.

40 Muhammed Jamal Khalifa, arrest in San Francisco, document supplied to the author, undated.

41 Ibid.

42 Based on estimates by military and civilian security and intelligence agencies and national police and law enforcement authorities, February 2002.

43 Interview, Al Qaeda member, March 2001.

44 United States of America *v.* Osama Bin Laden *et al.* Southern District of New York., February 6, 2001.

45 Sean O' Neill, "The Extremist Network that Sprang from 'Londonistan'", *Daily Telegraph*, January 3, 2002, p. 14.

46 Peter Bergen, *Holy War, Inc.*, pp. 1-6.

47 Dominic Kennedy, Daniel McGory, James Bone, and Richard Ford, "The Fingerprints of Terror", *The Times*, November 24, 2001, p. 1.

48 The Ladenese Epistle: Declaration of War (I) October 2, 1996, MSANews<http://msanews.mynet.net/MSANEWS/199610/19961012.3html>

49. Nick Fielding, "Al Qaeda's Satellite Phone Records Revealed", *Sunday Times*, 24 March, 2002, and John Sweeney, "Bin Laden connected to London dissident", BBC News (internet version), Sunday, 10 March, 2002.

50 Simon Apiku, "Wanted: Terrorists Living Abroad", *Middle East Times*, January 27, 1999.

51 "The Fingerprints of Terror".

52 "Man says he was recruited by Bin Laden for suicide attack on US Embassy in Paris", Associated Press, October 2, 2001.

53 Interview, central London, March 2001.

54 Tactical Interrogation Report of Muhammed Afroz, arrested on October 2, 2001.

Intelligence Bureau, New Delhi, India, p. 1.
[55] Ibid. p.2
[56] Ibid., p.3
[57] Ibid., p.3
[58] Ibid., p. 4
[59] Interviews, DST, 1999-2001, and with Gerard Chaliand, France's leading expert on guerrilla warfare, 1997-2002.
[60] *El Fath el Moubine*, no. 25, Dec 30, 1994.
[61] "French Court Jails Islamists", BBC, September 15, 1999.
[62] Ibid.
[63] Interview, Military Security, Algiers, January 2002. Also see reference to "martydom operation" in Shaikh Abu Hamza al-Misri, *Khawaraij and Jihad*, including a full chapter about the massacre in Algeria, Ibn Umar (ed.), Birmingham, Makhtabah al-Ansar, 2000, fn 130.
[64] Peter Harclerode, *Secret Soldiers, Special Forces in the War against Terrorism*, London, Cassell, 2000, ch. 12.
[65] Italian intelligence officer, interview, Mont Coulmeyer, October 2000.
[66] GIA statement in *Al Hayat*, Arabic daily, London, reproduced in AFP, June 27, 1999.
[67] "Algeria Week in Review", *North Africa Journal*, Africa News Service, June 4, 1999 p 1.
[68] Many cell members of the network lived at this hotel.
[69] *World Insurgency and Terrorism*, London: Jane's Informational Group, January-April 2001, p. 245.
[70] Inerview, Magnus Ranstorp, CSTPV, University of St Andrews, July 2001.
[71] *El-Watan*, March 31, 1999 and *Middle East International*, January 30, 1998.
[72] *Keesings Archive*, March 1997 and BBC News, February 18, 1998.
[73] Interview, intelligence officer, based on communication transcripts between Osama and Hattab monitored in mid-February 1999.
[74] Author's interview with Phillip Miguex, DST operative, Paris, 2000.
[75] Shaikh Abu Hamza al-Misri, *Khawaraij and Jihad*. Abu Hamza refers to the group as Salafists and not as GSPC.
[76] Emerson Vermaat, "Bin Laden's Terror Networks in Europe", unpublished manuscript, February 2002, p. 17.
[77] "Gang de Roubaix: La Jeunesse De Dumont A l'Etude," TF1.Fr (FrenchTV), October 4, 2001, http://www.tf1.fr/news/france/0,822213,00.html and "Bin Laden's Invisible Network", *Newsweek*, International Edition, October 29, 2001, p. 50.
[78] Yonah Alexander and Michael S. Swetnam, *Osama bin Laden's al-Qaida: Profile of a Terrorist Network*, New York, Transnational Publishers, 2001, p. 26.
[79] Romana Abels and Kustaw Bessems, *Extremisten Zin Juist Vaak Intelligent*, Trouw, Netherlands, pp. 13-15. The author is grateful to Harm Botje for translating the original Dutch text into English.
[80] Transcript of Osama Bin Laden video tape, mid-November 2001, recovered in Afghanistan. Transcript and annotations independently prepared by George Michael, translator, Diplomatic Language Services, and Kassem M. Wahba, Arabic language program coordinator, School of Advanced International Studies, Johns Hopkins University.
[81] Emerson Vermaat, "Bin Laden's Terror Networks in Europe", p. 7.
[82] Jose Maria Irujo, "Otro Miembro De Al Qaeda Visito Espana Antes De Un Atentado", *El Pais*, Madrid, November 25, 2001.
[83] Interview, former Al Qaeda member, 1999.
[84] Larry Neumeister, "Five More Indicted in Embassy Bombings", Associated Press, December 21, 2000.
[85] David Bamber, Chris Hastings, and Rajeev Syal, "Bin Laden British Cell had Plans for Nerve Gas Attack on European Parliament", *The Sunday Telegraph*, London, September 16, 2001, p. 1 and David E. Kaplan and Andrew Marshall, *The Cult at the End of the*

World: The Incredible Story of Aum, London, Arrow Books, 1996, p. 1.
[86] Interview, former Al Qaeda member, January 2001 and classified intelligence reports from European and North American agencies on Al Qaeda's use of chemical weapons in 2001.
[87] Andres English, "Operation Al Muhajirun," *Hamburger Abendblat*, October 11, 2001, and Peter Finn and Sarah Delaney, "Al Qaeda's Links Deepen in Europe," *Washington Post*, October 31, 2001.
[88] Nestor Cerda, "Al Qaeda's Infrastructure in Spain", unpublished report, January 2002, p. 2.
[89] USA *v.* Zacarias Moussaoui, US District Court for the Eastern District ofVirginia, Alexandria, December 2001.
[90] Ibid.
[91] Tawfig Tabib, "interview with Sheikh al-Mujahideen Abu Abdel Aziz", *Al-Sirat Al-Mustaqeem* (The Straight Path), no. 33, Safar 1415, August,1994
[92] Ibid.
[93] According to a claim made by a journalist from a reputed German news magazine, a female colleague saw him in Bosnia in 1993. Interview, journalist, *Stern*, October 2001.
[94] *Non-Governmental Charitable Organisations*, p. 2.
[95] Mark Huband, "Bankrolling Bin Laden".
[96] Foreign intelligence source.
[97] *Non-Governmental Charitable Organisations*, p. 5.
[98] Lamya Radi, "Leader of Albanians' Group Accuses US Intelligence of Kidnapping 12 Fundamentalists and Handing them Over to the Egyptian Authorities", Haekstep, *Al-Quds al-Arabi*, February 2, 1999.
[99] Thomas Friedman, "Abu Zubaydah is identified as the new operations chief of Al Qaeda", *New York Times*, February 13, 2002.
[100] According to a foreign intelligence source, after the raid the organisation relocated to Ljubljana.
[101] John K. Cooley, *Unholy Wars*, p. 178.
[102] Ibid., p. 175.
[103] Ibid., p. 180.
[104] *The Jihad Fixation*, p. 329.
[105] Islambouli, sentenced to death in 1981 and to life with hard labour in 1999 in Egypt, is in Afghanistan.
[106] *Jane's World Insurgency and Terrorism* (January-April 2000), pp. 248 and 570.
[107] Ali Rahnema (ed.), *Pioneers of Islamic Revival,* London, Zed Books, 1994.
[108] "Osama Bin Laden: His Links to the Egyptian Terrorist Groups", European Intelligence Agency, 2000, p. 16.
[109] "Algerian Terrorism, Terrorist Group Profiles", Dudley Knox Library, Naval Postgraduate School, p. 1 http://web.nps.navy.mil/~library/tgp/algerian.html
[110] Steve Macko, "The Year in Algerian and Egyptian Terrorism", *ERRI Daily Intelligence Report* — ERRI Risk Assessment Services — December 26, 1997, vol. 3, p. 360.
[111] "Fourteen killed in Algeria Attack," AP, June 11, 1999.
[112] "Activities in Algeria", *Nida'ul Islam*, July-September 1996.
[113] For Arabic copy of declaration, see Shaikh Abu Hamza al-Misri, *Khawaraij and Jihad*, pp. 341-3.
[114] Ibid., pp. 154-5.
[115] Ibid., fn 134.
[116] Briefing on GSPC by Metropolitan Police Special Branch, New Scotland Yard, January 2001.
[117] Two *katibats* (brigades), el-Ahoual and al-Fourkan, were active in early and mid-2000.
[118] Interview, military security, Algiers, January 2002.
[119] *World Insurgency and Terrorism, Jane's Informational Group*, January-April 2001, p. 248

and Luis Martinez, *The Algerian Civil War 1990-1998*, London, Hurst, 1998, p. 209, fn 28.
[120] *Background on Osama Bin Laden and Al-Qa'ida*, p. 11.
[121] *Al Qaeda Infrastructure in Sudan*, p. 10.
[122] Mark Hosenball and Daniel Klaidman, "Periscope: Calling Al Qaeda: Questions about Iran", *Newsweek*, February 25, 2002, p. 6.
[123] Ibid.
[124] Judy Pasternak and Stephen Braun, "Response to Terror", *Los Angeles Times*, January 20, 2002
[125] Ibid.
[126] Ibid.
[127] Jean-Charles Brisard and Guillaume Dasquie, *Ben Laden, La Verite Interdite*, Denoel Impacts, Paris, 2001, p. 244.
[128] Peter Arnett, Transcript of Osama bin Laden Interview, CNN, March 1997.
[129] Mark Huband, "Bankrolling Bin Laden".
[130] Ibid.
[131] Muhammed Jamal Khalifa's parents are Jomady Khalifa and Jonnadi Jamal.
[132] With its headquarters in Jeddah, the Saudi government, private organisations, and individuals financed the IIRO.
[133] Sitta Jihada Awang is a former official of the International Relief and Information Centre of the Philippines.
[134] "Muhammed Khalifa's Network in the Philippines", Directorate for Intelligence, Philippine National Police, pp. 1-6.
[135] According to a Western intelligence source, Khalifa was in the Netherlands from September 22-27, 1994, where he met with representatives of the Egyptian Islamic Group; Islamic Salvation Front of Algeria, and Muwafaq Foundation.
[136] Ibid., pp. 1-6.
[137] "Special report on Mohammad Jamal Khalifa", Directorate for Intelligence, National Headquarters, Philippine National Police, Camp Crame, Quezon City and other reports on the Mohammad Khalifa network in the Philippines.
[138] Magnus Ranstorp, *Hizbollah in Lebanon: The Politics of the Western Hostage Crisis*, London, Macmillan, 1997, p 68.
[139] Interview, former head of Italian Intelligence, February 2000.
[140] Interview, US intelligence community, February 2000.
[141] Ibid.
[142] Hala Jaber, *Hezbollah - Born With A Vengeance: Inside The World's Most Secretive and Deadly Organisation*, London, Fourth Estate, 1997, p. 80.
[143] *Annual Report, Patterns of Global Terrorism,* Department of State, Washington, DC, 2001 and previous reports.
[144] Interview, Magnus Ranstorp, CSTPV, University of St Andrews, March 2002.
[145] Neil Barnett, "Islamist Groups Take Root in the Balkans, The Czech Connection", *Jane's Intelligence Review*, January 2002, p. 22.
[146] Al Qaeda specialist, Western security and intelligence agency, Asia-Pacific Centre for Security Studies, Hawaii, February 2002.
[147] Ibid.
[148] *Al Qaeda Infrastructure in Sudan*, European Intelligence Agency, 2001, p. 5.
[149] Interviews, Israeli security and intelligence agencies, September 2000.
[150] Yoni Fighel and Yael Shahar, "The Al-Qaida-Hezbollah Connection", February 26, 2002, www.ict.org.il. *See also* Shaul Shay, *The Endless Jihad: The Mujahidin, the Taliban and Bin Laden*, Herzliya, Israel International Policy Institute for Counter-Terrorism, 2002, p. 135.
[151] Ibid.
[152] Ibid.
[153] Ibid.

154 Ibid.
155 Michael Elliott, "The Shoe Bomber's World", *Time*, February 25, 2002, p. 5.
156 Elaine Shannon, "The explosives: Who built Reid's shoes?", *Time*, February 25, 2002. p. 50.
157 Interview, Israeli bomb disposal division, Israeli police, May 2000. .
158 Abul Bara' Hassan Salman, Deputy Emir, Eritrean Islamic Jihad Movement , "The Governing Regimes Acts Inimically Against the Eritrean People", *Nida'ul Islam*, February-March 1998.
159 Ibid.
160 Ibid.
161 Rashid Muhammed Husein, spokesperson of the office of foreign affairs and media for the Islamic Union of Mujahideen in Ogadin, "Jihad in Ogadin — I", *Nada'ul Islam*, March-April 1996.
162 Abu Yaser, spokesperson for external relations and the media in the Islamic Union of Mujahideen in Ogadin, "Jihad in Ogadin — II", *Nada'ul Islam*, July-August 1997.
163 "Assassination Attempt in Ogadin", *Nida'ul Islam*, July-September 1996.
164 Bushra Hussein, "Islamic Coalition in Somalia", *Nida'ul Islam*, September-October 1997
165 "Islamic Coalition in Somalia", *Nida'ul Islam*, September-October 1997.
166 Abul Bara' Hassan Salman, "The Governing Regimes Acts Inimically Against the Eritrean People", *Nida'ul Islam*, February-March 1998.
167 *Background on Osama Bin Laden and Al-Qa'ida*, CIA, Washington DC, 1998, p. 10.
168 Tactical Interrogation report of Maulana Masood Azhar, Indian Intelligence Bureau, New Delhi, n.d..
169 Ibid.
170 Jenny Hailes, "Somalia Provides Unsafe Haven for Extremist Islamic Groups", *Jane's Intelligence Review*, vol. 14, no 1, pp. 16-17.
171 J. Stephen Morrison, "Africa and the War on Terrorism", House International Relations Committee, Capitol Hill Hearing Testimony, Washington, DC, November 15, 2001.
172 J. Pasternak and S. Braun, "Response to Terror".
173 Abu Yaser, spokesperson for external relations and the media in the Islamic Union of Mujahideen in Ogadin, "Jihad in Ogadin — II", *Nada'ul Islam*, July-August 1997.
174 *Al Qaeda Infrastructure in Sudan*, European Intelligence Agency, 2001, p. 5.
176 Ibid.
177 *Responsibility for the terrorist atrocities in the United States on 11 September 2001: Britain's case against Bin Laden*, UK government release, October 4, 2001, 21 pp
178 Islamic Liberation Army of the People of Kenya, August 11, 1998, Arabic script, issued in London, London, p. 1.
179 Ibid.
180 Ibid.
181 United States of America *v.* Osama Bin Laden *et al.*, Southern District of New York, 18 October 2001.
182 Ibid.
183 Rahimullah Yusufzai, "Confusion about US attacks in Afghanistan", Peshawar, *The News*, August 21, 1998.
184 *Al Qaeda Infrastructure in Sudan*, European Intelligence Agency, 2001, p. 5.
185 Ibid.
186 Ibid., p. 21
187 Mario Daniel Montoya, "War on Terrorism Reaches Paraguay's Triple Border", *Jane's Intelligence Review*, vol. 13, no. 12, London, December 2001, p 12.
188 Ibid., p. 12.
189 Daniel Sobelman, "Israel Takes Special Interest in Triple Border Area", *Jane's*

Intelligence Review, vol. 13, no. 12, London, December 2001, p. 14.
190 Ibid, p. 15.
191 Interviews, Directorate of Military Intelligence, Bogota, Colombia April 2001.
192 Interview, British Intelligence, London, February 2001.
193 Mario Daniel Montoya, "War on Terrorism Reaches Paraguay's Triple Border", p. 14.
194 Interviews with military, police and intelligence officials, Bogota, Colombia, April 2001.

CH. 4: ASIA: Al QAEDA'S NEW THEATRE

1 Ahmed Rashid, "The Fires of Faith in Central Asia", *World Policy Journal*, Spring 2001 internet version, pp. 137-48. See also Ahmed Rashid, *Jihad: The Rise of Militant Islam in Central Asia*, New Haven, Yale University Press, 2002, p. 6.
2 Ahmed Rashid, "The Fires of Faith in Central Asia", p. 6.
3 "Uzbek Anti-Government Activist Sheltered in Afghanistan", Itar-Tass, Islamabad, February 3, 2001, p. 1.
4 Interviews, Japanese diplomats and businessmen, Kazakhastan, Kyrgyzstan and Uzbekistan, March 2001.
5 Maria Utyaganova, "IMU Incursion in Central Asia: Earlier and Larger?", Central Asia and the Caucasus, March 28, 2001, p. 2.
6 "Tajikistan denies Uzbek militants hole up in Pamir Foothills," Dushanbe, January 17, 2001, Intar-Tass.
7 Ahmed Rashid, "Western Powers Bolster Tajikistan as it faces Renewed Threats to Stability and Security," *Central Asia and the Caucasus*, May 23, 2001, p. 1.
8 Stephen Blank, "Rumors of War in Central Asia", *Central Asia and the Caucasus*, May 9, 2001, p. 1.
9 For instance the Kyrgyzstan President Akayev said he feared an invasion of 5,000 Islamists from Afghanistan and Tajikistan. Ahmed Rashid, "Central Asia Summary: Recent Developments in Kazakhstan, Kyrgyzstan and Turkmenistan", *Eurasian Insight*, January 18, 2001, p. 4
10 Considering the low cost of living of that region, $100 per month would be a very good salary.
11 Rahul Bedi, "The Chinese Connection", *Jane's Intelligence Review*, vol. 14, no. 2, February 2002.
12 Ibid.
13 Ibid.
14 www.parliament.the-stationery-office.co.uk/pa/cm199900/cmselect/cmfaff/574/574ap20.htm
15 Interviews with security and intelligence officials in Almaty and Bishkek, March 2001.
16 Julie Sirrs, *The Taliban's Foreign Fighters*, Committee for a Free Afghanistan, USA, November 11, 2000, p. 19.
17 Ibid.
18 Ibid.
19 Mark Fineman and Richard C. Paddock, "Response to Terror: Indonesia Cleric Tied to '95 Anti-U.S. Plot", *Los Angeles Times*, February 7, 2002
20 *Muhammed Jamal Khalifa, Biographical Profile*, Directorate for Intelligence, Philippine National Police, p. 3.
21 Ibid. p. 3.
22 *Responsibility for the terrorist atrocities in the United States on 11 September 2001: Britain's*

case against Bin Laden, UK government release, October 4, 2001, 21 pp
23 Interviews, members of the Pakistani and Philippines intelligence communities, Islamabad and Manila, 1995-6.
24 Ramzi Ahmed Yousef, intelligence report, Kuwait, 1996.
25 "Comprehensive Report on Suspected Terrorist Support Network – Case Operations Kamikaze and Quarter Moon", secret, n.p., n.d, p. 1.
26 Interviews. Philippines intelligence community, 1999
27 *Terrorism in the United States: 30 Years of Terrorism, A Special Retrspective Edition*, Counter Terrorism Threat Asssessment and Warning Unit, Counter Terrorism Division, FBI Publication no. 0308, p. 52.
28 Mark Fineman and Richard C. Paddock, "Response to Terror: Indonesia Cleric Tied to '95 Anti-U.S. Plot", *Los Angeles Times*, February 7, 2002
29 *Tactical Interrogation Report of Abdul Hakim Murad*, Manila, January 1995.
30 *Comprehensive Report on Suspected Terrorist Support Network*, p. 1.
31 *Terrorism in the United States*, p. 52.
32 Fineman and Paddock, "Response to Terror".
33 *Terrorism in the United States*, p. 52.
34 *Special Report on Mohammad Jamal Khalifa*, Directorate for Intelligence, Philippine National Police, Manila, n.d., p. 3.
35 Ibid.
36 Ibid.
37 Interview, confidential French source, Paris, 1999.
38 *Comprehensive Report on Suspected Terrorist Support Network*, p. 2.
39 Ibid.
40 Interview, Commodore Ruben G. Domingo, Commander Philippine Fleet, Naval Base Caviti, November 2001.
41 Interview, confidential French source, Paris, 1999.
42 Interview, MILF Vice-Chairman, January 2002.
43 Interview, MILF chairman, Hashim Salamat, BBC, February 7, 1999
44 Interview, signals intelligence officer, Western intelligence agency, 1998-9.
45 *Report on JI*, Singapore: Government of Singapore, January 2002.
46 Ibid.
47 Ibid.
48 Copy of video in author's possession.
49 *Report on JI*, Singapore: Government of Singapore, January 2002.
50 Interview, Philippine National Police, Task Force Sanglah.
51 "Special Report on Arrested International Terrorist Fathur Rohman", p. 3.
52 Ma Concepcion Clamor, "Terrorism and South East Asia: A Philippine Perspective", Transnational Violence and Seams of Lawlessness in the Asia-Pacific: Linkages to Global Terrorism, Asia-Pacific Centre for Security Studies, Hawaii, February 19-21, 2002, pp. 10-11.
53 Interview, Philippine National Police, Task Force Sanglah, Camp Crame, Quezon City, Manila, January 2002.
54 Ma Concepcion Clamor, "Terrorism and South East Asia: A Philippine Perspective", pp. 10-11.
55 Interview, Philippine National Police, Task Force Sanglah, Camp Crame, Quezon City, Manila, January 2002.
56 Ibid.
57 Ibid.
58 Ibid.
59 Ma Concepcion Clamor, "Terrorism and South East Asia: A Philippine Perspective", pp. 10-11.
60 Interview, Philippine National Police, Task Force Sanglah, Camp Crame, Quezon City,

Manila, January 2002.
[61] Ibid.
[62] "Suharto's Policy Towards the Islamic Movement", Sydney, *Nida'ul Islam*, February-March 1997.
[63] Ibid.
[64] Ibid.
[65] Rajiv Chandrasekaran, "Clerics Groomed Students for Terrorism – Malaysian Police say Indonesians Quietly Recruited for Al Qaeda-linked group", *Washington Post*, February 7, 2002.
[66] Ibid.
[67] Ibid.
[68] Ibid.
[69] Abu Bakar Basir, "Indonesia, Democracy, Priests, Parliament and Self-made Gods", *Nida'ul Islam*, October-November 1996
[70] Ibid.
[71] Mark Fineman and Richard C. Paddock, "Response to Terror: Indonesia Cleric Tied to '95 Anti-U.S. Plot", *Los Angeles Times*; February 7, 2002
[72] Ibid.
[73] Ibid.
[74] Transcript, communication monitored by an Asian intelligence agency, 1996.
[75] Patrick Sennyah, Ainon Mohd and Hyati Hayatudin, "KMM's Opposition Link", *New Straits Times*, October 12, 2001.
[76] Zachary Abuza, "Tentacles of Terror, Al Qaeda's Southeast Asian Linkages", Transnational Violence and Seams of Lawlessness in the Asia-Pacific: Linkages to Global Terrorism, Asia-Pacific Centre for Security Studies, Hawaii, February 19-21, p. 31
[77] Simon Elegant, "Getting Radical", *Time Asia*, September 10, 2001.
[78] Interviews, Malaysian security and intelligence authorities, January 2002.
[79] "MILF Linkages with Domestic and Foreign Non-Government and People's Organisations (NGOs-POs)", Directorate for Intelligence, Philippine National Police, p.1., n.d, and other sources.
[80] Chandrasekaran, "Clerics Groomed Students for Terrorism".
[81] Richard S. Ehrlich, City Times, 90 minute taped interview, n.d., Malaysia. >>Ehrlich.tripod.com<<
[82] Ibid.
[83] Interviews, Indonesian intelligence community, Jakarta, November 2001.
[84] "Suharto's Policy Towards the Islamic Movement".
[85] Ibid.
[86] Ibid. Since Suharto's fall the policy has changed.
[87] Ibid
[88] "Al Qaeda infrastructure in Indonesia", Indonesian Intelligence (secret), February 2002.
[89] Ibid.
[90] Ibid.
[91] Ibid.
[92] Ibid.
[93] Setiyar *et al.*, "Evil Deeds on a Holy Night", pp. 22-3, and Johan Budi S.P. *et al.*, "Christmas Night Marred by Terror", *Tempo*, Indonesia, January 9-15, 2001, pp. 20-1.
[94] Interview, Indonesian intelligence officers, February 2002.
[95] Confidential source, Indonesia, November 2001.
[96] "Al Qaeda infrastructure in Indonesia".
[97] Ibid.
[98] Interviews with civilian and military security and intelligence agencies, Jakarta, Indonesia, November 2001.

[99] "Muslim Groups Hunt for Americans", *The Jakarta Post*, September 24, 2001.
[100] Ibid.
[101] "MILF Linkages with Domestic and Foreign Non-Government and People Organisations".
[102] "Ja'far Released from Detention, Put Under House Arrest", *The Jakarta Post*, May 16, 2001.
[103] Interview, Jakarta, November 2001.
[104] "Lasykar Jihad Protests to 'The Jakarta Post'", *The Jakarta Post*, January 10, 2001.
[105] "Terrorist Threat a Concern in RI", *The Jakarta Post*, September 3, 2001.
[106] "Police officer who supervised the visitations informed the press" and "Ja'far Demands Deployment of Militias in Ambon", May 10, 2001.
[107] Ibid.
[108] Karim Raslan, "Indonesia to the Rescue Against Radicalism", *The Jakarta Post*, September 21, 2001.
[109] "MILF Linkages with Domestic and Foreign Non-Government and People Organisations".
[110] Peter Chalk, "Thailand," in Jason Isaacson and Colin Rubenstein (eds), *Islam in Asia: Changing Political Realities*, Washington DC and Melbourne, AJC and AIJAC, 1999, 166.
[111] Ibid.
[112] See "Terrorist Report Prompted Closure," *The Bangkok Post*, November 21, 1999; "US Embassy Closes Amid Security Alert," *The Bangkok Post*, November 28, 1998.
[113] Julie Sirrs, *The Taliban's Foreign Fighters*, Committee for a Free Afghanistan, USA, November 11, 2000, p. 9
[114] Ibid.
[115] Ibid.
[116] Rahul Bedi, "Nuclear Scientists in Myanmar", *Jane's Intelligence Review*, March 2002, vol. 14 no. 3, p . 2.
[117] Interview, Japanese police officers, January 2002.
[118] http://www.islam.org.au/articles/15/LADIN.HTM.
[119] Tactical Interrogation Report of Muhammed Afroz, arrested on October 2, 2001, Intelligence Bureau, New Delhi, India, p.2.
[120] Ibid. p.3.
[121] *Patterns of Global Terrorism*, Washington, DC, State Department, 1998.
[122] Ibid.
[123] Interview, George Fernandes, Minister of Defence, India, November 2001
[124] Interview, counter-insurgency expert in Kashmir, November 2001
[125] Ibid.
[126] Interview, Ajai Sahni, Institute of Conflict Management, New Delhi, November 2001.
[127] Interviews, US Intelligence community, February 2001.
[128] Interview, Ajai Sahni.
[129] Owais Tohid, 'Bin Laden to be protected, say Pakistani Islamists,' AFP, Karachi, February 13, 1999.
[130] Ibid.
[131] Ibid.
[132] Tactical Interrogation reports of Hezb members, Intelligence Bureau, New Delhi, 2000-2001
[133] Tactical Interrogation Report of Muhammed Iqhlaque, Intelligence Bureau, New Delhi, August 2000.
[134] Interview, B. Raman, Former Additional Secretary, Research and Analysis Wing, New Delhi, November 2001.
[135] Hatkat-ul Mujahidin statement, July 18, 1999, n.p.
[136] Harkat-ul Mujahidin statement, May 2, 2001, n.p.

137 Interview, B. Raman.
138 M.J. Gohel, "Profile of Sheikh Omar", Asia-Pacific Foundation, London, February 2002.
139 Ibid.
140 Ibid.
141 Ibid.
142 Tactical Interrogation Report, Ahmad Omar Saeed Sheikh, arrested in October 1994, Indian Intelligence Bureau, New Delhi, India, p. 2.
143 Ibid., p. 3.
144 Ibid., p. 6.
145 Ibid., p. 7.
146 Ibid., p. 8.
147 Ibid., p. 15
148 Ibid., p. 16
149 Ibid., p. 16
150 Interview, Brigadier Jamsheed Ali, Inter-Services Intelligence, Pakistan, 1995..
151 *Patterns of Global Terrorism*, Washington DC, State Department, 1998.
152 S.K. Ghosh, *Pakistan's ISI: Network of Terror in India*, New Delhi, A.P.H. Publishing Corporation, 2000, pp. 155-95.
153 Interview, Ajai Sahni.
154 Paul Watson and Sidhhartha Barua, "Response to Terror: Worlds of Exremism and Terror Collide in an Indian Jail", *Los Angeles Times*, February 8, 2002.
155 Ibid.
156 Sandeep Unnithan and Mohammad Waqas , "The Al Qaida Training Camps: Terror Academy", *India Today*, January 21, 2002.
157 *Kal Roos ko bikharte dekha tha, Ab India toot ta dekhenge, Hum barq-e-jehad ke sholon mein, America ko jalta dekhenge*: Original text.
158 Full text of a letter signed by Osama bin Ladin dated September 24, 2001 and faxed to the al-Jazeera television news channel, later read on-air.
159 Ibid.
160 Shaheen Akhtar, "Geo-Strategic Implications of Terrorism in South Asia – Pakistan's Perspective", Transnational Violence and Seams of Lawlessness in the Asia-Pacific: Linkages to Global Terrorism, Asia-Pacific Centre for Security Studies, Hawaii, February 19-21, p. 16.
161 Ibid.
162 Amjad Bashir Siddiqi, "ISI asked to help police arrest sectarian terrorists", *The News*, Islamabad, January 13, 2002.
163 Rana Mubashir, "16 Jihadis freed for lack of evidence", *The News*, Islamabad, January 25, 2002.
164 Confidential source, January 2000.
165 Al Jazeera TV, Qatar, October 14, 2001.
166 Afghan Islamic Press, Kandahar, October 26, 2001.
167 Tactical Interrogation Report of Muhammed Afroz, p.1.
168 Notice to Airmen (NOTAM). Disseminated in Pakistan, India and Sri Lanka, February 24, 2002.
169 "Mumbai is on alert: Chechen terrorist may be in town," *Indian Express*, New Delhi, January 31, 2002.
170 Interview, Indian intelligence, February 2002.
171 Ibid.
172 Interview, Major Shahriar Rashid, Bangladesh Military.
173 Interviews, Directorate General of Forces Intelligence (DGFI) and National Security Intelligence (NSI), Bangladesh, and other foreign agencies, January-February, 2002.

NOTES TO CH. 5: THE AL QAEDA THREAT AND THE INTERNATIONAL RESPONSE

[1] Bruce Hoffman, *Inside Terrorism*, London, Victor Gollancz, 1998, p. 124; and Paul Wilkinson, *Terrorism Versus Democracy, The Liberal State's Response*, London, Frank Cass, 2001, p. 190.
[2] Ayman al-Zawahiri, *Knights Under the Prophet's Banner - Meditations on the Jihadist Movement,* London, *Al-Sharq al-Awsat* (in Arabic), December 2, 2001.
[3] Ibid.
[4] Ibid.
[5] Ibid.
[6] Ibid.
[7] "The Wills of the New York and Washington Battle Martyrs". This is the Al Qaeda video in which al-Zawahiri took credit for the 9/11 attacks. It includes footage of Ahmed Ibrahim al-Haznawi (*alias* Alghamdi), one of the hijackers of UA93 that crashed in Pennsylvania, pleading with God to accept him as a martyr, the background being a montage of a burning WTC. The film was released by Al Jazeera satellite television station, Qatar, to Western networks, on April 15, 2002. The entire film was broadcast on Al Jazeera on April 18, 2002.
[8] Ayman al-Zawahiri, "Knights Under the Prophet's Banner".
[9] Tayseer Allouni [the Kabul correspondent of Al-Jazeera], transcript of an interview with Osama Bin Laden, October 21, 2001, translated from Arabic by the Institute for Islamic Studies and Research (www.alneda.com).
[10] Ayman Al Zawahiri, "Knights Under the Prophet's Banner".
[11] Anthony Davis, "How the Afghan War was Won: Key Dates in the Campaign", *Jane's Intelligence Review*, London, vol. 14, no. 2, February 2002, p. 11.
[12] Zahid Hussain and Katty Kay, "Bin Laden Aide Held by US after Pakistan Raids", *The Times*, April 1, 2002, p. 16.
[13] Ahmed Rashid, *Jihad: The Rise of Militant Islam in Central Asia*, p. 4.
[14] "The Wills of the New York andWashington Battle Martyrs".
[15] Tayseer Allouni, transcript of a an interview with Osama Bin Laden, October 21, 2001 (www.alneda.com).
[16] "The Wills of the New York and Washington Battle Martyrs".
[17] Ayman al-Zawahiri, *Knights Under the Prophet's Banner.*
[18] Ibid.
[19] Barry Desker and Kumar Ramakrishna, "Forging an Indirect Strategy in Southeast Asia", *The Washington Quarterly*, vol. 25, no. 2 (Spring 2002), pp. 161-76.
[20] Interview with Lt.-Col. Mike Dolamore, MBE, RL, Director, UK Counter-Terrorism School, March 2002.
[21] Jeffery MacMorray, "Pakistan allowed to Boost US Imports", *Pakistan Today*, February 16, 2002.
[22] Tayseer Allouni, transcript of a an interview with Osama Bin Laden, October 21, 2001 (www.alneda.com).
[23] Robert Baer, *See No Evil, The True Story of a Ground Soldier in the CIA's War on Terrorism*, New York: Crown Publishers, 2002, p. 119.
[24] Interview with Pat Duecy, Director, Joint Intelligence Task Force for Counter-Terrorism, Pentagon, Washington DC, March 2002.
[25] "Muslim Reaction – Liberal's Hour", *The Economist*, London, December 30, 2001.

[26] Andrea Stone, "In poll, Islamic World says Arabs not involved in 9/11", *USA Today*, February 27, 2002, p.1.
[27] Ibid.
[28] Ibid.
[29] Ibid.
[30] Ibid.
[31] Tayseer Allouni [the Kabul correspondent of Al-Jazeera], transcript of a an interview with Osama Bin Laden, October 21, 2001, translated from Arabic by the Institute for Islamic Studies and Research (www.alneda.com).
[32] Ibid.
[33] Bruce Hoffman, "The Emergence of New Terrorism", Workshop on the New Dimensions of Terrorism, March 2002, Institute for Defence and Strategic Studies, Singapore, p. 2.
[34] Brian Jenkins, "The Organization Men: Anatomy of a Terrorist Attack", in James F. Hoge, Jr. and Gideon Rose, *How Did This Happen? Terrorism and the New War* New York, Public Affairs, 2001, p. 5.
[35] Bruce Hoffman, "The Emergence of New Terrorism", p. 2, fn 5.
[36] *The Wills of the New York and Washington Battle Martyrs.*
[37] Dato Seri Dr Mahathir bin Mohamad, Inaugural Address, The Extraordinary Session of the Islamic Conference of Foreign Ministers on Terrorism, Palace of the Golden Horses, Kuala Lumpur, Malaysia, April 1, 2002.

INDEX